THE
KINGDOM
OF THE
CULTS
HANDBOOK

Other Books by Walter Martin

The Kingdom of the Cults

The Kingdom of the Cults Study Guide

The Kingdom of the Occult

Through the Windows of Heaven: 100 Powerful Stories and Teachings from Walter Martin, the Original Bible Answer Man

The Christian and the Cults

Christian Science

Essential Christianity

Herbert W. Armstrong and the Worldwide Church of God

Jehovah of the Watchtower

Jehovah's Witnesses

The Maze of Mormonism

Mormonism

New Age Cults

The New Cults

The Riddle of Reincarnation

The Rise of the Cults

Screwtape Writes Again

Walter Martin Speaks Out on the Cults

Walter Martin's Cults Reference Bible

THE
KINGDOM
OF THE
CULTS
HANDBOOK

QUICK REFERENCE GUIDE *to* ALTERNATIVE BELIEF SYSTEMS

WALTER MARTIN
WITH JILL MARTIN RISCHE

BETHANYHOUSE
a division of Baker Publishing Group
Minneapolis, Minnesota

Published by Bethany House Publishers
11400 Hampshire Avenue South
Bloomington, Minnesota 55438
www.bethanyhouse.com

Bethany House Publishers is a division of
Baker Publishing Group, Grand Rapids, Michigan

Printed in the United States of America

Library of Congress Cataloging-in-Publication Control Number: 2019946584

ISBN 978-0-7642-3271-8

This volume is an abridgment with Jill Martin Rische of *The Kingdom of the Cults* sixth edition.

Unless otherwise indicated, Scripture quotations are from the King James Version of the Bible.

Scripture quotations identified BSB are from the Berean Study Bible, (BSB) © 2016, 2018, 2019 by Bible Hub and Berean.Bible.

Scripture quotations identified ESV are from The Holy Bible, English Standard Version® (ESV®), copyright © 2001 by Crossway, a publishing ministry of Good News Publishers. Used by permission. All rights reserved. ESV Text Edition: 2016

Scripture quotations identified NASB are from the New American Standard Bible® (NASB), copyright © 1960, 1962, 1963, 1968, 1971, 1972, 1973, 1975, 1977, 1995 by The Lockman Foundation. Used by permission. www.Lockman.org

Scripture quotations identified NIV are from the Holy Bible, New International Version®. NIV®. Copyright © 1973, 1978, 1984, 2011 by Biblica, Inc.™ Used by permission of Zondervan. All rights reserved worldwide. www.zondervan.com. The "NIV" and "New International Version" are trademarks registered in the United States Patent and Trademark Office by Biblica, Inc.™

Scripture quotations identified NKJV are from the New King James Version®. Copyright © 1982 by Thomas Nelson, Inc. Used by permission. All rights reserved.

Scripture quotations identified RSV are from the Revised Standard Version of the Bible, copyright 1946, 1952 [2nd edition, 1971] National Council of the Churches of Christ in the United States of America. Used by permission. All rights reserved worldwide.

Cover design by LOOK Design Studio

19 20 21 22 23 24 25   7 6 5 4 3 2 1

Contents

Preface

Since the very first publication of *The Kingdom of the Cults* in 1965, many readers have requested a handbook-style mini-version of the original volume, suitable for times of sharing their faith, for a Bible study, or as a supplement for students and instructors. June 26, 2019, marks the thirtieth anniversary of my father's new life with the Lord, and it seems like the perfect time to introduce something special.

The new abridged edition of Walter Martin's classic work conveys his unique theological insights and key historical facts in a clear, concise way. It is meant to engage both loyal supporters and a new audience searching for accuracy in a quick-answer format. Each chapter includes central beliefs, provides specific biblical answers to doctrine, and concludes with an *Explore* element and a *Discuss* section that summarizes the reading material in a question-and-answer format. In addition to this, a *Dig Deeper Study Guide* is available at waltermartin.com.

In the case of the appendices, two new topics have been introduced that rely on Walter Martin's theological exposition of Satanism and the Pantheistic New Age. Historical elements were added in order to present a strong defense against the emergence of two particularly strong aggressors against the Church of Jesus Christ.

I would like to include a special thanks to all those involved in bringing this volume from idea to realization; to those who continue to "put up a good fight for the faith," as my father would always say; and to everyone worldwide who read and taught *The Kingdom of the Cults* in an effort to educate others to take a stand. Your love and support mean a great deal to me and to my family.

Fifty-four years after its first publication, *The Kingdom of the Cults* still meets the urgent need of the Church to obey the Scriptural injunction to "earnestly contend for the faith which was once delivered unto the saints" (Jude 3). Walter Martin once wrote that we have no time to sit on the sidelines as evil invades the Church and pervades the world. "We have had *enough* of 'just be positive and preach the Gospel' or 'Don't offend people by defending your Christian faith or criticizing false teachings; God will protect the church.' Throughout history, every time the Church has failed to defend the faith, false doctrines and heretical teachings have plagued us. Only the church militant can become the church triumphant. The challenge is here; the time is now!"

Jill Martin Rische
April 12, 2019

Acknowledgments

Special thanks are due Dr. Martin's widow, Darlene Martin, for her faithfulness in preserving her husband's classic text on American cults and to researcher-author Kurt Van Gorden for his invaluable expertise.

1

The Kingdom of the Cults

Quick Facts on the Kingdom of the Cults

- The term *cult* is not derogatory but descriptive of religious groups that differ in belief or practice from culturally accepted norms.

- Theologically, a cult is a group of people gathered around someone's *interpretation* of the Bible.

- All doctrine must be weighed against Divine revelation, the Word of God.

- Cults are a challenge to the Church to affirm the great principles and foundations of the Gospel of Christ, and to make them meaningful to the present generation.

Historical Perspective

It has been said of the United States that it is "the great melting pot" for the people of the world. And the contents of that pot would not be complete unless it also included the religions of those masses that now make up the populace of America. This writer has spent over forty years of his life in research and fieldwork among the religions of America, and this volume, limited as it is by the vastness and complexity of the problem itself, constitutes his evaluation of that vibrant brand of religion that has come to be recognized by many as the "Kingdom of the Cults."[1]

1. It is my conviction that the reader is entitled to know the theological position from which this volume is written so that there will be no misconceptions as to the ground for my evaluation. I am

Dr. Charles C. Braden states:

By the term cult I mean nothing derogatory to any group so classified. A cult, as I define it, is any religious group which differs significantly in one or more respects as to belief or practice from those religious groups which are regarded as the normative expressions of religion in our total culture.[2]

From a theological viewpoint, the cults contain many major deviations from historical Christianity. Yet, paradoxically, they continue to insist that they are entitled to be classified as Christians.

Examples

1. Jehovah's Witnesses are, for the most part, followers of the interpretations of Charles T. Russell and J. F. Rutherford.
2. The Christian Scientist of today is a disciple of Mary Baker Eddy and her interpretations of Scripture.
3. The Mormons adhere to those interpretations found in the writings of Joseph Smith and Brigham Young.
4. The Unity School of Christianity follows the theology of Charles and Myrtle Fillmore.

While I am in agreement that cults represent the earnest attempt of millions of people to find the fulfillment of deep and legitimate needs of the human spirit that most have not found in established churches, I feel there is still much more to be said.[3] It has been wisely observed by someone that "a man who will not stand for something is quite likely to fall for almost anything." So I have elected to stand on the ramparts of biblical Christianity as taught by the apostles, defended by the church fathers, rediscovered by the reformers, and embodied in what is sometimes called Reformed Theology.

It is the purpose of this book then, to evaluate the so-called cults and -isms that today are found in abundance in America and, in quite a number

a Baptist minister, an evangelical holding to the inerrancy of Scripture, and teach in the fields of Biblical Theology, Comparative Religion, and Apologetics.

2. Charles S. Braden and John C. Schaffer, *These Also Believe* (New York: The Macmillan Company, 1949), xii. Preface, Dr. Braden NU Emeritus Professor 1954, John C. Schaffer, lecturer 1955, Scripps 1954–56. Dr. Charles Braden was emeritus professor at Northwestern University, and co-author, John C. Schaffer, was a lecturer and visiting professor at Scripps College.

3. Braden and Schaffer, *These Also Believe*, xii.

of cases, on the great mission fields of the world. My approach to the subject is threefold: (1) *historical analysis* of the salient facts connected with the rise of the cult systems; (2) *theological evaluation* of the major teachings of those systems; and (3) *apologetic contrast* from the viewpoint of biblical theology, with an emphasis upon exegesis and doctrine.

Cults contain many major deviations from historical Christianity yet continue to insist that they are entitled to be classified as Christians.

It is not my desire in any sense to make fun of adherents of cult systems, the large majority of whom are sincere, though I am not adverse to humor when it can underscore a point. A study of the cults is a serious business. They constitute a growing trend in America—a trend that is away from the established Christian churches and the historic teachings of the Bible—an emphasis upon autosoteric efforts, or the desire to save one's self apart from biblical revelation.

It is most significant that those who have written on the cults have only recently stressed the authority of the Scriptures as a criterion for measuring either the truth or falsity of cultic claims. When this book first appeared in 1965, it was the first to make such a stress on such a large scale. Since then my example has been followed, and the Christian is now in a position to readily find the Scripture's verdict on the cults. Dr. Marcus Bach, who has written extensively from a liberal viewpoint on the cults, summed up this attitude of tolerance apart from scriptural authority when he wrote,

Somehow I felt I must become a representative of the average churchgoer everywhere in America, whose heart was with me in my seeking. If the Jehovah's Witnesses have some heavenly tip-off that the world is coming to an end in 1973,[4] we want to tell our friends about it in plenty of time! If Father Divine is really God, we want to know about it! If Unity is building a new city down in Missouri, we Americans want to get in on the ground floor! If that man in Moscow, Idaho, talked with God, actually and literally, we have a right to know how it's done! Certainly these modern movements suggest that there was a vital, if not always coherent, moving force back of them, giving luster and drive to their beliefs. I decided that I would not concern

4. They most recently decided on September of 1975, to their later dismay. This new false prophecy cost them thousands of members.

myself so much with the rivalry among groups as with their realization. I would devote myself more to the *way* than to the *why* of their doctrine. Let others turn ecclesiastical microscopes on them or weigh them in the sensitive scale of final truth; I would content myself with the age-old verdict of Gamaliel: "If this work be of men, it will come to naught; but if it be of God, we cannot overthrow it."

I decided to set forth on my own with no strings attached and no stipend from any university, no commission from any church, no obligation to any individual or group, no bias, no preconceived judgment, no illusions.

"All roads that lead to God are good." As I began my adventure, the fervor of this naïve and youthful conviction rushed over me once more.[5]

Dr. Bach admits more in this statement than perhaps he intended, for though it is a laudable aim to become "representative of the average churchgoer everywhere in America," his use of the word *if* in the reference to the teachings of the cults indicates that the final truth, grounded in the authority of Scripture and the revelation of Jesus Christ, has not been obtained by the Christian church, and that other sources must be investigated in order to ascertain the whole truth of the Christian message. We are in full agreement that "these modern movements suggest that there was a vital, if not always coherent, moving force back of them, giving luster and drive to their beliefs." But since the cult systems vigorously oppose the Christian church, particularly in the realm of Christology and soteriology, perhaps it is not at all out of order to suggest "that force" is the same that opposed our Lord and the apostles and has consistently opposed the efforts of the Christian church, the force described by the apostle Paul as "the god of this world" (2 Corinthians 4:4).

Theological Evaluation

Liberal scholars, then, have devoted themselves more to the way than to the why of the doctrines of the cults, and they have adopted the statement of Gamaliel as their creed. It will be remembered that Gamaliel counseled the Jews not to oppose the Christians for "if this counsel or this work be of men, it will come to naught: But if it be of God, ye cannot overthrow it" (Acts 5:38–39). Let it not be forgotten that Gamaliel's advice is *not* biblical

5. Marcus Bach, *They Have Found a Faith* (Indianapolis: The Bobbs-Merrill Company, 1946), 19–21.

theology; and if it were followed in the practical realm of experience as steadfastly as it is urged, then we would have to recognize Islam as "of God" because of its rapid growth and reproductive virility throughout the world. We would have to acknowledge Mormonism (six people in 1830 to 16 million in 2018) in the same category as Islam, something which most liberals are unwilling to do, though some have not hesitated to so declare themselves.

We do not suggest that we "turn ecclesiastical microscopes" on the cults, but rather that they be viewed in the light of what we know to be divine revelation, the Word of God, which itself weighs them, "in the sensitive scale of final truth" for it was our Lord who taught, "If you believe not that I AM, you will die in your sins" (John 8:24). And the final criterion today as always must remain, "What think ye of Christ? whose son is he?" (Matthew 22:42).

> Jesus' claim was absolute, and allegiance to Him, as the Savior of the world, takes precedence over all claims of men and religions.

I must dissent from the view that "all roads that lead to God are good" and believe instead the words of our Lord, "I am the way, the truth, and the life: no man cometh unto the Father, but by me" (John 14:6). It should be carefully noted that Jesus did not say, "I am one of many equally good ways" or "I am a better way than the others, I am an aspect of truth; I am a fragment of the life." Instead, His claim was absolute, and allegiance to Him, as the Savior of the world, was to take precedence over all the claims of men and religions.

I should like to make it clear that in advancing criticism of some of the views of liberal scholars in the field of cults and -isms, I do not discount their many valuable contributions. And no singular study, regardless of the time involved and the thoroughness of the investigation, can review all the data and evaluate all the facts necessary to completely understand the origin and development of cultism. My approach is quite honestly theological in its orientation with the aim of contrast and reaffirmation in view. Dr. Jan Van Baalen is correct when he says that "the cults are the unpaid bills of the church."[6] They are this and more, for they are a challenge to the Church to affirm once again the great principles and foundations of the Gospel of Christ and to make them meaningful to the present generation. There can be no doubt that the great trend in religion is syncretistic, or a

6. Van Baalen, Jan Karel, *The Chaos of Cults* (London: Pickering & Inglis Ltd., 1962), 14.

THE KINGDOM OF THE CULTS HANDBOOK

type of homogenization of religions, such as the great historian Arnold Toynbee has more than once suggested.

We are consistently being told in books, articles, council pronouncements, and ecumenical conclaves that we must "play down the things that divide us and emphasize those things which make for unity." This is all well and good if we are speaking about a firm foundation of doctrinal, moral, and ethical truth, and if we are speaking about true unity within the body of Christ. But if, as some suggest, this be broadened to include those who are not in agreement with the essentials of biblical Christianity, we must resolutely oppose it.[7]

Biblical Perspective

The age that saw the advent of Jesus Christ was an age rich in religion, stretching from the crass animism and sex worship of the great majority of the world to the Roman pantheon of gods and the Greek mystery religions. One need only peruse Gibbon's *Decline and Fall of the Roman Empire* to become acutely aware of the multiplicity of gods and goddesses, as well as of philosophical and ethical systems that pervaded the religious horizon in that era of history. Judaism had withdrawn itself from any extensive missionary activity, burdened as the Jews were by the iron rule of an unsympathetic Roman paganism.

The Law of God had been interpreted and reinterpreted through commentaries and rabbinical emendations to the place where our Lord had to say to the religious leaders of His day, "Why do ye also transgress the commandment of God by your tradition? . . . Thus have ye made the commandment of God of none effect by your tradition" (Matthew 15:3, 6).

Into this whirlpool of stagnant human philosophy and perverted revelation came the Son of God who, through His teachings and example, revealed that there was such a thing as divine humanity, and through His miraculous powers, vicarious death, and bodily resurrection, cut across the maze of human doubts and fears, and was lifted up, to draw all men unto Him. It has been wisely observed that men are at liberty to reject

7. Today, that opposition grows ever weaker. The National Council of Churches now accepts not only the Community of Christ—formerly the Reorganized Church of Jesus Christ of Latter Day Saints—but several other cults as well. The World Council of Churches, which constitutes the spearhead of the ecumenical movement throughout the world, consistently denies membership to the cults under study in this volume on the grounds that they do not recognize or worship Jesus Christ as God and Savior, but permits serious doctrinal error.

Jesus Christ and the Bible as the Word of God; they are at liberty to oppose Him; they are at liberty to challenge it. But they are not at liberty to *alter* the essential message of the Scriptures, which is the good news that God does care for the lost souls of His children, and so loved us as to send His only Son that we might live through Him.

> Men . . . are not at liberty to alter the essential message of the Scriptures.

In keeping with this Gospel of God's grace, our Lord not only announced it but He prophesied the trials and tribulations that would encompass His followers, both within the Church and without, and one of the greatest of all these trials would, our Lord taught, be the challenge of false prophets and false christs who would come in His name and deceive many (Matthew 24:5). So concerned was Christ in this area that He at one time declared,

> Beware of false prophets, which come to you in sheep's clothing, but inwardly they are ravening wolves. Ye shall know them by their fruits. Do men gather grapes of thorns, or figs of thistles? Even so every good tree bringeth forth good fruit; but a corrupt tree bringeth forth evil fruit. A good tree cannot bring forth evil fruit, neither can a corrupt tree bring forth good fruit. Every tree that bringeth not forth good fruit is hewn down, and cast into the fire. Wherefore by their fruits ye shall know them. Not every one that saith unto me, Lord, Lord, shall enter into the kingdom of heaven; but he that doeth the will of my Father which is in heaven. Many will say to me in that day, Lord, Lord, have we not prophesied in thy name? and in thy name have cast out devils? and in thy name done many wonderful works? And then will I profess unto them, I never knew you: depart from me, ye that work iniquity (Matthew 7:15–23).

Christ pointed out that the false prophets would come. There was not a doubt in the mind of the Son of God that this would take place, and the history of the heresies of the first five centuries of the Christian church bear out the accuracy of His predictions. Christ further taught that the fruits of the false prophets would also be apparent, and that the Church would be able to detect them readily. Let us never forget that "fruits" from a corrupt tree can also be doctrinal, as well as ethical and moral. A person may be ethically and morally "good" by human standards, but if he sets his face against Jesus Christ as Lord and Savior, and rejects Him, his fruit is corrupt and he is to be rejected as counterfeit. The Apostle John understood this when he wrote, "They went out from us, but they were not of us; for if they had been of us, they would no doubt have continued with us: but they went out, that they might be made manifest that they were not all of us" (1 John 2:19).

The Bible, then, does speak of false prophets, false christs, false apostles and "deceitful workers, transforming themselves into the apostles of Christ. And no marvel; for Satan himself is transformed into an angel of light. Therefore it is no great thing if his ministers also be transformed as the ministers of righteousness; whose end shall be according to their works" (2 Corinthians 11:13–15).

We cannot afford to hold any concept of the purveyors of erroneous doctrines different from that held by our Lord and the apostles, and we must, as Paul states, "abhor that which is evil; cleave to that which is good" (Romans 12:9). In the light of this teaching, it is extremely difficult for this writer to understand how it is possible to cleave to that which is good without an abhorrence of that which is evil.

The biblical perspective, where false teachers and false teachings are concerned, is that we are to have compassion and love for those who are enmeshed in the teachings of the false prophets, but we are to vigorously oppose the teachings, with our primary objective the winning of the soul and not so much the argument. It must never be forgotten that cultists are souls for whom Jesus Christ died, for "he is the propitiation for our sins: and not for ours only, but also for the sins of the whole world" (1 John 2:2).

Today, the kingdom of the cults stretches throughout the world, its membership in the millions, with about 15 million cult members in the United States alone.[8] The Church of Jesus Christ has badly neglected both the evangelizing and refuting of the various cult systems, although there is cause for some optimism.[9]

8. A recent, significant drop in overall cult membership statistics can be verified in the Pew Research Center statistics. "Chapter 1: The Changing Religious Composition of the U.S.," Pew Research Center, accessed April 7, 2018, http://www.pewforum.org/2015/05/12/chapter-1-the -changing-religious-composition-of-the-u-s/.

9. "Religious Landscape Study," Pew Research Center, accessed April 7, 2018, http://www .pewforum.org/religious-landscape-study/. The membership growth rate of Latter Day Saints, Jehovah's Witnesses, and other cults has slowed considerably. Today in the United States, Christianity statistically outpaces the kingdom of the cults, but we are still facing a dangerous exponential rise in numbers of cult followers in Latin America and Third World countries. South Africa is especially vulnerable due to political chaos and racial tensions. It has emerged recently as a battlefront against both well-known cults and neo-gnostic heresies. Islam and Buddhist religions, as well as New Age and Pagan movements, also claim increases in membership worldwide, so the problem faces us and continues to grow. The kingdom of the cults is expanding.

Our purpose in this volume is to further awaken interest to this tremendously important field of Christian missionary effort among the cults, to point out the flaws in the various cult systems, to provide the information that will enable Christians both to answer cultists and to present effectively to them the claims of the Gospel of Christ, with a deep concern for the redemption of their souls. It is also the aim of this book to so familiarize the reader with the refreshing truths of the Gospel of Christ that he may see the great heritage that is ours in the Christian faith and be challenged more effectively to both live and to witness for the Savior.

The American Banking Association has a training program that exemplifies this aim of the author. Each year it sends hundreds of bank tellers to Washington in order to teach them to detect counterfeit money, which is a great source of a loss of revenue to the Treasury Department. It is most interesting that during the entire two-week training program, no teller touches counterfeit money. Only the original passes through his hands. The reason for this is that the American Banking Association is convinced that if a man is thoroughly familiar with the original, he will not be deceived by the counterfeit bill, no matter how much like the original it appears.[10] It is the contention of this writer that if the average Christian would become familiar once again with the great foundations of his faith, he would be able to detect those counterfeit elements so apparent in the cult systems, which set them apart from biblical Christianity.

Charles W. Ferguson, in his provocative volume *The New Books of Revelation*, describes the advent of modern cult systems as "the modern Babel." He goes on to state,

It should be obvious to any man who is not one himself, that the land is overrun with messiahs. I refer not to those political quacks who promise in one election to rid the land of evil, but rather to those inspired fakirs who promise to reduce the diaphragm or orient the soul through the machinery of a cult religion. Each of these has made himself the center of a new theophany, has surrounded himself with a band of zealous apostles, has hired a hall for a shrine and then set about busily to rescue truth from the scaffold and put it on the throne.[11]

10. This example remains relevant but the American Banking Association discontinued the training program.
11. Charles W. Ferguson, *The New Books of Revelation* (Garden City: Doubleday, Doran and Co., 1928), 1.

Ferguson did the Christian church a great service in the late 1920s by focusing attention upon the rise of the cults. His observations were pithy and to the point, and though they cannot always be endorsed from a biblical standpoint, there can be little doubt that he put his finger upon the cults as a vital emergent force in American Protestantism with which the church of Jesus Christ must reckon. It is with this force that we now come to deal, confident that on the authority of the Scriptures, the Christian church has the answers, and in the Gospel of Christ, a Savior who can provide the cultist with something no cult system has ever been able to originate—peace with God and fellowship with the Father and with His Son, Jesus Christ.

The cults have capitalized on the failure of the Christian church to understand their teachings and to develop a workable methodology both to evangelize and to refute cult adherents. Within the theological structure of the cults there is considerable truth, all of which, it might be added, is drawn from biblical sources, but so diluted with human error as to be more deadly than complete falsehood.

The cults have also emphasized the things that the Church has forgotten, such as divine healing (Christian Science, Unity, New Thought), prophecy (Jehovah's Witnesses and Mormonism), and a great many other things that in the course of our study we will have opportunity to observe. But let it never be forgotten that where the Gospel of Jesus Christ is proclaimed in power and with what Dr. Frank E. Gaebelein has called "a compelling relevancy," cults have made little or no headway. This has led Dr. Lee Belford, professor of comparative religions at New York University, to state,

> The problem is essentially theological where the cults are concerned. The answer of the church must be theological and doctrinal. No sociological or cultural evaluation will do. Such works may be helpful, but they will not answer the Jehovah's Witness or Mormon who is seeking biblical authority for either the acceptance or rejection of his beliefs.[12]

The problem, then, is complex. There is no simple panacea, but it constitutes a real challenge to Christianity that cannot be ignored or neglected any longer—for the challenge is here and the time is now.

---

12. Dr. Martin knew Dr. Belford personally from his days as a student at New York University.

/————————————— **Explore** —————————————\

Doctrine
Soteriology
Christology
Theology

/————————————— **Discuss** —————————————\

1. The authority of the Scriptures is the criterion for measuring truth or error in all cultic claims. What is the *inerrancy* of Scripture? Are we required to defend it?

   _____

   _____

2. The Bible is controversial—some call it a collection of stories and a "stumbling block" to belief. They avoid talking to unbelievers about creation, the flood, and other supernatural events the world calls *myths*. What approach did Jesus take? Which did Paul take?

   _____

   _____

3. How do liberal scholars take Gamaliel's advice out of context? How does God view someone who is a doctrinally sound teacher but has little money and few followers?

   _____

   _____

/————————————— **Dig Deeper** —————————————\

See *The Kingdom of the Cults Study Guide* available at WalterMartin.com.

2

Scaling the Language Barrier

Quick Facts on Scaling the Language Barrier

- Define key words and standard doctrinal phrases.
- Compare definitions with contexts.
- Learn the terminology of major cult systems.
- Present a clear testimony of regenerative experience with Jesus Christ.

Historical Perspective

The scientific age in which we live has, in the very real sense of the term, given rise to a new vocabulary that, unless it is understood, can create enormous problems in the realm of communication. The revolutions in culture that have taken place in the vocabularies of technology, psychology, medicine, and politics have not left untouched the religions of the world in general and the theology of Christianity in particular.

Writing in *Eternity* magazine, noted theologian Dr. Bernard Ramm calls attention to this particular fact when evaluating the theological system of the late Dr. Tillich, leading theological luminary of our day and former professor of theology at the University of Chicago's Divinity School. Dr. Ramm charges that Tillich has so radically redefined standard theological terms that the effect upon Christian theology is nothing short of cataclysmic. "Such biblical notions of sin, guilt, damnation, justification, regeneration, etc., all come out retranslated into a language that is foreign to the meaning of these concepts in the Scriptures themselves."[1]

Dr. Ramm is quite right in his observations, for any student of Paul Tillich's theology and, for that matter, the theology of contemporary neo-liberalism and neoorthodoxy will concede immediately that, in the theological framework of these two systems of thought, the vocabulary of what has been rightly termed by Dr. Edward Carnell as "classical orthodoxy" undergoes what can only be termed radical redefinition. Just how this is effected is worthy of another chapter, but no one informed on the subject seriously questions that this is what has occurred.

It is therefore possible for the modern theologians to use the terminology of the Bible and historical theology, but in an entirely different sense from that intended by the writers of Scripture.

Before attempting to examine the non-Christian cult systems contained in this volume, one must face the fact that the originators and promulgators of cult theology have done exactly the same thing to the semantic structure of Christian theology as did the modern theologians. So it is possible for a Jehovah's Witness, a Christian Scientist, or a Mormon, for example, to utilize the terminology of biblical Christianity with absolute freedom, having already redesigned these terms in a theological framework of his own making and to his own liking, but almost always at direct variance with the historically accepted meanings of the terms.

The student of cultism, then, must be prepared to scale the language barrier of *terminology*. First, he must recognize that it does exist, and second, he must acknowledge the very real fact that unless terms are defined when one is either speaking or reading cult theology, the semantic jungle which the cults have created will envelop him, making difficult, if not impossible, a proper contrast between the teachings of the cults and those of orthodox Christianity.

On countless occasions, the author has been asked, "Why is it that when I am talking with a cultist he seems to be in full agreement with what I am saying, but when we have finished talking, I am aware of a definite lack of communication, almost as though we were not talking the same language?"

The answer to this question is, of course, that we have not been communicating, because the vocabulary of the cults is not the vocabulary

1. Bernard Ramm, *Eternity* (November 1963): 33.

of the Bible by definition. Only the Lord knows how many fruitless hours have been spent attempting to confront cultists with the claim of the Gospel, when five short minutes of insistence upon definitions of the terms employed in conversation (particularly concerning the nature of God and the person, nature, and work of Jesus Christ) would have stripped the cult theology of one of its most potent tools, that of theological term-switching. Through the manipulation of terminology, it is therefore obvious that the cultist has the Christian at a distinct disadvantage, particularly in the realm of the great fundamental doctrines of biblical theology. The question then, is how can the interested Christian solve that problem, if indeed it can be solved at all? In short, is there some common denominator that one can use when faced with a cultist of any particular variety, and if so, how does one put this principle into practice?

> The vocabulary of the cults is not the vocabulary of the Bible.

The cults capitalize on the almost total inability of the average Christian to understand the subtle art of redefinition in the realm of biblical theology. Human nature being what it is, it is only natural that Christian ministers as well as laymen should desire a panacea to the irritating and, at times, frustrating problem of cult terminology. Unfortunately, however, no such panacea exists. But lest we become discouraged with the prospect of facing the ever-multiplying bodies of non-Christian cults unprepared for this conflict (and make no mistake, this is spiritual conflict), proper usage of definitions as a practical tool will rob the cultist of at least two of his advantages: surprise and confusion.

Theological Evaluation

The Riddle of Semantics

The problem of semantics has always played an important part in human affairs, for by its use or abuse entire churches, thrones, and governments have been erected, sustained, or overthrown. In the late George Orwell's stirring novel *1984*, he points out that the redefinition of common political terms can lead to slavery when allowed to pass unchallenged by a lethargic populace. It is a classic illustration of the dangers of perverted semantics.

Trick terminology is a powerful propaganda weapon. The communist dictatorship of China, rejected by *Russian* theorists as incalculably brutal and inept, dares to call itself the People's Republic of China. As history testifies, the people have very little, if any, say in the actual operation of communism. If democracy is the rule of the people, the Chinese communists have canonized the greatest misnomer of all time!

Both the Chinese communists and the Russians paid a terrible price for not defining terminology, and for listening to the siren song of Marxism without carefully studying and analyzing the atheistic collectivism through which the music came.

Applying this analogy to the field of cults, it is at once evident that a distinct parallel exists between the two systems. For cultism, like communism, plays a type of hypnotic music upon a semantic harp of terminological deception. And there are many who historically followed these strains down the broad road to spiritual eternal judgment. There is a common denominator then, and it is inextricably connected with language and the precise definition of terminology. It is what we might call the key to understanding cultism.

The key to understanding cultism is recognizing and neutralizing redefined terms.

Precisely how to utilize the key that will help unlock the jargon of cult semantics is best illustrated by the following facts, drawn from over thirty years of research and practical fieldwork with cultists of every variety.

The average non-Christian cult owes its very existence to the fact that it has utilized the terminology of Christianity, has borrowed liberally from the Bible (almost always out of context), and sprinkled its format with evangelical clichés and terms wherever possible or advantageous. Up to now this has been a highly successful attempt to represent their respective systems of thought as "Christian."

On encountering a cultist, always remember that you are dealing with a person who is familiar with Christian terminology, and who has carefully redefined it to fit the system of thought he or she now embraces.

A concrete example of a redefinition of terms can be illustrated in the case of almost any of the Gnostic cult systems that emphasize healing and hold in common a pantheistic concept of God (Christian Science, New Thought, Unity, Christ Unity Science, Metaphysics, Religious Science, Divine Science).

Biblical Perspective

This semantic maze in full operation is awesome to behold. Cult adherents will begin talking at length about God and Christ. They will speak especially about love, tolerance, forgiveness, the Sermon on the Mount and, as always, the out-of-context perversion of James' "faith without works is dead."

It should be noted that hardly ever will such cultists discuss the essential problem of evil, the existence of personal sin, or the necessity of the substitutionary atonement of Christ as the sole means of salvation from sin, through the agency of divine grace and the exercise of faith. In fact, they conscientiously avoid such distasteful subjects like the proverbial plague and discuss them only with great reluctance.

Of course, there are exceptions to this rule, but on the average, it is safe to assume that reticence will characterize any exploration of these touchy issues. Both Christian Science and Unity talk of God as Trinity but their real concept of God is a pantheistic abstraction. For example, *Life*, *Truth*, and *Love* constitute the triune divine principles in Christian Science.

The historic doctrine of the Trinity is seldom, if ever, considered without careful redefinition. The *Metaphysical Bible Dictionary*, published by the Unity School of Christianity, demonstrates this masterpiece of redefinition. Unity redefines exhaustively many of the cardinal terms of biblical theology, much as Mary Baker Eddy did in her Glossary of Terms in the book *Science and Health With Key to the Scriptures*.

The reader will be positively amazed to find what has happened to biblical history, the person of Adam, the concept of human sin, spiritual depravity, and eternal judgment. One thing, however, will emerge very clearly from this study: Unity may use the terminology of the Bible, but by no stretch of the imagination can the redefinition be equated with the thing itself.

Another confusing aspect of non-Christian cultists' approach to semantics is the manner in which they will surprise the Christian with voluminous quotations from no less authority than the Bible, and give the appearance of agreeing with nearly every statement the Christian makes in attempting to evangelize. Such stock phrases as "We believe that way too; we agree on this point" or the more familiar: "Mrs. Eddy, Mr. or Mrs. Fillmore, Mr. Evans, Dr. Buchman, Joseph Smith, or Brigham Young says exactly the same thing; we are completely in agreement." All such tactics based upon the juggling of terms usually have the effect of frustrating the average Christian, for he is unable to put his finger on what he knows is error, and is repeatedly tantalized by the seeming agreement that he knows does *not* exist. He is therefore often forced into silence because he is unaware of what the cultist is actually doing. Often, even though he may be aware of this in a limited sense, he hesitates to plunge into a discussion for fear of ridicule because of an inadequate background or a lack of biblical information.

The solution to this perplexing problem is far from simple. The Christian must realize that for every biblical or doctrinal term *he* mentions, a redefinition light flashes on in the mind of the cultist, and a lightning-fast redefinition is accomplished. Realizing that the cultist will apparently agree with the doctrine under discussion while firmly disagreeing in reality with the historical and biblical concept, the Christian is on his way to dealing effectively with cult terminology. This amazing operation of terminological redefinition works very much like a word association test in psychology.

It is simple for a cultist to spiritualize and redefine the clear meaning of biblical texts and teachings so as to be in apparent harmony with the historic Christian faith. However, such a harmony is at best a surface agreement, based upon double meanings of words that cannot stand the test of biblical context, grammar, or sound exegesis.

Language is, to be sure, a complex subject; all are agreed on this. But one thing is beyond dispute, and that is that in context words mean just what they say. Either we admit this or we must be prepared to surrender all the accomplishments of grammar and scholastic progress and return to writing on cave walls with charcoal sticks in the tradition of our alleged stone-age ancestors. To illustrate this point more sharply, the experience of everyday life points out the absurdity of terminological redefinitions in every way of life.

In context words mean just what they say.

In the realm of medicine, a doctor who announces that he will perform an open-heart operation, then proceeds in the presence of his colleagues to remove the gall bladder, and then attempts to defend his action by the claim that open-heart surgery actually means removal of the gall bladder in his vocabulary, could not practice medicine for long! Open-heart surgery is delicate repair of the heart muscle. Removal of the gall bladder is, by definition, surgery of another type. In law and in medicine, therefore, terms are what they are by definition. On the business and professional

SCALING THE LANGUAGE BARRIER

level this also holds true. But to the cultists words do not always mean what they have always meant by definition in specific context. And just as the American Bar Association will not tolerate confusion of terminology in the trial of cases, and as the American Medical Association will not tolerate redefinition of terminology in diagnostic and surgical medicine, so also the Church of Jesus Christ has every right not to tolerate the gross perversions and redefinitions of historical, biblical terminology simply to accommodate a culture and a society that cannot tolerate an absolute standard or criterion of truth, even if it be revealed by God in His Word and through the true witness of His Spirit.

The major cult systems, then, change the definition of historical terms without a quibble. They answer the objections of Christian theologians with the meaningless phrase "You interpret it your way and I'll interpret it mine. Let's be broad-minded. After all, one interpretation is as good as another."

A quick survey of how cults redefine Christian terminology illustrates this important observation:

Cult	Term	Cult Definition	Christian Definition
Mormonism	God	Many gods and goddesses	One Triune God
Jehovah's Witnesses	Jesus Christ	Not god, created by Jehovah; Jesus is Michael, the archangel.	God the Son, Second person of the Trinity; Creator of all
Christian Science	Sin	Illusion, error, not real	Disobedience to God
New Age	Salvation	Becoming One with the universe/god	Reconciliation with God by means of Christ's atonement and resurrection

Is it any wonder that orthodox Christians feel called upon to openly denounce such perversions of clearly defined and historically accepted biblical terminology, and claim that the cults have no rights—scholastically, biblically, or linguistically—to redefine biblical terms as they do?

We ought never to forget for one moment that things are what they are by definition. Any geometric figure whose circumference is $2\pi r$ is by definition circular. Any two figures whose congruency can be determined by the application of angle-side-angle, side-angle-side, or side-side-side is, by definition, a triangle.

To expand this, we might point out that any formula that expresses hydrogen to be in two parts and oxygen to be in one is water, and hydrogen to be in two parts, sulfur in one part, and oxygen in four parts is sulfuric acid. H_2O can never be H_2SO_4. Nor can the Atonement become *at-one-ment* as the theology of the Gnostic cults (Christian Science, Unity, New Thought) explains it. It simply cannot be, if language means anything.

To spiritualize texts and doctrines or attempt to explain them away on the basis of the nebulous word *interpretation* is scholastic dishonesty, and it is not uncommonly found in leading cult literature. Cultists are destined to find out that the power of Christianity is not in its terminology but in the relationship of the individual to the historic Christ of revelation. The divine-human encounter must take place. One must become a new creation in Christ Jesus, and the emptying of Christian terminology of all its historic meanings serves only the purpose of confusion and can never vitiate the force of the Gospel, which is the Person of the Savior performing the historic function of redeeming the sinner by grace.

The Christ of Scripture is an eternal, divine personality who cannot be dismissed by a flip of the cultist's redefinition switch, regardless of how deftly it is done. The average Christian will do well to remember the basic conflict of terminology that he is certain to encounter when dealing with cultists of practically every variety.

Whenever a Christian encounters a cultist then, certain primary thoughts must be paramount in his mind: (1) he must strive to direct the conversation to the problem of terminology and maneuver the cult adherent into a position where he must define his usage of terms and his authority, if any, for drastic, unbiblical redefinitions, which are certain to emerge; (2) the Christian must then compare these "definitions" with the various contexts of the verses upon which the cultist draws support of his doctrinal interpretations; (3) he must define the words *interpretation* and *historic orthodoxy*, and standard doctrinal phrases such as *the new birth, atonement, context, exegesis, eternal judgment,* etc., so that no misunderstanding will exist when these things come under discussion, as they inevitably will; (4) the Christian must attempt to lead the cultist to a review of the importance of properly defining terms for all important doctrines involved, particularly the doctrine of personal redemption from sin, which most cult systems define in a markedly unbiblical manner; (5) it is the responsibility of the Christian to present a clear testimony of his own regenerative experience with Jesus Christ in terminology that has been carefully clarified regarding the necessity of such regeneration on the part of the cultist in the light of the certain reality of God's inevitable justice.

It may be necessary also, in the course of discussing terminology and its dishonest recasting by cult systems, to resort to occasional polemic utterances. In such cases, the Christian should be certain that they are tempered with patience and love, so that the cultist appreciates that such tactics are motivated by one's personal concern for his eternal welfare, and not just to "win the argument."

Let it never be forgotten that cultists are experts at lifting texts out of their respective contexts without proper concern for the laws of language or the established principles of biblical interpretation. There are those of whom Peter warns us, who "wrest . . . scriptures, unto their own destruction" (2 Peter 3:16). This is an accurate picture of the kingdom of the cults in the realm of terminology.

Semantics

Looking back over the picture of cult semantics, the following facts emerge:

1. The average cultist knows his own terminology very thoroughly. He also has a historic knowledge of Christian usage and is therefore prepared to discuss many areas of Christian theology intelligently.

2. The well-trained cultist will carefully avoid definition of terms concerning cardinal doctrines such as the Trinity, the Deity of Christ, the Atonement, the Bodily Resurrection of our Lord, the process of salvation by grace and justification by faith. If pressed in these areas, he will redefine the terms to fit the semantic framework of orthodoxy unless he is forced to define his terms explicitly.

3. The informed Christian must seek for a point of departure, preferably the authority of the Scriptures, which can become a powerful and useful tool in the hands of the Christian, if properly exercised.

4. The concerned Christian worker must familiarize himself to some extent with the terminology of the major cult systems if he is to enjoy any measure of success in understanding the cultist's mind when bearing a witness for Christ.

We have stressed heavily the issue of terminology and a proper definition of terms throughout this entire chapter. It will not have been wasted effort if the reader has come to realize its importance and will be guided accordingly when approaching the language barrier—an extremely formidable obstacle both to evangelizing cultists and to giving a systematic and effective defense of the Christian faith against their perversions.

/————————————————— **Explore** —————————————————\

Theological Framework
Classical Orthodoxy (Cardinal Doctrines)
Neoorthodoxy
Neoliberalism

/————————————————— **Discuss** —————————————————\

1. What happens when historically accepted terms are redefined? In medicine? In mathematics? In theology?

   —————————————————————————————————————

   —————————————————————————————————————

2. When cult adherents redefine Christian terms, Christians must point to biblical verses and focus on *context*. Why?

   —————————————————————————————————————

   —————————————————————————————————————

3. Why is it important to talk about personal redemption from sin and the justice of God?

   —————————————————————————————————————

   —————————————————————————————————————

4. Was Jesus polemic? If so, what biblical event demonstrates this? (chapter and verse)

_____

_____

Dig Deeper

See *The Kingdom of the Cults Study Guide* available at WalterMartin.com.

3

The Psychological Structure of Cultism

Quick Facts on the Psychological Structure of Cultism

- Recognize that all cult belief systems manifest closed-mindedness, intolerance, and antagonism on a personal level.
- Become a source of neutral, objective data.
- Communicate love and sincerity to those in virtual isolation from the Christian message.
- Avoid terms certain to evoke a theologically conditioned reflex and sever the lines of communication.

Historical Perspective

The history of cultism generally begins with an authoritarian pronouncement on the part of the founder or founders. This in turn is institutionalized during their lifetime or after their death into a dogmatic system that requires absolute faith in the supernatural authority of those who received the initial revelation and whose writings and pronouncements are alleged to have transmitted it.

It is extremely difficult, when approaching the study of the field of non-Christian cults, to accurately appraise such groups without some knowledge of the psychological factors involved in both their formation and growth.

Each cult has what might be called its own "belief system" that follows a distinct pattern and, allowing for obvious differences of personality that exist in any group, can be analyzed and understood in relation to its particular theological structure. Individuals share certain psychological traits in common with fellow cult members.

Examples

1. The Jehovah's Witnesses represent those cult systems that put strong emphasis upon eschatology and prophecy.
2. The Mormons represent those that emphasize priestly authority, secret rituals, and symbols.
3. Christian Science represents the Gnostic cults that ground their experience in metaphysical pantheism and physical healing.

Charles Taze Russell claimed that his writings were indispensable to the study of the Bible for Jehovah's Witnesses. He taught that to study the Bible apart from his inspired comments was to go into spiritual darkness, and that concentration on his writings—even at the expense of studying the Bible—would most certainly lead one into deeper spiritual illumination within two years.

Cult adherents share certain psychological traits in common with fellow members.

When Joseph Smith Jr., the Mormon prophet, and his successor, Brigham Young, wished to implement doctrines or changes of practice in the Mormon Church, they prefaced their remarks with proclamations that God had revealed to them the necessity of such doctrines or practices among the "saints."

Mary Baker Eddy, the founder of Christian Science, also conformed to this pattern by requiring her followers to regard her book *Science and Health With Key to the Scriptures* as a divine revelation, and her religion as a "higher, clearer, and more permanent revelation than before."[1] Mrs. Eddy did not hesitate to state that she would blush to write of this work as she did, if she were its author apart from God.[2]

1. Georgine Milnine, *The Life of Mary Baker G. Eddy and the History of Christian Science* (Grand Rapids: Baker Book House, 1937). Quoted from Mrs. Eddy's personal letter to a student.
2. Mary Baker Eddy, *The First Church of Christ, Scientist, and Miscellany* (Boston: Trustees Under the Will of Mary Baker Eddy, 1941), 1, 15. (First published in 1913.)

Analyzing Cult Belief Systems

There are three regions or levels that psychologists generally recognize in any belief or disbelief system:[3]

1. The first or central region is that which encompasses the individual's basic primitive outlook on the world in which he lives and asks such questions as, "Is the world a threatening place or is it an accepting place?"
2. The second or intermediate region is the area of authority. In other words, whose authority is a person willing to accept in matters pertaining to the functions of life?
3. Finally, there is the peripheral region, which penetrates into the details of the structure of living. The details may vary or change according to the specific content the authority, once accepted, may invoke.

Cult belief systems share much in common:

Closed-mindedness—They are not interested in a rational cognitive evaluation of the facts. The organizational structure interprets the facts to the cultist, generally invoking the Bible and/or its respective founder as the ultimate source of its pronouncements. Such belief systems are in isolation; they never shift to logical consistency. They exist in what we might describe as separate compartments in the cultist's mind and are almost incapable of penetration or disruption if the individual cultist is completely committed to the authority pattern of his organization.

Antagonism on a personal level—The cultist almost always identifies his dislike of the Christian message with the messenger who holds such opposing beliefs.

The identification of opposing beliefs with the individual in the framework of antagonism leads the cultist almost always to reject the individual as well as the belief, a problem closely linked with closed-mindedness and one that is extremely difficult to deal with in general dialogue with cultists.

Hostility—The first step in a systematic undercutting of the problem of hostility is to emphasize theology as the real source of antagonism. Theoretically, if one could drive a wedge between the cult adherent and the personality of the Christian, it would be possible to deal with the individual

3. Milton Rokeach, *The Open and Closed Mind* (New York: Basic Books, 1960).

cultist by becoming a *neutral*, objective source of data. The Christian would then be a person who maintains a system of theology opposed to theirs but is not personally antagonistic toward the cultist.

Such a procedure can go a long way toward allaying hostility. Once someone thoroughly "brainwashed" psychologically by his own authority system—The Watchtower Society, Mrs. Eddy's books, the writings of Joseph Smith and Brigham Young—is confronted by a Christian he can accept on a personal basis apart from differences of theological opinion, the possibility of communication improves markedly.

In effect, the cultist is faced with a dilemma: "How can this person (the Christian) be such an acceptable personality yet not share my theology?" He or she begins to wonder how it is possible for the Christian to accept him as a person and yet not accept his beliefs. This can be the beginning of rapport in the realm of personal evangelism.

Indoctrination—Almost all systems of authority in cult organizations indoctrinate their disciples to believe that anyone who opposes their beliefs cannot be motivated by anything other than satanic force or blind prejudice and ignorance. A cultist's encounter with Christians who do not fit this pattern can produce startling results. A discerning Christian who gives every indication of being unprejudiced, reasonably learned, and possessed of a *genuine love* for the welfare of the cultist himself (which is easily detectable in the Christian's concern for his soul and spiritual well-being) can have a devastating effect upon the conditioning apparatus of any cult system.

Delusion—Above all else, Christians must learn that most cults consider that they have freed their adherents from religious exploitation, which they almost always accuse historic Christianity of practicing. In this connection it becomes a vital necessity to demonstrate genuine interest in the cultist as a person for the sake of himself and his personal redemption, rather than as a possible statistic for any given denomination.

Isolationism—The prime task of Christians who would be effective witnesses for Christ in the midst of the kingdom of the cults is that they be free from all appearance of guile and ulterior motivation, remembering that our main task is to communicate to those who are in virtual isolation from the Christian message.

This isolationism, which can be extreme, must be considered in preparing one's presentation of the Gospel. It is a very real mental and emotional chain that has a stronghold on the cultist's ability to discern truth from error, light from darkness. If the tragedy of Jonestown on November 18, 1978, when over 900 cult followers of "Rev." Jim Jones committed forced suicide, has taught us anything, it has taught us the despair and isolationism of cultists. The following quote from *People's Temple—People's Tomb* illustrates this graphically:

> A sealed note found on the cult commander's body, apparently written by a follower just prior to the ritual suicide, gave additional credence to this theory. "Dad," the note said, "I see no way out. I agree with your decision—I fear only that without you the world may not make it to communism. For my part I am more than tired of this wretched, merciless planet and the hell it holds for so many masses of beautiful people—thank you for the ONLY life I've known."[4]

It is important to remember that the cultic psychological patterns evidenced in manic proportions at Jonestown are present to some degree in each and every cult.

Dogmatism—Almost without exception, all cultic belief systems manifest a type of institutional dogmatism and a pronounced intolerance for any position but their own. This no doubt stems from the fact that non-Christian cult systems that wish to be identified with Christianity almost always claim authority on supernatural grounds.

We do not wish to imply that there is no such thing as an authoritative dogmatism that is valid and true (such as the teachings of Jesus Christ), but rather that cult systems tend to invest with the authority of the supernatural whatever pronouncements are deemed necessary to condition and control the minds of their followers.[5]

Intolerance—The problem of intolerance is closely linked to institutional dogmatism or authoritarianism. Those systems that embody this line of reasoning are resistant to change and penetration since the cults thrive on conformity, ambiguity, and extremeness of belief.

Compartmentalization—Within the structure of non-Christian cult systems, one can observe the peaceful coexistence of beliefs that are beyond a shadow of a doubt logically contradictory. In terms of psychological analysis, it would come under the heading "compartmentalization." In

4. Phil Kerns, *People's Temple—People's Tomb* (Plainfield: Logos International, 1979), 205.
5. Some interesting studies of institutional dogmatism can be found in such books as George Orwell's *1984*, Eric Hoffer's *The True Believer*, and Richard Crossman's volume *The God That Failed*.

1984, George Orwell describes this as "double think." Milton Rokeach, commenting on this, illustrates the point admirably:

> In everyday life we note many examples of "double think"; expressing an abhorrence of violence and at the same time believing it is justifiable under certain conditions; affirming a faith in the common man and at the same time believing that the masses are stupid; being for democracy but also advocating a government run by an intellectual elite; believing in freedom for all but also believing that certain groups should be restricted; believing that science makes no value judgments, but also knowing a good theory from a bad theory and a good experiment from a bad experiment. Such expressions of clearly contradictory beliefs will be taken as one indication of isolation in the belief system. . . . A final indicator of isolation is the outright denial of contradiction. Contradictory facts can be denied in several ways: on grounds of face absurdity ("it is absurd on the face of it"), "chance," "the exception that proves the rule," and "the true facts are not accessible, and the only available sources of information are biased."[6]

Examples

1. Jehovah's Witnesses are well aware of the fact that the Watchtower organization under the leadership of Judge Rutherford maintained that Abraham, Isaac, and Jacob would return to earth before the close of the 1920s, and even bought a home for the patriarchs to dwell in (San Diego, California, Beth Sarim, "the house of princes").

2. At the same time Jehovah's Witnesses are fully aware of the fact that the patriarchs did not materialize on schedule, they cling tenaciously to the same principles of prophetic interpretation that conceived and brought forth the now-defunct interpretations of previous Watchtower leaders. How tenaciously they do cling is evident from their latest fiasco, a prediction that the Battle of Armageddon would occur in 1975. It obviously hasn't occurred yet, but faithful Jehovah's Witnesses are still pounding on the doors of America, telling of the "light" they receive through Jehovah's organization.

3. Well-informed Mormon historians and theologians are equally aware that the first edition of *The Book of Mormon* and the present edition

6. Milton Rokeach, *The Open and Closed Mind* (New York: Basic Books, 1960), 36, 37.

of *The Book of Mormon* are quite different in 3,913[7] separate instances (over 25,000 including punctuation changes), the first edition having been revised and corrected by Joseph Smith and his successors over the last one hundred and fifty years. Yet both the errors and the revisions of *The Book of Mormon* are heralded as divine revelation by Mormons. This is another example of the peaceful coexistence of logical contradiction within the belief system of Mormonism that permits the isolation or compartmentalization of conflicting evidence or concepts.

4. Another example of contradiction is the fact that the Christian Science Church has known for many years that though Mary Baker Eddy spoke vigorously against doctors and drugs—as well as vigorously affirming the unreality of pain, suffering, and disease—she herself was frequently attended in her declining years by doctors. She received injections of morphine for the alleviation of pain, wore glasses, and had her teeth removed when they became diseased. But still the Christian Science Church insists upon the validity of Mrs. Eddy's teachings that deny the very practices Mrs. Eddy herself exemplified. This is a classic example of isolation, which might justly come under the heading of "physician, heal thyself!"

Theological Evaluation

There are many other instances of psychological aberration in cult belief systems but it is apparent that we are confronted with those who believe not the Gospel, "lest the light of the glorious gospel of Christ, who is the image of God, should shine unto them" (2 Corinthians 4:4). The Apostle Paul described them as victims of the master psychologist and propagandist of the ages described by our Lord as "the prince of this world" and by Paul as "the god of this age." The one who by the sheer force of his antagonism to the truth of divine revelation in the person of Jesus Christ has psychologically "blinded the minds" of those who will not believe the Gospel.

This is a psychological blindness and a spiritual blindness brought about by the isolation of man from God through the rebellion of human nature

7. Jerald and Sandra Tanner, *3,913 Changes in the Book of Mormon* (Salt Lake City: Utah Lighthouse Ministry, 1996), Introduction. See also http://www.utlm.org/onlinebooks/3913intro .htm).

and the repeated violation of divine law. These are factors that cannot be ignored, for they are a direct reflection of the forces that from "the heavenlies" dominate the world in which we live (Ephesians 6:10–12).

The Psychological Conditioning Process

The cult systems of Jehovah's Witnesses, Mormonism, and Christian Science condition their adherents to respond to the "outside world" of unbelievers.

In the case of Jehovah's Witnesses, the literature of the Watchtower is replete with examples of a psychological conditioning that elicits a definite pattern of religious reflexes in response to a given stimulus. As Pavlov's dog salivated at the sound of a bell that represented food, so a true Jehovah's Witness will spiritually and emotionally salivate whenever the Watchtower rings the conditioning bell of Russellite theology. The example that I believe best demonstrates this is taken in context from Watchtower publications and speaks for itself:

> In Christendom, as surprising as it may seem to some, the false religious teachings create traditions, and commands of men are both directly and indirectly responsible for the physical and spiritual miseries of the poor, notwithstanding Christendom's showy display of charity.[8]
>
> . . . Haters of God and His people are to be hated, but this does not mean that we will take any opportunity of bringing physical hurt to them in the spirit of malice or spite, for both malice and spite belong to the devil, whereas, pure hatred does not.
>
> We must hate in the truest sense, which is to regard with extreme and active aversion, to consider as loathsome, odious, filthy, to detest. Surely any haters of God are not fit to live on His beautiful earth. . . .
>
> Jehovah's enemies are recognized by their intense dislike for His people and the work these are doing. For they would break it down and have all of Jehovah's Witnesses sentenced to jail or concentration camps if they could. Not because they have anything against the Witnesses personally, but on account of their work. They publish blasphemous lies and reproach the holy name Jehovah. Do we not hate those who hate God? We cannot love those hateful enemies, for they are fit only for destruction.[9]

8. *The Watchtower*, December 1, 1951, 731.
9. Judge J. F. Rutherford, *Reconciliation* (Brooklyn, NY: Watchtower Bible and Tract Society, 1928), 85.

According to the Watchtower, the clergy of Christendom are obviously the villains and are the object of "pure hatred." Just how pure hatred differs from good old-fashioned hatred the Watchtower never gets around to explaining, but it is clear that Christendom (all historic denominations and churches) led by the allegedly corrupt clergy has foisted the "satanically conceived" Trinity doctrine and the doctrines of hell and eternal punishment upon the unsuspecting masses of mankind. Clergymen are therefore always suspect, and their theology is to be regarded as untrustworthy and inspired by Satan.

The doctrines of hell and eternal punishment that stimulate fear of judgment are "unreasonable" and not in accord with the Watchtower concept of the character of God.

The doctrine of the Trinity is satanic in origin, according to the Watchtower, and all these doctrines must be rejected and hated as false.

The Watchtower attaches a polemic significance to certain common theological terms—Holy Trinity, Deity of Christ, Hell, Eternal Punishment, Christendom, immortal soul, etc. Every time one of these terms is mentioned by anyone, the reflex action on the part of the Jehovah's Witnesses is instantaneous and hostile.

If we couple this with the Watchtower's heavy emphasis upon the fulfillment of prophecy and a distorted eschatology, the sense of urgency they radiate about Armageddon—which they believe will solve all these problems by annihilating the clergy and all organized religion—begins to make sense, and the reason for their actions becomes clear.

This entire pattern of preconditioning must be understood so that the Christian can avoid, where possible, direct usage of terms that will almost certainly evoke a theologically conditioned reflex and sever the lines of communication.

An intricate part of the Jehovah's Witness belief system is the conviction that Christians will always attack Jehovah's Witnesses on a personal as well as a religious level. The Witnesses readily assume a martyr or persecution complex the moment any antagonism is manifested toward Russell, Rutherford, their theology, the Watchtower, or themselves. It is apparently a comfortable, somewhat heroic feeling to believe that you are standing alone against the massed forces of "the devil's organization" (a Watchtower synonym for Christendom).

This illusion is made to seem all the more real when unthinking Christians unfortunately accommodate the Witnesses by appearing overly aggressive toward the Watchtower theology or the Witnesses personally.

In the light of Jehovah's Witnesses' insistence upon "pure hatred," one wonders how they live with their own New World Translation of Matthew 5:43–44, which reads,

> You heard that it was said you must love your neighbor and hate your enemy. However, I say to you: continue to love your enemies and pray for those persecuting you; that you may prove yourselves sons of your Father who is in the heavens.

The Watchtower, then, does not hesitate to accuse the clergy and Christendom of provoking all kinds of evil; in fact, they have not hesitated to suggest that Christendom encouraged and did nothing to prevent the two great world wars: "Had Christendom chosen to do so, she could easily have prevented World Wars 1 and 2."[10]

Biblical Perspective

Some of the basic motivations of the Watchtower are clearly seen in stark contrast with the teachings of Holy Scripture and reveal that there is more than a spiritual disorder involved. Indeed, there exist deep psychological overtones, which cannot be considered healthy in any sense of the term.

Jehovah's Witnesses are preoccupied with Armageddon, the theocracy, the end of the age, and "pure hatred," but the Mormons have quite different psychological and theological emphases.

At the very core of Mormon theology there is a tremendous emphasis upon authority as it is invested in the priesthood, rituals, and symbols presided over by the hierarchy of the Mormon Church. Mormons are taught from their earliest days that the priesthood has the key to authority, and that one of the marks that identifies the "restoration" of the true church of Jesus Christ on earth is the fact that this priesthood exists and perpetuates that authority.

A devout Mormon will wear symbolic underclothing, which perpetually reminds him of his responsibility and duties as a Mormon.

There is a tremendous emphasis upon baptism for the remission of sins, tithing, and voluntary missionary service—all of these bind Mormons into a tight, homogeneous circle, escape from which, apart from severe spiritual as well as economic penalties, is virtually impossible.

10. *The Watchtower*, December 1, 1951, 731.

Every Mormon is indoctrinated with the concept that his is the true Christian religion, or to use their terms, "the restoration of Christianity to earth."

The secret rites in the Mormon temples, the rituals connected with baptism for the dead, and the secret handshakes, signs, and symbols bind the average Mormon and his family into what might be called in psychological terms the "in group." Apart from acceptance by this group the average Mormon can find no peace or, for that matter, community status or prestige.

Instances of discrimination against Mormons who have experienced true Christian conversion are not infrequent in Mormon-dominated areas, where a man can lose his business very easily by incurring the disfavor of the Mormon Church.

The social welfare program of the Mormons is another excellent inducement to Mormons to remain faithful, since if the "breadwinner" of the family is injured, loses his job, or dies, the church undertakes the care and support of his family. So effective is this work that during the Great Depression of the 1930s, no Mormon family went hungry and no soup kitchens or bread lines disfigured the domain of Mormondom.

The Mormons also conscientiously invoke the biblical principle of helping each other. They lend to each other, work for each other, and cooperate toward the common goal of bringing "restored Christianity" to the masses of mankind. These and other forces make Mormonism a family-centered religion, which ties the faith of the church to the indissoluble bonds of family unity and loyalty.

This forges an incredibly complex system of pressures and intertwining values over which is superimposed the theological structure of the Mormon Church, which stands between the *average* Mormon and the attainment of "exaltation" or progression to godhood.

With such great psychological, economic, and religious forces concentrated upon him, it is a courageous person indeed who shakes off these varied yokes and steps into the freedom of a genuine experience with the Son of God. But a growing number are doing just this as the Spirit of God continues to call out the church, which is Christ's body.

Christian Science, unlike the two other cults we have considered, is neither interested in bestowing godhood on its adherents (Mormonism) nor pushing the eschatological panic button of Armageddon (Jehovah's Witnesses).

Christian Science is an ingenious mixture of first-century Gnostic theology, eighteenth-century Hegelian philosophy, and nineteenth-century idealism woven into a redefined framework of Christian theology with an emphasis upon the healing of the body by the highly questionable practice of denying its objective material reality.

In Christian Science there is a complete separation between the objective world of physical reality (matter) and the spiritual world of supernatural existence (mind). Mrs. Eddy taught that "man as God's idea is already saved with an everlasting salvation."[11]

It is unnecessary for Christian Scientists to think of themselves as sinners in need of a salvation they believe is already theirs by virtue of the fact that "man is already saved" because he is a reflection of the divine mind.

In Christian Science, there are disturbing psychological aberrations. Mrs. Eddy demanded of her followers that they abstain from any critical contact with the non-spiritual elements of the illusory material world. She forbade the reading of "obnoxious literature," lest Christian Scientists become convinced that the physical body and its diseases, suffering, and inevitable death were real.

There is in Christian Science a subconscious repression, a conscious putting out of one's mind certain things that are disconcerting to the entire configuration of psychological patterns of conditioning.

Christian Scientists are conditioned to believe in the nonexistence of the material world even though their senses testify to its objective reality. They continually affirm that matter has no true existence, and thus, in a very real sense, entertain a type of religious schizophrenia. One side of their personality testifies to the reality of the material world and its inexorable decay, while the conditioning process of Christian Science theology hammers relentlessly to suppress this testimony and affirm that the only true reality is spiritual or mental.

In Margaret Mitchell's classic novel *Gone with the Wind*, Scarlett O'Hara, the heroine, when confronted with the harsh realities of life in the wake of the Civil War, repeatedly states, "I'll think about that tomorrow," as if not thinking about it today would eliminate the reality of its claim at that moment.

11. Mary Baker Eddy, *Miscellaneous Writings* (Boston: Trustees under the Will of Mary Baker Eddy, 1924), 261. First published, 1896.

When working with sensory data, Christian Scientists totally disassociate their religious convictions, for if they did not, they would not continue to feed, clothe, or house their bodies. But in still another sense, they attempt to master the all-too-obvious frailties of the body by the application of a religion which denies the material reality of that body. A psychologist of the behaviorist school in one sense does the same thing. In the office he may talk about "conditioning" and may associate everything, including his home, with mechanistic psychology; however, at home he still loves his wife and children, and doesn't respond in that same manner. This is one of the chief reasons why Christian Scientists sometimes appear to be almost immune to the conviction of personal guilt as a result of sin.

Guilt implies the threat of judgment and a standard that is the basis of that judgment; hence the reality of the concept of sin, which is transgression of the law of God. Christian Scientists desperately want only a "good" world, a pleasant place full of happiness, life, love, and security. This they can have only if they deny the empirical evidence of the opposites of those concepts.

In effect, they affirm the reality of "good" at the expense of the antithesis of "good," as if by denying the existence of evil one had annihilated evil! There can be no doubt that there is "selective perception" in the mind of the Christian Scientist, which enables him to select those things which are of a metaphysical nature, disassociate them from the sense perception of the physical world, and still maintain his idealistic philosophy and Gnostic theology. This he accomplishes by repressing or suppressing any evidence to the contrary.

By following Mrs. Eddy's advice and avoiding what she would call "obnoxious literature," i.e., evidence that controverts the idealism of Christian Science philosophy, Christian Scientists avoid facing the damaging data of physical reality. It is in effect an act of unconscious suppression, utilized in order to escape the data.

In the kingdom of the cults, we are actually seeing a mosaic of abnormal conditioned behavior patterns that express themselves in a theological framework, utilizing Christian terms perverted by redefinition and represented as "new insight," when in truth they are only old errors with new faces.

The defense mechanisms on a psychological level are apparent when one considers the background and vocabulary of the cult systems. There exists, beyond a shadow of a doubt, an abnormal behavior syndrome operating in the mentality of most cultists, which causes the cultist (in the case of Christian Scientists) to build his theological system upon a preconditioned and artificially induced criterion of evaluation, i.e., the divine mission and inspiration of Mary Baker Eddy. In the case of other cultists, the names Joseph Smith, "Pastor" Russell, Brigham Young, or any other cult authority figure could be supplied, and the conditioned reflex would be virtually the same.

There are many more observations that could be made, but space will not permit. It is my hope that in observing and analyzing the facets of cult behavior patterns already discussed, the reader may obtain a deeper insight and appreciation of the psychological structure of cultism as it continues to influence a growing segment of professing Christendom, which is ill-prepared for the subtleties and dangers of such psychological and theological deviations.

Explore

Authoritarian
Pantheism
Metaphysical
Hegelian philosophy
Gnostic

Discuss

1. Why are psychological factors important?

2. What do cult belief systems have in common?

3. What is conditioning?

_____

_____

4. What does the Bible say about the human heart and how does this influence our choices?

_____

_____

⊢———————————— **Dig Deeper** ————————————⟍

See *The Kingdom of the Cults Study Guide* available at WalterMartin.com.

4

Jehovah's Witnesses

Quick Facts on Jehovah's Witnesses

- Jesus is not Jehovah God; he is the first and only direct creation of God and the agent through which Jehovah made all other things.

- Jesus' true followers are known by their worship of the true and almighty God, Jehovah, who is not a Trinity.

- Jesus was raised from the dead, not with a physical body, but as a mighty spirit Creature.

- The second "coming" of Jesus was an invisible spiritual presence that began in 1914.

- The dead exist only in God's memory: the wicked will not be punished with conscious torment but will be extinguished forever.

Historical Perspective

Charles Taze Russell was the founder of what is now known as the Jehovah's Witnesses cult and the energetic administrator that brought about its far-flung organization. The name Jehovah's Witnesses was taken at Columbus, Ohio, in 1931, to differentiate between the Watchtower organization run by Judge Rutherford, Russell's successor, and those who remained as true followers of Russell as represented by The Dawn Bible Students and the Laymen's Home Missionary Movement.

Russell apparently controlled the entire financial power of the Society and was not accountable to anyone. He was proven to be a perjurer under oath, a sworn adversary of historical Christianity, and a scholastic fraud.

C. T. Russell was born on February 16, 1852, the son of Joseph L. and Anna Eliza Russell, and spent most of his early years in Pittsburgh and Allegheny, Pennsylvania, where at the age of twenty-five he was known to be manager of several men's furnishings stores. At an early age he rejected the doctrine of eternal torment, probably because of the severe indoctrination he had received as a Congregationalist, and as a result of this act entered upon a long and varied career of denunciation aimed at "Organized Religions." In 1870, at the age of eighteen, Russell organized a Bible class in Pittsburgh, which in 1876 elected him "Pastor" of the group. From 1876 to 1878 the "Pastor" was assistant editor of a small Rochester, New York, monthly magazine, but he resigned when a controversy arose over Russell's counterarguments on "the atonement" of Christ.

> The Society has become a great disseminator of propaganda and a challenge to the zeal of every Christian.

Shortly after leaving his position, Russell founded *The Herald of the Morning* (1879), which developed into today's *The Watchtower Announcing Jehovah's Kingdom*. From 6,000 initial issues, the publication has grown to 69,804,000 bimonthly copies (six annually) in 334 languages.[1] The other Watchtower periodical, *Awake!* has a bimonthly circulation of 64,905,000 per month in 184 languages.[2]

The Watchtower Bible and Tract Society claims to have 120,053 congregations throughout the world in 240 different lands. They boast that they have published 220 million New World Translation Bibles and 40 billion pieces of literature in 900 languages from their inception through 2017. Its literature is distributed by the individual Jehovah's Witness, called a "publisher," who is often seen on the street or going door-to-door—some 8.4 million volunteers participate. Missionary activity is carried on by pioneer publishers, of whom there are 1.2 million workers.[3] The Society

1. Self-reported statistics. *The Watchtower*, Vol. 139, No. 1, 2018, 2.
2. *Awake!*, Vol. 99, No. 1, 2018, 2.
3. Current statistics can be found on the official JW.org website, "2017 Grand Totals," accessed February 22, 2018, https://www.jw.org/en/publications/books/2017-service-year-report/2017-grand-totals.

has become a great disseminator of propaganda and a challenge to the zeal of every Christian.

Russell continued his teachings until his death on October 31, 1916, aboard a transcontinental train in Texas. The former pastor had a remarkable life, highly colored with legal entanglements, but not without success in his chosen field. Russell's obituary reads, in part,

> A year after this publication, *The Watch Tower*, had been established, Russell married Maria Ackley in Pittsburgh. She had become interested in him through his teachings, and she helped him in running the Watchtower.
>
> Two years later, in 1881, came "The Watch Tower Bible and Tract Society," the agency through which in later years "Pastor" Russell's sermons were published (as advertisements) in newspapers throughout the world. This Society progressed amazingly under the joint administration of husband and wife, but in 1897 Mrs. Russell left her husband. Six years later, in 1903, she sued for separation. The decree was secured in 1906 following sensational testimony and "Pastor" Russell was scored by the courts.
>
> There was much litigation then that was quite undesirable from the "Pastor's" point of view regarding alimony for his wife, but it was settled in 1909 by the payment of $6,036 to Mrs. Russell. The litigation revealed that "Pastor" Russell's activities in the religious field were carried on through several subsidiary societies and that all of the wealth that flowed into him through these societies was under the control of a holding company in which the "Pastor" held $990 of the $1,000 capital and two of his followers the other $10.[4]

Russell apparently controlled the entire financial power of the Society and was not accountable to anyone.[5] The *Brooklyn Daily Eagle* led the fight to expose the hypocrisy of "Pastor" Russell, and nothing could be more appropriate than their on-the-spot testimony as to his many fraudulent claims.[6] Russell carried on many such advertising stunts, and despite his protestations about earthly governments and laws being organizations of the devil, he was always the first to claim their protection when it was convenient for him to do so.

4. *Brooklyn Daily Eagle*, November 1, 1916 obituary column. The *Brooklyn Daily Eagle* was a newspaper of local and national importance which ran from 1841–1955. See *History of the Brooklyn Daily Eagle*, https://www.bklynlibrary.org/brooklyn-collection/history-brooklyn-daily -eagle for more information. The *Eagle* is a significant historical source in and of itself, but its importance increases even more when we consider that Brooklyn, New York, was an integral part of early Watchtower history. Its headquarters was first established there in 1908.
5. See chapter 4 of *The Kingdom of the Cults* for details on Charles Russell's scandals.
6. *Brooklyn Daily Eagle* citations are available in Chapter 4 of *The Kingdom of the Cults*.

Recent History

Upon Russell's death the helm of leadership was manned by Judge Joseph Franklin Rutherford, who acquitted himself nobly in the eyes of the Society by attacking the doctrines of "organized religion" with unparalleled vigor, and whose radio talks, phonograph recordings, numerous books, and resounding blasts against Christendom reverberated down the annals of the organization until his death on January 8, 1942, from cancer, at his palatial mansion, "Beth Sarim" or "House of Princes," in San Diego, California. He was seventy-two. Rutherford's career was no less amazing than Russell's, for the judge was an adversary of no mean proportions, whether in action against "organized religion," which he termed "rackets," or against those who questioned his decisions in the Society.

Throughout the years following Russell's death, Rutherford rose in power and popularity among the "Russellites," and to oppose him was tantamount to questioning the authority of Jehovah himself. An example of this one-man sovereignty concerns the friction that occurred in the movement when Rutherford denounced Russell's pyramid prophecies scheme as an attempt to find God's will outside the Scriptures (1929). Many followers of Russell's theory left the Society as a result of this action by Rutherford, only to be witheringly blasted by the vituperative Judge, who threatened that they would "suffer destruction" if they did not repent and recognize Jehovah's will as expressed through the Society.

Rutherford also approached at times the inflated egotism of his predecessor Russell, especially when in his pamphlet *Why Serve Jehovah?* he declared in effect that he was the mouthpiece of Jehovah for this age and that God had designated his words as the expression of divine mandate. It is indeed profitable to observe that Rutherford, as do all would-be "incarnations of infallibility," manifested unfathomable ignorance of God's express injunctions, especially against the preaching of "any other gospel" (Galatians 1:8–9). It was under the leadership of the judge that the Russellites adopted the name "Jehovah's Witnesses" (1931), partly to distinguish Rutherford's group from the splinter groups that arose after Russell's death.

In comparing Russell and Rutherford it must be noted that the former was a literary pygmy compared with his successor. Russell's writings were distributed, some fifteen or twenty million copies of them, over a period of sixty years, but Rutherford's in half that time were many times that amount.

The prolific judge wrote over one hundred books and pamphlets, and his works as of 1941 had been translated into eighty languages.

Thus, he was the Society's second great champion who, regardless of his many failings, was truly an unusual man by any standard. Russell and Rutherford are the two key figures in the Society's history, and without them it is doubtful that the organization would ever have come into existence.

One of the most distressing traits manifested in the literature and teachings of Jehovah's Witnesses is their seemingly complete disregard for historical facts and dependable literary consistency. At the same time, however, they condemn all religious opponents as "enemies of God"[7] and perpetrators of what they term "a racket."[8]

Historically, Jehovah's Witnesses have quoted "Pastor" Russell numerous times since his death in 1916. The following is a token sample of what we can produce as concrete evidence. In 1923, seven years after the "pastor's" demise, Judge J. F. Rutherford, heir to the Russellite throne, wrote a booklet some fifty-odd pages in length, entitled *World Distress: Why and the Remedy*. In this informative treatise, the new president of The Watch Tower Bible and Tract Society and the International Bible Students quoted "Pastor" Russell no fewer than *sixteen* separate times; referred to his books *Studies in the Scriptures* at least twelve times; and devoted six pages at the end of the booklet to advertising these same volumes. Further than this, in a fifty-seven-page pamphlet published in 1925, entitled *Comfort for the People*, by the same Rutherford, "His Honor," in true Russellite character, defines clergymen as "dumb dogs (D. D.)," proceeds to quote "Pastor" Russell's prophetical chronology (AD 1914),[9] and then sums up his tirade against Christendom universal by recommending Russell's writing in four pages of advertisements at the back of the book.

Jehovah's Witnesses in the Divine Purpose was published still later and gave high praise to Russell as well. The Society's debt to Russell as founder and to his teachings as foundational is still acknowledged in Watchtower publications such as their 1979 publication, *Jehovah's Witnesses in the Twentieth Century*. In the Internet age, they devote a small portion of their website to Russell as the one who began the modern-day Watchtower Bible

7. J. F. Rutherford, *Deliverance* (Brooklyn: Watchtower Bible and Tract Society, 1926), 91.
8. J. F. Rutherford, *Religion* (Brooklyn: Watchtower Bible and Tract Society, 1927), 88, 104, 133, 137, 140–141, etc.
9. Jehovah's Witnesses still hold to it today and teach it as dogma.

and Tract Society.[10] They credit Jesus as the "Founder of Christianity" and then they draw the line from Christ to Russell.[11]

Theological Evaluation

Doctrines of Jehovah's Witnesses

1. There is one solitary being from all eternity, Jehovah God, the Creator and Preserver of the Universe and of all things visible and invisible.

2. The Word or Logos is "a god," a mighty god, the "beginning of the Creation" of Jehovah and His active agent in the creation of all things. The Logos was made human as the man Jesus and suffered death to produce the ransom or redemptive price for obedient men.

3. The Bible is the inerrant, infallible, inspired Word of God as it was originally given, and has been preserved by Him as the revealer of His purposes.

4. Satan was a great angel who rebelled against Jehovah and challenged His Sovereignty. Through Satan, sin and death came upon man. His destiny is annihilation with all his followers.

5. Man was created in the image of Jehovah but willfully sinned, hence all men are born sinners and are "of the earth." Those who follow Jesus Christ faithful to the death will inherit the heavenly Kingdom with Him. Men of good will who accept Jehovah and His Theocratic Rule will enjoy the "new earth"; all others who reject Jehovah will be annihilated.

6. The atonement is a ransom paid to Jehovah God by Christ Jesus and is applicable to all who accept it in righteousness. In brief, the death of Jesus removed the effects of Adam's sin on his offspring and laid the foundation of the New World of righteousness including the Millennium of Christ's reign.

7. The man Christ Jesus was resurrected a divine spirit creature after offering the ransom for obedient man.

10. "Who Was the Founder of Jehovah's Witnesses?," accessed February 18, 2018, https://www.jw.org/en/jehovahs-witnesses/faq/founder.
11. For most of their history, the Watchtower has limited their association with Russell, but this line from Christ to Russell avoids even the Apostles themselves and the early Church Fathers!

8. The soul of man is not eternal but mortal, and it can die. Animals likewise have souls, though man has the preeminence by special creation.

9. Hell, meaning a place of "fiery torment" where sinners remain after death until the resurrection, does not exist. This is a doctrine of "Organized Religion," not the Bible. Hell is the common grave of mankind, literally *sheol* (Hebrew), "a place of rest in hope" where the departed sleep until the resurrection by Jehovah God.

> The man Christ Jesus was resurrected a divine spirit creature.

10. Eternal Punishment is a punishment or penalty of which there is no end. It does not mean "eternal torment" of living souls. Annihilation, the second death, is the lot of all those who reject Jehovah God, and it is eternal.

11. Jesus Christ has returned to earth AD 1914, has expelled Satan from Heaven, and is proceeding to overthrow Satan's organization, establish the Theocratic Millennial Kingdom, and vindicate the name of Jehovah God. He did not return in a physical form and is invisible as the Logos.

12. The Kingdom of Jehovah is Supreme, and as such cannot be compatible with present Human Government ("Devil's Visible Organization"), and any allegiance to them in any way which violates the allegiance owed to Him is a violation of the Scripture.

The Holy Trinity

1. "The obvious conclusion is, therefore, that Satan is the originator of the Trinity doctrine" (*Let God Be True*, Brooklyn: Watchtower Bible and Tract Socieety, 1946 ed., 101).

2. "Sincere persons who want to know the true God and serve Him find it a bit difficult to love and worship a complicated, freakish-looking, three-headed God" (*LGBT*, 102).

3. "Any trying to reason out the Trinity teaching leads to confusion of mind. So the Trinity teaching confuses the meaning of John 1:1–2; it does not simplify it or make it clear or easily understandable" (*"The Word," Who Is He? According to John*, 7).

Deity of Christ

1. "The true Scriptures speak of God's Son, the Word, as 'a god.' He is a 'mighty god,' but not the Almighty God, who is Jehovah" (*The Truth Shall Make You Free*, Brooklyn: Watchtower Bible and Tract Society, 1943, 47).
2. "In other words, he was the first and direct creation of Jehovah God" (*The Kingdom Is at Hand*, Brooklyn: Watchtower Bible and Tract Society, 1944, 46–47, 49).
3. "The Bible shows that there is only one God . . . greater than His Son . . . and that the Son, as the Firstborn, Only-begotten, and 'the creation by God,' had a beginning. That the Father is greater and older than the Son is reasonable, easy to understand, and is what the Bible teaches" (*From Paradise Lost to Paradise Regained*, Brooklyn: Watchtower Bible and Tract Society, 1958, 164).
4. "As chief of the angels and next to the Father, he [Christ] was known as the Archangel (highest angel or messenger), whose name, Michael, signifies 'Who as God' or 'God's Representative'" (*Studies in the Scriptures*, Brooklyn: International Bible Student Association, 1911 ed., 5:84).

   "Being the only begotten Son of God . . . the Word would be a prince among all other creatures. In this office he [Christ] bore another name in heaven, which name is 'Michael'. . . . Other names were given to the Son in course of time" (*TTSMYF*, 49).

The Holy Spirit

1. "As for the 'Holy Spirit,' the so-called 'third Person of the Trinity,' we have already seen that it is not a person, but God's active force" (*The Truth That Leads to Eternal Life*, Brooklyn: Watchtower Bible and Tract Society, 1968, 24).
2. "The Bible's use of 'holy spirit' indicates that it is a controlled force that Jehovah God uses to accomplish a variety of his purposes. To a certain extent, it can be likened to electricity, a force that can be adapted to perform a great variety of operations" (*Should You Believe in the Trinity?*, Brooklyn: Watchtower Bible and Tract Society, 2006, 20).
3. "No, the holy spirit is not a person and it is not part of a Trinity. The holy spirit is God's active force that he uses to accomplish his will. It

is not equal to God but is always at his disposition and subordinate to him" (*SYBITT*, 23).

The Virgin Birth

1. "Jesus was conceived by a sinless, perfect Father, Jehovah God. . . . The perfect child Jesus did not get human life from the sinner Adam, but received only a human body through Adam's descendant Mary. Jesus' life came from Jehovah God, the Holy One. . . . Jehovah took the perfect life of his only-begotten Son and transferred it from heaven to . . . the womb of the unmarried girl Mary. . . . Thus God's Son was conceived or given a start as a human creature. It was a miracle. Under Jehovah's holy power the child Jesus, conceived in this way, grew in Mary's womb to the point of birth" (*FPLTPR*, 126–127).
2. "Jesus' birth on earth was not an incarnation. . . . He emptied himself of all things heavenly and spiritual, and God's almighty spirit transferred his Son's life down to the womb of the Jewish virgin of David's descent. By this miracle he was born a man. . . . He was not a spirit-human hybrid, a man and at the same time a spirit person. . . . He *was* flesh" (*What Has Religion Done for Mankind?*, Brooklyn: Watchtower Bible and Tract Society, 1951, 231).
3. "While on earth, Jesus was a human, although a perfect one because it was God who transferred the life-force of Jesus to the womb of Mary" (*Should You Believe in the Trinity?*, 14).

The Atonement

1. "That which is redeemed or bought back is what was lost, namely, perfect human life, with its rights and earthly prospects" (*Let God Be True*, 114).
2. "The human life that Jesus Christ laid down in sacrifice must be exactly equal to that life which Adam forfeited for all his offspring: it must be a perfect human life, no more, no less. . . . This is just what Jesus gave . . . for men of all kinds" (*You May Survive Armageddon into God's New World*, Brooklyn: Watchtower Bible and Tract Society, 1955, 39).
3. "Jesus, no more and no less than a perfect human, became a ransom that compensated exactly for what Adam lost—the right to perfect

human life on earth. . . . The perfect human life of Jesus was the 'corresponding ransom' required by divine justice—no more, no less. A basic principle even of human justice is that the price paid should fit the wrong committed. . . . So the ransom, to be truly in line with God's justice, had to be strictly an equivalent—a perfect human, 'the last Adam.' Thus, when God sent Jesus to earth as the ransom, he made Jesus to be what would satisfy justice, not an incarnation, not a god-man, but a perfect man, 'lower than angels'" (*Should You Believe in the Trinity?*, 15).

Salvation by Grace

1. "We have learned that a person could fall away and be judged unfavorably either now or at Armageddon or during the thousand years of Christ's reign or at the end of the final test . . . into everlasting destruction" (*From Paradise Lost to Paradise Regained*, 241).
2. "Make haste to identify the visible theocratic organization of God that represents his king, Jesus Christ. It is essential for life. Doing so, be complete in accepting its every aspect" (*The Watchtower*, October 1, 1967: 591).
3. "To receive everlasting life in the earthly Paradise we must identify that organization and serve God as part of it" (*The Watchtower*, February 15, 1983: 12).

The Resurrection of Christ

1. "This firstborn from the dead was raised from the grave, not a human creature, but a spirit" (*Let God Be True*, 276).
2. "Jehovah God raised him from the dead, not as a human Son, but as a mighty immortal spirit Son. . . . For forty days after that he materialized, as angels before him had done, to show himself alive to his disciples" (*LGBT*, 40).
3. "Jesus did not take his human body to heaven to be forever a man in heaven. Had he done so, that would have left him even lower than the angels. . . . God did not purpose for Jesus to be humiliated thus forever by being a fleshly man forever. No, but after he had sacrificed his perfect manhood, God raised him to deathless life as a glorious spirit creature" (*LGBT*, 41).

The Triune Deity[12]

One of the greatest doctrines of the Scriptures is that of the Triune Godhead (*tes Theotetos*) or the nature of God himself. To say that this doctrine is a "mystery" is indeed inconclusive, and no informed minister would explain the implications of the doctrine in such abstract terms. Jehovah's Witnesses accuse "the clergy" of doing just that, however, and it is unfortunate to note that they are, as usual, guilty of misstatement in the presentation of the facts and even in their definition of what Christian clergymen believe the Deity to be.

First of all, Christian ministers and Christian laypersons do not believe that there are "three gods in one" (*Let God Be True*, 100), but *do* believe that there are three Persons all of the same Substance—coequal, coexistent, and coeternal. There is ample ground for this belief in the Scriptures, where plurality in the Godhead is very strongly intimated if not expressly declared. Let us consider just a few of these references.

In Genesis 1:26 Jehovah is speaking of Creation, and He speaks in the plural: "Let *us* make man in *our* image, after *our* likeness." Now it is obvious that God would not create man in His image and the angels' images if He were talking to them, so He must have been addressing someone else— and who but His Son and the Holy Spirit who are equal in Substance could He address in such familiar terms? Since there is no other god but Jehovah (Isaiah 43:10–11), not even "a lesser mighty god" as Jehovah's Witnesses affirm Christ to be, there must be a unity in plurality and Substance or the passage is not meaningful. The same is true of Genesis 11:7, when God said at the Tower of Babel, "Let *us* go down," and also of Isaiah 6:8, "Who will go for *us*? . . ." These instances of plurality indicate something deeper than an interpersonal relationship; they strongly suggest what the New Testament fully develops, namely, a Tri-Unity in the One God. The claim of Jehovah's Witnesses that the early church Fathers, including Tertullian and Theophilus, propagated and introduced the threefold unity of God into Christianity is ridiculous and hardly worth refuting. Any unbiased study of the facts will convince the impartial student that before Tertullian or

---

12. Jehovah's Witnesses take great delight in pointing out that the word "Trinity" does not appear as such in the Bible. They further state that since it is not a part of Scripture, it must be of pagan origin and should be discounted entirely. What the Witnesses fail to understand is that the very word *Jehovah*, which they maintain is the only true name for God, also does not appear as such in the Bible, but is an interpolation of the Hebrew consonants *YHWH* or *JHVH*, any vowels added being arbitrary. Thus it is seen that the very name by which they call themselves is just as unbiblical as they suppose the Trinity to be.

Theophilus lived, the doctrine was under study and considered sound. No one doubts that among the heathen (Babylonians and Egyptians) demon gods were worshiped, but to call the Triune Godhead a doctrine of the devil (*Let God Be True*, 101), as Jehovah's Witnesses do, is blasphemy and the product of untutored and darkened souls.

In the entire chapter titled "Is there a Trinity?" (*Let God Be True*, 100–101), the whole problem as to why the Trinity doctrine is "confusing" to Jehovah's Witnesses lies in their interpretation of "death" as it is used in the Bible. To Jehovah's Witnesses, death is the cessation of consciousness, or *destruction*. However, no single or collective rendering of Greek or Hebrew words in any reputable lexicon or dictionary will substantiate their view. Death in the Scriptures is "separation" from the body as in the case of the first death (physical), and separation from God for eternity as in the second death (the lake of fire, Revelation 20). Death never means annihilation, and Jehovah's Witnesses cannot bring in one word in context in the original languages to prove it does. A wealth of evidence has been amassed to prove it does not. I welcome comparisons on this point.

The rest of the chapter is taken up with childish questions—some of which are painful to record. "Who ran the universe the three days Jesus was dead and in the grave?" (death again portrayed as extinction of consciousness) is a sample of the nonsense perpetrated on gullible people. "Religionists" is the label placed on all who disagree with the organization's views regardless of the validity of the criticism. Christians do not believe that the Trinity was incarnate in Christ and that they were "three in one" as such during Christ's ministry. Christ voluntarily limited himself in His earthly body, but heaven was always open to Him and He never ceased being God, Second Person of the Trinity. At His baptism the Holy Spirit descended like a dove, the Father spoke, and the Son was baptized.

What further proof is needed to show a threefold unity? Compare the baptism of Christ (Matthew 3:16–17) with the commission to preach in the threefold Name of God (Matthew 28:19) and the evidence is clear and undeniable. Even in the Incarnation itself (Luke 1:35) the Trinity appears (see also John 14:16 and 15:26). Of course it is not possible to fathom this great revelation completely, but this we do know: There is a unity of Substance, not three gods, and that unity is One in every sense, which no reasonable person can doubt after surveying the evidence. When Jesus said, "My Father is greater than I," He spoke the truth, for in the form of a servant (Philippians 2:7) and as a man, the Son was subject to the Father willingly; but upon His resurrection and in the radiance of His glory taken again from whence He veiled it (2:7–8). He showed forth His deity when He declared, "All authority is surrendered to me in heaven and earth" (Matthew 28:18); proof positive of His intrinsic nature and unity of Substance. It is evident that the Lord Jesus Christ was never inferior—speaking of His nature—to His Father during His sojourn on earth.

Jehovah's Witnesses vs. the Scriptures, Reason, and the Trinity

Every major cult and non-Christian religion that seeks to deride orthodox theology continually attacks the doctrine of the Trinity. Jehovah's Witnesses (the Russellites of today) are the most vehement in this endeavor, and because they couch their clever misuse of terminology in scriptural contexts, they are also the most dangerous. Throughout the whole length and breadth of the Watchtower's turbulent history, one "criterion" has been used in every era to measure the credibility of any biblical doctrine. This "criterion" is *reason*. During the era of "Pastor" Russell, and right through until today, reason has always been "the great god" before whom all followers of the Millennial Dawn[13] movement allegedly bow with unmatched reverence. In fact, the "great paraphraser," as Russell was once dubbed, even went so far as to claim that reason—or the ability to think and draw conclusions—opened up to the intellect of man the very character of God himself!

Think of it—according to the "pastor," God's nature is actually openly accessible to our feeble and erring reasoning powers. In the first volume of the *Millennial Dawn* series (later titled *Studies in the Scriptures*), "Pastor" Russell makes God subject to our powers of reasoning. Wrote the "pastor": "Let us examine the character of the writings claimed as inspired (The Bible), to see whether their teachings correspond with the character we have *reasonably* imputed to God" (p. 41). Here it is plain to see that for Russell, man's understanding of God's character lies not in God's revelation of himself to be taken by faith, but in our ability to reason out that character subject to the laws of our reasoning processes.

Russell obviously never considered Jehovah's Word as recorded in the fifty-fifth chapter of Isaiah the prophet, which discourse clearly negates man's powers of reasoning in relation to the divine character and nature of his Creator.

---

13. Name originally given to the movement by Russell in 1886.

For my thoughts are not your thoughts, neither are your ways my ways, saith the Lord. For as the heavens are higher than the earth, so are my ways higher than your ways, and my thoughts than your thoughts (Isaiah 55:8–9).

By this statement God certainly did not say reason and thought should be abandoned in the process of inquiry, but merely that no one can know the mind, nature, or thoughts of God in all their fullness, seeing that man is finite and He is infinite. The term *reason* and derivatives of it (*reasonable, reasoning, reasoned*, etc.) are used eighty-eight times in the English Bible, and only *once* in all these usages (Isaiah 1:18) does God address man. Jehovah's Witnesses maintain that since God said, "Come now and let us reason together," He therefore gave reason a high place, even using it himself to commune with His creatures. While this is true, it is only so in a limited sense at best.

God never said, "Reason out the construction of my spiritual substance and nature" or "Limit my character to your reasoning powers." Nevertheless, Jehovah's Witnesses, by making Christ (the Logos, John 1:1) "a god" or "a mighty god," but not "Jehovah God," have done these very things. In the reference quoted above (Isaiah 1:18), Jehovah showed man the way of salvation and invited him to be redeemed from sin. God never invited him to explore His deity or probe into His mind. The Apostle Paul says, "For who hath known the mind of the Lord? or who hath been his counselor? or who hath first given to him, and it shall be recompensed unto him again? For of him, and through him, and to him, are all things: to whom be glory for ever" (Romans 11:34–36).

But now let us examine this typical propaganda from the Watchtower's arsenal and see if they really do follow "Pastor" Russell and his theory of reason. In this article,[14] "The Scriptures, Reason, and the Trinity," the Witnesses constantly appeal to *reason* as the standard for determining what God thinks. The following are quotations that we believe illustrate this point beyond doubt. In addition, we will compare the statements of this article at strategic points with a much more recent publication, *Should You Believe in the Trinity?*[15] to show that the teaching has remained consistent over time.

1. "To hold that Jehovah God the Father and Christ Jesus His Son are coeternal is to fly in the face of reason" (*Watchtower*). Notice that reason

14. *The Watchtower* (January 1, 1973).
15. *Should You Believe in the Trinity?* (Brooklyn: Watchtower Bible and Tract Society, 1989), 15–26.

is used as the "yardstick" to determine the validity of a scriptural doctrine. The more recent publication remarks concerning the Trinity: "Is such reasoning hard to follow? Many sincere believers have found it to be confusing, contrary to normal reason, unlike anything in their experience" (*Should You Believe in the Trinity?*, 3).

2. "Jehovah God says, 'Come now, and let us reason together' (Isaiah 1:18). The advocates of the Trinity admit that it is not subject to reason or logic, and so they resort to terming it a 'mystery.' But the Bible contains no divine mysteries. It contains 'sacred secrets.' Every use of the word 'mystery' and 'mysteries' in the *King James Version* comes from the same Greek root word meaning 'to shut the mouth,' that is to keep secret. There is a vast difference between a secret and a mystery. A secret is merely that which has not been made known, but a mystery is that which cannot be understood.

"However, contending that since the Trinity is such a confusing mystery it must have come from divine revelation creates another major problem. Why? Because divine revelation itself does not allow for such a view of God: 'God is not a God of confusion.' In view of that statement, would God be responsible for a doctrine about himself that is so confusing that even Hebrew, Greek, and Latin scholars cannot really explain it?" (*Believe*, 5).

Once again the interested reader must pay close attention to the Witnesses' favorite game of term-switching. *The Watchtower* makes a clever distinction between the term *mystery* and the term *secret* and declares that "the Bible contains no divine mysteries." In view of the seriousness of this Watchtower exercise in semantics, we feel obliged to destroy their manufactured distinction between *secret* and *mystery*, by the simple process of consulting the dictionary.

Mystery is defined as (1) "Secret, something that is hidden or unknown"; *Secret* is defined as (1) "Something secret or hidden; mystery." Surely this is proof conclusive that the Bible contains "divine mysteries" as far as the meaning of the term is understood. It must also be equally apparent that Jehovah's Witnesses obviously have no ground for rejecting the word *mystery* where either the Bible or the dictionary are concerned. We fail to note any "vast difference" between the two words, and so does the dictionary. The truth is that the Watchtower rejects the Trinity doctrine and other cardinal doctrines of historical Christianity not because they are mysterious, but because Jehovah's Witnesses are determined to reduce Jesus, the Son of God, to a creature or "a second god," all biblical evidence notwithstanding. They still follow in "Pastor" Russell's footsteps, and one needs no dictionary to substantiate that.

3. "Jehovah God by His Word furnishes us with ample *reasons* and logical bases for all regarding which he expects us to exercise faith. . . . We can make sure of what is right only by a process of reasoning on God's Word."

Here indeed is a prime example of what Jehovah's Witnesses continually represent as sound thinking. They cannot produce even one shred of evidence to bolster up their unscriptural claim that God always gives us reason for those things in which He wants us to "exercise faith." Biblical students (even "International" ones)[16] really grasp at theological straws in the wind when they attempt to prove so dogmatic and inconclusive a statement.[17]

The Watchtower widely cries that they will meet all persons with an open Bible, but to this date not one of their alleged authorities has materialized despite our numerous invitations. We of orthodox Christianity do not desire to maliciously attack anyone's faith merely for the "joy" of doing it; but we must be faithful to our Lord's command to "preach the word and contend for the faith." As long as the Watchtower continues to masquerade as a Christian movement and attack, without biblical provocation or cause, orthodox Christian theology with such articles as "The Scripture, Reason, and the Trinity," etc., so long will our voice be raised in answer to their consistent misrepresentations. God granting us the grace, we can do no other but be faithful to Him "who is the faithful and true witness, the *source* through whom God's creation came" (Revelation 3:14, Knox Version)—His eternal Word and beloved Son, Jesus Christ, our Lord.

Jehovah's Witnesses and the Holy Spirit

Though it is rudimentary to any study of the Bible, the personality and deity of the Holy Spirit must constantly be defended against the attacks of the Watchtower.

The Watchtower, as has been seen, denies the Holy Spirit's personality and deity, but the following references, only a few of many in Scripture, refute their stand completely:

16. Russellism, which rejected Rutherford, still exists under various names, such as Free Bible Students, the Laymen's Home Missionary Movement (Paul Johnson), and International Bible Students.
17. This argument is continued in chapter 4 of *The Kingdom of the Cults* (2019).

(1) *Acts 5:3–4.* In verse three, Peter accuses Ananias of lying *to* the Holy Spirit, and in verse four he declares the Holy Spirit to be God, an equation hard for the Watchtower to explain, much less deny. Who else but a person can be lied to?

(2) *Acts 13:2, 4.* In this context the Holy Spirit *speaks* and *sends*, as He does in 21:10–11, where He *prophesies* Paul's imprisonment. Only a personality can do these things, *not* "an invisible active force," as the Jehovah's Witnesses describe Him.

(3) *2 Samuel 23:2–3.* This serves as a good Old Testament example of the Holy Spirit's person and deity. David's introduction to his prophecy has the Holy Spirit as the speaker (person, His word) and He is also the "God of Israel." It is the same speaker throughout this introduction, the Holy Spirit, the God of Israel.

(4) Finally, such references as *John 14:16–17, 26; 16:7–14* need no comment. *He* is a divine person and He is God (Genesis 1:2).

The New World Translation of the Bible

In any dealings one may have with the Watchtower or its numerous representatives, it is a virtual certainty that sooner or later in the course of events the Watchtower's "translation" of the Bible will confront the average prospective convert. This translation of the entire Bible is called the *New World Translation of the Holy Scriptures.* It is usually abbreviated as NWT.

The "translation" has had wide distribution on all six continents. Jehovah's Witnesses boast that their "translation" is "the work of competent scholars" and further that it gives a clarity to the Scriptures that other translations have somehow failed to supply. Such stupendous claims by the Watchtower involve the necessity of a careful examination of their "translation" so that it may be weighed by the standards of sound biblical scholarship. An exhaustive analysis of this work is impossible in this limited space, but we have selected some of the outstanding examples of fraud and deceit from the *New World Translation.* These examples should discourage any fair-minded individual from placing much value upon the Jehovah's Witnesses' Bible.

> The New World Bible translation committee had no known translators with recognized degrees.

THE KINGDOM OF THE CULTS HANDBOOK

The New World Bible translation committee had no known translators with recognized degrees in Greek or Hebrew exegesis or translation. In fact, Frederick W. Franz, then representing the translation committee and later serving as the Watchtower Society's fourth president, admitted under oath that he could not translate Genesis 2:4 from the Hebrew.[18]

Biblical Perspective

The Watchtower "translation" speaks for itself and shows more clearly than pen can the scholastic dishonesty and lack of scholarship so rampant within its covers. In order to point out these glaring inconsistencies, the author has listed four prime examples of the Watchtower's inaccuracies in translating the New Testament.

The Watchtower's Scriptural Distortions

(1) The first major perversion that Jehovah's Witnesses attempt to foist upon the minds of the average reader is that it has remained for them as "God's true Witnesses" to restore the divine Old Testament name *Jehovah* to the text of the Greek New Testament. But let us observe this pretext as they stated it in their own words:

> The evidence is, therefore, that the original text of the Christian Greek Scriptures has been tampered with, the same as the text of the LXX [the Septuagint—a Greek translation of the Old Testament] has been. And, at least from the third century AD onward, the divine name in tetragrammaton [the Hebrew consonants YHWH usually rendered "Jehovah"] form has been eliminated from the text by copyists. . . . In place of it they substituted the words *kyrios* (usually translated "the Lord") and *theos*, meaning "God" (*New World Translation of the Christian Greek Scriptures*, 1950, 18).

The "evidence" that the Witnesses refer to is a papyrus roll of the LXX, which contains the second half of the book of Deuteronomy and which does have the tetragrammaton throughout. Further than this, the Witnesses refer to Aquila (AD 128) and Origen (ca. AD 250), who both utilized the tetragrammaton in their respective *Version* and *Hexapla*. Jerome, in the

18. A section of the Franz court transcript is available for review in chapter 4 of *The Kingdom of the Cults* (2019).

fourth century, also mentioned the tetragrammaton as appearing in certain Greek volumes even in his day. On the basis of this small collection of fragmentary "evidence," Jehovah's Witnesses conclude their argument:

> It proves that the original LXX did contain the divine name wherever it occurred in the Hebrew original. Considering it a sacrilege to use some substitute such as *kyrios* or *theos*, the scribes inserted the tetragrammaton at its proper place in the Greek version text (12).

The whole case the Witnesses try to prove is that the original LXX and the New Testament autographs all used the tetragrammaton (p. 18) but owing to "tampering" all these were changed; hence, their responsibility to restore the divine name. Such is the argument, and a seemingly plausible one to those not familiar with the history of manuscripts and the Witnesses' subtle use of terms.

To explode this latest Watchtower pretension of scholarship completely is an elementary task. It can be shown from literally thousands of copies of the Greek New Testament that not *once* does the tetragrammaton appear, not even in Matthew, which was possibly written in Hebrew or Aramaic originally, therefore making it more prone than all the rest to have traces of the divine name in it—yet it does not! Beyond this, the roll of papyrus (LXX) that contains the latter part of Deuteronomy and the divine name only proves that one copy did have the divine name (YHWH), whereas all other existing copies use *kyrios* and *theos*, which the Witnesses claim are "substitutes." The testimonies of Aquila, Origen, and Jerome, in turn, only show that *sometimes* the divine name was used, but the general truth upheld by all scholars is that the Septuagint, with minor exceptions, always uses *kyrios* and *theos* in place of the tetragrammaton, and the New Testament never uses it at all. Relative to the nineteen "sources" the Watchtower uses in their Foreword (30–33) for restoring the tetragrammaton to the New Testament, it should be noted that they are all translations from Greek (which uses *kyrios* and *theos*, not the tetragrammaton) back into Hebrew, the earliest of which is AD 1385, and therefore they are of no value as evidence.

These cold logical facts unmask once and for all the shallow scholarship of Jehovah's Witnesses, whose arrogant pretension that they have a sound basis for restoring the divine name (Jehovah) to the Scriptures while inferring that orthodoxy suppressed it centuries ago is revealed to be a hollow scholastic fraud. After arduously arguing in favor of restoring Jehovah to the New Testament, the Watchtower admits that there is no evidence for it in the Greek text: "Manuscripts of the book of Revelation . . . have God's name in its abbreviated form, 'Jah,' (in the word 'Hallelujah'). But apart from that, no ancient Greek manuscript that we possess today of the books from Matthew to Revelation contains God's name [the tetragrammaton] in full."[19]

No reasonable scholar, of course, objects to the use of the term Jehovah in the Bible. But since only the Hebrew consonants YHWH appear without vowels, pronunciation is at best uncertain, and dogmatically to settle on *Jehovah* is straining at the bounds of good linguistics. When the Witnesses arrogantly claim then to have "restored" the divine name (Jehovah), it is almost pathetic. All students of Hebrew know that any vowel can be inserted between the consonants (YHWH or JHVH), so that theoretically the divine name could be any combination from JoHeVaH to JiHiViH without doing violence to the grammar of the language in the slightest degree. So much then for this, another empty claim of the Watchtower's pseudo-scholars.

(2) *Colossians 1:16.* "By means of him all [other][20] things were created in the heavens and upon the earth, the things visible and the things invisible, no matter whether they are thrones or lordships or governments or authorities" (NWT, 1984).

In this particular rendering, Jehovah's Witnesses attempt one of the most clever perversions of the New Testament texts that the author has ever seen. Knowing full well that the word *other* does not occur in the Greek text, or for that matter in any of the three verses (16, 17, 19) where it has been added, the Witnesses deliberately insert it into the translation in a vain attempt to make Christ a creature and one of the "things" He is spoken of as having created. The 1950 release of the *New World Translation of the Christian Greek Scriptures* added "other" four times in Colossians 1:16–19 without brackets or otherwise indicating that it was not in the Greek text.[21] In 1961, they added brackets to the word *other* after Christian scholars complained about their dishonesty. It remained that way for fifty years, but in 2013, they returned to their 1950 dishonest practice of

19. *The Divine Name That Will Endure* (Brooklyn: Watchtower Bible and Tract Society, 1997), 23.
20. Brackets are part of the NWT text itself.
21. New World Translation committee explained in 1961 that the brackets for "other" in Colossians and elsewhere, are to "enclose words inserted to complete or clarify the sense in the English text." See *New World Translation*, Foreword, 1961 edition, 6.

inserting "other" into the translated text as if it were in the original Greek. Far from *clarifying* God's Word here, these unwarranted additions serve only to further the erroneous presupposition of the Watchtower that our Lord Jesus Christ is a creature rather than the Eternal Creator.

The entire context of Colossians 1:15–22 is filled with superlatives in its description of the Lord Jesus as the "image of the invisible God, the first begetter [or 'original bringer forth'—Erasmus] of every creature." The Apostle Paul lauds the Son of God as *Creator* of all things (v. 16) and describes Him as existing "before all things" and as the one by whom "all things consist" (v. 17). This is in perfect harmony with the entire picture Scripture paints of the eternal Word of God (John 1:1) who was made flesh (John 1:14) and of whom it was written: "All things were made by him; and without him was not any thing made that was made" (John 1:3). The writer of the book of Hebrews also pointed out that God's Son "[upholds] all things by the word of his power" (Hebrews 1:3) and that He is Deity in all its fullness, even as Paul wrote to the Colossians: "For . . . in him should all fullness [of God] dwell" (Colossians 1:19).

The Scriptures, therefore, bear unmistakable testimony to the creative activity of God's Son, distinguishing Him from among the "things" created, as *the* Creator and Sustainer of "all things."

Jehovah's Witnesses, therefore, have no conceivable ground for this dishonest rendering of Colossians 1:16–17 and 19 by the insertion of the word *other*, since they are supported by no grammatical authorities, nor do they dare to dispute their perversions with competent scholars lest they further parade their obvious ignorance of Greek exegesis.

(3) *Matthew 27:50*. "Again Jesus cried out with a loud voice, and yielded up his breath" (NWT, 1961 edition).

Luke 23:46. "And Jesus called with a loud voice and said: Father, into your hands I entrust my spirit" (NWT, 1961 edition).

For many years the Watchtower has been fighting a vain battle to redefine biblical terms to suit their peculiar theological interpretations. They have had some measure of success in this attempt in that they have taught the rank and file a new meaning for tried and true biblical terms, and it is this trait of their deceptive system that we analyze now in connection with the above quoted verses.

The interested student of Scripture will note from Matthew 27:50 and Luke 23:46 that they are parallel passages describing the same event, namely, the crucifixion of Jesus Christ. In Matthew's account, the Witnesses had no difficulty substituting the word *breath* for the Greek *spirit* (*pneuma*), for in their vocabulary this word has many meanings, none of them having any bearing upon the general usage of the term, i.e., that of an immaterial, cognizant nature, inherent in man by definition and descriptive of angels through Creation. Jehovah's Witnesses reject this immaterial nature in man and call it "breath," "life," "mental disposition," or "something wind like." In fact, they will call it anything but what God's Word says it is, an invisible nature, eternal by creation, a spirit, made in the image of God (Genesis 1:27). Sometimes, and in various contexts, spirit (*pneuma*) can mean some of the things the Witnesses hold, but context determines translation, along with grammar, and their translations quite often do not remain true to either.

Having forced the word *breath* into Matthew's account of the crucifixion to make it appear that Jesus only stopped breathing and did not yield up His invisible nature upon dying, the Witnesses plod on to Luke's account, only to be caught in their own trap. Luke, learned scholar and master of Greek that he was, forces the Witnesses to render his account of Christ's words using the correct term *spirit* (*pneuma*), instead of "breath" as in Matthew 27:50. Thus in one fell swoop the entire Watchtower fabric of manufactured terminology collapses, because Jesus would hardly have said: "Father, into thy hands I commit my *breath*"—yet if the Witnesses are consistent, which they seldom are, why did they not render the identical Greek term (*pneuma*) as "breath" both times, for it is a parallel account of the same scene!

The solution to this question is quite elementary, as all can clearly see. The Witnesses could not render it "breath" in Luke and get away with it, so they used it where they could and hoped nobody would notice either it or the different rendering in Matthew. The very fact that Christ dismissed His spirit proves the survival of the human spirit beyond the grave, or as Solomon so wisely put it: "Then shall the dust return to the earth as it was: and the spirit shall return unto God who gave it" (Ecclesiastes 12:7). For over a third of a century, the Watchtower perpetrated a lie in their translation of Matthew; however, Christians who expose the truth about the Watchtower are having an effect, because the word "breath" was changed to the correct translation of "spirit" in 1984 and it remained so in 2013.

The Second Coming of Christ

(4) Second Thessalonians most vividly portrays the Witnesses at their crafty best, as they desperately attempt to make Paul teach what in all his

writings he most emphatically denied, namely, that Christ would come *invisibly* for His saints.

In his epistle to Titus, Paul stressed the importance of "looking for that blessed hope, and the glorious appearing of the great God and our Savior Jesus Christ" (2:13), something he would not have been looking for if it was to be a secret, invisible *parousia* or "presence."

Paul, contrary to the claims of Jehovah's Witnesses, never believed in an invisible return, nor did any bona fide member of the Christian church up until the fantasies of Charles Taze Russell and his *parousia* nightmare, as a careful look at Paul's first epistle to the Thessalonians plainly reveals. Said the inspired apostle:

> For this we say unto you by the word of the Lord, that we which are alive and remain unto the *coming* of the Lord shall not prevent them which are asleep.
>
> For the Lord himself shall *descend* from heaven [visible] with a shout [audible], with the voice of the archangel, and with the trump of God: and the dead in Christ shall rise first (1 Thessalonians 4:15–16, brackets are author's).

Here we see that in perfect accord with Matthew 26 and Revelation 1, Christ is pictured as *coming* visibly, and in this context no reputable Greek scholar alive will allow the use of "presence"; it must be "coming." (See also 2 Thessalonians 2:8).

For further information relative to this subject, consult any standard concordance or Greek lexicon available, and trace Paul's use of the word "coming." This will convince any fair-minded person that Paul never entertained the Watchtower's fantastic view of Christ's return.

These things being clearly understood, the interested reader should give careful attention to those verses in the New Testament that do not use the word *parousia* but are instead forms of the verb *elthon* and those related to the word *erchomai* (see Thayer, 250) and which refer to the Lord's coming as a visible manifestation. These various texts cannot be twisted to fit the Russellite pattern of "presence," since *erchomai* means "to come," "to appear," "to arrive," etc., in the most definite sense of the term. (For reference, check Matthew 24:30 in conjunction with Matthew 26:64—*erchomenon*; also John 14:3— *erchomai*; and Revelation 1:7— *erchetai*).

Once it is perceived that Jehovah's Witnesses are only interested in what they can make the Scriptures say, and not in what the Holy Spirit has already perfectly revealed, then the careful student will reject entirely Jehovah's Witnesses and their Watchtower "translation." These are as "blind leaders of the blind" (Matthew 15:14), "turning the grace of God into lasciviousness, and denying the only Lord God, and our Lord Jesus Christ" (Jude 4). Further, that they wrest the Scriptures unto their own destruction (2 Peter 3:16), the foregoing evidence has thoroughly revealed for all to judge.

Recently the Jehovah's Witnesses "reinterpreted" their prophetic scheme to downplay the significance of 1914. As the Watchtower Society approached the new millennium, it had to somehow account for the fact that the Battle of Armageddon had yet to occur, even though, according to the Society's interpretation, it was supposed to happen within the lifetime of those born by 1914.

For decades the *Awake!* masthead contained the statement, "Most important, this magazine builds confidence in the Creator's promise of a peaceful and secure new world *before the generation that saw the events of 1914 passes away.*"[22] However, the November 8, 1995, issue (as well as all subsequent issues) states, "Most important, this magazine builds confidence in the Creator's promise of a peaceful and secure new world *that is about to replace the present wicked lawless system of things.*"[23] This is but the latest in a multitude of reinterpretations by the Watchtower to extend their erroneous end times scenario into successive decades as their "prophetic" prowess fails. Following is a chart that shows the successive replacement teachings of the Watchtower over the years.

Teaching	Statement	Source
"Beginning of the End" in 1799 (later changed to 1914).	"1799 definitely marks the beginning of 'the time of the end.' . . . 'The time of the end' embraces a period from AD 1799, as above indicated, to the time of the complete overthrow of Satan's empire. . . . We have been in 'the time of the end' since 1799."	*The Harp of God* (Brooklyn: Watchtower Bible and Tract Society, 1928 ed.), 235–236, 239.
Christ's "Invisible Presence" begins in 1874 (later changed to 1914).	"The time of the Lord's second presence dates from 1874. . . . From 1874 forward is the latter part of the period of 'the time of the end.' From 1874 is the time of the Lord's second presence."	*The Harp of God*, 236, 239–240.

22. Emphasis added.
23. Emphasis added.

Teaching	Statement	Source
The Battle of Armageddon ends in 1914 (later changed to "still future").	"The 'battle of the great day of God Almighty' (Rev. 16:14), which will end in AD 1914 with the complete overthrow of earth's present rulership, is already commenced."	Charles Taze Russell, *Studies in the Scriptures*, 2:101.
The Battle of Armageddon will end shortly after 1914.	"In the year 1918, when God destroys the churches wholesale and the church members by millions, it shall be that any that escape shall come to the works of Pastor Russell to learn the meaning of the downfall of 'Christianity.'"	Charles Taze Russell, *Studies in the Scriptures*, 7:485.
The Battle of Armageddon will come around 1925.	"The date 1925 is even more distinctly indicated by the Scriptures because it is fixed by the law God gave to Israel. Viewing the present situation in Europe, one wonders how it will be possible to hold back the explosion much longer; and that even before 1925 the great crisis will be reached and probably passed."	*The Watch Tower*, July 15, 1924, 211.
1914 is the starting date for the last generation before the Battle of Armageddon.	"The thirty-six intervening years since 1914, instead of postponing Armageddon, have only made it nearer than most people think. Do not forget: 'This generation shall not pass, till all these things be fulfilled'" (Matthew 24:34).	*The Watchtower*, November 1, 1950, 419.
People who were present and understood the events of 1914 will live to see the Battle of Armageddon.	"Jesus said, 'This generation will by no means pass away until all these things occur.' Which generation is this, and how long is it? . . . The 'generation' logically would not apply to babies born during World War I. It applies to Christ's followers and others who were able to observe that war and the other things that have occurred in fulfillment of Jesus' composite 'sign.' Some of such persons 'will by no means pass away until' all of what Christ prophesied occurs, including the end of the present wicked system."	*The Watchtower*, October 1, 1978, 31.
Anyone *born* by 1914 will live to see Armageddon.	"If Jesus used 'generation' in that sense and we apply it to 1914, then the babies of that generation are now seventy years old or older. And others alive in 1914 are in their eighties or nineties, a few even having reached one hundred. There are still many millions of that generation alive. Some of them 'will by no means pass away until all things occur'" (Luke 21:32).	*The Watchtower*, May 14, 1984, 5.

75

Teaching	Statement	Source
Anyone who sees the events signaling the End, regardless of any relationship to 1914, will see the Battle of Armageddon.	"Eager to see the end of this evil system, Jehovah's People have at times speculated about the time when the 'great tribulation' would break out, even tying this to calculations of what is the lifetime of a generation since 1914. However we 'bring a heart of wisdom in' not by speculating about how many years or days make up a generation. . . . 'This generation' apparently refers to the peoples of earth who see the sign of Christ's presence but fail to mend their ways."	*The Watchtower*, November 1, 1995, 17–20.

The Watchtower Bible and Tract Society still has not learned to refrain from prophesying falsely. In The Watchtower, January 1, 1997, (11), it once again raises expectations among its followers that the Battle of Armageddon is just around the corner:

In the early 1920s, a featured public talk presented by Jehovah's Witnesses was entitled "Millions Now Living Will Never Die." This may have reflected over-optimism at that time. But today that statement can be made with full confidence. Both the increasing light on Bible prophecy and the anarchy of this dying world cry out that the end of Satan's system is very, very near!

The Watchtower further refers to the coming end in this way: "Soon, all the distress that Satan and his demons have brought upon earth's inhabitants will end by divine intervention. Then God's promised new world of righteousness will bring about a permanent end to the causes behind hopelessness and suicide."[24]

The Deity of Jesus Christ

Throughout the entire content of inspired Scripture, the fact of Christ's identity is clearly taught. He is revealed as Jehovah God in human form (Isaiah 9:6; Micah 5:2; Isaiah 7:14; John 1:14; 8:58; 17:5 [cf. Exodus 3:14]; Hebrews 1:3; Philippians 2:11; Colossians 2:9; and Revelation 1:8, 17–18; etc.). The deity of Jesus Christ is one of the cornerstones of Christianity, and as such has been attacked more vigorously throughout the ages than any other single doctrine of the Christian faith. Adhering to the old

24. *The Watchtower*, September 15, 2000, 4.

Arian heresy of the fourth century AD, which Athanasius the great church Father refuted in his famous essay "On the Incarnation of the Word," many individuals and all cults steadfastly deny the equality of Jesus Christ with God the Father, and hence, the Triune deity. Jehovah's Witnesses, as has been observed, are no exception to this infamous rule. However, the testimony of the Scriptures stands sure, and the abovementioned references alone put to silence forever this blasphemous heresy, which in the power of Satan himself deceives many with its "deceitful handling of the Word of God."

The deity of Christ, then, is a prime answer to Jehovah's Witnesses, for if the Trinity is a reality, which it is, if Jesus and Jehovah are "One" and the same, then the whole framework of the cult collapses into a heap of shattered, disconnected doctrines incapable of even a semblance of congruity. We will now consider the verses in question, and their bearing on the matter.

1. (a) *Isaiah 7:14.* "Therefore the Lord [Jehovah] himself shall give you a sign; Behold, a virgin shall conceive, and bear a son, and shall call his name Immanuel" (literally, "God" or "Jehovah with us," since Jehovah is the only God).

(b) *Isaiah 9:6.* "For unto us a child is born, unto us a son is given: and the government shall be upon his shoulder: and his name shall be called Wonderful, Counsellor, The mighty God, The everlasting Father, The Prince of Peace."

(c) *Micah 5:2.* "But thou, Bethlehem Ephratah, though thou be little among the thousands of Judah, yet out of thee shall he come forth unto me that is to be ruler in Israel; whose goings forth have been from of old, from everlasting."

Within the realm of Old Testament Scripture, Jehovah, the Lord of Hosts, has revealed His plan to appear in human form and has fulfilled the several prophecies concerning this miracle in the person of Jesus Christ. Examination of the above listed texts will more than convince the unbiased student of Scripture that Jehovah has kept His promises and did become man, literally "God with us" (Matthew 1:23; Luke 1:32–33; John 1:14).

The key to Isaiah 7:14 is the divine name "Immanuel," which can only be rightly rendered "God with us"; and since there is no other God but Jehovah by His own declaration (Isaiah 43:10–11), therefore Jesus Christ and Jehovah God are of the same Substance in power and eternity, hence equal. This prophecy was fulfilled in Matthew 1:22–23; thus there can be no doubt that Jesus Christ is the son of the virgin so distinctly portrayed in Isaiah 7:14. Jehovah's Witnesses can present no argument to refute this plain declaration of Scripture, namely that Jehovah and Christ are "One" and the same, since the very term "Immanuel" ("God" or "Jehovah with us") belies any other interpretation.

Isaiah 9:6 in the Hebrew Bible is one of the most powerful verses in the Old Testament in proving the deity of Christ, for it incontestably declares that Jehovah himself planned to appear in human form. The verse clearly states that all government will rest upon the "child born" and the "son given" whose identity is revealed in the very terms used to describe His attributes. Isaiah, under the inspiration of the Holy Spirit, describes Christ as "Wonderful, Counsellor, The mighty God, The everlasting Father, The Prince of Peace"—all attributes of God alone. The term "mighty God" is in itself indicative of Jehovah since not only is He the only God (Isaiah 43:10–11), but the term "mighty" is applied to Him alone in relation to His deity. Jehovah's Witnesses dodge this verse by claiming that Christ is *a* mighty god, but not *the* Almighty God (Jehovah). This argument is ridiculous on the face of the matter. However, Jehovah's Witnesses insist that since there is no article in the Hebrew text, "mighty," therefore, does not mean Jehovah. The question arises: Are there two "mighty Gods"? This we know is absurd; yet Jehovah's Witnesses persist in the fallacy, despite Isaiah 10:21, where Isaiah (*without* the article) declares that "Jacob shall return" unto the "mighty God," and we know that Jehovah is by His own word to Moses "the God of Jacob" (Exodus 3:6). In Jeremiah 32:18 (*with* the article) the prophet declares that He (Jehovah) is "the Great, the Mighty God" (two forms of saying the same thing; cf. Isaiah 9:6; 10:21; Jeremiah 32:18). If we are to accept Jehovah's Witnesses' view, there must be two mighty Gods; and that is impossible, for there is only one true and mighty God (Isaiah 45:22).

The prophet Micah, writing in Micah 5:2, recording Jehovah's words, gives not only the birthplace of Christ (which the Jews affirmed as being the City of David, Bethlehem), but he gives a clue as to His identity—namely, God in human form. The term "goings forth" can be rendered "origin,"[25] and we know that the only one who fits this description, whose origin is "from everlasting" must be God himself, since He alone is the eternally existing one (Isaiah 44:6, 8). The overwhelming testimony of these verses

25. Brown, Driver, and Briggs, *Hebrew Lexicon of the Old Testament*, 426 [a] Item [2].

alone ascertains beyond reasonable doubt the deity of the Lord Jesus Christ, who became man, identified himself with us in His incarnation, and offered himself "once for all" a ransom for many, the eternal sacrifice who is able to save to the uttermost whoever will appropriate His cleansing power.

2. *John 1:1.* "In the beginning (or "origin," Greek, *Arche*) was the Word, (*Logos*) and the Word was with God, (*Ton Theon*) and the Word was God (*Theos*)."

Contrary to the translations of *The Emphatic Diaglott* and the *New World Translation of the Holy Scriptures*, the Greek grammatical construction leaves no doubt whatsoever that this is the only possible rendering of the text. The subject of the sentence is *Word* (*Logos*), the verb *was*. There can be no direct object following "was," since according to grammatical usage intransitive verbs take no objects but take instead predicate nominatives, which refer back to the subject—in this case, *Word* (*Logos*). In fact, the late New Testament Greek scholar Dr. E. C. Colwell formulated a rule that clearly states that a definite predicate nominative (in this case, *Theos*—God) never takes an article when it precedes the verb (was), as we find in John 1:1.[26] It is therefore easy to see that no article is needed for *Theos* (God), and to translate it "a god" is both incorrect grammar and poor Greek since *Theos* is the predicate nominative of *was* in the third sentence-clause of the verse and must refer back to the subject, *Word* (*Logos*). Christ, if He is the Word "made flesh" (John 1:14), can be no one else except God unless the Greek text and consequently God's Word be denied.

Jehovah's Witnesses, in an appendix in their *New World Translation* (773–777), attempt to discredit the proper translation on this point, for they realize that if Jesus and Jehovah are "One" in nature, their theology cannot stand since they deny that unity of nature. The refutation of their arguments on this point is conclusive.

The claim is that since the definite article is used with *Theon* in John 1:1b and not with *Theos* in John 1:1c, therefore the omission is designed to show a difference; the alleged difference being that in the first case the one true God (Jehovah) is meant, while in the second "a god," other than and inferior to the first, is meant, this latter "god" being Jesus Christ.

26. John Wenham, *The Elements of New Testament Greek* (Cambridge: Cambridge University Press, 1965), 35.

On page 776b the claim is made that the rendering "a god" is correct because "all the doctrine of sacred Scriptures bears out the correctness of this rendering." This remark focuses attention on the fact that the whole problem involved goes far beyond this text. Scripture does in fact teach the full and equal *deity* of Christ. Why then is so much made of this one verse? It is probably because of the surprise effect derived from the show of pseudo-scholarship in the use of a familiar text. Omission of the definite article with *Theos* does not mean that "a god" other than the one true God is meant. Let one examine these passages where the definite article is not used with *Theos* and see if the rendering "a god" makes sense: Matthew 3:9; 6:24; Luke 1:35, 78; 2:40; John 1:6, 12–13, 18; 3:2, 21; 9:16, 33; Romans 1:7, 17–18; 1 Corinthians 1:30; 15:10; Philippians 2:11–13; Titus 1:1, and many, many more. The "a god" contention proves too weak and is inconsistent. To be consistent in this rendering of "a god," Jehovah's Witnesses would have to translate every instance where the article is absent as "a god" (nominative), "of a god" (genitive), "to" or "for a god" (dative), etc. This they do not do in Matthew 3:9; 6:24; Luke 1:35, 78; John 1:6, 12–13, 18; Romans 1:7, 17, etc. (See the *New World Translation of the Holy Scriptures* and *The Emphatic Diaglott* at abovementioned references.)

You cannot honestly render *Theos* "a god" in John 1:1, and then render *Theou* "of God" (Jehovah) in Matthew 3:9, Luke 1:35, 78; John 1:6, etc., when *Theou* is the genitive case of the *same* noun (second declension), *without* an article and *must* be rendered (following Jehovah's Witnesses' argument) "of *a* god" not "of God" as both *The Emphatic Diaglott* and *New World Translation* put it. We could list at great length, but suggest consultation of the Greek New Testament by either D. Erwin Nestle or Westcott and Hort, in conjunction with *The Elements of Greek* by Francis Kingsley Ball[27] on noun endings, etc. Then if Jehovah's Witnesses must persist in this fallacious "a god" rendition, they can at least be consistent, *which they are not*, and render every instance where the article is absent in the same manner. The truth of the matter is that Jehovah's Witnesses use and remove the articular emphasis *whenever* and *wherever* it suits their fancy, regardless of grammatical laws to the contrary. In a translation as important as God's Word, every law must be observed. Jehovah's Witnesses have not been consistent in their observances of those laws.

27. Francis Kingsley Ball, *The Elements of Greek* (New York: Macmillan, 1948), 7, 14.

The writers of the claim have exhibited another trait common to Jehovah's Witnesses—that of half-quoting or misquoting a recognized authority to bolster their ungrammatical renditions. On page 776 in an appendix to the *New World Translation of the Christian Greek Scriptures*, when quoting Dr. A. T. Robertson's words, "Among the ancient writers O *Theos* was used of the god of absolute religion in distinction from the mythological gods," they fail to note that in the second sentence following, Dr. Robertson says, "In the New Testament, however, while we have *pros ton Theon* (John 1:1–2) it is far more common to find simply *Theos*, especially in the Epistles."

In other words, the writers of the New Testament frequently do not use the article with *Theos*, and yet the meaning is perfectly clear in the context, namely that the one true God is intended. Let one examine the following references where in successive verses (and even in the same sentence) the article is used with *one* occurrence of *Theos* and *not* with another form, and it will be absolutely clear that no such drastic inferences can be drawn from John's usage in John 1:1–2 (Matthew 4:3–4; 12:28; Luke 20:37–38; John 3:2; 13:3; Acts 5:29–30; Romans 1:7–8, 17–19; 2:16–17; 3:5; 4:2–3, etc.).

The doctrine of the article is important in Greek; it is *not* used indiscriminately. But we are *not* qualified to be sure in *all* cases what is intended. Dr. Robertson is careful to note that "it is only of recent years that a really scientific study of the article has been made."[28] The facts are not all known, and no such drastic conclusion, as the writers of the appendix note, should be dogmatically affirmed.

It is nonsense to say that a simple noun can be rendered "divine," and that one *without* the article conveys merely the idea of quality.[29] The authors of this note later render the same noun *Theos* as "a god," not as "a quality." This is a self-contradiction in the context.

In conclusion, the position of the writers of this note is made clear in an appendix to the *New World Translation of the Christian Greek Scriptures* (774); according to them it is "unreasonable" that the Word (Christ) should be the God with whom He was (John 1:1). Their own manifestly erring reason is made the criterion for determining scriptural truth. One need only note the obvious misuse in their quotation from

28. A. T. Robertson, *A Grammar of the Greek New Testament in the Light of Historical Research* (Nashville: Broadman Press, 1934), 755.
29. Appendix to the *New World Translation of the Christian Greek Scriptures*, 773–774.

Dana and Mantey (774–775). Mantey clearly means that the "Word was deity" in accord with the overwhelming testimony of Scripture, but the writers have dragged in the interpretation "a god" to suit their own purpose, which purpose is the denial of Christ's deity, and as a result a denial of the Word of God. The late Dr. Mantey publicly stated that he was quoted out of context, and he personally wrote the Watchtower, declaring, "There is no statement in our grammar that was ever meant to imply that 'a god' was a permissible translation in John 1:1," and "It is neither scholarly nor reasonable to translate John 1:1 'The Word was a god.'"[30]

The Resurrection of Christ

Jehovah's Witnesses, as has been observed, deny the bodily resurrection of the Lord Jesus Christ and claim instead that He was raised a "divine spirit being" or as an "invisible spirit creature." They answer the objection that He appeared in human form by asserting that He simply took human forms as He needed them, which enabled Him to be seen, for as the Logos He would have been invisible to the human eye. In short, Jesus did not appear in the *same* form that hung upon the cross since that body either "dissolved into gases or . . . is preserved somewhere as the grand memorial of God's love."[31] This, in spite of Paul's direct refutation in 1 Timothy 2:5, where he calls "the *man* Christ Jesus" our only mediator—some thirty years after the Resurrection!

The Scriptures, however, tell a completely different story, as will be evident when their testimony is considered. Christ himself prophesied His own bodily resurrection, and John tells us "He spake of the temple of His body" (John 2:21).

In John 20:24–26, the disciple Thomas doubted the literal, physical resurrection of Christ, only to repent (v. 28) after Jesus offered His body (v. 27), the same one that was crucified and still bore the nail prints and spear wound, to Thomas for his examination. No reasonable person will say that the body the Lord Jesus displayed was not His crucifixion body, unless he either ignorantly or willfully denies the Word of God. It was no other body "assumed" for the time by a spiritual Christ; it was the identical

30. Michael Van Buskirk, *The Scholastic Dishonesty of the Watchtower* (Santa Ana, CA: CARIS, 1976), 11.
31. Charles T. Russell, *Studies in the Scriptures*, Vol. V, 454.

form that hung on the tree—the Lord himself; He was alive and undeniably tangible, not a "divine spirit creature." The Lord foresaw the unbelief of men in His bodily resurrection and made an explicit point of saying that He was not a spirit but flesh and bones (Luke 24:39–44), and He even went so far as to eat human food to prove that He was identified with humanity as well as Deity. Christ rebuked the disciples for their unbelief in His physical resurrection (Luke 24:25), and it was the physical resurrection that confirmed His deity, since only God could voluntarily lay down and take up life at will (John 10:18). We must not forget that Christ prophesied not only His resurrection but also the nature of that resurrection, which He said would be bodily (John 2:19–21). He said He would raise up "this temple" in three days (v. 19), and John tells us "He spake of the temple of his *body*" (v. 21, emphasis added).

Jehovah's Witnesses utilize, among other unconnected verses, 1 Peter 3:18 as a defense for their spiritual resurrection doctrine. Peter declares that Christ was "put to death in the flesh, but quickened by the Spirit." Obviously, He was made alive in the Spirit and by the Spirit of God, for the Spirit of God: the Substance of God himself, raised up Jesus from the dead, as it is written, "But if the Spirit of him that raised up Jesus from the dead dwell in you" (Romans 8:11). The meaning of the verse then is quite clear. God did not raise Jesus a spirit but raised Him *by* His Spirit, which follows perfectly John 20:27 and Luke 24:39–44 in establishing the physical resurrection of the Lord.

The Watchtower quotes Mark 16:12 and John 20:14–16 as proof that Jesus has "other bodies" after His resurrection. Unfortunately for them, the reference in Mark is a questionable source. A doctrine should not be built around one questionable verse. The reason that Mary (in Mark 16) and also the Emmaus disciples (Luke 24) did not recognize Him is explained in Luke 24:16 (RSV): "Their eyes were kept from recognizing him," but it was "Jesus himself" (v. 15).

Jehovah's Witnesses also try to undermine our Lord's bodily resurrection by pointing out that the doors were shut (John 20:26) when Jesus appeared in the Upper Room. However, Christ had a "spiritual body" (1 Corinthians 15:50, 53) in His glorified state; identical in form to His earthly body, but immortal and thus capable of entering either the dimension of earth or of heaven with no violation to the laws of either one.

Paul states in Romans 4:24; 6:4; 1 Corinthians 15:15; etc., that Christ is raised from the dead, and Paul preached the physical resurrection and return of the God-man, not a "divine spirit being" without a tangible form. Paul also warned that if Christ is not risen, then our faith is in vain (1 Corinthians 15:14); to us who believe God's Word there is a Man in the Glory who showed His wounds as a token of His reality and whose question we ask Jehovah's Witnesses: Has a spirit flesh and bones as you see me have? (Luke 24:39).[32]

As I stated at the beginning of this point, it would be futile to refute all the errors of thought in the Jehovah's Witnesses' theology. Therefore, I have presented what I feel is sufficient evidence to show that man has an eternal soul and will abide somewhere, either in conscious joy or sorrow eternally, and that those who believe and trust in Christ as their personal Savior will "put on" that immortality when Jesus returns.

Regarding the Jehovah's Witnesses, we can only say as Paul said to the Corinthians in 2 Corinthians 4:3–4: "But if our gospel be hid, it is hid to them that are lost: In whom the god of this world hath blinded the minds of them which believe not, lest the light of the glorious gospel of Christ, who is the image of God, should shine unto them," and as he again states in 2 Thessalonians 2:10–11, "because they received not the love of the truth, that they might be saved. And for this cause God shall send them strong delusion, that they should believe a lie."

Honest study of this problem will reveal to any interested Bible student that man does possess an eternal immaterial nature, which was fashioned to occupy an everlasting habitation whether in conscious bliss or torment. This then is the nature and certain destiny of man.

Author's Note

The following partial list of references to the soul and spirit of man as drawn from the Old and New Testaments provides ample evidence that man is not just a combination of body and breath forming a living soul, as the Jehovah's Witnesses teach, but rather a soul, or spirit, possessing a corporeal form.

The Hebrew equivalent for soul as used in the Old Testament is *nephesh*, and for spirit *ruach*. The Greek equivalent for soul is *psuche* and for spirit *pneuma*.

32. For detailed arguments and misapplied texts see chapter 4 of *The Kingdom of the Cults* (2019).

1. It is an entity possessing the attributes of life (Isaiah 55:3). It is also separate from the body (Matthew 10:28; Luke 8:55; 1 Thessalonians 5:23; Hebrews 4:12; Revelation 16:3), i.e., it exists independent of material form.

2. A soul departs at the death of the form (Genesis 35:18).

3. The soul is conscious after death (Matthew 17:3; Revelation 6:9–11).

4. The soul of Samuel was conscious after death (1 Samuel 28:14–19).

5. Stephen had a spirit, which he committed to Christ at his death (Acts 7:59).

6. There is definitely a spirit and soul of man (Isaiah 57:16).

7. The spirit is independent of the body (Zechariah 12:1).

8. The spirit, the soul of man, does that which only a personality can do; it "wills" (*prothumon*) (Matthew 26:41).

9. We are instructed to worship in the spirit (John 4:23; Philippians 3:3) because God is a spirit.

10. The spirit of man has the attribute of personality, the ability to testify (Romans 8:16, 26), and also the faculty of "knowing" (1 Corinthians 2:11).

11. The spirit can be either saved or lost (1 Corinthians 5:5). It belongs to God, and we are instructed to glorify Him in it (1 Corinthians 6:20).

12. The spirit or soul goes into eternity and is a conscious entity (Galatians 6:8).

13. Christ is with our spirit (2 Timothy 4:22), for the spirit is the life of the body (James 2:26).

14. We are born of God's Spirit, and as such are spirits ourselves (John 3:5–6).

These references will suffice to show that the immaterial nature of man is far from the combination of breath and flesh that Jehovah's Witnesses maintain.

Jehovah's Witnesses thrive on the confusion they are able to create, and in their door-to-door canvassing they accentuate this trait by demonstrating extreme reluctance to identify themselves as emissaries of the Watchtower until they have established a favorable contact with the prospective convert. To put it in the terms of the vernacular, until they have "made their pitch" they are careful to conceal their identity.

In short, Jehovah's Witnesses may be proud to be the only people standing for "Jehovah God," but they are not above neglecting to tell prospective converts their real affiliation if it will help their cause. If evangelical Christianity continues to virtually ignore the activities of Jehovah's Witnesses, it does so at the peril of countless souls. Therefore, let us awaken to their perversions of Scripture and stand fast in the defense of the faith "once delivered unto the saints" (Jude 1).

Explore

Direct Creation
Spirit Creature
Russellism
New World Translation

Discuss

1. What did Charles Taze Russell and Judge Franklin Rutherford have in common? How were they different?

2. Was Jesus ever inferior to God?

3. Who is the Jesus of the Jehovah's Witnesses?

4. Point to three Bible verses that teach the Christian doctrine of the Trinity.

_____

_____

/————————————————— **Dig Deeper** ——————————————\

See _The Kingdom of the Cults Study Guide_ available at WalterMartin.com.

5

Christian Science

Historical Perspective

For decades Christian Science was the matriarch of the Mind Science family. With a large and growing membership, secular and religious respect, and great wealth, the Mother Church dominated the Mind Science movement, more important in almost all respects than Unity School of Christianity, Mind Science, Religious Science, Divine Science, and their other siblings. However, during the 1960s a trend became apparent. Christian Science was losing members and income at a steady and significant rate.

By the mid-seventies Christian Science members and even the public media were aware that the decline was long-term and steady. Since the mid-1980s, it has solidified its public image as a benign Christian denomination of thoughtful, spiritually mature people who enjoy a rather intellectual, quiet faith.

This faith gives them peace with God without any of the unappealing aspects of traditional Christianity, such as the existence of hell, the doctrine of the Trinity, or the incarnation, resurrection, and atonement of Jesus Christ.

The next couple of decades will tell whether Christian Science will be able to survive. Its forces are much diminished from what they once were. Only time will tell if the small core of faithful members will endure and spur growth in excess of attrition. Yet, even now, the Christian Science cult is a powerful force with which evangelical Christians everywhere must deal. We shall examine its roots, founder, growth, and controversies, and contrast its teachings with the clear word of Scripture.

Mary Ann Morse Baker—better known among the band of faithful Christian Scientists as Mary Baker Eddy, "Mother" and Leader, the "Discoverer and Founder" of Christian Science. She was born in Bow, New Hampshire, in the year 1821 in the humble surroundings of a New Hampshire farmhouse, and reared a strict Congregationalist by her parents, Mark and Abigail Baker. The life of young Mary Baker, until her twenty-second year, was marked with frequent illnesses of both emotional and physical nature,[1] and the then infant science of mesmerism was often applied to her case with some success.

In December of 1843, at the age of twenty-two, the future Mrs. Eddy was married to George W. Glover, a neighboring businessman, whose untimely death of yellow fever in Wilmington, South Carolina, some seven months later reduced his pregnant wife to an emotional and highly unstable invalid, who, throughout the remaining years of her life, relied from time to time upon the drug morphine as a medication.[2]

To be sure, no informed person believes that Mrs. Eddy was a "dope addict," but much evidence from incontrovertible sources is available to show beyond doubt that throughout her life Mrs. Eddy made repeated use of this drug.[3]

After a brief and disastrous second marriage, Mary Baker Glover Patterson married Asa G. Eddy when Mrs. Eddy was fifty-six years of age. Asa Eddy's death of a coronary thrombosis prompted Mrs. Eddy to commit a

1. Georgine Milmine, *The Life of Mary Baker G. Eddy and the History of Christian Science* (Grand Rapids, MI: Baker Book House, 1937), 3–25.
2. *New York World*, October 30, 1906.
3. Ernest Sutherland Bates and John V. Dittemore, *Mary Baker Eddy: The Truth and the Tradition* (New York: Knopf, 1932), 41, 42, 151, 445.

nearly fatal mistake where Christian Science was concerned. She contested the autopsy report, and the physician she chose confirmed her conviction that Asa died of "arsenic poisoning mentally administered."[4] Such a radical report prompted an inquiry into the credentials of Mrs. Eddy's physician, Dr. C. J. Eastman, dean of the Bellevue Medical College, outside Boston. It was found that "Doctor" Eastman was running a virtual abortion mill, and had no medical credentials whatever to justify his title. He was sentenced to ten years in prison upon his conviction, and the Bellevue Medical College closed. Mrs. Eddy had contradicted her own advice concerning autopsies.[5] And she would have been far better off to have practiced in this instance what she preached and to have abandoned Asa's remains to the scrap heap of mental malpractice, but the error was virtually unavoidable since Mrs. Eddy was not to be outdone by any medical doctor. She was an expert healer by her own admissions; the autopsy was therefore inevitable.

Mrs. Eddy's letter to the *Boston Post* dated June 5, 1882, in which she accused some of her former students of mentally poisoning Asa Eddy with malicious mesmerism in the form of arsenic mentally administered is one of the most pathetic examples of Mrs. Eddy's mental state ever recorded and one which the Christian Science Church would like to forget she ever wrote.

The Influence of P. P. Quimby

The real history of Christian Science, however, cannot be told unless one P. P. Quimby of Portland, Maine, be considered, for history tells us that as Mrs. Eddy was the mother of Christian Science, so Phineas Parkhurst Quimby was undoubtedly its father. "Dr." Quimby in the late 1850s entitled his system of mental healing "The Science of Man," and used the terms "The Science of Christ" and "Christian Science" for some time before Mrs. Eddy gratuitously appropriated the terminology as her own, something she dared not do while the old gentleman was alive and her relationship to him known to all.

Mrs. Eddy's relationship to Dr. Quimby began when she arrived in Portland, Maine, in 1862 and committed herself to his care for treatment of "spinal inflammation." In November of that same year Mrs. Eddy noised

4. *Boston Post*, June 5, 1882.
5. See *Science and Health with Key to the Scriptures* by Mary Baker Eddy (Boston: Trustees under the Will of Mary Baker G. Eddy, 1934), 196, and the 1881 edition, vol. 1, 269.

abroad to all men that P. P. Quimby had healed her of her infirmity. Said the then adoring disciple of Quimby, "I visited P. P. Quimby and in less than one week from that time I ascended by a stairway of 182 steps to the dome of the City Hall and am improving ad infinitum."[6]

In later years Mrs. Eddy's recollection of Quimby was somewhat different from her earlier echoes of praise, and she did not hesitate to describe him as a very "unlearned man," etc. Dr. Quimby termed his ideas "Science of Health." Mrs. Eddy entitled her book *Science and Health with Key to the Scriptures*, and published it in 1875 filled with numerous plagiarisms from the manuscripts of P. P. Quimby and by the writings of Francis Lieber, a German-American publisher and authority on the philosophy of Hegel.[7] For full documentation on Mrs. Eddy's plagiarism from Quimby the reader is urged to study the first four chapters of my book *The Christian Science Myth*, which documents exhaustively the entire controversy and proves beyond a shadow of a doubt that Mrs. Eddy plagiarized a great part of her work from Quimby and other sources, and then had it all copiously edited by the Rev. J. H. Wiggin, a retired Unitarian minister.[8]

> Mrs. Eddy plagiarized a great part of her work from Quimby and other sources.

Our authority for exposing this plagiarism on the part of "Mother" Eddy is none other than Mrs. Eddy herself, who wrote, "When needed tell the truth concerning a lie. The evasion of truth cripples integrity, and casts thee down from the pinnacle. . . . A dishonest position is far from Christianly scientific."[9] In addition, Mrs. Eddy made the following statement on the subject of plagiarism: "There is no warrant in common law and no permission in the gospel for plagiarizing an author's ideas and their words."[10] So it appears that out of her own mouth Mrs. Eddy has condemned plagiarism, a practice from which she seemed to have extreme difficulty abstaining.

6. Portland *Evening Courier*, November 7, 1862.

7. It should be noted here that although Eddy appears to have plagiarized a significant portion of Quimby's material, she did not agree with all of his conclusions. Eddy and Quimby disagreed on the existence of matter, the role of religion, and their perception of God. The basic distinction between the idealism of Eddy differs substantially with the mind-material dualism of Quimby.

8. Wiggin revealed his part in her deceptive plan via the posthumous publication of an interview he gave to one Livingstone Wright, later published as a pamphlet entitled *How Reverend Wiggin Rewrote Mrs. Eddy's Book*.

9. *Science and Health*, 448.

10. Mary Baker Eddy, *Retrospection and Introspection* (Boston: Estate Trustees, 1891), 76.

The Figment of Divine Authorship

According to an authorized statement published by the Christian Science Publishing Society of Boston, Eddy, after a fall on a slippery sidewalk February 1, 1866, was pronounced "incurable" and given three days to live by the attending physician, Dr. Alvin M. Cushing. The third day, allegedly her last on earth, Eddy (the statement makes out) cried for a Bible, read Matthew 9:2, and rose completely healed. Thus the statement claims "she discovered" Christian Science. This is the story maintained by the organization today, as a comment on the First Church of Christ, Scientist website states:

> In 1866 [Eddy] was severely injured in a fall, and turned to the Bible as she had been accustomed to doing. All she had pondered in the past came strongly and clearly to her as she read an account of one of Jesus' healings. She was immediately healed. Convinced that God had healed her, she spent the next several years searching the Scriptures to understand the principle behind her healing. She named her discovery Christian Science and explained it in 1875 when she first wrote *Science and Health*.[11]

Corroborating this new story, Eddy in her book *Retrospection and Introspection* (38) declares that in February of 1866 (one month after Quimby's death), she was mortally injured in a sidewalk fall and was not expected to live. She, however, vanquished the angel of death in this skirmish, and on the third day emerged triumphant over her bodily infirmity. These two statements, the interested reader will note, substantiate each other in every detail; it is therefore most unfortunate that they should both be falsehoods. Mrs. Eddy never discovered Christian Science in the manner claimed, never was in danger of losing her life in the manner described, and never "rose the third day healed and free" as she maintained.

Two incontrovertible facts establish these truths beyond doubt:

1. Dr. Alvin M. Cushing, the attending physician at this "illness" of Mrs. Eddy, denied under oath in a 1,000-word statement that he ever believed or said that she was in a precarious physical condition.[12] Moreover, Dr. Cushing stated (contrary to the claims of Christian Scientists) that Eddy always enjoyed robust health and that he further

11. Christian Science website, http://www.tfccs.com/GV/QANDA/MBEQ2.jhtml.
12. Entire statement documented in Milmine, 84–86.

attended her in August of the same year four separate times and administered medicine to her for bodily ailments.

2. Julius Dresser (pupil of the late "Dr." Quimby) received a letter from Eddy dated February 15, 1866, two weeks *after* her alleged "recovery" from the fall on an icy sidewalk. In this letter Eddy alludes to the fall and claims Dr. Cushing resigned her to the life of a cripple. Eddy wrote:

> Two weeks ago I fell on the sidewalk and struck my back on the ice, and was taken for dead, came to consciousness amid a storm of vapors from cologne, chloroform, ether, camphor, etc., but to find myself the helpless cripple I was before I saw Dr. Quimby. The physician attending said I had taken the last step I ever should, but in two days I got out of my bed alone and will walk; but yet I confess I am frightened . . . Now can't you help me? . . . I think I could help another in my condition . . . yet I am slowly failing. . . .[13]

Barring the obvious medical error of a doctor administering chloroform and ether to an unconscious person, Eddy's account once again demonstrates her ability to think in paradoxes and contradict all reason and logical expression. The accounts are therefore spurious and complete fabrications.

Horace T. Wentworth, with whose mother Eddy lived in Stoughton while she was teaching from the *Quimby Manuscripts* (1867–1870), has made the following statement, and no Christian Scientist has ever refuted it:

> As I have seen the amazing spread of this delusion and the way in which men and women are offering up money and the lives of their children to it, I have felt that it is a duty I owe to the public to make it known. I have no hard feelings against Mrs. Eddy, no axe to grind, no interest to serve; I simply feel that it is due the thousands of good people who have made Christian Science the anchorage of their souls and its founder the infallible guide of their daily life, to keep this no longer to myself. I desire only that people who take themselves and their helpless children into Christian Science shall do so with the full knowledge that this is not divine revelation but simply the idea of an old-time Maine healer.

13. F. W. Peabody, *The Religio-Medical Masquerade*, 80–81.

Further than this statement, Wentworth has also recorded as incontestable evidence the very copy of P. P. Quimby's *Manuscripts* from which Eddy taught during the years of 1867 through 1870 that contains corrections in Eddy's own handwriting. Note, please, all this is undeniable fact—yet Eddy maintains that she *alone* "discovered and founded" the Christian Science religion. What a historical perversion the prophetess of Christian Science has attempted to perpetrate. Let it also be remembered that Eddy claimed for Quimby's theories, which she expanded, Divine import, owning that she only copied what God Almighty spoke.[14]

From the home of the Wentworths in Stoughton, Massachusetts, where she taught from the Quimby manuscripts, Eddy went on to Lynn, Massachusetts, where she completed her "writing" of *Science and Health*, which she published in 1875. After leaving Lynn, largely because of the revolt of most of her students, Eddy came to Boston and opened what later became "The Massachusetts Metaphysical College" (571 Columbus Avenue), where she allegedly taught some 4,000 students at $300 per student over a period of eight years (1881–1889). One cannot help but wonder what would induce a reasonably intelligent person to spend that amount of money for a course that never lasted the length of a college half-semester and which was taught by a staff hardly qualified intellectually to instruct the ninth grade. Eddy herself knew comparatively nothing of biblical history, theology, philosophy, or the ancient languages. Christian Science sources have attempted for years to prove that Eddy was a scholar in these fields, but the Rev. J. H. Wiggin, her literary adviser for some years, and himself an excellent scholar, has gone on record as saying that she was grossly ignorant of the subjects in question.

When Eddy left the thankless community of Lynn, Massachusetts, she was then sixty-one years old and possessed fewer than fifty persons she could call "followers." As the calendar neared 1896, however, the indomitable will and perseverance of Mary Baker Eddy began to pay sizable dividends. Her churches and societies numbered well over 400 and the membership in them eventually increased from 800 to 900 percent.

Eddy's reign had very little internal opposition and hence went unchallenged during her lifetime, but after her decease a definite scramble for control of her empire ensued.

14. *Christian Science Journal*, January, 1901.

Theological Evaluation

The following are some major doctrines of historical orthodoxy and the contradictory quotations from Eddy's writings:

I. The Inspiration of the Bible—Referring to Genesis 2:7

1. Referring to Genesis 2:7: Is this addition to His creation real or unreal? Is it the truth, or is it a lie concerning man and God? It must be a lie (*Science and Health*, 524).
2. . . . the manifest mistakes in the ancient versions; the thirty thousand different readings in the Old Testament, and the three hundred thousand in the New—these facts show how a mortal and material sense stole into the divine record, with its own hue darkening, to some extent, the inspired pages (139).

II. The Doctrine of the Trinity and the Deity of Christ

1. The theory of three persons in one God (that is, a personal Trinity or Triunity) suggests polytheism, rather than the one ever-present I am (256).
2. The Christian who believes in the First Commandment is a monotheist. Thus he virtually unites with the Jew's belief in one God and recognizes that Jesus Christ is not God, as Jesus himself declared, but is the Son of God (361).
3. The spiritual Christ was infallible; Jesus, as material manhood, was not Christ (*Miscellaneous Writings*, 84).

III. The Doctrine of God and the Holy Spirit

1. The Jewish tribal Jehovah was a man-projected God, liable to wrath, repentance, and human changeableness (*S & H*, 140).
2. God. The great I am; the all-knowing, all-seeing, all-acting, all-wise, all-loving, and eternal; Principle; Mind; Soul; Spirit; Life; Truth; Love; all substance; intelligence (*S & H*, 587).
3. (1) God is All-in-all. (2) God is good. Good is Mind. (3) God, Spirit, being all, nothing is matter. . . . GOD: Divine Principle, Life, Truth, Love, Soul, Spirit, Mind (*S & H*, 113, 115).

IV. The Virgin Birth of Christ

1. God is indivisible. A portion of God could not enter man; neither could God's fullness be reflected by a single man, else God would be manifestly finite, lose the deific character, and become less than God (*S & H*, 336).

2. Jesus, the Galilean Prophet, was born of the Virgin Mary's spiritual thoughts of Life and its manifestation (*The First Church of Christ Scientist and Miscellany*, 1913, 1941, 261).

> The sick are not healed merely by declaring there is no sickness, but by knowing that there is none.

V. The Doctrine of Miracles

1. The sick are not healed merely by declaring there is no sickness, but by knowing that there is none (*S & H*, 447).

2. Sickness is part of the error that Truth casts out. Error will not expel error. Christian Science is the law of Truth, which heals the sick on the basis of the one Mind, or God. It can heal in no other way, since the human, mortal mind so-called is not a healer, but causes the belief in disease (*S & H*, 482).

3. The so-called miracles contained in Holy Writ are neither supernatural nor preternatural. . . . Jesus regarded good as the normal state of man, and evil as the abnormal. . . . The so-called pains and pleasures of matter were alike unreal to Jesus; for he regarded matter as only a vagary of mortal belief and subdued it with this understanding (*Miscellaneous Writings*, 199–200).

VI. The Atonement of Jesus Christ

1. The material blood of Jesus was no more efficacious to cleanse from sin when it was shed upon "the accursed tree" than when it was flowing in His veins as he went daily about his Father's business (*S & H*, 25).

2. The real atonement—so infinitely beyond the heathen conception that God requires human blood to propitiate His justice and bring His mercy—needs to be understood (*No and Yes*, 54).

VII. The Death and Resurrection of Christ

1. Jesus' students, not sufficiently advanced to understand fully their Master's triumph, did not perform many wonderful works until they saw him after his crucifixion and learned that he *had not died* (*S & H*, 45–46).
2. His disciples believed Jesus to be dead while he was hidden in the sepulchre, whereas he was alive, demonstrating within the narrow tomb the power of Spirit to overrule mortal, material sense (44).

VIII. The Creation of Matter and Its Reality

1. There is . . . no intelligent sin, evil mind, or matter: and this is the only true philosophy and realism (*No and Yes*, 38).
2. There is no life, truth, intelligence nor substance in matter. All is infinite Mind and its infinite manifestation, for God is All-in-all (*S & H*, 468).

IX. The Existence of Sin, Sickness, and Death

1. DEVIL. Evil; a lie; error; neither corporeality nor mind; the opposite of Truth; a belief in sin, sickness, and death; animal magnetism or hypnotism; the lust of the flesh (*S & H*, 584).
2. DEATH. An illusion, the lie of life in matter; the unreal and untrue; the opposite of Life.

    Matter has no life, hence it has no real existence. Mind is immortal. The flesh, warring against the Spirit; that which frets itself free from one belief only to be fettered by another, until every belief of life where Life is not yields to eternal Life. Any material evidence of death is false, for it contradicts the spiritual facts of being (584).

As the preceding quotations indicate, the teachings of Christian Science are vastly different than those generally understood to comprise the fundamental teaching of historical Christianity.

Theoretically, Eddy was an absolute idealist who denied outright the existence of matter from the tiniest insect to the most gigantic star in the celestial galaxies. But practically speaking, Eddy was a calculating materialist, an individual who thoroughly enjoyed all the material comforts derived from denying their existence. Hundreds of thousands of faithful Christian Scientists supplied their "leader" with all that money could buy and every material benefit available, yet Eddy continually affirmed the nonexistence of these material blessings by teaching in effect that they really did not exist to be enjoyed—they were "illusions of mortal mind," she said. In Eddy's philosophy all that exists is "Mind" (God) and "It" is "Good"; matter has no "real" existence at all. It should be mentioned here that Eddy never defined matter to the satisfaction of any qualified logician, so it must be assumed that she meant those elements that were recognizable to the five senses.

However, Eddy's vaunted metaphysical allegiance to this alleged rule crumbles weakly under the relentless hammering of sound logical principles. Let us see if the rule of inversion is always valid by applying it to similar constructions.

All rabbits are quadrupeds—(inverted) all quadrupeds are rabbits. Now, of course, any intelligent person can easily see that this inversion leads to a false conclusion, since dogs, cats, horses, and elephants are all quadrupeds and it is obvious they have no relation to the rabbit family. No rational person could therefore long entertain such logical absurdity, but it is exactly this kind of reasoning that forms the basis of Eddy's philosophy and the entire foundation of Christian Science practice. Sin, sickness, and death are equally relegated to these peculiar logical dungeons of Christian Science reasoning processes and then represented as "illusions of mortal mind." Regarding this phantom "mortal mind," Eddy wrote:

> At best, matter is only a phenomenon of mortal mind, of which evil is the highest degree; but really there is no such thing as *mortal mind*—though we are compelled to use the phrase in the endeavor to express the underlying thought (*Unity of Good*, 50).

These are strange words indeed, are they not—giving a name to an illusion that does not exist, representing it as evil, which is equally nonexistent, and then blaming it for all physical woes, which cannot exist, since there is no reality or existence apart from Mind, or God? This type of reasoning is considered sound thinking by Christian Scientists the world over; however, the reader is urged to form his own conclusions dictated by the obvious facts that matter is demonstrably "real" and its decay and death are an ever-present problem.

The syllogisms—(1) God is all, God is Mind, therefore Mind is all; and (2) Mind is all, matter is not Mind, therefore matter has no existence—are only escape mechanisms from the objective world of material reality to the subjective world of idealism, which can never answer the problems of evil, sin, sickness, or material death since they are negated by the assumption that only Mind exists and it is immaterial, therefore not included in material categories. By denying even that portion of the mind that recognizes these physical realities, and calling it "mortal mind," Eddy has forever isolated herself and Christian Science from the realm of objective reality, since the mind that truly rejects the existence of matter must never allow for the limitations of matter, which constitute physical existence. But in practice, no Christian Scientist holds these tenets as an absolute—they all clothe, feed, and house the "illusion of mortal mind" called their bodies, and many go to dentists and surgeons for the filling of imaginary cavities and the setting of nonexistent bones.

If these facts are not proof positive that the entire philosophy of Christian Science in principle and practice is a huge philosophical hoax, then the author despairs of man's ability to analyze available evidence and arrive at logical conclusions. Even in its basic propositions, the Eddy philosophy is a sorry foundation for faith by all standards and an almost unbelievable imposition upon the principles of sound logic.

Biblical Perspective

Inspiration and Authority of the Bible

Christian Science, as a theology, and all Christian Scientists, for that matter, both affirm that the Bible is God's Word and quote Eddy to "prove" that their whole religion is based upon the teachings of Scripture. Eddy said:

> The Bible has been my only authority. I have had no other guide in "the straight and narrow way" of Truth (*Science and Health*, 126).

However, Eddy and Christian Science have repudiated and contradicted this affirmation numerous times (see *Miscellaneous Writings*, 169–170, and

Science and Health, 517, 537, etc.), and in reality have perverted the clear teachings of the Bible to serve their own ends.

In Psalm 119 we read, "For ever, O Lord, thy word is settled in heaven. . . . Thy word is very pure. . . . Thy word is true from the beginning." The prophet Isaiah reminds us, "The word of our God shall stand for ever" (Isaiah 40:8), and Christ himself confirmed these great truths when he said, "The scripture cannot be broken. . . . Heaven and earth shall pass away, but my words shall not pass away" (John 10:35; Matthew 24:35). It will be remembered also that the Apostle Paul stamped with divine authority the testimony of the Scriptures when he wrote, "All scripture is given by inspiration of God, and is profitable for doctrine, for reproof, for correction, for instruction in righteousness" (2 Timothy 3:16).

Coupled with these unassailable voices of testimony as to the Bible's authority, it is evident from the words of Jesus himself and the writings of His disciples and apostles that He believed in the authority of the Old Testament most emphatically and even alluded to Old Testament characters and events, thus establishing the authenticity and trustworthiness of the Old Testament.

The Bible declares that *it*, not Eddy and Christian Science, is the supreme authority on the activities of God and His relationship to man. Christian Science employs every art and method of paradoxical reasoning to escape the dilemma with which it is faced. It switches terminology around until the terms in question lose all logical meaning, and it spiritualizes texts until they are literally milked dry of any divine revelation whatsoever. To the average Christian Scientist, the Bible is a compilation of ancient writings "full of hundreds of thousands of textual errors. . . . Its divinity is . . . uncertain, its inspiration . . . questionable. . . . It is made up of metaphors, allegories, myths, and fables. . . . It cannot be read and interpreted literally. . . ."[15] Consequently, Christian Scientists believe, owing to the utter and hopeless confusion that the Bible allegedly engenders without a qualified interpreter, that it is necessary to have someone interpret the Bible for them. Eddy is the divinely appointed person to fulfill this task. Through *Science and Health*, she, they affirm, "rediscovered the healing principle of Jesus and His disciples, lost since the early Christian era," and has *blessed the world* with Christian Science—the "Divine Comforter." To all Christian Scientists, then, since they swear allegiance to Eddy, "the material record

15. I. M. Haldeman, *Christian Science in the Light of Holy Scripture*, 377.

of the Bible . . . is no more important to our well-being than the history of Europe and America" (*Miscellaneous Writings*, 170).

The reader is asked to compare this supposedly "Christian" view with the foregoing scriptural references and the words of Christ and the Apostle Paul, who said and wrote respectively:

Sanctify them through thy truth: thy *word* is truth (John 17:17).

But continue thou in the things which thou hast learned and hast been assured of, knowing of whom thou hast learned them; and that from a child thou hast known the *holy scriptures*, which are able to make thee wise unto salvation through faith which is in Christ Jesus (2 Timothy 3:14–15).

We are told in the words of Peter:

Knowing this first, that no prophecy of the scripture is of any private interpretation. For the prophecy came not in old time by the will of man: but holy men of God spake as they were moved by the Holy Ghost (2 Peter 1:20–21).

By these things, of course, we do not mean that God dictated or mechanically reproduced the Bible, or even that He wrote tangibly, using the hands of men as an adult guides the hand of a child,

> **The Bible declares that it, not Eddy and Christian Science, is the supreme authority on the activities of God and His relationship to man.**

but that God spoke and caused to be recorded truly and without error those things necessary for our salvation and an understanding of His sovereign purposes and love. The Bible is the inspired Word of God, and is wholly dependable in whatever fields it speaks. This, of course, holds true only for the original manuscripts of the Bible of which we have excellent reproductions. No scholar to our knowledge, however, holds to the infallibility of copies or translations, which sometimes suggest textual difficulties. The Bible, therefore, stands paramount as God's revelation to man, the simple presentation of infinite values and truths clothed in the figures of time and space. Christian Science, by denying many of these truths and the veracity of the Bible itself in favor of Eddy's "interpretations," disobeys directly the injunction of God to "study" and "believe" His Word, which alone is able to make us "wise unto salvation through faith in Christ Jesus."

The Doctrine of the Trinity and the Deity of Christ

One prominent trait of all non-Christian religions and cults is their pointed denial of the scriptural doctrine of the Trinity and the deity of Jesus Christ. Christian Science ranges high in this category on the basis that it unequivocally denies the true deity of our Lord and the triunity of the Godhead (Colossians 2:9). Eddy said, and most decisively so, that "the theory of three persons in one God (that is, a personal Trinity or Triunity) suggests polytheism, rather than the one ever-present I AM" (*Science and Health*, 256). Going beyond this declaration Eddy also wrote: "Jesus Christ is not God, as Jesus himself declared, but is the Son of God" (*S & H*, 361), and she crowned this travesty with the astounding "revelation" that "Life, Truth, and Love constitute the triune Person called God" (*S & H*, 331). Thus it was that with one sweep of an unblushing pen, a vindictive, ignorant, untrained, and egocentric old woman banished the God of the Bible from her religion forever. It is hardly necessary to examine at length the doctrine of the Trinity and the deity of Christ to refute Eddy's vague ramblings, but it is profitable, we believe, to review those passages of Scripture that so thoroughly unmask the pronounced shallowness of the Christian Science contentions.

"Let *us* make man in *our* image, after *our* likeness" (Genesis 1:26).

"Let *us* go down, and there confound their language" (Genesis 11:7).

"Who will go for *us*?" (Isaiah 6:8).

Then we could mention Genesis 18, where Abraham addresses God personally as Lord (Jehovah) over ten times; the obvious plurality of the Godhead is strongly implied if not expressly declared by the use of three angels to represent God. The fact that God intended to beget a Son after the flesh and of the line of David by virgin birth (Isaiah 7:14; 9:6; Micah 5:2; Matthew 1:23; Luke 1:35; cf. Psalm 2:7; Hebrews 1:5; 5:5; Acts 13:33), that this Son in the likeness of flesh was His eternal Word (John 1:1, 14, 18), and that He is true deity (Colossians 2:9; Philippians 2:8–11; Revelation 1:8, 17–18; Hebrews 1:1–4, etc.) and a separate person from God the Father is all indicative of the truth that Jesus Christ was truly the God-man of prophecy and the personal Messiah of Israel. It is fruitful to note also that Eddy recognizes the "true" God not as Jehovah but as "I AM" (*S & H*, 256), apparently oblivious of the fact that the word *Jehovah* is itself taken from the Hebrew verb form "to be" (Exodus 3:14), literally "I was, I am, I continue to be" or as the Jews render it "the Eternal"—(*YHWH*

THE KINGDOM OF THE CULTS HANDBOOK

the tetragrammaton). Keeping with this vein of thought it will be easily recognized that Jesus identified himself with the same "I AM" or Jehovah—and, in fact, claimed in no uncertain terms that He was that "I AM" (John 8:58), for which the Jews were ready to stone Him to death on the grounds of blasphemy (John 8:59 and 10:30–33).

As to Eddy's argument that Jesus was God's Son, not God, the answer is painfully simple when thoroughly analyzed. The solution is briefly this: Christ was God's Son by nature, not creation, as we are; hence, His intrinsic character was that of Deity—His attributes were Divine—He possessed "all power," etc. (Matthew 28:18). He therefore could not be a true Son unless He were truly divine; therefore, He could not be the Son of God at all without at once being "God the Son," i.e., of the very nature of His Father. The Scriptures declare God's Son is Deity—"The mighty God . . . the everlasting Father" (Isaiah 9:6), or "the image of . . . God" (Colossians 1:15) . . . Impress of His Substance . . . radiance of His glory" (Hebrews 1:1–3), etc. Innumerable testimonies as to His divinity are given, far too exhaustive to record here, but evidence nonetheless and beyond disputation. To reduce the Trinity so evident at Christ's baptism and the Great Commission ("In the name of the Father, and of the Son, and of the Holy Ghost," Matthew 28:19) to three of Eddy's choice terms, "Life, Truth, and Love," and declare all else "suggestive of heathen gods" (*Science and Health*, 256) is a prime demonstration of crass indifference to biblical terminology and historical theology—an emphatic Christian Science attitude instituted by Eddy.

John tells us that Christ was by His own admission *equal* in deity to God the Father (John 5:18; cf. Philippians 2:8–11; Colossians 2:9; Hebrews 1:3), yet inferior in position and form during His earthly ministry (John 14:28) as a man. The Eternal Word voluntarily humbled himself, became human and subject to our limitations, even to the death of the cross, the Bible tells us, but never for a moment did He cease to be what by nature and inheritance He always was and will be, God the Son, second person of the Trinity, eternal Creator and Savior of the sons of men.

Therefore, let us remember most clearly that Christian Science offers a dual Christ, a great man inspired by the "Christ idea" as Eddy would have it, one who never really "died" at all for our sins.

The Scriptures hold forth as a ray of inextinguishable light the deity of our Lord and the Trinity of God. We must therefore be ever vigilant in our defense of the personal Jesus who is our personal Savior, lest the impersonal Christ of Christian Science be allowed further opportunity to counterfeit the Christ of the Bible. This counterfeit, so widely taught in Christian Science, is merely another false theory that masquerades under the banner of the Christian religion and attempts to subvert the true Christian faith.

The Personality of God the Father and the Holy Spirit

In Christian Science theology, if it be properly understood, the term "God" is merely a relative one and bears no resemblance whatsoever to the Deity so clearly revealed in the Bible. As has been amply shown, Eddy interchanges the terms *Life, Truth, Love, Principle, Mind, Substance, Intelligence, Spirit, Mother,* etc. with that of *God;* thus, Christian Science contends that God is impersonal, devoid of any personality at all. Biblically speaking, of course, this is a theological and historical absurdity since the core of Jehovah's uniqueness was His personal nature—I AM—indicative of a reflective and constructive Mind. Jesus repeatedly addressed His Father as a direct object, "I" and "Thou," postulating a logical subject/object relation in communication and at least twice the Father answered Him (see Matthew 3:17 and Luke 9:35), establishing His independence of person. This would have been impossible if God were circumscribed by Eddy's theology, for only a personality or cognizant ego can think reflectively, carry on conversation, and use the personal pronouns "I" or "He," etc.

The God of the Old Testament and the New is a personal, transcendent Being, not an impersonal spirit or force, and man is created in His image, that of a personal, though finite, being. The higher animals, to whatever degree they "think," are incapable of rationality and, also unlike man, of the faculty of "knowing," as Descartes once put it: "Cogito ergo sum" ("I think, therefore I am").

But far surpassing this elementary distinction between the God of Christianity and that of Christian Science is the inescapable fact that the God of the Bible does what only a personality can do, and these traits forever separate Him from the pantheistic god of Christian Science, which is incapable by definition of performing these things. Briefly, God is described as capable of doing the following things:

1. *God remembers.* "I, even I, am he that blotteth out thy transgressions for mine own sake, and will not remember thy sins" (Isaiah 43:25; also compare Psalm 79:8; Jeremiah 31:20; Hosea 8:13).

2. *God speaks.* "I am the Lord: that is my name: and my glory will I not give to another, neither my praise to graven images" (Isaiah 42:8; see also Genesis 1:26; Isaiah 43:10–13; 44:6; Matthew 17:5; Hebrews 1:1).

3. *God hears, sees, and creates.* "And God saw that the wickedness of man was great in the earth" (Genesis 6:5); "God heard their groaning" (Exodus 2:24); "and when the people complained . . . and . . . the Lord heard it" (Numbers 11:1); "In the beginning God created the heaven and the earth" (Genesis 1:1).

4. *God "knows," i.e., He has a mind.* "The Lord knoweth them that are his" (2 Timothy 2:19); "God is greater than our heart, and knoweth all things" (1 John 3:20); "For I know the thoughts that I think toward you, saith the Lord" (Jeremiah 29:11).

5. *God will judge the world.* "Therefore I will judge you . . . saith the Lord God" (Ezekiel 18:30); "Therefore thus saith the Lord God unto them; Behold, I, even I, will judge" (Ezekiel 34:20); "For we must all appear before the judgment seat of Christ" (2 Corinthians 5:10).

6. *God is a personal Spirit.* "God is a Spirit: and they that worship him must worship him in spirit and in truth" (John 4:24); "I am the Almighty God; walk before me, and be thou perfect" (Genesis 17:1); God's Son is declared to be the "express image of his person" (Hebrews 1:3), therefore God is a person.

7. *God has a will.* "Thy will be done in earth, as it is in heaven" (Matthew 6:10); "Prove what is that good, and acceptable, and perfect, will of God" (Romans 12:2); "He that doeth the will of God abideth for ever" (1 John 2:17); "Lo, I come to do thy will, O God" (Hebrews 10:7, 9).

From this brief résumé of some of God's attributes, the interested reader can doubtless see the vast difference between the God and Father of our Lord Jesus Christ and the "Divine Principle" of Eddy's Christian Science. Psychologically speaking, a principle cannot remember; "Life, Truth, and Love" cannot speak audibly; nor can "Substance, Mind, or Intelligence" hear, see, create, know, judge, or will. The God of the Bible does these things; the god of Christian Science cannot. It is admitted, of course, that a mind or an intelligence can do these things, but Eddy does not recognize the existence of personality in the Deity, and only a personality has a mind or an intelligence.

Eddy's god (Principle) cannot create nor can it exert a will because Principle or even a principle, if you desire, does not possess a will by any logical definition. The god of Christian Science is an *it*, neuter in gender—merely a name—incapable of metaphysical definition or understanding outside of the maze that is Christian Science theology. The Apostle Paul triumphantly reminds us, "I know whom I have believed, and am persuaded that he is able to keep that which I have committed unto him against that day" (2 Timothy 1:12). The true Christian has a personal relationship with his Lord; he prays through Christ and the power of the Holy Spirit; he asks that it might be given; indeed, personal contact is the very source of the Christian's life and spiritual peace. Christian Scientists have no such contact and consequently no real spiritual life or peace, only the riddles and incoherencies of Eddy and a basic uncertainty about good health.

Concerning the doctrine of the Holy Spirit and the attitude of Christian Science toward it, little need be said, since Eddy's attitude was so obvious, but at the risk of repetition a short review may be profitable. As a matter of course, Eddy denied both the personality and office of the Holy Spirit and for His exalted ministry substituted "Divine Science" (*Science and Health*, 55).

To refute such a decided perversion of Scripture and historical theology one need only recall who the writers of the Bible, and Christ himself, considered the Holy Spirit to be in respect to personality and power. In the sixteenth chapter of John's gospel, Jesus instructed His disciples about their new ministry and duties and promised them a "Comforter" who would strengthen and guide them after His ascension. To quiet their fears, Jesus told them that it was essential to the coming of the Comforter, who issued forth from the Father, that He (Jesus) go away. The Lord said:

> If I go not away, the Comforter will not come unto you; but if I depart, I will send him unto you. And when he is come, he will reprove the world of sin, and of righteousness, and of judgment (vv. 7–8).

It is useful to observe that the Greek text uses the masculine pronoun "He" and also "Him" for the Holy Spirit and ascribes to Him a will (v. 7) and the power to "reprove" the world of "sin, righteousness, and judgment" (v. 8). "Divine Science" has not, will not, and cannot do any of these things because it denies the reality of sin, hence, excluding the need for righteousness, and teaches in place of judgment the pernicious unbiblical doctrine of man's inherent goodness. The Holy Spirit, therefore, is a person with a will and divine power to regenerate the soul of man (John 3) and glorify Jesus Christ. It should also be remembered that He does what only a person can do—He teaches us (Luke 12:12), He speaks to us (Acts 13:2), He thinks and makes decisions (Acts 15:28), and He moves us to do the will of God as He has moved holy men of God to serve in the past (2 Peter 1:21). Further than this, the Holy Spirit can be lied to (Acts 5:5), He can be grieved (Ephesians 4:30), and He is often resisted (Acts 7:51). All these things denote dealings with a personality, not an impersonal force, and certainly not "Divine Science." Beyond these things, the Holy Spirit sanctifies and separates us from sin and prays to the Father for us that we might be freed from great temptations (Romans 8:26).

Certainly these points of evidence disprove the meager attempts of Christian Science to reduce the third person of the Trinity to a metaphysical catchword ("Divine Science"), and reveal clearly for all to see the semantic deception Eddy has utilized in attempting to undermine this great scriptural truth.

The Miracles of Christ

The doctrine of the virgin birth of Jesus Christ is indissolubly joined with that of the validity of Old Testament prophecy concerning the Messiah of Israel. Isaiah the prophet tells us that "a virgin shall conceive, and bear a son, and shall call his name Immanuel" (7:14), and that this child was to be miraculous in every sense of the word. Indeed, so unique was this child to be that to Him alone of all the sons of men is the name God applied, the "mighty God" to be specific, the "everlasting Father," the "Prince of Peace" (9:6). We are told that He shall reign forever (v. 7), and that the zeal of God himself will bring this to pass. Unfolding further the panorama of Old Testament prophecy, we are told that the child in question will be the Son of David (9:7), of royal lineage, and that He will be born in Bethlehem of Judea (Micah 5:2). Even more remarkable than these rays of light from God, the Scriptures further tell us that He was to be crucified for the sins of Israel and the world (Isaiah 53; cf. Daniel 9:26), and that He would rise again to life and come in power to sift the sons of men with eternal judgment (Psalm 22; cf. Zechariah 12:10).

But these facts are all a matter of history, which Jesus of Nazareth fulfilled to the letter, and which only remain to be consummated at His triumphant return as Judge of the world. Both Matthew and Luke declare the human fulfillment of God's plan in Mary's conception of the Christ child (Matthew 1:18–25; cf. Luke 1:30–38). Thus the physical existence of Jesus Christ is a biologically established fact. Christian Science vehemently denies this fact and teaches instead that Mary conceived the spiritual idea of God and named it Jesus (*Science and Health*, 29). Denying as she did the reality of the physical universe, this was a strangely logical step for Eddy as opposed to her usual contempt for all logical form whatsoever. But be that as it may, all the wanderings of Eddy's mind, be they from Dan to Beersheba, can never change the testimony of Old and New Testament Scripture that a demonstrably "real" child was born to Mary, not an "idea," that this child existed as a concrete physical being apart from His divine nature and is now forever, for our sake, both God and man in Jesus Christ. The Virgin Birth, therefore, is a well-supported biblical doctrine, which contradicts most forcibly the false concept Eddy has incorporated into the Christian Science religion.

Respecting the miracles performed by Christ during His earthly ministry, Christian Scientists, whether they admit it or not, must logically deny that they were miracles in the first place and discount them as merely "illusions of the mortal mind." Eddy states that disease, sin, sickness, and death are all illusions; they are not "real" because only Mind (God) is real and Mind is spiritual, not material. Therefore, following Christian Science theology to its "logical" conclusions, since the "illusion of disease" can exist only in "the illusion called matter," which is itself existent only in the illusion called "mortal mind"—which Eddy denies exists anyway—there were no miracles at all because there was no corporeal body to be diseased, hence no need for a cure. Eddy wrote:

> The sick are not healed merely by declaring there is no sickness, but by knowing there is none (*Science and Health*, 447).

This reasoning on the part of Christian Science theology presupposes the assumption that there is no evil, since God—Good—is all that really exists. Unfortunately, it places them in the untenable position of having to account for the origin of the *idea* of evil, for even an illusion must have some basis in experience. Notwithstanding the circularity of this Christian Science argument, the Scriptures send a fresh breath of intellectual honesty into their account of Christ's true attitude toward disease, its reality, and cure. The Lord Jesus never told the disintegrating leper as Mrs. Eddy's practitioner would, "You have no disease, it cannot exist, only God is good and He is all, etc." Rather, He recognized the physical decay and by an act of sovereign grace restored the damaged tissue with one short phrase: "I will, be thou clean." It will be recalled that the leper in question said, "Lord, if thou wilt, thou canst make me clean" (Matthew 8:2–3). Christ's answer included none of Eddy's "Divine Science" or treatments by paid "quacktitioners," as they are sometimes called. He merely restored the form His power had originally created (Colossians 1:16) and destroyed the bacteria responsible for the disease. Jesus never healed by denying the reality of the disease He intended to cure. Rather, He affirmed its reality and glorified God for its cure.

You will remember that at the raising of Lazarus (John 11), Christ waited until his friend was physically dead beyond question (four days) and then restored to the function of life every cell of his decaying body and glorified God for the victory over man's second oldest enemy.[16] We should note in this connection that Jesus did not deny the reality of death, as do Christian Scientists. He did not consider it "an illusion"; rather, He verbally confirmed it: "Lazarus is dead" (John 11:14).

Christian Science finds no support for its denial of the physical miracles of Christ; deny the physical though they may, the facts are established. Should further proof be desired, however, the reader is urged to consult the following biblical references which prove, we believe, that the miracles of Christ were physical realities, the result of supernatural intervention on the part of God in behalf of His erring creatures:

1. *Matthew 8:14–15*. The healing of Peter's mother-in-law.
2. *Matthew 8:26–27*. Christ stills the tempest.
3. *Matthew 9:2, 6–7*. Jesus heals the palsied man.
4. *Matthew 9:27–30*. Christ restores the sight of two blind men.
5. *Mark 1:32–34*. Jesus heals the sick and casts out devils.
6. *John 2:1–11; John 6:10–14*. The miracles of changing water to wine and the feeding of five thousand people.

Concluding this discussion, it should be noted in reference to John 2:1–11 and 6:10–14 that Christ would hardly have created wine from water

16. Satan occupies the dubious honor of being the first.

or multiplied loaves and fishes to quench the thirst and satisfy the hunger of nonexistent bodies or "illusions of mortal mind," to quote Eddy. The nature of all Christ's miracles was that of a divine/human encounter, comprising empirically verified physical events to meet human needs—whether hunger, thirst, or suffering—not "illusions," as the theology of Christian Science attempts to make the gullible believe.

The Vicarious Atonement of Christ

There is no doctrine found within the pages of the Bible that is better supported or substantiated than that of the substitutionary death of Christ for the sins of the world. As far back in the biblical record as Exodus, Moses wrote of God's symbolic use of blood for purification and sacrifice. It will be recalled that Jehovah delivered the Israelites from Egypt by causing all the firstborn of the nation, including Pharaoh's own son, to fall under the shadow of sudden death (Exodus 12). The Jews were instructed in this instance to sprinkle the blood of the young lamb on the doorposts and lintels of their homes, and God promised, "When I see the blood, I will pass over" (Exodus 12:13). The Lord also instituted the animal sacrifices of the Levitical era and expressly stated: "It is the blood that maketh an atonement [covering] for the soul" (Leviticus 17:11). Following this typology through into the New Testament, we find that Jesus was called "the Lamb of God, which taketh away the sin of the world" (John 1:29), and further, that His blood shed upon the cross is our atonement or "covering" for sin, even for the sins of all mankind (Matthew 26:28; Romans 5:6–8; Ephesians 1:7; Colossians 1:20; etc.).

The believer in Christ, therefore, is saved by grace alone, through faith in His blood and its efficacy for the cleansing of all sin (Romans 3:25). John, the beloved disciple, reminds us in his powerful epistle, "The blood of Jesus Christ his Son cleanseth us from all sin" (1 John 1:7), and Peter no less resoundingly declares, "Ye were not redeemed with corruptible things, as silver and gold . . . but with the precious blood of Christ, as of a lamb without blemish and without spot" (1 Peter 1:18–19). Indeed, like a crimson cord binding all the Bible into one compact testimony, the trail of blood courses from Genesis to Revelation, testifying from the mouths of unimpeachable witnesses the wondrous story of God's redemptive love. Listen for a moment to the record of Scripture, and the picture comes clearly into focus: God loved us and sent His Son to be our Savior.

"Christ died for the ungodly," Paul triumphantly cries, and "without shedding of blood there is no remission of sins" (Romans 5:6; Hebrews 9:22); He purchased the church with His own blood (Acts 20:28), Luke informs us, and John adds to the witness by declaring that Christ "washed us from our sins in His own blood" (Revelation 1:5). This was not a pagan sacrifice to placate the wrath of a heathen god's justice, as Eddy wrote, but a sacrifice offered "through the eternal Spirit" to free the sons of men from the curse of sin and open the path of salvation by which we can have "boldness to enter into the holiest by the blood of Jesus . . . a new and living way" to the very throne room of God our Father (Hebrews 10:19–20).

Contrasting this picture of concrete biblical theology with the views of Christian Science, no better illustration of Eddy's repudiation of this doctrine can be shown than that which comes from her own pen. In speaking of the Atonement, Eddy said:

The material blood of Jesus was no more efficacious to cleanse from sin when it was shed upon "the accursed tree," than when it was flowing in his veins (*Science and Health*, 25).

According to Eddy, Jesus, the disciples and apostles, and the early Christian theologians did not understand the meaning of the vicarious Atonement, but she did! Eddy wrote:

He atoned for the terrible unreality of a supposed existence apart from God (*No and Yes*, 55).

The efficacy of the crucifixion lies in the practical affection and goodness it demonstrated for mankind (*Science and Health*, 24).

This is, of course, the opposite of anything the Bible teaches. When Jesus said, "This is my flesh which I shall give for the life of the world," and "This is my blood shed for many for the remission of sin," Eddy would have us believe that He anticipated no sacrifice for man's sin at all, but merely martyrdom for "the terrible unreality of a supposed existence apart from God." Further comment on this problem is not deemed necessary in the light of the obvious denial by Christian Science of this historically accepted biblical doctrine, so strongly supported by the Scriptures of both Testaments.

The Death, Resurrection, and Ascension of Christ

In our age of advanced medicine, we read of many miracles ascribed to the labors of medical science; but all these advancements, marvelous though they may be, have only delayed the inevitable decay and death of the body and have yet to guarantee us physical immortality. The Scriptures clearly teach us that "it is appointed unto men once to die, but after this the judgment" (Hebrews 9:27), even as they tell us that our Lord himself physically died at Calvary (Philippians 2:8). In fact, the death of Jesus upon the cross is more thoroughly substantiated from biblical and secular history than is His birth, which makes it even more difficult to believe that rational persons would deny it. However, Eddy and Christian Science do deny it, hence the necessity of refuting their illogical contentions.

Joseph of Arimathea, it will be remembered, requested the dead body of Jesus from Pontius Pilate (Matthew 27:58) and properly prepared it for burial (vv. 59–60), as was the custom of the Jews. One thing that Joseph knew above anything else in the gathering shadows of the Sabbath that marked the solemn hour rent by bitterness, sorrow, and fear, was that the body of the Galilean prophet he buried was physically incapable of life; Jesus of Nazareth was dead. The absolute terror and doubt that gripped the immediate followers of Jesus could have come only from the personal knowledge that He had perished under the unbelieving Judeo-Roman conspiracy and that their cause was without a visible leader and apparently doomed to failure. The Apostle Paul tells us repeatedly, "Christ died" (Romans 5:6); Peter recounts that He "bare our sins in his own body on the tree" (1 Peter 2:24), and John testifies that the soldiers "saw" when they came to Jesus "that he was dead already" (John 19:33). Certainly such intimate accounts cannot be lightly dismissed, yet Eddy and Christian Science boldly assert "His disciples believed Jesus to be dead while he was hidden in the sepulchre, whereas he was alive" (*Science and Health*, 44), and once again Eddy states:

Jesus' students . . . did not perform many wonderful works until they saw him after his crucifixion and learned that he had not died (*Science and Health*, 45–46).

The issue therefore is a clean-cut one. The Bible says Christ died upon the cross; Eddy and Christian Science say He did not. For those who call themselves Christians, the choice is not a difficult one to make, and for those who are not Christians we are certain they will accept the words of the Scripture in preference to Eddy anyhow, if only on general principles and the testimony of history.

The resurrection of Christ is treated on a similar basis by the Christian Science religion, which affirms that He never rose from the dead physically any more than He died physically, Eddy deliberately perverting numerous texts of Scripture to glean support for her wobbly propositions.

So it is that we learn how Christian Science often attempts to change the obvious meaning of texts. In the twentieth chapter of John's gospel, the resurrected Jesus, to prove to the doubting Thomas that He was not a spirit but genuine "flesh and bones," presented His body bearing the imprint of nails and spear for the disciple's examination. To His disciple at another time Jesus also said, "Handle me . . . for a spirit hath not flesh and bones, as ye see me have" (Luke 24:39). The resurrection of Christ and its startling revelation—namely, that He was who He claimed to be, the Son of God—is the one factor that most probably accounts for the rapid rise of Christianity's power over the lives of men. Here was a genuine opportunity to believe in a Savior who proved His divinity by vanquishing death, and who promised the same victory to those who believe and preach His Gospel. It is no wonder Satan has so strenuously opposed this doctrine of Scripture, for upon it hangs the verity of our salvation. As Paul puts it, "If Christ be not raised, your faith is vain; ye are yet in your sins" (1 Corinthians 15:17). Eddy and Christian Science may oppose this truth vigorously—as indeed they do—but the Gospel of Christ will not be hindered by mere denials, and their unbelief does not in any sense nullify the truth of God as the Scriptures so powerfully declare it:

> But now is Christ risen from the dead, and become the firstfruits of them that slept. For since by man came death, by man came also the resurrection of the dead. For as in Adam all die, even so in Christ shall all be made alive[17] (1 Corinthians 15:20–22).

As to the doctrine of the ascension of Christ into heaven, physically, another denial is vouchsafed from the pen of Eddy. By the same method she uses to spiritualize the resurrection of Christ, Eddy also spiritualizes His ascension. She describes it thusly:

17. Or to more properly grasp the sense of the Greek, "As in Adam all die, so then through Christ shall all be resurrected."

[The disciples'] dear Master would rise again in the spiritual realm of reality, and ascend far above their apprehension. As the reward for his faithfulness, he would disappear to material sense in that change which has since been called the ascension (*Science and Health*, 34).

Now, to any alert Bible student, the ascension of Christ was a physical one; the disciples saw Him carried into the heavenlies visibly; it was not merely an upward stroke on the "spiritual scale" of existence, as Eddy put it, but a change of position from one sphere to another, visible in part to the human eye. In connection with this, one need only remember the testimony of the angels who escorted their Lord to His throne:

Ye men of Galilee, why stand ye gazing up into heaven? this same Jesus, which is taken up from you into heaven, shall so come in like manner as ye have seen him go into heaven (Acts 1:11).

Beside these great declarations of Scripture, the confused writing of Eddy is conspicuously immature and inadequate because, as always, the Bible, which is the supreme Christian authority, confirms the truth as it really happened, not as Christian Science has imagined it happened.

The Existence of Satan, Evil, and Sin

Probably one of the most obvious doctrines of biblical theology is that of the origin, existence, and final disposition of evil. From Genesis to Revelation one can distinguish the powers set in array against God and His people, powers whose ultimate end is spiritual judgment of the most terrible order. We are told in the Scriptures that Satan or Lucifer, the "god of this world," was once a mighty and perfect angelic son of God whose dazzling and wondrous countenance earned for him the titles "son of the morning" and "Covering Cherub" (Isaiah 14:12; Ezekiel 28:14). The Scriptures also tell us that this powerful angel secretly cherished the desire to usurp the throne of his Maker (Isaiah 14:13–14), and upon gathering numerous supporters he rebelled against the sovereignty of Jehovah. The outcome of this wicked rebellion was the driving from heaven of Satan and the fallen angels that followed him, and he was subsequently allowed dominion over the celestial universe for reasons best known to God and himself, hence his title "prince of the power of the air" (Ephesians 2:2).

With this rebellion commenced the beginning of all evil or sin, i.e., that which is opposed to the will of God. After his rout in the heavenly encounter, Satan extended his kingdom over the heavenlies and earth, determined to disrupt, if possible, the plans of God. In the Garden of Eden Satan's desires reached fruition, and he succeeded in spiritually corrupting the future parents of the human race, Adam and Eve (Genesis 3). As punishment for this sin against the Lord, Satan was sentenced to a humiliating defeat by the "Seed" of the very creatures he had so willfully wronged (Genesis 3:15). This promised Seed who would bruise the head of Satan was to be the Messiah of Israel, who we have already seen is the Lord Jesus Christ. The final judgment of Satan will come after his complete and utter defeat at Armageddon, when he and all his followers from the ancient days of his heavenly citizenship will then be cast into the lake of fire, there to suffer eternally the righteous judgment of God (Revelation 20:10).

Despite this graphic biblical portrayal of Satan available for all to see, Eddy and Christian Science energetically deny his existence referring to him as "another elusive personification" (*Science and Health*, 81). Further establishing her contention that evil is nonexistent, Eddy flatly states:

> Hence, evil is but an illusion, and it has no real basis. Evil is a false belief. God is not its author. The supposititious parent of evil is a lie (*Science and Health*, 480).
>
> There never was a moment in which evil was real (*No and Yes*, 24).

Since Christian Science denies the origin of evil or Satan, it is only logical that it should deny evil, and sin as the result of evil. Concerning sin Eddy wrote:

> The only reality of sin, sickness, or death is the awful fact that unrealities seem real to human, erring belief, until God strips off their disguise. They are not true, because they are not of God (*S & H*, 472).
>
> Sin, sickness, and death are to be classified as effects of error. Christ came to destroy the belief of sin (*S & H*, 473).

Placing this declaration on a level plane with the biblical definition and development of the doctrine of sin, it is seen to be at complete odds with the biblical record. John reminds us that sin, far from being an "illusion" or a nonexistent force, is in reality a very potent enemy of man. "Sin," writes John, "is the transgression of the law," and further, "All unrighteousness is sin" (1 John 3:4; 1 John 5:17). Paul also admonishes, "For the wages of sin is death" (Romans 6:23). One can hardly be expected to believe that the Christian Science teaching about sin is truthful when both John and Paul, inspired spokesmen of God, so clearly contradict it. The Bible innumerable times declares: "All have sinned, and come short of the glory of God" (Romans 3:23), and, "If we say we have not sinned, we make him [God] a liar, and his word is not in us" (1 John 1:10). As to the personality and power of a personal force of evil (Satan), the Bible equally establishes his existence as opposed to Eddy's denials. Jesus, it will be remembered, spoke with Satan, who tempted Him (Luke 4:5–6). This could hardly have been an illusion, even of the Christian Science variety, and the Lord also announced that He had come "to destroy the works of the devil," whom He described as a liar and a "murderer from the beginning" who "abode not in the truth" . . . "a liar and the father of it" (John 8:44). Eddy's devil, as her literary advisor, the Rev. J. H. Wiggin, so aptly put it, was Malicious Animal Magnetism, which she invented to explain away the rather obvious fact that evil and sin existed despite her affirmations to the contrary. This doctrine eventually became a mania with Eddy and drove her to irrational behavior and fantastically absurd demonstrations of temper, illness, and rapid excursions to different communities "when she felt the fiend closing in."

The Scriptures, therefore, give more than convincing proof "that God will judge sin" and that it is not an illusion but an ever-present enemy, of which all men, even Christian Scientists, must reap the wages in the end. It is comforting to know from a biblical standpoint that though "the wages of sin is death . . . the gift of God is eternal life through Jesus Christ our Lord" (Romans 6:23).

Biblical Texts Helpful in Refuting Christian Science Theology

1. *The Authority of the Bible.* Psalm 119:140; Isaiah 40:8; Matthew 24:35; John 10:35; 17:17; 2 Timothy 3:16.
2. *The Trinity and the Deity of Christ.* Genesis 1:26; 11:7; 18:1–33; Exodus 3:14; Isaiah 6:8; 9:6; John 1:1, 14; 8:58; Colossians 1:15; 2:9; Hebrews 1:3; Revelation 1:7–8, 16.
3. *The Personality of the Holy Spirit.* Luke 12:12; John 16:7–8; Acts 13:2.
4. *The Virgin Birth and Miracles of Jesus.* Isaiah 7:14; 9:6; Micah 5:2; Matthew 1:18–25; Luke 1:30–38; Matthew 8:14–15, 26–27; 9:2, 6–7, 27–30; Mark 1:32–34; John 2:1–11; 6:10–14.

5. *The Atonement, Death, and Resurrection of Christ.* Exodus 12:13; Leviticus 17:11; Psalm 22; Isaiah 53; Daniel 9:26; Matthew 26:28; 28:5–7; Luke 24:39; John 1:29; 19:33; Romans 5:6–8; Ephesians 1:7; Colossians 1:20.

6. *The Doctrine of Eternal Retribution.* Matthew 13:42, 50; 22:13; Mark 9:44, 46, 48; Luke 3:17; Revelation 20:10.

7. *The Doctrine of Christian Prayer.* Matthew 6:5–15; 7:7–11; Luke 18:1; Philippians 4:6; 1 Thessalonians 5:17; James 5:16.

8. *The Doctrine of Sin.* Romans 3:23; 6:23; 1 John 1:10; 3:4; 5:17.

9. *Jesus is the Christ (Messiah) of God.* John 4:25, 26; 1 John 2:22.

10. *God is not pantheistic in any sense.* Acts 17:24–28; Romans 1:25.

11. *God is neither male nor female.* Jeremiah 7:18; 1 Corinthians 8:6.

12. *Matter exists and is independent of spirit.* Matthew 10:28; Luke 24:39.

Explore

Mesmerism
Divine Principle
Mind-Material Dualism
Delusion

Discuss

1. What happened when Quimby entered the Christian Science picture?

2. Why does plagiarism matter?

3. According to Mary Baker Eddy, Jesus, the disciples and apostles, and the early Christian theologians did not understand the meaning of the vicarious Atonement, but she did. How did the biblical atonement differ from Eddy's version of it?

_____

_____

4. True or False: The death of Jesus upon the cross is more thoroughly substantiated from biblical and secular history than is His birth.

_____

_____

Dig Deeper

See *The Kingdom of the Cults Study Guide* available at WalterMartin.com.

6

Mormonism

Quick Facts on Mormonism

- The Bible is the Word of God insofar as it is correctly translated.
- There are three sacred books in addition to the Bible: the Book of Mormon, the *Doctrine and Covenants*, and the *Pearl of Great Price*.
- Mormonism is polytheistic in its core: many gods may rule over many planets.
- Jesus was not conceived by the Holy Spirit; he is the half brother of Lucifer.

Historical Perspective

The Church of Jesus Christ of Latter-day Saints (LDS) is distinctive among all the religious cults and sects active in the United States in that it has by far the most fascinating history, and one worthy of consideration by all students of religions originating on the American continent.

The Mormons is the common name for the Church of Jesus Christ of Latter-day Saints, with its headquarters in Salt Lake City, Utah. The Mormon Church's growth is due largely to their worldwide missionary program, numbering 16.2 million adherents in 2018.[1]

1. "Facts and Statistics," Newsroom, accessed April 5, 2018, https://www.mormonnewsroom .org/facts-and-statistics.

The average active Mormon is usually marked by many sound moral traits. He is generally amiable, almost always hospitable, and extremely devoted to his family and to the teachings of his church. Sad to say, however, the great majority of Mormons are in almost total ignorance of the shady historical and theological sources of their religion. They are openly shocked at times when the unglamorous and definitely unchristian background of the Mormon Church is revealed to them. This little-known facet of Mormonism is "a side of the coin" that innumerable Mormon historians have for years either hidden from their people or glossed over in an attempt to suppress certain verifiable and damaging historical evidences. Such evidence the author has elected to review in the interest of obtaining a full picture of Joseph Smith's religion.

> Mormon historians have for years either hidden from their people or glossed over verifiable and damaging historical evidences.

Early Mormon History

1. Joseph Smith Jr., "The Prophet," better known to residents of Palmyra, New York, as just plain "Joe Smith," was born in Sharon, Vermont, December 23, 1805, the fourth child of Lucy and Joseph Smith.

2. Joseph Smith Sr. was a mystic, a man who spent much of his time digging for imaginary buried treasure (he was particularly addicted to Captain Kidd's legendary hoard!). Besides this failing, he sometimes attempted to mint his own money, which at least once brought him into decided conflict with the local constabulary. This fact is, of course, well known to any informed student of Mormonism.[2]

In 1820, Joseph Smith Jr. claimed a heavenly vision that he said singled him out as the Lord's anointed prophet for this dispensation, though it was not until 1823, with the appearance of the angel Moroni at the quaking Smith's bedside, that Joe began his relationship to the fabulous "golden plates," or what was to become the Book of Mormon.

2. James H. Kennedy, *Early Days of Mormonism: Palmyra, Kirkland, and Nauvoo* (New York: Scribner's, 1888), 8.

According to Smith's account of this extraordinary revelation, which is recorded in the *Pearl of Great Price, Joseph Smith—History,* 1:29–54, the angel Moroni, the glorified son of one Mormon, the man for whom the famous book of the same name is entitled, appeared beside Joseph's bedside and thrice repeated his commission to the allegedly awestruck treasure hunter. Smith did not write this account down until some years later, but even that fails to excuse the blunder he made in transmitting the angelic proclamation. This confusion appears in the 1851 edition of the *Pearl of Great Price,* wherein Joseph Smith identifies the messenger as Nephi, an entirely different character found in the Book of Mormon.

This unfortunate crossing up of the divine communication system was later remedied by thoughtful Mormon scribes who have exercised great care to ferret out all the historical and factual blunders not readily explainable in the writings of Smith, Young, and other early Mormon writers. In current editions of the *Pearl of Great Price,* Moroni is identified as the nighttime visitor. However, the historical contradiction of whether Nephi or Moroni carried the message to Smith apparently makes little difference to the faithful.

What cannot be erased so easily is the original handwritten manuscript history of the church that contains this error, which was supervised by Joseph Smith during his lifetime.[3] Later, in 1842, these manuscripts formed the basis of the published history of Mormonism, again, overseen by Smith, where Nephi appears again as the revelatory angel.[4] The first edition of the *Pearl of Great Price* (1851), with the subtitle "Choice selections of revelations, translations, and narrations of Joseph Smith," also contained the name Nephi because the published history of Mormonism set this foundation.

In 1827 Smith claimed to receive the golden plates upon which the Book of Mormon is alleged to have been written. Shortly after this historic find, unearthed in the hill Cumorah, near Palmyra, New York, Smith began to "translate" the "reformed Egyptian"[5] hieroglyphics, inscribed thereupon by means of the "Urim and Thummim," a type of miraculous spectacles, which the angel Moroni had the foresight to provide for the budding seer.

3. A reproduction of the manuscript may be found in Jerald and Sandra Tanner's *Mormonism—Shadow or Reality* (Salt Lake City: Utah Lighthouse Ministry, 1987, fifth edition), 136.

4. "History of Joseph Smith," Times and Seasons, April 15, 1842, 3:753.

5. Reformed Egyptian is an undocumented language never seen by any leading Egyptologist or philologist who has ever been consulted on the problem. However, the Mormons still maintain their claim with the full knowledge that these are the facts.

THE KINGDOM OF THE CULTS HANDBOOK

A whirlwind of contradictory accounts swirled through Smith's early history, particularly concerning his seer stones, first vision, translational work, revelations, and priesthood restoration.

From the now hallowed state of Pennsylvania, immortalized by Smith's initiation into the priesthood of Aaron by John the Baptist, Joseph returned shortly to the home of Peter Whitmer in Fayette, New York, where he remained until the "translation" from the plates was completed and the Book of Mormon published and copyrighted in the year 1830. On April 6 of the same year, the prophet, in company with his brothers Hyrum and Samuel, Oliver Cowdery, and David and Peter Whitmer Jr., officially founded a "new religious society" entitled "The Church of Christ" in 1830 (renamed the Church of the Latter-day Saints in 1834 and finally as the Church of Jesus Christ of Latter-day Saints in 1838). Thus it was that one of the more virulent strains of American cults came into existence— Mormonism had begun in earnest.

Sidney Rigdon, Parley P. Pratt, and his younger brother, Orson Pratt, it should be noted, were almost from the day of their "conversions" slated for greatness in the Mormon hierarchy; and it is their writings, along with those of Brigham Young, Charles Penrose, and James Talmage, that best argue in favor of the Mormon cause even to this day.

Mormon Sacred Texts

Aside from the King James Version of the Bible, which the Mormons accept as part of the Word of God, "We believe the Bible to be the word of God as far as it is translated correctly" (*Pearl of Great Price, Eighth Article of Faith*).[6] To this they have added the *Doctrine and Covenants*, the *Pearl of Great Price*, and the initial volume, the Book of Mormon, all canonized as authorized Scripture—the "Four Standard Works." The last mentioned is a subject of this chapter since it occupies a pivotal place in Mormon theology and history and therefore must be carefully examined. A great deal of research on the part of a number of able scholars and organizations has already been published concerning the Book of Mormon, and we have

6. "The King James Version the LDS church uses is one they publish themselves. The church does their own chapter headings and cross-references, notes, and explanations, that take one to other LDS sources like other LDS scripture or the JST (Joseph Smith Translation of the Bible)." —Dr. Lynn Wilder, a former Brigham Young University professor and former Mormon (private correspondence). See also her autobiography at "Ex-Mormon Christians United for Jesus," http://www.unveilingmormonism.com/bio/.

MORMONISM

drawn heavily upon whatever documented and verifiable information was available. The task of validating the material was enormous, and so we have selected that information which has been verified beyond refutation and is available today in some of our leading institutions of learning (Stanford University, Union Theological Seminary, the Research Departments of the Library of Congress, the New York Public Library, and others).

It is a difficult task to evaluate the complex structure of the Book of Mormon, and the reader is urged to consider the bibliography included in the full version of *The Kingdom of the Cults* if he should desire further and more exhaustive studies.

Scientific Evidence against the Book of Mormon

In an attempt to validate and justify the claims of the Book of Mormon, the highest authority in Mormonism, Joseph Smith Jr., the Mormon prophet, related an event which, if true, would add significant weight to some of the Mormon claims in their sacred book. Fortunately, it is a fact on which a good deal of evidence can be brought to bear.

Smith put forth his claim in the book *Pearl of Great Price, Joseph Smith—History*, 1:62–64 (1982 edition), and it is worthwhile to examine it:

I commenced copying the characters off the plates. I copied a considerable number of them, and by means of the Urim and Thummim I translated some of them. . . . Mr. Martin Harris came to our place, got the characters which I had drawn off the plates, and started with them to the city of New York. For what took place relative to him and the characters, I refer to his own account of the circumstances, as he related them to me after his return, which was as follows: "I went to the city of New York, and presented the characters that had been translated, with the translation thereof, to Professor Charles Anthon, a gentleman celebrated for his literary attainments. Professor Anthon stated that the translation was correct, more so than any he had before seen translated from the Egyptian. I then showed him those which were not yet translated, and he said that they were Egyptian, Chaldaic, Assyriac, and Arabic; and he said they were true characters."

According to Joseph Smith, then, Martin Harris, his colleague, obtained from the learned Professor Charles Anthon of Columbia University a validation of Smith's translation of the reformed Egyptian hieroglyphic characters found on the plates that Moroni made available to him. The difficulty with Smith's statement is that Professor Anthon never said any such thing, and fortunately he went on record in a lengthy letter to Mr. E. D. Howe, a contemporary of Joseph Smith, who did one of the most thorough jobs of research on the Mormon prophet and the origins of Mormonism.[7]

Professor Anthon's letter is both revealing and devastating where Smith's and Harris's veracity are concerned. We might also raise the question as to how Professor Anthon could say that the characters shown to him by Martin Harris and authorized by Joseph Smith as part of the material copied from the revelation of the Book of Mormon were "Egyptian, Chaldaic, Assyriac, and Arabic" when the Book of Mormon itself declares that the characters were "reformed Egyptian," the language of the Nephites. Since the language of the Book of Mormon was known to "none other people," how would it be conceivably possible for Professor Anthon to have testified as to the accuracy of Smith's translation? To this date, no one has ever been able to find even the slightest trace of the language known as "reformed Egyptian"; and all reputable linguists who have examined the evidence put forth by the Mormons have rejected them as mythical.

Archaeological Evidence

The Book of Mormon purports to portray the rise and development of two great civilizations. As to just how great these civilizations were, some excerpts from the book itself adequately illustrate:

"The whole face of the land had become covered with buildings, and the people were as numerous almost, as it were the sand of the sea" (Mormon 1:7).

". . . fine workmanship of wood, in buildings, and in machinery, and also in iron and copper, and brass and steel, making all manners of tools" (Jarom 1:8; 2 Nephi 5:15).

". . . did multiply and spread . . . began to cover the face of the whole earth, from the sea south to the sea north, from the sea west to the sea east" (Heleman 3:8).

". . . had been slain . . . nearly two million [Jaredites]" (See Ether 15:2).

". . . their shipping and their building of ships, and their building of temples, and of synagogues and their sanctuaries" (Heleman 3:14. See also 2 Nephi 5:15–16; Alma 16:13).

7. For Professor Anthon's letter on the false claims of Joseph Smith Jr., see *The Kingdom of the Cults* (2019).

"... swords ... cimeters ... breastplates ... arm-shields ... shields ... head-plates ... armor" (See Alma 43:18–19; 3:5; Ether 15:15).

See 3 Nephi 8:9–10, 14; 9:4–6, 8: where cities and inhabitants were sunk in the depths of the sea and earth.

The Book of Mormon indicates the tremendous spread of the cultures of these races. There are numerous cities catalogued in the Book of Mormon, evidence that these were indeed mighty civilizations, which should, by all the laws of archaeological research into the culture of antiquity, have left vast amounts of "finds" to be evaluated.

But such is not the case. The Mormons have yet to explain the fact that leading archaeological researchers not only have repudiated the claims of the Book of Mormon as to the existence of these civilizations, but have adduced considerable evidence to show the impossibility of the accounts given in the Mormon Bible.

From the Smithsonian Institution in Washington:

1. The Smithsonian Institution has never used the Book of Mormon in any way as a scientific guide. Smithsonian archaeologists see no direct connection between the archaeology of the New World and the subject matter of the book.

2. The physical type of the Native American is basically Mongoloid, being most closely related to that of the peoples of eastern, central, and northeastern Asia. Archaeological evidence indicates that the ancestors of the present Native Americans came into the New World—probably over a land bridge known to have existed in the Bering Strait region during the last Ice Age—in a continuing series of small migrations beginning from about 25,000 to 30,000 years ago.

3. Present evidence indicates that the first people to reach this continent from the East were the Norsemen who briefly visited the northeastern part of North America around AD 1000 and then settled in Greenland. There is nothing to show that they reached Mexico or Central America.

4. One of the main lines of evidence supporting the scientific finding that contacts with Old World civilizations, if indeed they occurred at all, were of very little significance for the development of Native American civilizations is the fact that none of the principal Old World domesticated food plants or animals (except the dog) occurred in the

New World in Pre-Columbian times. Native Americans had no wheat, barley, oats, millet, rice, cattle, pigs, chickens, horses, donkeys, or camels before 1492. (Camels and horses were in the Americas, along with the bison, mammoth, and mastodon, but all these animals became extinct around 10,000 BC at the time the early big game hunters spread across the Americas.)[8]

From this evidence, it is clear that the cities mentioned in the Book of Mormon are imaginary, that elephants never existed on this continent, and that the metals described in the Book of Mormon have never been found in any of the areas of contemporary civilizations of the New World.

The DNA Factor

If the Lamanites, as the Book of Mormon claims, were the descendants of Nephi, who was a Jew of the Mediterranean Caucasoid type, then their descendants, Native Americans, would by necessity have the same blood factor genotypically, and phenotypic or apparent characteristics would be the same. But this is not at all the case. Instead, the Native American, so say anthropologists, is not of Semitic extraction and has the definite phenotypical characteristic of a Mongoloid. A thorough study of anthropology and such writers as W. C. Boyd (*The Contributions of Genetics to Anthropology*) and Bentley Glass, the gifted geneticist of Johns Hopkins University, reveals that Mormon findings based upon the Book of Mormon are out of harmony with the findings of geneticists and anthropologists. There simply is no foundation for the postulation that the Native American (Lamanites, according to the Mormons) is in any way related to the race to which Nephi (a Semite) allegedly belonged.

Corrections, Contradictions, and Errors

There is a great wealth of information concerning the material contained in the Book of Mormon and the various plagiarisms, anachronisms, false prophecies, and other unfortunate practices connected with it. At best we can give but a condensation of that which has been most thoroughly documented.

8. See the Institute for Religious Research at Irr.org for images of the Smithsonian correspondence, https://mit.irr.org/smithsonian-institution-statement-on-book-of-mormon.

Since the publication of the Book of Mormon in 1830, the first edition has undergone extensive "correction" in order to present it in its current form. Some of these "corrections" should be noted.

1. When compared with the 1830 edition, 1 Nephi 19:16–20 reveals more than twenty changes in the "inspired Book of Mormon," words having been dropped, spelling corrected, and words and phraseology added and turned about. This is a strange way to treat an inspired revelation from God.[9]

2. In Alma 28:14–29:11, more than eighteen changes may be counted from the original edition. Interestingly, in Alma 29:4, a phrase that claimed the book was "unalterable" was altered itself! The missing phrase, ". . . Yea, decree unto them that decrees which are unalterable . . ." was dropped from 1830 until it reappeared in 1981.

These are but a few of the examples from the approximately 4,000 word changes to be found in the Book of Mormon, so it is apparent that in no sense can it be accepted as the Word of God. The Scripture says, "The word of the Lord endureth for ever" (1 Peter 1:25); and our Savior declared, "Sanctify them through thy truth: thy word is truth" (John 17:17).

The record of the Scriptures rings true. The Book of Mormon, on the other hand, is patently false in far too many instances to be considered coincidence.

Plagiarisms—The King James Version

A careful examination of the Book of Mormon reveals that it contains thousands of words from the King James Bible. In fact, verbatim quotations, some of considerable length, have caused the Mormons no end of embarrassment for many years.

The comparisons of Moroni 10 with 1 Corinthians 12:1–11; 2 Nephi 14 with Isaiah 4; and 2 Nephi 12 with Isaiah 2 reveal that Joseph Smith made free use of his Bible to supplement the alleged revelation of the golden plates. The book of Mosiah, chapter 14, in the Book of Mormon, is a reproduction of the fifty-third chapter of Isaiah the prophet, and 3 Nephi 13 copies Matthew 6 almost word for word.

9. For a thorough comparison of the 1830 Book of Mormon with the 1920 text, see Jerald Tanner and Sandra Tanner, *3,913 Changes in the Book of Mormon* (Salt Lake City: Utah Lighthouse Ministry, 1996).

There are other instances of plagiarisms from the King James Bible, including paraphrases of certain verses. One of these verses (1 John 5:7) is reproduced in 3 Nephi 11:27. The only difficulty with the paraphrase here is that the text is considered by New Testament scholars to be an interpolation missing from all the major manuscripts of 1 John. Its presence in the King James Version of the Bible was enough for Smith to paraphrase it not knowing the difference.

Theological Evaluation

The Priesthoods

The Mormon church almost from its inception has claimed what no other church today claims to possess: the priesthoods of Aaron and Melchizedek.

In the theology of Mormonism, both the Melchizedek and Aaronic orders are considered to be one priesthood without beginning or end.

The Mormons maintain that Joseph Smith and Oliver Cowdery received the Aaronic priesthood from the hand of John the Baptist on May 15, 1829, and that "the Melchizedek priesthood was conferred upon Joseph Smith and Oliver Cowdery through the ministration of Peter, James, and John, shortly after the conferring of the Aaronic order."[10]

In the theology of Mormonism, both the Melchizedek and Aaronic orders are considered to be but one priesthood "without beginning of days or end of years" (*Doctrine and Covenants*, 84:17), and through the authority of this priesthood alone, they maintain, men speak and act in the name of the Lord for the salvation of humanity. In order that this may be clearly understood, the following quotation from the leading Mormon volume on the subject of the priesthood must be considered:

> This authoritative Priesthood is designed to assist men in all of life's endeavors, both temporal and spiritual. Consequently, there are divisions or offices of the Priesthood, each charged with a definite duty, fitting a special human need.

10. John A. Widtsoe, *The Priesthood and Church Government* (Salt Lake City: Deseret Book Company, 1939), 107.

The prophet Joseph Smith once said that all Priesthood is Melchizedek. That is to say that the Melchizedek Priesthood embraces all offices and authorities in the Priesthood. This is clearly stated in the *Doctrine and Covenants*, Section 107, Verse 5: "All other authorities or offices in the church are appendages to this (i.e., Melchizedek) Priesthood. . . ."

There are two Priesthoods spoken of in the Scriptures, viz., the Melchizedek and the Aaronic or Levitical. Although there are two Priesthoods, yet the Melchizedek Priesthood comprehends the Aaronic or Levitical Priesthood; and is the grand head, and holds the highest authority that pertains to the Priesthood, and the keys of the kingdom of God in all ages of the world to the latest posterity on the earth; and is the channel through which all knowledge, doctrine, the plan of salvation, and every important matter is revealed from heaven.[11]

The Mormon concept of the priesthood holds that God has placed in that church presidents, apostles, high priests, seventies, elders; and that the various offices all share specific authorities.

The president of the church, they maintain,

may hold and dispense the powers of the administrative responsibilities of that office, the power of the Priesthood is decentralized: first, according to offices and the jurisdictions of those respective offices; second, according to individual Priesthood-bearers. This means that while the church as a whole is delicately responsive to central authority for church-wide purposes, the central-local relationships in the organization do not restrict the full initiative and free development of either territorial divisions of the Church, individual quorums, groups of quorums, or the member as an individual. . . . The Priesthood provides a "functional" instrumentality for church government that is at once efficient and responsible in centralization, but flexible and decentralized in actual administration.[12]

It is therefore apparent that in Mormon theology the priesthood occupies a position of great importance and comprehends nearly every male member of the church above the age of twelve in one capacity or another; and therefore by necessity the refutation of the Mormon claims to its possession undercuts the very foundations of Mormonism.[13]

11. Widtsoe, *The Priesthood*, 102–103.
12. Widtsoe, *The Priesthood*, 103.
13. Until June 1978, men of African descent were denied the priesthood because of a teaching that they were under a curse for their lack of valiance in their premortal existence. Under this ban they were unable to attain the status of "exaltation" (godhood).

With the foregoing in mind, let us examine the Scriptures that most thoroughly refute the Mormon contentions. The Scripture indeed provides a wealth of information.

In the seventh chapter of the epistle to the Hebrews, Melchizedek, who was the king of Salem and priest of the Most High God, is mentioned briefly in connection with Abraham. The author of Hebrews points out that the priesthood of Melchizedek is superior to the Aaronic priesthood and the administrations of the Levites because Abraham, who was the father of the sons of Levi, paid tithe to Melchizedek. This establishes the fact that Melchizedek was superior to Abraham. The writer of Hebrews puts it this way: "And without all contradiction the less is blessed of the better. And here men that die receive tithes; but there he receiveth them, of whom it is witnessed that he liveth. And as I may so say, Levi also, who receiveth tithes, paid tithes in Abraham. For he was yet in the loins of his father, when Melchizedek met him" (7:7–10).

The establishment of the fact that the Melchizedek priesthood is superior to the Aaronic would be virtually meaningless if the writer of Hebrews had not gone on to say:

"If therefore perfection were by the Levitical priesthood (for under it the people received the law), what further need was there that another priest should rise after the order of Melchizedek, and not be called after the order of Aaron? For the priesthood being *changed*, there is made of necessity a change also of the law" (vv. 11–12, emphasis added).

The whole point of the seventh chapter of Hebrews, as any careful exegesis will reveal, is the fact that Jesus Christ, who is "a priest forever after the order of Melchizedek" (v. 17) has, by virtue of His sacrifice upon the cross, changed the priesthood of Aaron (v. 12), instituting in its place His own priesthood of the Melchizedek order.

Christ was not of the tribe of Levi and not of the priesthood of Aaron; He was of the tribe of Judah. This stinging truth demolishes the Mormon argument, for Jesus, being of Judah's tribe, could never possess the Levite tribal priesthood. The point of Hebrews is to teach that Jesus' priesthood is infinitely superior to that of Aaron. It is quite evident that the Levitical priesthood could not evolve into the Melchizedek priesthood, but that it passed away as symbolized by the tearing of the veil leading to the Holy of Holies at the crucifixion (Matthew 27:51).

The writer of Hebrews further states that Christ is our great High Priest and that He has "passed through the heavenlies" to "appear in the presence of God for us." In addition to this, it is declared that "Christ is not entered into the holy places made with hands, which are the figures of the true; but into heaven itself. . . . Nor yet that he should offer himself often, as the high priest entereth into the holy place every year with blood of others; for then must he often have suffered since the foundation of the world: but now once in the end of the world hath he appeared to put away sin by the sacrifice of himself" (Hebrews 9:24–26).

The previous reference is clearly to the truth that the old priesthood (Aaronic or Levitical), which enabled the priests to enter into the temple apartment once every year on the Day of Atonement, has become obsolete because Christ has once offered an eternal atonement for the sins of the whole world (1 John 2:2).

How significant indeed are these facts when placed beside the Mormon claim to possession of the Aaronic priesthood, which God's Word says has been "changed" and completely consummated in the Priest whose order is after Melchizedek, Jesus Christ himself.

Our Lord's priesthood is not dependent upon its continuation from father to son as the Aaronic was through the Levitical order, something necessitated by virtue of the fact that all men die; hence its transference. But the writer of Hebrews tells us that the Lord Jesus Christ arose "after the similitude of Melchizedek." He is "another priest, Who is made, not after the law of carnal commandment [which is temporary by nature], but after the power of an endless life" (Hebrews 7:15–16). The Greek word *akatalutos* is rightly translated "imperishable, indestructible, and indissoluble"; and in this context it refers to His life.[14] He was not consecrated a priest as were the Levites from father to son, but His priesthood is after the order of endless Being. His is an infinite priesthood because He is eternal.

All this background is of vital importance in refuting the Mormon claims to the perpetuity of the Aaronic priesthood, but even more so in refuting their concept of the Melchizedek priesthood, which they also claim to have received.

In the same chapter of Hebrews, a second Mormon claim is tersely dispensed with by the Holy Spirit in an emphatic and irrevocable manner.

By so much was Jesus made a surety of a better testament. And they truly were many priests, because they were not suffered to continue by reason

---

14. *Akatalutos* is translated as "indestructible" in AMP, ESV, HCSB, LEB, NASB, NET, NIV, NRSV; "indissoluble" in ASV (footnote), DARBY, JUB, WYC.

of death: But this man, because he continueth ever, hath an unchangeable priesthood. Wherefore he is able to save them to the uttermost that come unto God by him, seeing he ever liveth to make intercession for them. For such an high priest became us, who is holy, harmless, undefiled, separate from sinners, and made higher than the heavens; who needeth not daily, as those high priests, to offer up sacrifice, first for his own sins, and then for the people's: for this he did once, when he offered up himself. For the law maketh men high priests which have infirmity; but the word of the oath, which was since the law, maketh the Son, who is consecrated for evermore (vv. 22–28).

Particular attention should be paid to verse 24, which, in the Greek, is devastating to the Mormon claim. Verse 24, in Greek, as the Goodspeed translation literally reads, "But he continues forever, so his priesthood is untransferable."[15]

The Greek word *aparabatos* literally rendered as *untransferable*, carries the note of finality. Thayer's *Greek-English Lexicon*, in defining this word, puts it this way:

"Priesthood unchangeable and therefore not liable to pass to a successor," Hebrews 7:24.[16]

Since the word appears but once in New Testament Greek, there is not even the appeal to possible contextual renderings. Here is one instance where no amount of semantic juggling can escape the force of the context and grammar.

The writer of Hebrews, under the inspiration of the Holy Spirit, declares that the priesthood of Melchizedek is the peculiar possession of Jesus Christ, not only by virtue of the fact that He is God and possessed of imperishable life, but because it cannot be transferred to another. It consummated the Aaronic priesthood; it terminated the Levitical order; it resides in the Son of God; and by the will of His Father, it cannot be transferred. There is no escape from the force of these revelations of Scripture, and no exegetical theologian or commentator has ever held otherwise. Mormons have the right to claim any priesthood they wish, but what separates truth from error is when we compare what they say to the Bible.

15. The Mormon claim that Melchizedek conferred his priesthood on Abraham when the latter paid tithe to him (Genesis 18) finds no support in Scripture (*Priesthood and Church Government*, John A. Widtsoe, 109). Mormons should be pressed at this juncture for the biblical evidence, the absence of which affords further opportunity to undercut their already weakened position.
16. ". . . does not pass on to any successor," is the Weymouth translation. "Permanent" is a good translation as found in ESV, NIV, NASB, HCSB, NET.

The True Priesthood

In the opening sentences of the book of the Revelation, John the apostle makes an astounding statement when he declares:

"Blessing and peace to you from him who is, and was, and is coming, and from the seven spirits before his throne and from Jesus Christ, the trustworthy witness, the firstborn of the dead, the sovereign of the kings of the earth. To him who loves us and has released us from our sins by his own blood—he has made us a kingdom of priests for his God and Father—to him be glory and power forever" (John 1:4–6, Goodspeed).

How incisive is this plain declaration by apostolic authority? Jesus Christ, who is the sovereign of the kings of the earth, the One who continues to love us and who has released us from our sins through His own blood, has also made us (all believers) "a kingdom of priests for His God and Father." Here is the true priesthood indeed.

The Christian does not need temples with secret services, rituals, and mysteries. His priesthood knows no special offices or power to communicate with the dead—things that the Mormon priesthood most definitely claims. The Christian priesthood embraces all those who have been loosed from their sins by the blood of Jesus Christ, and who enjoy the perpetual love of the Lamb of God who takes away the sins of the world.

The authentic Christian priesthood is further developed in the writings of Peter, who affirms that "You are the chosen race, the *royal priesthood,* the consecrated nation, his own people, so that you may declare the virtues of him who has called you out of darkness into his wonderful light; you who were once no people, but are now God's people; once unpitied, but now pitied indeed" (1 Peter 2:9–10, Goodspeed).

In this context, the words of the apostle establish that long before there were any mythological Mormon priesthoods, there was a priesthood embracing all the redeemed, a "royal priesthood," neither of Aaron nor of Melchizedek. This priesthood is composed of all consecrated "ambassadors for Christ," to quote the Apostle Paul, whose task it is to exhort men to "be reconciled to God . . . knowing the terror of the Lord" (see 2 Corinthians 5:20, 11).

As has been observed, Mormonism places great stress upon the priesthood. But as we have also seen, it is not the priesthood described in the Scriptures. Instead, they have substituted the revelation of "prophet" Smith concerning a priesthood. Scripture reveals that the Aaronic priesthood has been changed (Hebrews 7:12), and the Melchizedek priesthood by its nature is "untransferable" (7:24). The resulting dilemma is that Mormons have no priesthood at all since their denial of the true deity of Jesus Christ and the nature of God rules out the possibility that they could share in the priesthood of all believers. In order for one to be one of the "kingdom of priests to God His Father" (Revelation 1:4–6) and a member of the "royal priesthood" (1 Peter 2:9–10), one must first have undergone personal regeneration in a saving encounter or experience with the only God-Man of Scripture—Jesus Christ. Mormon theology with its pantheon of gods, its perverted view of the Virgin Birth, and its outright condemnation of all churches as an "abomination" (*Joseph Smith—History* 1:19), removes itself from serious consideration as a form of Christianity. There is more to Christianity than the application of the Christian ethic. There is a great deal more to the Gospel than the similarity of terms, albeit redefined. Christianity is not merely a system of doctrinal pronouncements (though they are of vast importance). It is a living, vital experience with the God of the Bible as He was incarnate in the man from Nazareth. Mormonism, with its many doctrinal vagaries and outright denials of historic Christian teachings, disqualifies itself. And its priesthood, on which it places so much emphasis, is shown to be the antithesis of the divine revelation.

It is to be earnestly hoped that more Christians will acquaint themselves with the biblical evidence concerning the true priesthood in which we all participate. It is only when a thorough understanding of the fundamentals of Christian theology is obtained that it is possible to successfully encounter and refute the Mormon doctrine of the priesthood.

The Mormon Doctrine of God

It will be conceded by most informed students of Christianity that one cannot deny the existence of the one true God of Scripture and at the same time lay claim to being a Christian. The New Testament writers, as well as our Lord himself, taught that there was but one God, and all church theologians from the earliest days of church history have affirmed that Christianity is monotheistic in the strictest sense of the term. Indeed, it was this fact that so radically differentiated it and the parental Judaism from the pagan, polytheistic societies of Rome and Greece. The Bible is particularly adamant in its declaration that God recognizes the existence of no other "deities." In fact, on a number of occasions the Lord summed up His uniqueness in the following revelation:

> Ye are my witnesses, saith the Lord, and my servant whom I have chosen: that ye may know and believe me, and understand that I am he: before me there was no God formed, neither shall there be after me. I, even I, am the Lord; and beside me there is no saviour. . . . Thus saith the Lord the King of Israel, and his redeemer the Lord of hosts; I am the first, and I am the last; and *beside me there is no God.* . . . Ye are even my witnesses. Is there a God beside me? *yea, there is no God; I know not any.* . . . I am the Lord, and there is none else, *there is no God beside me:* I girded thee, though thou hast not known me. . . . *There is no God else beside me;* a just God and a Saviour; *there is none beside me.* Look unto me, and be ye saved, all the ends of the earth: *for I am God, and there is none else* (Isaiah 43:10–11; 44:6, 8; 45:5, 21–22, emphasis added).

Throughout the Old Testament, God is known by many titles. He is Elohim, Jehovah, Adonai, El Gebor, and He is also spoken of by combinations of names, such as Jehovah-Elohim, Jehovah-Sabaoth, etc. If the Hebrew Old Testament tells us anything, it is the fact that there is but one God: "Hear, O Israel: The Lord our God is one Lord" (Deuteronomy 6:4). And Jewish monotheism, as all know, at length gave birth to Christian monotheism, the one developing from the other by progressive revelation from God the Holy Spirit. It is not necessary to belabor the point; it is common knowledge that the facts as they have been stated are true. But as we approach our study of the Mormon concept of God, a subtle yet radical change takes place in the usage of the vocabulary of Scripture as we shall see.

It must also be admitted at the outset that the Bible does designate certain individuals as "gods," such as Satan, who is described by Christ as "the prince of this world" and elsewhere in Scripture as "the god of this world." It must be clearly understood, however, that whenever this term is assigned to individuals, to spirit personalities, and the like, metaphorical and contextual usage must be carefully analyzed so that a clear picture emerges. For instance, the Lord declared to Moses: "See, I have made thee a god to Pharaoh: and Aaron thy brother shall be thy prophet" (Exodus 7:1). The Hebrew indicates here, along with Exodus 4:16, "And he shall be thy spokesman unto the people: and he shall be, even he shall be to thee instead of a mouth, and thou shalt be to him instead of God," that a definite relationship was involved. The context also reveals that Moses, by virtue of the power invested in him by God, became in the eyes of Pharaoh "a god." Aaron in turn became a prophet of the "god" (Moses) that Pharaoh beheld because he was the spokesman for Moses. So metaphorical usage is obviously intended, from the very usage of the language and its contextual analysis. On this point all Old Testament scholars are agreed. But this should never cloud the issue that there is only one true and living God as the previous quotations readily attest.

The Truth about the God of the Mormons

In sharp contrast to the revelations of Scripture are the "revelations" of Joseph Smith, Brigham Young, and the succeeding Mormon "prophets." So that the reader will have no difficulty understanding what the true Mormon position is concerning the nature of God, the following quotations derived from popular Mormon sources will convey what the Mormons mean when they speak of "God."

1. "In the beginning, the head of the Gods called a council of the Gods; and they came together and concocted a plan to create the world and people it" (Joseph Smith, *Journal of Discourses*, 6:5).
2. "God himself was once as we are now, and is an exalted man" (Joseph Smith, *Journal of Discourses*, 6:3).
3. "The Father has a body of flesh and bones as tangible as man's: the Son also; but the Holy Ghost has not a body of flesh and bones, *but is* a personage of Spirit" (*Doctrine and Covenants*, 130:22).
4. "Gods exist, and we had better strive to be prepared to be one with them" (Brigham Young, *Journal of Discourses*, 7:238).
5. "As man is, God once was: as God is, man may become" (Prophet Lorenzo Snow, quoted in Milton R. Hunter, *The Gospel Through the Ages*, [Salt Lake City: Stevens & Wallis, 1945], 105–106).

It would be quite possible to continue quoting sources from many volumes and other official Mormon publications, but the fact is well established.

The Community of Christ (RLDS), which disagrees with the Utah church on the subject of polytheism, steadfastly maintains that Joseph Smith Jr. never taught or practiced either polygamy or polytheism, but the following direct quotation from Smith, relative to the plurality of gods and the doctrine that Mormon males may attain to godhood, vexes the Community of Christ church no end. But, it is a fact, nonetheless.

The following quotations are excerpted from a sermon published in the Mormon periodical *Times and Seasons* (August 15, 1844, 5:613–614) four months after Smith delivered it at the funeral of Elder King Follett, and only two months after Smith's assassination in Carthage, Illinois.

It is significant that the split in Mormonism did not take place for more than three and a half years. Apparently their ancestors did not disagree with Smith's theology, as they themselves do today. Nor did they deny that Smith preached the sermon and taught polytheism, as does the Community of Christ today. But the facts must speak for themselves. Here are the abovementioned quotes:

> I want you all to know God, to be familiar with him. . . . What sort of a being was God in the beginning?
>
> First, God himself, who sits enthroned in yonder heavens, is a man like unto one of yourselves . . . if you were to see him today, you would see him in all the person, image and very form as a man. . . .
>
> I am going to tell you how God came to be God. We have imagined that God was God from all eternity. These are incomprehensible ideas to some, but they are the simple and first principles of the gospel, to know for a certainty the character of God, that we may converse with him as one man with another, and that God himself; the Father of us all dwelt on an earth the same as Jesus Christ himself did . . . what did Jesus say? (mark it elder Rigdon) Jesus said, as the Father hath power in himself, even so hath the Son power; to do what? Why what the Father did, that answer is obvious. . . . Here then is eternal life, to know the only wise and true God. You have got to learn how to be Gods yourselves; to be kings and priests to God, the same as all Gods have done before you—namely, by going from a small degree to another, from grace to grace, from exaltation to exaltation, until you are able to sit in glory as doth those who sit enthroned in everlasting power. (Joseph Smith, *Journal of Discourses*, 6:3–4)

Tenth LDS President Joseph Fielding Smith notes that the King Follett sermon was given at the April conference of the Church in 1844 and was heard by around 20,000 people. The argument that Smith was misquoted is wrong because it was recorded by four scribes: Willard Richards, Wilford Woodruff, William Clayton, and Thomas Bullock. BYU professor

George W. Pace wrote in *The Encyclopedia of Mormonism* that Smith's two-hour-and-fifteen-minute message "may be one of the Prophet's greatest sermons because of its doctrinal teachings." (Daniel H. Ludlow, ed., *The Encyclopedia of Mormonism*, [New York: MacMillan Publishing Co., 1992], 772)

Mormon theology is polytheistic, teaching in effect that the universe is inhabited by different gods who procreate spirit children, which are in turn clothed with bodies on different planets, "Elohim" being the god of this planet (Brigham's teaching that Adam is our heavenly Father is now officially denied by Mormon authorities, but they hold firm to the belief that their God is a resurrected, glorified man). In addition to this, the "inspired" utterances of Joseph Smith reveal that he began as a Unitarian, progressed to tritheism (three gods), and graduated into full-fledged polytheism, in direct contradiction to the revelations of the Old and New Testaments as we have observed. The Mormon doctrine of the trinity is a gross misrepresentation of the biblical position, though they attempt to veil their evil doctrine in semi-orthodox terminology. We have already dealt with this problem, but it bears constant repetition lest the Mormon terminology go unchallenged.

On the surface, when they speak of the Father, Son, and Holy Ghost, they appear to be orthodox, but in the light of unimpeachable Mormon sources, Mormons speak with a duplicity of terms while knowing better. The truth of the matter is that Mormonism has never historically accepted the Christian doctrine of the Trinity; in fact, they deny it by completely perverting the meaning of the term. The Mormon doctrine that God the Father is a mere man is the root of their polytheism, and forces Mormons to deny not only the Trinity of God as revealed in Scripture, but the immaterial nature of God as pure spirit. Mormons have gone on record and stated that they accept the doctrine of the Trinity, but, as we have seen, it is *not* the Christian Trinity. God the Father does not have a body of flesh and bones, a fact clearly taught by our Lord (John 4:24, cf. Luke 24:39).

The Holy Spirit in Mormonism

Having discussed the nature and attributes of God in contrast to Mormon mythology and its pantheon of polygamous deities, it remains for us to understand what the Mormon teaching concerning the third person of the Christian Trinity is, since they deign to describe Him as "a personage of spirit."

In *Doctrine and Covenants* 20:37 the following statement appears: "All those who humble themselves . . . and truly manifest by their works that they have received of the Spirit of Christ unto the remission of their sins, shall be received by baptism into his church."

Joseph Smith the prophet was the recipient of this alleged revelation and he is to be believed at all costs; yet the same Joseph Smith translated the Book of Mormon, which unreservedly declared:

"Yea, blessed are they who shall . . . be baptized, for they shall . . . receive a remission of their sins. . . . Behold, baptism is unto repentance to the fulfilling of the commandments unto the remission of sins" (3 Nephi 12:2; Moroni 8:11).

In one instance, Smith taught that baptism follows the initial act—remission of sins—and in the second instance, the initial act—remission of sins—reverses its position and follows baptism. According to Talmage, "God grants the gift of the Holy Ghost unto the obedient; and the bestowal of this gift follows faith, repentance, and baptism by water. . . . The apostles of old promised the ministration of the Holy Ghost unto those only who had received baptism by water for the remission of sins" (*The Articles of Faith*, 163).

The question naturally arises: When, then, is the Holy Spirit bestowed? Or indeed, can He be bestowed in Mormon theology when it is not determined whether the remission of sins precedes baptism or follows it? Here again, confusion on the doctrine of the Holy Spirit is evidenced in Mormon thinking.

It would be possible to explore further the Mormon doctrine of the Holy Spirit, especially the interesting chapter in President Charles Penrose's book *Mormon Doctrine Plain and Simple or Leaves From the Tree* (Salt Lake City: G. Q. Canon, 1897), in which he refers to the Holy Spirit as "it" more than twenty times—devoid of personality, although, in the usual polytheistic Mormon scheme, endowed with Deity. Penrose closes his comment by stating, "As baptism is the birth of water, so confirmation is the birth or baptism of the Spirit. Both are necessary to entrance into the Kingdom of God. . . . The possessor of the Holy Ghost is infinitely rich; those who receive it can lose it, and are of all men the poorest. But there are various degrees of its possession. Many who obtain it walk but measurably in its light. But there are few who live by its whisperings, and approach by its mediumship into close communion with heavenly beings of the highest order. To them its light grows brighter every day" (18–19).

Mormonism, then, for all its complexities and want of conformity to the revelation of God's Word, indeed contradicts the Word of God repeatedly, teaching in place of the God of pure spiritual substance (John 4:24) a flesh-and-bone Deity and a pantheon of gods in infinite stages of progression. For Mormons, God is restricted to a narrow, rationalistic, and materialistic mold. He cannot be incomprehensible, though Scripture indicates that in many ways He most certainly is. "My thoughts are not your thoughts, neither are your ways my ways, saith the Lord. For as the heavens are higher than the earth, so are my ways higher than your ways, and my thoughts than your thoughts" (Isaiah 55:8–9). Mormon theology complicates and confounds the simple declarations of Scripture in order to support the polytheistic pantheon of Joseph Smith and Brigham Young. It is obvious, therefore, that the God of the Bible and the "god" of the Mormons, the "Adam-god" of Brigham Young and the flesh-and-bone deity of Joseph Smith are not one and the same; by their nature all monotheistic and theistic religions stand in opposition to Mormon polytheism. Christianity in particular repudiates as false and deceptive the multiplicity of Mormon efforts to masquerade as "ministers of righteousness" (2 Corinthians 11:15).

The Virgin Birth of Christ

One of the great doctrines of the Bible, which is uniquely related to the supreme earthly manifestation of the Eternal God, is the doctrine of the Virgin Birth of Jesus Christ. In one very real sense, this doctrine is indissolubly linked with that of the Incarnation, being, so to speak, the agency or instrument whereby God chose to manifest himself. Time and again the Bible reminds us that Deity was clothed with humanity in the manger of Bethlehem, and Christians of all generations have revered the mystery prefigured by the cryptic words of Isaiah the prophet:

> Behold, a virgin shall conceive, and bear a son, and shall call his name Immanuel. . . . For unto us a child is born, unto us a son is given: and the government shall be upon his shoulder: and his name shall be called Wonderful, Counselor, The mighty God, The everlasting Father, The Prince of Peace (Isaiah 7:14; 9:6).

The Apostle Paul refers numerous times to the deity of our Lord, declaring that "in Him dwelleth all the fullness of the Godhead bodily" (Colossians 2:9).

Attempts to minimize the Virgin Birth of Christ or to do away with it altogether, as some liberal theologians have energetically tried to do, have consistently met with disaster. This is true because the simple narratives of this momentous event recorded in Matthew and Luke refuse to surrender to the hindsight reconstruction theories of second-guessing critics.

Some persons have, on the other hand, decided upon a middle course where this doctrine is concerned. They affirm its biological necessity. In a word, Matthew and Luke, who had access to eyewitness testimonies (Mary, Joseph, Elizabeth, etc.), never really believed the teaching as recorded; rather it was a pious attempt to endow Christ with a supernatural conception in order to add glory to His personality. Regardless of how distasteful the unbiblical concepts of liberal and so-called neoorthodox theologians may be concerning the Virgin Birth of our Savior, no group has framed a concept of the Virgin Birth doctrine in the terms employed by the Mormon prophet Brigham Young. Mormon doctrine concerning the Virgin Birth of Christ was first delivered in the pronouncements of Brigham Young and has been consistently found in the teachings of all General Authorities throughout their history. It has never been contradicted and consequently represents the doctrine of the Mormon Church.

Relative to the doctrine of the Virgin Birth of Christ, Brigham Young has unequivocally stated, "When the Virgin Mary conceived the child Jesus, the Father had begotten him in his own likeness. He was *not* begotten by the Holy Ghost. And who was the Father? He is the first of the human family; and when he took a tabernacle [body], it was begotten by his Father in heaven, after the same manner as the tabernacles of Cain, Abel, and the rest of the sons and daughters of Adam and Eve; from the fruits of the earth, the first earthly tabernacles were originated by the Father, and so on in succession. . . . Jesus, our elder brother, was begotten in the flesh by the same character that was in the garden of Eden, and who is our Father in Heaven" (*Journal of Discourses*, 1:50–51).

Now, in order to understand what "prophet" Young was saying, another of his pronouncements found in the same context should be considered:

When our father Adam came into the garden of Eden, he came into it with a celestial body, and brought Eve, *one of his wives*, with him. . . . He *is our* FATHER *and our* GOD, *and the only God with whom* WE *have to do* (*Journal of Discourses*, 1:50–51).

As we have seen in the Mormon doctrine of "God," Mormon theology teaches that polytheism is the divine order. Belief in many gods is the cornerstone of their theology, and polygamous gods they are. Parley P. Pratt, a leading Mormon writer whose books are recommended by Mormon publishing houses as representing their theological views, also writes concerning this doctrine:

> Each of these Gods, including Jesus Christ and his Father, being in possession of not merely an organized spirit but also a glorious immortal body of flesh and bones . . . (*Key to the Science of Theology*, ed. 1978, 23).

Added to this polytheistic picture are other official Mormon sources, many of whom confirm the sexual conception of Jesus enunciated by Young and many others. Wrote Apostle James Talmage in *The Articles of Faith*:

> His [Christ's] unique status in the flesh as the offspring of a mortal mother [Mary] and of an immortal, or resurrected and glorified, Father [Elohim] (ed. 1974, 473).

Brigham Young, therefore, taught this unbiblical doctrine of which he spoke openly more than once as the following shows:

> When the time came that His first-born, the Saviour, should come into the world and take a tabernacle (body), the Father came Himself and favoured that spirit with a tabernacle instead of letting any other man do it (*Journal of Discourses*, 4:218).

> The birth of the Saviour was as natural as are the births of our children; it was the result of natural action. He partook of flesh and blood—was begotten of his Father, as we are of our fathers (*Journal of Discourses*, 8:115).

The base polytheism of Mormonism was never more clearly dissembled than in the foregoing statements, and Young's classification of the Father as a glorified, resurrected "man" cannot be misunderstood. The phrase "any *other* man" rules out the efforts of Mormon apologists to defend Young and unmasks the entire anti-Christian teaching.

We see, then, the Mormon teaching concerning our Lord's birth is a revolting distortion of the biblical revelation and one that is in keeping with the Mormon dogma of a flesh-and-bone god. In Mormon thinking, as reflected in the authoritative declarations of one of their prophets, our Savior was produced, not by a direct act of the Holy Spirit, but by actual sexual relations between "an immortal or resurrected and glorified Father" and Mary—a blasphemous view, which takes its place beside the infamous mythology of Greece, wherein the gods fathered human sons through physical union with certain chosen women.

Brigham Young further declared: "He (Christ) was *not* begotten by the Holy Ghost. . . . Jesus, our elder brother, was begotten in the flesh by the same character that was in the garden of Eden, and who is our Father in Heaven" (*Journal of Discourses*, 1:50–51). There can be no mistaking the fact that the Adam-God doctrine is meant here, no matter how vehemently the Mormon apologists of today may deny that it was ever taught. The language is too clear, the cross-reference easily demonstrable, and the denial of His conception by the Holy Spirit evident for all to see.

According to the revelation of the Virgin Birth as recorded within the Scripture, our Lord was conceived by a direct act of God the Holy Spirit, wholly apart from human agency. The Scripture is explicit in declaring that this conception took place while Mary was "espoused to Joseph, *before* they came together.*" Matthew, therefore, flatly contradicts Brigham Young in no uncertain terms, declaring: "She was found with child by the Holy Spirit" (Matthew 1:18). And the angel Gabriel, who appeared to Joseph to reassure him concerning the divine origin of Christ's conception, reiterated this fact by declaring, "That which is conceived in her is *of* the Holy Spirit" (v. 20).

Luke, the beloved physician, in his narrative of the Virgin Birth, describes the revelation of our Lord's conception in unmistakable terms: "The Holy Ghost shall come upon thee, and the power of the Highest shall overshadow thee: therefore also that holy thing which shall be born of thee shall be called the Son of God" (Luke 1:35).

Some Mormon apologists have attempted to prove from this verse, however, that the phrase "the power of the Highest shall overshadow thee" in fact refers to the Mormon god's impregnation of Mary, thus proving "the truthfulness" of Brigham Young's assertion. But as we shall see from Matthew's account, this is an impossible contention and is unworthy of further refutation.

It is true that many debates have been instigated over the nature of the Virgin Birth of Christ, but the Christian position has always been based upon a literal acceptance of the event as recorded in the first chapters of Matthew and Luke. It might be noted that even liberal and neoorthodox scholars have repudiated the grossly polytheistic and pagan concept enunciated by Brigham Young and handed down through Mormon theology.

We would do well to remember "prophet" Young's denials, "He (Jesus) was not begotten by the Holy Ghost. . . . Jesus, our elder brother, was begotten in the flesh by the same character that was in the garden of Eden, and who is our Father in Heaven," and contrast them with the reliable testimony of the Word of God:

> When as his mother Mary was espoused to Joseph, before they came together, she was found with child of the Holy Ghost. . . . The angel of the Lord appeared unto him in a dream, saying, Joseph, thou son of David, fear not to take unto thee Mary thy wife: for that which is conceived in her is of the Holy Ghost (Matthew 1:18–20).

The Mormon Church today finds itself, no doubt, in a very difficult position where this errant teaching concerning our Lord's conception is concerned. Some Mormons with whom the author has spoken repudiate vehemently Brigham Young's doctrine of the Virgin Birth, maintaining that he never really taught such a thing; but upon being faced with statements from Young's *Journal of Discourses* and quotations from Mormon periodicals and magazines between the years 1854 and 1878, particularly, they are forced to admit that such was the teaching of their church under Brigham Young. Then, not wanting to appear as though they lack loyalty to President Young, they lapse into silence or reluctantly affirm it.

One Mormon writer and historian, B. H. Roberts, writing in the *Deseret News* (July 23, 1921, Section 4:7) went so far as to deny that the Mormon church taught the Adam-God doctrine or the doctrine of the Virgin Birth as pronounced by Young. Mr. Roberts wrote in answer to the charge of the Presbyterian Church that "the Mormon church teaches that Adam is God . . . and that Jesus is his son by natural generation":

> As a matter of fact, the "Mormon" church does not teach that doctrine. A few men in the "Mormon" church have held such views: and several of them quite prominent in the councils of the church. . . . Brigham Young and

others *may* have taught that doctrine but *it has never been accepted by the church as her doctrine.*

The unfortunate thing about Mr. Roberts' statement is that (1) he was not empowered to speak for the church, and (2) he is in direct conflict with the teachings of his church on the subject of prophetic authority, not to mention Talmage's *Articles of Faith* previously cited. He also used a carefully qualified term when he said that "Brigham Young and others *may* have taught that doctrine." As we have seen, Brigham Young *did* teach that doctrine; and according to the Mormon faith, Brigham Young was a prophet of God as was Joseph Smith, in the same category as Jeremiah, Ezekiel, or Daniel. So the fact that Brigham taught it—and no General Authority has ever contradicted it—demonstrates that it is the doctrine of the Mormon Church, despite any claims to the contrary.

The Mormon Savior

The record of the Bible concerning the Savior of the world, the Lord Jesus Christ, is well-known to students of the Scriptures. In Christian theology, there is but one God (Deuteronomy 6:4; 1 Corinthians 8:4–6), and Jesus Christ is His eternal Word made flesh (John 1:1; 1:14). It was the function of the second person of the Trinity, upon His reception by the sons of men, to empower them to be the sons of God (John 1:12); and this, the Scripture teaches, came about as a result of God's unmerited favor and His great love toward a lost race.

The Lord Jesus offered one eternal sacrifice for all sins, and His salvation comes not by the works of the law or any human works whatever (Galatians 2:16; Ephesians 2:9), but solely by grace through faith (Ephesians 2:8). The Savior of the New Testament revelation existed eternally as God; lived a holy, harmless, and undefiled life, separate from sinners; and "knew no sin." He was "a man of sorrows, and acquainted with grief" (Isaiah 53:3), "the Lamb of God, which taketh away the sin of the world" (John 1:29).

The savior of Mormonism, however, is an entirely different person, as their official publications clearly reveal. The Mormon "savior" is not the second person of the Christian Trinity, since, as we have previously seen, Mormons reject the Christian doctrine of the Trinity, and he is not even a careful replica of the New Testament Redeemer. In Mormon theology,

Christ as a preexistent spirit was not only the spirit brother of the devil (as alluded to in the *Pearl of Great Price*, *Moses* 4:1–4 and later reaffirmed by Brigham Young in the *Journal of Discourses*, 13:282), but celebrated his own marriage to "Mary and Martha, and the other Mary," at Cana of Galilee, "whereby he could see his seed, before he was crucified" (Apostle Orson Hyde, *Journal of Discourses*, 4:259; 2:82). As we have seen previously, the Mormon concept of the Virgin Birth alone distinguishes their "Christ" from the Christ of the Bible.

In addition to this revolting concept, Brigham Young categorically stated that the sacrifice made upon the cross by Jesus Christ in the form of His own blood was ineffective for the cleansing of *some* sins. Brigham went on to teach the now suppressed but never officially repudiated doctrine of "blood atonement."

To better understand Young's limitation of the cleansing power of Christ's blood, we shall refer to his own words:

> Suppose you found your brother in bed with your wife, and you put a javelin through both of them, you would be justified, and they would atone for their sins, and be received into the kingdom of God. I would at once do so in such a case; and under such circumstances, I have no wife whom I love so well that I would not put a javelin through her heart, and I would do it with clean hands.
>
> There is not a man or woman, who violates the covenants made with their God, that will not be required to pay the debt. The blood of Christ will never wipe that out, your own blood must atone for it; and the judgments of the Almighty will come, sooner or later, and every man and woman will have to atone for breaking their covenants. . . . All mankind love themselves, and let these principles be known by an individual, and he would be glad to have his blood shed. . . . I could refer you to plenty of instances where men have been righteously slain, in order to atone for their sins. . . . This is loving our neighbor as ourselves; if he needs help, help him; and if he wants salvation and it is necessary to spill his blood on the earth in order that he may be saved, spill it (*Journal of Discourses*, 3:247; 4:219–220).

So clear-cut was Brigham's denial of the all-sufficiency and efficiency of the atoning sacrifice of Christ in the foregoing quotation that Mormons have had to develop an argument "to explain" what the prophet really meant. It is their contention that a criminal is "executed to atone for his crimes and this is all Brigham Young meant."

However, they completely omit any discussion of the fact that Young's statement is not dealing with this subject at all. Young's statement declared that what Christ's blood could *not* cleanse, a man's own blood atonement could. This teaches that in some instances human sacrifice, which Brigham states took place and which he sanctioned, were efficacious where Christ's blood was not.

The Mormons want no part of the biblical doctrine of the all-sufficiency of Christ's Atonement, in the words of John: "The blood of Jesus Christ his Son cleanses us from *all* unrighteousness" (1 John 1:7, emphasis added). This both contradicts Young and reveals the true biblical teaching.

There can be no doubt from the biblical record that it is in Jesus Christ that we have redemption and that His blood is the means of the cleansing of the conscience (Hebrews 9:14) and of the loosening from sin (Revelation 1:5). It is the very basis of our justification (Romans 5:9).

The Christ of the Mormons cannot save, for He is as the Apostle Paul describes him, "another Jesus," the subject of "another gospel," and the originator of a "different spirit," whose forerunner (the angelic messenger, Moroni) was anticipated by the apostle (Galatians 1:8–9), and who along with the entire revelation is to be considered "anathema" or more literally from the Greek, "cursed" by God.

It may be difficult for some to grasp what is in fact an incredible concept, but Mormonism fits perfectly into the descriptions given by the Word of God. The greatest of the apostles, in his second letter to the Corinthian church, after mentioning a counterfeit Jesus, gospel, and spirit, goes on to state that such occurrences should not come as a surprise to the Christian church.

"For such are false apostles, deceitful workmen, transforming themselves into apostles of Christ, and it is not surprising, for Satan himself transforms himself into an angel of light. It is therefore no great marvel if his servants also transform themselves as servants of righteousness whose end will be according to their works" (2 Corinthians 11:13–15, from the Greek).

This is harsh language indeed, but it is the language of God's choosing and it cannot be ignored by anyone who takes seriously the revelations of Scripture and apostolic authority.

Mormonism, with its apostles, priesthood, temples, secret signs, symbols, handshakes, and mysteries, claims to be "the church of the restoration"; but at its heart, in its doctrine of the Messiah, it is found to be contrary to every major biblical pronouncement.

Salvation by Grace?

It is common to find in Mormon literature the statement that "all men are saved by grace alone without any act on their part." Although this appears to be perfectly orthodox, it is necessary to study *all* the Mormon statements relative to this doctrine in order to know precisely what they mean.

In one such official Mormon publication, the Mormons give their own interpretation:

> Grace is simply the mercy, the love and the condescension God has for his children, as a result of which he has ordained the plan of salvation so that they may have power to progress and become like him. . . . All men are saved by grace alone without any act on their part, meaning that they are resurrected and become immortal because of the atoning sacrifice of Christ. . . . In addition to this redemption from death, all men, by the grace of God, have the power to gain eternal life. This is called salvation by grace coupled with obedience to the laws and ordinances of the gospel. Hence Nephi was led to write: "We labor diligently to write, to persuade our children, and also our brethren, to believe in Christ, and to be reconciled to God; for we know that it is by grace that we are saved *after all we can do.*"
>
> Christians speak often of the blood of Christ and its cleansing power. Much that is believed and taught on this subject, however, is such utter nonsense and so palpably false that to believe it is to lose one's salvation. Many go so far, for instance, as to pretend and, at least, to believe that if we confess Christ with our lips and avow that we accept Him as our personal Saviour, we are thereby saved. His blood, without other act than mere belief, they say, makes us clean. . . . Finally in our day, he has said plainly: "My blood shall not cleanse them if they hear me not." Salvation in the kingdom of God is available because of the atoning blood of Christ. But it is received only on condition of faith, repentance, baptism, and *enduring to the end in keeping the commandments of God.*[17]

The above quotation is a typical example of what might be termed theological double-talk, which in one breath affirms grace as a saving principle and in the next declares that it is "coupled with obedience to the law and ordinances of the gospel," and ends by declaring that confession of Christ

17. Bruce R. McConkie, *What the Mormons Think of Christ* (Salt Lake City: Bookcraft, 1973), 27–33, emphasis added.

and acceptance of Him as "personal Savior" is "utter nonsense" and "palpably false." McConkie decries the fact that Christ's blood "without other act than mere belief . . . makes us clean."[18]

The biblical position is, however, quite clear in this area; we are saved by grace alone, as previously mentioned, but it in no way enables us to "have power to progress and become like Him." As we have seen, in the Mormon sense such a progression refers to becoming a god, not to the Christian doctrine of sanctification, or of the life of the believer being brought into conformity to the Holy Spirit as clearly enunciated in the epistle to the Romans (chapters 8 and 12).

Mr. McConkie's assertion—that "salvation by grace" must be "coupled with obedience with the laws and ordinances of the gospel" in order for a person to be saved—introduces immediately the whole Mormon collection of legalistic observances and requirements. In the end, salvation is not by grace at all, but it is in reality connected with human efforts: "baptism, and enduring to the end in keeping the commandments of God."[19]

This is not the Christian doctrine of redemption that the Apostle Peter described graphically when he wrote:

> Forasmuch as ye know that ye were not redeemed with corruptible things, as silver and gold, from your vain conversation received by tradition from your fathers; but with the precious blood of Christ, as of a lamb without blemish and without spot. . . . Being born again, not of corruptible seed, but of incorruptible, by the word of God, which liveth and abideth for ever (1 Peter 1:18–19, 23).

In diametric opposition to the Mormon concept, the confession of Christ with the lips and the acceptance of Him as "our personal Savior" is indeed the very means of personal salvation. It is the biblical record which states that "with the heart man believeth unto righteousness; and with the mouth confession is made unto salvation" (Romans 10:10). The gospel's command is "believe on the Lord Jesus Christ, and thou shalt be saved" (Acts 16:31). This is, of course, totally foreign to what the Mormons would have us believe. Jesus Christ did not die merely to ensure our resurrection, as Mr. McConkie declares, but He died to reconcile us to God, to save us by grace, to redeem us by blood, and to sanctify us by His Spirit. But such

18. McConkie, *What the Mormons Think of Christ*, 31.
19. McConkie, *What the Mormons Think of Christ*, 33.

biblical doctrines the Mormons most decidedly reject. It appears that they cannot conceive of a God who could save apart from human effort, and Nephi's statement betrays this: "For we know it is by grace that we are saved *after all we can do*" (2 Nephi 10:24).

In Mormonism, it is they who must strive for perfection, sanctification, and godhood. Grace is merely incidental.

It was no less an authority than Brigham Young who taught concerning salvation:

"But as many as received Him, to them gave he power to *continue* to be the sons of God" (*Journal of Discourses*, 12:100–101).

In Brigham's theology, "instead of receiving the gospel to become the sons of God, my language would be—to receive the gospel that we may continue to be the sons of God. Are we not all sons of God when we are born into this world? Old Pharaoh, King of Egypt, was just as much a son of God as Moses and Aaron were His sons, with this difference—he rejected the word of the Lord, the true light, and they received it."

In agreement with their doctrine of the preexistence of souls, the Mormons believe that they are already the sons of God and that the acceptance of God merely enables them to "continue to be the sons of God," a direct contradiction of the biblical record which states:

"But as many as received him, to them gave he power to become the sons of God, even to them that believe on his name" (John 1:12).

The Apostle Paul points out, with devastating force, the fact that "they which are the children of the flesh, these are *not* the children of God: but the children of the promise are counted for the seed" (Romans 9:8, emphasis added).

The apostle, with equal certainty, affirms that only those who are led by God's Spirit can be called the sons of God (Romans 8:14). It is difficult to see how in any sense of the term, "Old Pharaoh, King of Egypt, was just as much a son of God as Moses and Aaron were His sons," as Brigham Young declared.

The biblical teaching is that "ye are all the children of God *by faith* in Christ Jesus" (Galatians 3:26, emphasis added), a fact Brigham obviously overlooked.

It is one of the great truths of the Word of God that salvation is not of him that wills or of him that strives, but of God who shows mercy (Romans 9:16), and that Jesus Christ has redeemed us from the curse of the law, having become a curse for us (Galatians 3:13).

It was the teaching of our Lord that "all that the Father giveth me shall come to me; and him that cometh to me I will in no wise cast out" (John 6:37), and the salvation which He still offers to lost men is "not by any works of righteousness which we have done, but according to his mercy he saved us" (Titus 3:5).

In the Mormon religion, they boldly teach universal salvation, for as Mr. Evans, the Mormon apostle and spokesman, put it: "Mormons believe in universal salvation that all men will be saved, but each one in his own order."[20]

It is the teaching of the Scriptures, however, that not all men will be saved, and that at the end of the ages some shall "go away into everlasting punishment: but the righteous into life eternal" (Matthew 25:46).

The somber warnings of the Apostle John stand arrayed against the Mormon doctrine of universal salvation:

> And I saw the beast, and the kings of the earth, and their armies, gathered together to make war against him that sat on the horse, and against his army. And the beast was taken, and with him the false prophet that wrought miracles before him, with which he deceived them that had received the mark of the beast, and them that worshipped his image. These both were cast alive into a lake of fire burning with brimstone. . . . And the devil that deceived them was cast into the lake of fire and brimstone, where the beast and the false prophet are, and shall be tormented day and night for ever and ever. . . . And whosoever was not found written in the book of life was cast into the lake of fire. . . . But the fearful, and unbelieving, and the abominable, and murderers, and whoremongers, and sorcerers, and idolaters, and all liars, shall have their part in the lake which burneth with fire and brimstone: which is the second death. . . . The same shall drink of the wine of the wrath of God, which is poured out without mixture into the cup of his indignation; and he shall be tormented with fire and brimstone in the presence of the holy angels, and in the presence of the Lamb: And the smoke of their torment ascendeth up for ever and ever: and they have no rest day nor night, who worship the beast and his image, and whosoever receiveth the mark of his name (Revelation 19:19–20; 20:10, 15; 21:8; 14:10–11).

By no conceivable stretch of the imagination is universal salvation to be found in these passages where the Greek words in their strongest form indicate torment, judgment, and eternal fire that defies human chemical analysis.

20. Leo Rosten, *A Guide to the Religions of America* (New York: Simon & Schuster, 1963), 136.

The Mormon doctrine of "celestial marriage" derived from their original concept of polygamy and substituted for it in 1890, when they were forced to abandon this immoral conduct lest Utah not be given statehood, is tied to their doctrine of salvation. The Mormons believe that the family unit will endure into the eternal ages, hence their insistence upon the sealing of Mormon men to many women, and the sealing of their families. It was for this reason that there are many special rites and ceremonies instituted in behalf of the dead (particularly relatives); hence, their practice of baptism for the dead and laying on of hands (for the bestowing of the gift of the Holy Ghost), all by proxy.

The Resurrection

Mormons also believe in the bodily resurrection of all men and in salvation in a threefold heaven. In Mormon theology, there are three heavens: the telestial, the terrestrial, and the celestial.

Bruce McConkie states that "most adults" will go to the telestial kingdom and that it is composed of "the endless hosts of people of all ages who have lived after the manner of the world; who have been carnal, sensual, and devilish; who have chosen the vain philosophies of the world rather than accept the testimony of Jesus; who have been liars and thieves, sorcerers and adulterers, blasphemers and murders" (*Mormon Doctrine*, 1966, 778).

The second kingdom (the terrestrial) will be inhabited by Christians who did not accept the Mormon message, Mormons who did not live up to their church's requirements, and men of good will of other religions who rejected the revelations of the Latter-day Saints (*Mormon Doctrine*, 1966, 784).

The highest or celestial heaven is itself divided into three levels. Only in this highest level is godhood or the possession of a kingdom for one's self and one's family to be gained. This particular estate has as its prerequisite the candidate's having been sealed by celestial marriage in a Mormon temple while upon the earth. Even in the celestial kingdom, godhood is by slow progression, and in the end each who becomes a god will, with his family, rule and populate a separate planet of his own.

Biblical Perspective

It is almost superfluous to comment that this entire scheme of the consummation of Mormon salvation is the antithesis of the biblical revelation, which knows nothing of godhood, either constituted or progressive, and which teaches instead that in heaven the destiny of the redeemed will be the special providence of God himself, which "eye hath not seen, nor ear heard," and which has "never entered into the mind of men" for these are "the things which God hath prepared for them that love Him" (1 Corinthians 2:9). God has revealed many of these things to us by His Spirit; but as Paul so eloquently puts it, we "see through a glass, darkly; but *then* face to face" (1 Corinthians 13:12, emphasis added).

Let us understand clearly, then, that salvation in the biblical sense comes as the free gift of God by grace alone through faith in the vicarious sacrifice of Christ upon the cross. The Lord Jesus Christ said, "He that hears my word and believes Him that sent me *has* eternal life, and shall never come into judgment; but has passed out of death into life" (John 5:24, emphasis mine, from the Greek).

> Salvation in the biblical sense comes as the free gift of God by grace alone through faith in the vicarious sacrifice of Christ upon the cross.

The command of the Gospel to all men everywhere is to repent. "Because [God] hath appointed a day, in which he will judge the world in righteousness by that man whom he hath ordained; whereof he hath given assurance unto all men, in that he hath raised him from the dead" (Acts 17:31).

The Scriptures disagree with the Mormons in their insistence upon good works as a *means* of salvation. The book of James clearly teaches (chapter 2) that good works are the *outgrowth* of salvation and justify us before men, proving that we have the faith that justifies us before God (Romans 4 and 5).

No Mormon can today claim that he *has* eternal life in Christ. This is the very power of the Gospel, which is entrusted to Christ's church (Romans 1:16–17). Let us therefore use it in an attempt to bring them to redemptive knowledge of the true Christ of Scripture and the costly salvation He purchased for us with His own blood.

John, the beloved apostle, has summed it up:

> If we receive the witness of men, the witness of God is greater: for this is the witness of God which he hath testified of his Son. He that believeth on the Son of God hath the witness in himself: he that believeth not God

hath made him a liar; because he believeth not the record that God gave of his Son. And this is the record, that God hath given to us eternal life, and this life is in his Son. He that hath the Son hath life; and he that hath not the Son of God hath not life. These things have I written unto you that believe on the name of the Son of God; that ye may know that ye have eternal life, and that ye may believe on the name of the Son of God. And this is the confidence that we have in him, that, if we ask any thing according to his will, he heareth us: And if we know that he hear us, whatsoever we ask, we know that we have the petitions that we desired of him. . . . And we know that we are of God, and the whole world lieth in wickedness. And we know that the Son of God is come, and hath given us an understanding, that we may know him that is true, and we are in him that is true, even in his Son Jesus Christ. This is the true God, and eternal life (1 John 5:9–15, 19–20).

Let us follow in his train, "for the hour is coming in which no one can work," and the Mormons, too, are souls for whom Christ died.

We have seen in the preceding pages how the Mormon religion utilizes biblical terms and phrases and even adopts Christian doctrines in order to claim allegiance to the Christian faith. Mormons have also come to lay much stress upon public relations and take pains to make certain that they do not use language that might reveal the true nature of their theological deviations. We have also seen that the Mormon Church considers itself alone the true church of Christ in our age, and further that they consider all other groups to be Gentiles and apostates from the true Christian religion.

We further read the words of Joseph Smith himself, whom all Mormons are bound to recognize as the prophet of God, equal if not superior to any of the Old Testament prophets.

Wrote "prophet" Smith concerning an alleged interview with the deity:

My object in going to inquire of the Lord which of all the sects was right, that I might know which to join. No sooner, therefore, did I get possession of myself, so as to be able to speak, then I asked the Personages who stood above me in the light, which of all the sects was right and which I should join.

I was answered that I must join none of them, for they were all wrong, and the Personage who addressed me said that all their creeds were an abomination in His sight; that those professors were all corrupt; that: "they draw near to me with their lips, but their hearts are far from me, they teach for doctrines the commandments of men, having a form of godliness, but they deny the power thereof."

He again forbade me to join any of them; and many other things did he say unto me, which I cannot write at this time."[21]

In addition to this statement of Smith's, Twelfth Mormon Prophet Spencer W. Kimball gave the following comment:

Latter-day Saints are true Christians. We cannot understand how anyone could question our being Christians. . . . We are the true followers of Jesus Christ; and we hope the world will finally come to the conclusion that we are Christians, if there are any in the world" (*Teachings of Spencer W. Kimball* [Salt Lake City: Bookcraft, 1982], 434).

From these facts it is evident for all to see that Mormonism strives with great effort to masquerade as the Christian church complete with an exclusive message, infallible prophets, and higher revelations for a new dispensation that the Mormons would have us believe began with Joseph Smith Jr.

But it is the verdict of both history and biblical theology that Joseph Smith's religion is a polytheistic nightmare of garbled doctrines draped with the garment of Christian terminology. This fact, if nothing else, brands it as a non-Christian cult system.

Those who would consider Mormonism would be greatly profited by a thoughtful consideration of the facts and evidence previously discussed, lest they be misled into the spiritual maze that is Mormonism.

Explore

Celestial Sireship
Prophetic Mantle
Aaronic Priesthood
Celestial Kingdom

21. Joseph Smith, *History*, 1:18–20.

Discuss

1. Was God once a man?

2. Who is the Jesus of the Mormons?

3. Does the history of Joseph Smith Jr. matter?

4. What does the DNA of Native Americans tell us about Mormonism?

Dig Deeper

See *The Kingdom of the Cults Study Guide* available at WalterMartin.com.

7

Spiritism—the Cult of Antiquity

Quick Facts on Spiritism

- Spiritism teaches the fatherhood of God and the brotherhood of man.
- Humans experience a continuous existence and a path of endless progression.
- There is a communion of spirits and ministry of angels.
- Divinity dwells in all.

Historical Perspective

By far the oldest form of religious cult extant today, and certainly one of the deadliest where the certainty of divine judgment is concerned, is that of Spiritism, often erroneously referred to as "Spiritualism." However, in speaking of this cult, it is sometimes necessary to use that term in order to communicate in the vernacular of our day.

Worldwide religion statistics note that those who describe their beliefs as Spiritism or Spiritualism can be reasonably estimated conservatively in the hundreds of millions worldwide.[1] Spiritism is finding new life, even in what is referred to as the scientific age of physics and quantum mechanics!

---

1. Spiritism is often incorporated into a belief system. A Hindu or an agnostic may also be a practicing spiritist. For general worldwide religion statistics see *The Global Religious Landscape* (2012), Pew Research Center, https://unitedcor.org/sites/default/files/edit-contentfile/butte _county/International%20-%20Pew%20Religious%20Study.pdf.

Since the First World War the religious horizons of the globe have seen the rapid rise of various forms of Spiritism, a religion unique in that it offers contact with and information from beings beyond the grave. Much of contemporary Spiritism has been exposed by competent professionals as fraudulent. The classic exposé was by Houdini and Dunninger (*Magic and Mystery*).[2] Other exposés include that by former "psychic" M. Lamar Keene (*The Psychic Mafia*)[3] and a joint investigation by a Christian physician, Paul Meier, and a Christian magician, Danny Korem (*The Fakers*).[4]

However, not all psychic or spiritistic phenomena are phony. There is a spiritual dimension that cannot be ignored. Authentic Spiritists draw their power from the one the Bible calls "a roaring lion" who seeks "whom he may devour" (1 Peter 5:8), who is Satan. Spiritism, as we shall see, directly contradicts the Bible, God's Word. As well as constituting something akin to consumer fraud, Spiritism also constitutes biblical heresy.

> The direct testimony of Holy Scripture is that Spiritism is the masquerade of demonic forces pretending to be departed spirits.

In contemporary American life, so acute and complete is the recognition of supernatural sensitivity of communication and spirit manifestations that universities fund psychic research and studies of perception that transcend the normal senses. All are calibrated to achieve the same end—confirmation of what God has forbidden—the exploration of the psychic dimension.

The greatest of all source books on the subject of Spiritism is, of course, the Bible, which gives a historical outline of Spiritism in a most concise and dependable form.

Beginning graphically in Exodus, Scripture reveals that the ancient Egyptians were practitioners of cultism of magic sorcery and necromancy, which were utilized by the priests of the demon gods of Egypt to duplicate the miracles of Moses when he appeared before Pharaoh with the divine command (Exodus 7:11, 22; 8:18).

The attitude of God toward those who practice the forbidden sin is also clearly outlined in Scripture. The Lord ordered the death penalty for all sorcerers as recorded in Exodus 22:18 and Leviticus 20:27, to cite two specific instances. The Old Testament also named as those cursed by God,

2. Houdini and Dunninger, *Magic and Mystery* (New York: Weathervane Books, 1967).
3. M. Lamar Keene, *The Psychic Mafia* (New York: St. Martin's Press, 1976).
4. Paul Meier and Danny Korem, *The Fakers* (Grand Rapids: Baker Book House, 1980).

persons consorting with "familiar spirits" and "wizards" (Leviticus 19:31 and 20:6), in our language demons and mediums.

In company with these violators of divine command, Daniel the prophet often speaks of the magicians, sorcerers, soothsayers, and astrologers (Daniel 1:20; 2:2, 27; 4:7 and 5:7), who specialized along with the Chaldeans in the art of interpreting dreams and visions. The prophet Isaiah also speaks of ancient Spiritists as casting sorceries upon Israel (Isaiah 8:19; 19:3; 47:9), and King Saul, before his apostasy, under God's command drove such practitioners from Israel (1 Samuel 28:3, 9), as did the righteous King Josiah after him (2 Kings 23:24, 25).

The Scriptures likewise bear record that Manassah's downfall came about as the result of his delving into Spiritism (2 Kings 21:6; 2 Chronicles 33:6) and his ensuing practice of idolatry in defiance of the command of God. The Bible then presents a devastating résumé of man's forbidden desire to uncover the hidden spiritual mysteries of the universe, even if witchcraft, divination, or enchantments must be employed to further his unholy quest. Egyptians, Babylonians, Chaldeans, and the Canaanites, the Scriptures tell us, all practiced Spiritism, which practice, in one form or another, continued through the ages. In 1848 Spiritism received its modern rebirth at Hydesville, New York, in the persons of Kate and Margaret Fox, two of the best known of the nineteenth-century promulgators of Spiritism.

Modern Spiritism

Modern Spiritism had its birth, as far as most church historians are concerned, on March 31, 1848. On that date Mrs. John Fox of Hydesville, New York, heard peculiar noises in the upstairs rooms and cellar of her home. Margaret and Kate Fox seemed to be peculiarly sensitive to these noises, and through this sensitivity they developed into mediums, and their communications became known as "The Rochester Rappings."

Some time afterward, the Fox sisters allegedly stated that the noises originated from their cracking the joints of their toes, but modern-day Spiritists scorn this explanation, and today in Lilydale, New York, the Fox sisters' cottage has become a spiritualistic shrine, with a large marker, "There Is No Death," reaffirming the ancient practices of those whom God condemned as practitioners of abominations (Deuteronomy 18:9–12).

The roster of those interested in Spiritism is not inconsiderable. Dr. Bach lists a number of "great names" interested in psychic phenomena and research, names such as James Fenimore Cooper; William Cullen Bryant; Robert Dale Owen; Daniel Webster; Harriet Beecher Stowe; Elizabeth Barrett Browning; Horace Greeley; Elisha Cane; Sir Oliver Lodge, English physicist and author; E. Lee Howard, former pastor of the historic Congregational Church at Painesville, Ohio; Sherwood Eddy, world traveler and writer; Sir Arthur Conan Doyle and Sir William Crooks, the last of whom was honored with degrees from at least five English universities and was inventor of the Crooks tube and discoverer of thallium. According to Bach, "Crooks reported 'that he had seen manifestations of levitation, and heard accordions play without being touched by human hands; had seen a luminous hand write upon the wall, and a medium handle live coals with bare hands.' All of this he had subjected to scientific tests to prove there were forces at work which could not be explained by any known physical law."

While some of these names might be readily challenged, we are concerned only with the judgments of the Bible, in which we are admonished to "prove [test] all things; hold fast that which is good" (1 Thessalonians 5:21).

It is interesting to note that Spiritism has made its strongest appeal to those who have suffered great loss, and after each great war, Spiritism always seems to be on the upgrade following the death of loved ones. As Houdini and Dunninger stated in their classic exposé of fraudulent mediums: "The fact remains that a great number of self-styled mediums have played upon the credulity and sufferings of a public anxious to believe anything—anything which seems to assure continued life to those who have been loved, and who have passed the barrier of this life."[5]

The history of Spiritism literally spans the ages, but throughout it all, two things remain constant. The first is that Spiritism is to be found everywhere posing as a universal, common denominator for all religious groups, not excepting Judaism and Christianity. It teaches the continuity of life and the eternal progression of man toward perfection in the spirit realm. Second, the Eternal God has condemned its practice in the sternest possible terms, maintaining that the interpretation of the supernatural realms belongs solely to Him (Genesis 40:8), and that those who practice intrusion into these realms are worthy of death (Exodus 22:18).

We are repeatedly warned in the strongest terms not to seek after mediums and not to dabble in the realms of divine dominion (Leviticus 19:31). Only

5. Houdini and Dunninger, *Magic and Mystery*, 17.

the deluded prefer the doctrines of demons to faith in the Word of God, and, as we shall see, the doctrines of Spiritism are precisely of such a nature.

Verified Instances of Spiritistic Phenomena

Below is an instance of Spiritistic phenomena that I accept as indicative of true occultic/demonic involvement as described by the Bible.[6] It, I feel, has sound evidence attesting to its validity. There are many Christians, unfortunately, who suffer from the illusion that all Spiritism, or Spiritistic evidence, is fraudulent, and prefer to rest in the falsely secure belief that Spiritism can never be demonically empowered.

I do believe that much Spiritistic evidence is manufactured and comes from overactive imaginations or outright deception on the part of the "performer." Spiritism, legitimate or fraudulent, is big business. The lure of easy money is more than enough to draw many unsuspecting would-be mediums into occultic and/or deceptive Spiritistic practices. Ex-psychic M. Lamar Keene said of the largest Spiritist camp, Chesterfield, that it was "spiritualism's answer to Disneyland. That first season of mine, more than 65,000 pilgrims crowded onto the grounds from here, there, and everywhere. They spent more than a million dollars to commune with their beloved dead."[7]

Case Study

An example of spiritistic demonstration is recorded by J. Arthur Hill in his book, *Spiritualism: Its History, Phenomena, and Doctrine*,[8] wherein Mr. Hill cites the case of Daniel Douglas Home, medium extraordinary, who practiced communication and levitation:

> In 1885, Daniel D. Home, a young man of Scottish-American descent, arrived in the British Isles, and it is in the case of Home and his claims of spiritistic mediumship, that the objective observer finds evidence of supernatural manifestations that has been challenged by no one who has thoroughly investigated the life of Mr. Home.

6. For additional information on verified instances of Spiritistic phenomena, see chapter 7 of *The Kingdom of the Cults* (2019).
7. Keene, *The Psychic Mafia*, 43.
8. J. Arthur Hill, *Spiritualism: Its History, Phenomena, and Doctrine* (New York: George Doran, 1919), 74, 75.

There are many instances recorded of Home's ability to communicate with forces beyond this earth, but the physical phenomena or manifestations of spirit influence which reveal themselves in Home's fantastic ability, are the best testimonies to his possession by supernatural powers.

Sir Wm. Crooks, famed British scientist and acknowledged authority on the phenomena of spiritualism, testified that beyond a shadow of a doubt in the case of Mr. Home, there was "definitely the operation of some agency unknown to science."

In the presence of Sir William and Home, "an accordion placed under the table and untouched by the medium, played tunes, and could manage a few notes, though no tune, when it was held by Mr. Crooks himself. A lath of wood on a table, three feet from Home, rose 10 inches and floated about in the air for more than a minute, moving gently up and down as if it were on rippling water, the medium's hands, meanwhile, being held by Mrs. Walter Crooks and Mrs. William Crooks. A pencil on the table stood up on its point and tried to write, but fell down: the lath then slid across to it and buttressed the pencil, while it tried again. Tables slid about, untouched. Luminous clouds were seen and materialized hands, which carried flowers about. And Home himself was lifted into the air, thus paralleling the levitations of many saints. All this in a fair light, usually one gas burner.

The most famous of the levitations, however, occurred in 1868, at 5, Buckingham Gate, London, in the presence of Lords Lindsay and Adare, and Captain Wynne. Home floated or appeared to float out of one window and in at another. The windows were 76 inches apart, 85 feet above the ground, and there was no ledge or foothold between them. . . . It is difficult to believe that the whole of Home's phenomena were due to fraud or hallucination. As we so often have to say, certainty concerning matters of history, which are vouched for only by a few people, most or all of whom are now dead, is not attainable, and when the alleged events are of a kind to which our own experience supplies no parallel, it is easiest to suppose that the things were done fraudulently somehow. But we must admit that this conclusion is due to prejudice, for in any other matter we should unhesitatingly accept as final the word of so distinguished a man of science as Sir William Crooks, especially when supported by such massive testimony.

It must be noted that not every investigator of psychic phenomena accepts the validity of this particular event. Houdini and Dunninger remained unconvinced, as have some others.[9]

9. Houdini and Dunninger, *Magic and Mystery*, 97.

There are many other instances which we could cite to demonstrate the claims of Spiritists, that they do indeed make contact with powers beyond this earth, and such claims are doubtless quite valid. The question is, are such contacts approved of in the Word of God, and if not, then is not the practice of such contacts disobedience to the expressed will of God, and harmful to the soul of man?

Theological Evaluation

As we have noted, the Bible speaks emphatically on this very point, and as we move on to discuss doctrinal content and contrasts of Spiritistic teachings with those of Christianity, we shall be better able to understand the divine viewpoint where Spiritism and the practices of Spiritists are concerned.

Death does indeed have a sting for mankind that can only be removed by faith in the resurrection of Jesus Christ, which makes possible the resurrection of those who believe in Him (1 Corinthians 15:55–57).

It might also be profitably recalled that in his epistle to the Romans, the Apostle Paul spoke quite markedly of the reality of sin, evil, and spiritual death or separation from fellowship with God. Chapters five and six particularly point out that Christ alone restores man to fellowship, and this He did by ruining Satan's power. (See Hebrews 2:14.) In the revelation of the New Testament, death is indeed the result of sin. (See also Genesis chapter 3.) It is a part of the divine purpose that God has permitted to take place and has provided a solution for: i.e., its eventual destruction by resurrection, in Christ. Although it is a part of the divine purpose, it is not neutral; it is indeed the "last enemy" to be destroyed (1 Corinthians 15:26).

Death does indeed have a sting for mankind that can only be removed by faith in the resurrection of Jesus Christ.

Though we may also find ourselves in agreement with the statement of Mr. Hill concerning Daniel Home and his supernatural powers, we ought not to forget that Home was a true Spiritist-medium who denied the Deity of Jesus Christ, the Atonement and the bodily resurrection of our Lord. The powers that controlled him (Spiritists are wrong when they claim to control the spirits) were not powers from God. On the contrary, they were the demonic spirits spoken of and condemned in the

Bible. The Father of Spirits, God Almighty, will be the eventual judge of him who is known as "the prince of the powers of the air," Satan.

The Theology of Spiritism

Its "Seven Principles" have been set forth as follows.

I. The Fatherhood of God
II. The Brotherhood of Man
III. Continuous Existence
IV. Communion of Spirits and Ministry of Angels
V. Personal Responsibility
VI. Compensation and Retribution Hereafter for Good and Evil Done on Earth
VII. A Path of Endless Progression

Secretary of the Spiritualists' National Union,
The Seven Principles of Spiritualism, 2, 3

———

1. Spiritualism is the Science, Philosophy and Religion of continuous life, based upon the demonstrated fact of communication, by means of mediumship, with those who live in the Spirit world.
2. A Spiritualist is one who believes, as the basis of his or her religion, in the communication between this and the spirit world by means of mediumship, and who endeavors to mold his or her character and conduct in accordance with the highest teachings derived from such communion.

National Spiritualist Association,
Definitions, 1914, 1919

———

Infinite Intelligence pervades and controls the universe, is without shape or form and is impersonal, omnipresent and omnipotent.

It teaches that the spark of divinity dwells in all.

Every soul will progress through the ages to heights, sublime and glorious, where God is Love and Love is God.

"What Spiritualism Is and Does,"
Spiritualist Manual, 1940

———

I am here tonight as one of the founders of Spiritualism to denounce it as an absolute falsehood from beginning to end, as the flimsiest of superstitions, the most wicked blasphemy known to the world.—R. B. Davenport, (*The Deathblow to Spiritualism*, 1888, 76; cf. *The New York Daily Tribune*, for Oct. 22. See also *New York World*, Oct. 21, 1888).

LeRoy Edwin Froom, Spiritualism Today,
Washington D. C.: Review and Herald, 1963, 6

Biblical Perspective

The basic teachings of Spiritism, as demonstrated by their literature and contrasted with Christian truths, reveal that Spiritism cannot in any sense qualify as Christianity. In fact, it is a particularly virile form of cultism, opposed in almost every specific to the historic doctrines of the Christian faith.

Perhaps the most striking example in the New Testament of the immutable attitude of God toward Spiritism and mediums is recorded in the thirteenth chapter of the book of Acts and merits careful scrutiny:

> Now there were in the church that was at Antioch certain prophets and teachers; as Barnabas, and Simeon that was called Niger, and Lucius of Cyrene, and Manaen, which had been brought up with Herod the tetrarch, and Saul. As they ministered to the Lord, and fasted, the Holy Ghost said, Separate me Barnabas and Saul for the work whereunto I have called them. And when they had fasted and prayed, and laid their hands on them, they sent them away. So they, being sent forth by the Holy Ghost, departed unto Seleucia; and from thence they sailed to Cyprus. . . . And when they had gone through the isle unto Paphos, they found a certain sorcerer, a false prophet, a Jew, whose name was Barjesus: Which was with the deputy of the country, Sergius Paulus, a prudent man; who called for Barnabas and Saul, and desired to hear the word of God.
>
> But Elymas the sorcerer (for so is his name by interpretation) withstood them, seeking to turn away the deputy from the faith. Then Saul, (who also is called Paul) filled with the Holy Ghost, set his eyes on him. And said, O full of all subtilty and all mischief, thou child of the devil, thou enemy of all righteousness, wilt thou not cease to pervert the right ways of the Lord? And now, behold, the hand of the Lord is upon thee, and thou shalt be blind, not seeing the sun for a season. And immediately there fell on him a mist

and a darkness; and he went about seeking some to lead him by the hand (Acts 13:1–4, 6–11).

The context of this chapter indicates that Paul and Barnabas were set apart specifically by the Holy Spirit (vv. 2, 4) to preach the Word of God as the Spirit directed. In the course of discharging the duties assigned to them by the Holy Spirit, they found a certain magician or medium, a false prophet, a Jew, whose name was Barjesus (v. 6).

We learn from the account that this man deliberately obstructed the preaching of the Gospel to the deputy of the country, Sergius Paulus, a man of integrity who desired to hear the Word of God (v. 7). The judgment of God fell upon this man (v. 11). But it is not significant until it is noted that in verses 9 and 10 the judgment was preceded by the announcement that Paul was "filled with the Holy Spirit," when he set his eyes upon him. Paul's scathing denunciation of the medium identifies him as a destructive, mischievous son of Satan, the enemy of all divine righteousness, and the perverter or twister of the right pathway of the Lord.

The Scripture reminds us that we are the temple of the Holy Spirit (1 Corinthians 6:19). The Spirit of God dwells within each Christian, and Scripture assures us that "greater is he that is in you, than he that is in the world" (1 John 4:4).

The Christian, then, can never be possessed by demonic forces; he is constantly shielded and protected by the power of the indwelling Spirit. There is no demonic force that can withstand the presence and power of the Holy Spirit. This is why in the thirteenth chapter of Acts, the Scripture reminds us that Paul dealt with forces of darkness in his capacity as a believer filled with the Holy Spirit, and with complete assurance and confidence that God's power, grace, and all-pervading presence would give him the victory over any medium, false prophet, or "son of Satan" (as the Holy Spirit, through Paul, so graphically describes Barjesus).

As we close our study of Spiritism, three important factors can be gleaned from the comparison of Spiritism historically and theologically with the Gospel of Jesus Christ.

First, Spiritism as a cult has been from its beginning in opposition to the Judeo-Christian religions. In order for one to embrace its teachings, every major doctrine of the Christian faith must be rejected, including the inspiration and final authority of the Bible, the doctrines of the Trinity, the Deity of Christ, the Virgin Birth, Vicarious Atonement, and Bodily Resurrection of our Lord from the grave. The biblical doctrine of salvation by grace alone, through faith in Christ, apart from the works of the Law, is anathema to Spiritist theology, which relies on progressive evolution or growth in the "spirit world" to attain final perfection.

> **The Christian can never be possessed by demonic forces; he is constantly shielded and protected by the power of the indwelling Spirit.**

No informed student of Spiritism for a moment denies these things, and the previously noted quotations taken from bona fide Spiritist publications more than substantiate the validity of this contention.

Second, it cannot be forgotten that amidst the vast majority of Spiritistic phenomena which are fraudulent, there are truly supernatural manifestations. Authorities have given credence to a number of those which do not readily admit to natural or trick explanations. True Spiritism, then, can produce supernatural manifestations, which the Bible describes as originating in demonic forces, and thus under the judgment of God (Deuteronomy 18:9–11; Leviticus 19:31; 20:6; 1 Samuel 28:3–9; 2 Kings 21:6; 2 Chronicles 33:6; and Isaiah 47:9).

Third, Christians must realize that Spiritism is practiced by persons who willfully ignore the God of the Bible and His declared means of making men holy, i.e., the sending of His Son into the world that the world through Him might be saved (John 3:16, 36).

In the spirit of Christian love, we are committed to bear witness to Spiritists, refute their teachings, and confront them with the Christ of Calvary, who alone can "take away the sins of the world" (John 1:29). Spiritism properly understood, is indeed a cult of antiquity, but its motivating force comes from Satan who said long ago, in pristine Eden, "You shall not surely die," and of whom Jesus Christ said, "He is a liar" and "a murderer from the beginning and obeyed not the truth" (John 8:44).

Explore

Familiar Spirits
Psychic Phenomena
Mediumship
Progressive Evolution

/———————————————— **Discuss** ————————————————\

1. What does Spiritism teach?

2. Is there no such thing as a ghost?

3. What did Jesus teach us about demons during His ministry on earth?

4. Is it possible to be a Christian and a medium?

/———————————————— **Dig Deeper** ————————————————\

See *The Kingdom of the Cults Study Guide* available at WalterMartin.com.

8

The Theosophical Society

Quick Facts on the Theosophical Society

- Theosophy teaches a pantheistic, impersonal Supreme Being.
- It draws its authoritative teachings from Hindu, Buddhistic, and early Gnostic sources.
- Jesus Christ is not unique: Jesus is a reincarnated being separate from "christ." All men become christs.
- Reincarnation is the way of salvation.

Historical Perspective

Theosophy as a cult system derives its name from the Greek term *theosophia* meaning literally, divine wisdom. And, in the words of J. H. Russell, its teachings are:

At the same time religious, philosophic, and scientific . . . [postulating] one eternal, immutable, all-pervading principle, the root of all manifestation. From that one existence comes forth periodically the whole universe, manifesting the two aspects of spirit and matter, life and form, positive and negative, "the two poles of nature between which the universe is woven." Those two aspects are inseparably united; therefore all matter is ensouled by life while all life seeks expression through forms. All life being fundamentally one with the life of the Supreme Existence, it contains in germ all the characteristics of its source, and evolution is only the unfolding of those divine potentialities brought about by the conditions afforded in the various kingdoms of nature. The visible universe is only a small part of this field of evolution.[1]

> Theosophy may be recognized at the outset as a pantheistic form of ancient Gnosticism.

Theosophy may be recognized at the outset as a pantheistic form of ancient Gnosticism, which attempts to embrace religious, philosophical, and scientific truth as it is found in all religio-philosophical sources.[2]

According to the views of theosophists, their Society "is a growing system of thought, the result of careful study and research," and further "it is nothing less than the bedrock upon which all phases of the world's thought and activity are founded."[3] The "Three Declared Objects" of the Theosophical Society include:

1. To form a nucleus of the universal brotherhood of humanity without distinction of race, creed, sex, caste, or color.
2. To encourage the comparative study of religion, philosophy, and science.
3. To investigate unexplained laws of nature and the powers latent in humanity.[4]

This noble ideal dreams of a brotherhood of all faiths, or, if we may use the term, a type of homogenized religion, in which all men will agree to the cardinal tenets of Theosophy in one degree or another. In this respect, it is related to Spiritism, Rosicrucianism, Baha'ism, and the Great I AM cults.

The term "theosophy" was introduced, to the best knowledge of reputable scholars, in the third century by a noted philosopher, Ammonius Saccas, the teacher of Plotinus, the great Roman philosopher. Theosophy,

1. J. H. Russell, "Theosophy," *The New Schaff-Herzog Encyclopedia of Religious Knowledge* (Grand Rapids, MI: Baker Book House, 1977), repr., 11:407.
2. "Some Basic Concepts of Theosophy," *The Theosophical Society*, https://www.theosociety.org/pasadena/ts/h_tsideas.htm. The Pasadena, California, International Headquarters explains: "A primary idea is the *essential oneness* of all beings. Life is everywhere throughout the cosmos because all originates from the same unknowable divine source. Consequently, everything from the subatomic to plants, animals, humans, planets, stars, and galaxies is alive and evolving. Each is divine at its root and expresses itself through spiritual, intellectual, psychological, ethereal, and material ranges of consciousness and substance."
3. Irving S. Cooper, *Theosophy Simplified* (Wheaton, Ill.: The Theosophical Press, 1964), 7th ed., 22–23.
4. "The Theosophical Society," https://www.theosociety.org/pasadena/ts/h_tsociety.htm.

however, has a long history traceable directly to the Orient, particularly India, where the Upanishads and Vedas, or Hindu Scriptures, form the basis for no small part of the doctrines. The writings of Gautama Buddha and the early Christian Gnostics also heavily influenced the formulation of theosophical doctrines.

Theosophy claims to be a universal world religion of a distinct nature. But any careful study of its eclectic background readily reveals that much of its "original theology" is borrowed from easily recognizable sources. The modern American history of Theosophy began with the activities of the young and mystically inclined Russian Madam Helena Blavatsky, in the year 1875, in New York City.

Helena Petrovna was born in Ekaterinoslav, Russia, in 1831, the daughter of Peter Hahn, the son of the noble Von Hahn family of Germany. At the age of seventeen, Helena married the Czarist general Blavatsky, a cultured gentleman many years her senior, whom she promptly left after only three months of marriage. It is a known fact that Madam was notoriously short of patience and had a violent temper. It is asserted by at least one of her biographers that she married General Blavatsky merely to spite her acid-tongued governess, who, in a moment of sarcasm, declared that even the noble old gentleman would not marry a shrew like Helena. To her credit, Madam Blavatsky repented quite hastily of her revenge upon the governess, but she had already beguiled the general and was forced into a position of compliance with matrimony.[5]

Shortly after her separation from General Blavatsky, Helena embarked upon a long career of travel that eventually led her into the field of mystical religion, which she studied from Tibet, India, and Egypt to Texas, Louisiana, Cuba, and Canada, settling eventually in New York long enough to found, in the year 1875, the Theosophical Society, in conjunction with Colonel H. S. Olcott and W. Q. Judge, two ardent devotees.

In 1879, Madam Blavatsky left the United States for India, and later died in London, England, in 1891. W. Q. Judge split the Society in 1895, and then saw his organization also divided into the "Universal Brotherhood and Theosophical Society" and "The Theosophical Society in America."

Helena Blavatsky was a woman of tremendous physical proportions with piercing, almost hypnotic eyes, and she ruled the Theosophists during her

5. Baseden G. Butt, *Madam Blavatsky* (London: Marchand Bros., 1926), 13.

life, and in many areas even after her death, through her literary works—principally *The Secret Doctrine*, which is still regarded as divinely inspired interpretations or oracular instructions by most loyal Theosophists.

Annie Besant (1847–1933) was the most prominent of all the British Theosophical luminaries, and one destined to become a bright star in the political fortunes of India. Among her many accomplishments, Besant founded the Central Hindu College at Benares, India, in 1898, and also the Indian Home Rule League in 1916. In the year 1917, she was elected president of the Indian National Congress and was almost always regarded as a powerful figure in Indian politics. In 1889, Mrs. Besant, a native of London, became enthralled by the personality and teachings of Madam Blavatsky and forthwith became a devout pupil and disciple.

Theological Evaluation

According to the literature of the theosophical cult as represented chiefly by Helena Blavatsky, Annie Besant, I. C. Cooper, A. P. Sinnett, L. W. Rogers, and C. W. Leadbeater, there is a great fraternity of "Mahatmas" or "Masters," who are highly evolved examples of advanced reincarnations whose dwelling place is somewhere in the far reaches of remote Tibet.[6] These divine beings possessed Madam Blavatsky and utilized her services to reach the generations now living upon the earth with the restored truths of the great religions of the world, which have been perverted by mankind. In this highly imaginative picture, the Theosophists add seven planes of progression through which the souls of men must progress on their way to the Theosophists' "heaven" or Devachan.

In keeping with the Theosophists' concept of heaven in the final analysis, is the Nirvana of Buddhism, where the absorption of the personality or the soul into a type of world soul eventually extinguishes personal cognizance—the Theosophists also have their "hell," which, oddly enough, resembles the Roman Catholic purgatory, with indescribable tortures and degrees of degradation.

The name for this intermediate state of existence where the departed souls suffer for their past sins while awaiting reincarnation, or the chance to start living in a new body, is Kamaloka, where the atmosphere is "gloomy, heavy,

6. See H. P. Blavatsky, *Theosophical Glossary* (Los Angeles: The Theosophy Company, 1892, 1973).

dreary, depressing to an inconceivable extent . . . the man who is full of evil passions *looks* the whole of them; bestial appetites shape the astral body into bestial forms, and repulsively human animal shapes are the appropriate clothing of brutalized human souls. No man can be a hypocrite in the astral world and cloak foul thoughts with a veil of virtuous seeming; whatever a man is that he appears to be in outward form and semblance, radiant in beauty if his mind be noble, repulsive in hideousness if his nature be foul."[7]

Contrary to the Christian doctrines of redemption and punishment, Theosophy offers no forgiveness for sin except through reincarnations.

Contrary to the Christian doctrines of redemption and punishment, Theosophy offers no forgiveness for sin except through myriads of reincarnations ever progressing toward Devachan, and no eternal retribution for man's rebellion or sin, only the evolutionary terrors of Kamaloka.

The Theosophical Society maintains that it has three primary objectives, which are "(1) to form a nucleus of the brotherhood of humanity, without distinction of race, creed, sex, caste, or color; (2) to encourage the study of comparative religion, philosophy, and science; (3) to investigate the unexplained laws of nature and the powers latent in man. Assent to the first of these objects is required for membership, the remaining two being optional. 'The Society has no dogmas or creed, is entirely nonsectarian, and includes in its membership adherents of all faiths and of none, exacting only from each member their tolerance for the beliefs of others that he would wish them to exhibit toward his own.'"[8]

Theosophy makes no demands of absolute allegiance to any religion or religious leader, and it is resolutely opposed to any form of dogmatism, particularly that type manifested by the Son of God, who said, "I am the way, the truth, and the life: no man cometh unto the Father, but by me" (John 14:6).

God and Man in Theosophy

In common with Christian Science, Unity, and other pantheistic theologies, Theosophy conceives of God in strictly impersonal terms, while

7. Annie Besant, *The Ancient Wisdom: An Outline of Theosophical Teachings* (London: Theosophical Publishing Society, 1897), 92–93.
8. Russell, *Schaff-Herzog*, 408–409.

asserting that man is, in a spiritual sense, part of God. L. W. Rogers put it this way, when he wrote,

In divine essence, latent power and potential spirituality, man is an image of God, because he is part of Him. The same idea is more directly put in the Psalms, with the assertion "ye are gods." If the idea of the immanence of God is sound, then man is a literal fragment of the consciousness of the Supreme Being, is an embryo-god, being destined to ultimately evolve his latent powers into perfect expression. The oneness of life was explicitly asserted by Jesus. . . . It is an unqualified assertion that humanity is a part of God as leaves are part of the tree, not something a tree has created, in the sense that a man creates a machine, but something that is an emanation of the tree and is a living part of it. Thus only has God made man. Humanity is a growth, a development, an emanation, an evolutionary expression of the Supreme Being. . . . It is simplicity itself when we think of the solar system as simply an emanation of the Supreme Being, as something generated from a central life, an expression of that life which gives rise to the poles within it that we know as consciousness and matter. The human soul is an individualized fragment of that divine life . . . is literally a spark of the divine fire, and latent within it are the characteristics of that central light from which it originated. The theosophical conception of the soul is that it is literally an emanation from God, and since it is therefore of its own essence, it becomes clear why Theosophists assert that man is a god in the making.[9]

In keeping with this position, Mrs. Besant once declared, "Man is spiritual intelligence, a fragment of divinity clothed in matter."[10] Mrs. Besant's adopted son, Krishnamurti, once declared that all of us are a part of God and must dig down within ourselves to find the God within us.

These pantheistic views of the Deity are drawn from the deadly trinity of Hinduism, Buddhism, and Gnosticism. And one wonders why Theosophy even attempts to use Christian terms at all, except when it is realized that it is easier to reach the Western mind in terms of the Christian religion than in the language of Hinduism, Buddhism, and Gnosticism. So this is the obvious reason for the utilization of redefined Christian terminology by Theosophists.

9. L. W. Rogers, *Elementary Theosophy* (Wheaton, IL: The Theosophical Press, 1956), 22–25; 19–20.
10. Annie Besant, *Man's Life in Three Worlds* (London: Theosophical Publishing Society, 1899), 3.

Concerning the deity of Jesus Christ and His unique place as *the* Savior of the world, Theosophy declares that all men are innately divine, "so that in time all men become Christs."[11]

The clearest position on this subject, however, is declared by Rogers, who summed up the views of Theosophy where our Lord and His mission are concerned when he wrote,

> Most readers will probably agree that a world teacher known as the Christ did come, and that he founded a religion nearly 2,000 years ago. Why do they think so? They reply that God so loved the world that he sent his son the Christ to bring it light and life. If that is true, how can we avoid the conclusion that he or his predecessors, must have come many times before. The belief that he came but once is consistent only with the erroneous notion that Genesis is history, instead of allegory . . . when a new era in human evolution begins, a world teacher comes in a voluntary incarnation and founds a religion that is suited to the requirements of the new age. Humanity is never left to grope along alone. All that it can comprehend and utilize is taught in the various religions. World teachers, the christs and saviours of the age, have been appearing at propitious times since humanity began existence. . . . In the face of such facts, what becomes of the assertion that God so loved the world that he sent his son to help ignorant humanity about 2,000 years ago—but never before? What about the hundreds of millions of human beings who lived and died before that time? Did he care nothing for them? Did he give his attention to humanity for a period of only 2,000 years and neglect it for millions of years? Has anybody believed that God in his great compassion sent just *one* world teacher for that brief period. . . . If God so loved the world that he sent his son 2,000 years ago, he sent him, or some predecessor very many times before.
>
> Supermen are not myths or figments of the imagination. They are as natural and comprehensive as human beings. In the regular order of evolution, we shall ourselves reach their level and join their ranks, while younger humanity shall attain our present state. As they rose, we too shall rise. Our past has been evolution's night. Our present is its dawn. Our future shall be its perfect day. . . . That is the magnificent future the Theosophist sees for the human race.[12]

The refutation of these non-Christian concepts concerning God and the Lord Jesus Christ are clearly found in various places in the Bible. The

11. Annie Besant, *Is Theosophy Anti-Christian?* (London: Theosophical Publishing Society, 1901), 16.
12. Besant, *Anti-Christian*, 260–263.

personality of God and the deity of Christ are forcefully set forth along with many of the other things that Theosophists deny. The God of the Bible created man and is separate and distinct from him (Genesis 1:27). He is a cognizant ego or personality (Exodus 3:14; Isaiah 48:12; John 8:58), and He is triune—three separate persons—Father, Son, and Holy Spirit, yet one in essence or nature (Deuteronomy 6:4; Galatians 3:20). The God of the Bible cannot be equated with the God of Theosophy, nor can Jesus Christ be redefined so that Christ becomes innately divine, "so that in time all men become Christs."[13] Neither the laws of language, logic, nor biblical theology can permit such extravagances as the Theosophists must insist upon to arrive at such inconceivable equations.

The Theosophist, in his depersonalization of God, however, fails to recognize that man is a cognizant, reflective ego, and that he is a creation of God, in the divine spiritual image, debased though he may be by sin. How is it possible to claim for the creation what is not possessed by the Creator, namely, personality? Are we to assume that the creation, even though part of the divine, is greater in that part, i.e., the possession of ego and personality, than the divine itself? To use the analogy of Rogers, is the spark greater than the flame, the ray greater than the source from which it emanated? Of course not! So, then, neither is man greater than God. If man possesses personality and ego, and the Theosophists grant this, then God, by definition, must be personality and ego—a disconcerting fact, but a fact nonetheless!

The Bible gives much evidence to this effect by underscoring the personality of God in terms of attributes that only a personality can manifest. These traits forever separate Him from the pantheistic God of Theosophy, which is incapable, by definition, of performing these things.

1. *God remembers.* "I, even I, am he that blotteth out thy transgressions for mine own sake, and will not remember thy sins" (Isaiah 43:25).

2. *God creates.* "In the beginning God created the heavens and the earth" (Genesis 1:1).

3. *God knows, i.e., He has a mind.* "The Lord knoweth them that are his" (2 Timothy 2:19). "For I know the thoughts that I think toward you, saith the Lord" (Jeremiah 29:11).

13. Besant, *Anti-Christian*, 16.

4. *God is a personal Spirit.* "I am the Almighty God; walk before me, and be thou perfect" (Genesis 17:1).

5. *God has will.* "Lo, I come to do thy will, O God" (Hebrews 10:9).

From this brief résumé of some of God's attributes, the interested reader can doubtless see the vast difference between the God and Father of our Lord Jesus Christ and the impersonal God of Theosophy. Theosophy's God is not a personal being. He cannot remember, He cannot create, He cannot will, He cannot know, because He is not a personality, but an impersonal "it," an abstract, pantheistic principle, not the God of divine revelation.

Theosophy makes the grave error of all Gnostic cults: It divides Jesus and Christ, making Jesus only the outer man and Christ a divine consciousness immanent within Him and within all men, to a greater or lesser degree. For Theosophists, Jesus is not *the* Christ of divine revelation, as distinct from the Christ who is immanent within all men. They do not understand that the word *Christ* (*Christos* in the Greek) is a title corresponding to the Hebrew *Messiah.* It is not a force, essence, or divine spark, as any careful reading of a good Greek lexicon will speedily reveal. In the sixteenth chapter of Matthew's gospel, the Apostle Peter affirmed this truth by pointing out in his confession of faith, "Thou art the Christ, the Son of the living God" (Matthew 16:16). And John reminds us, "Who is a liar but he that denieth that Jesus is the Christ? He is antichrist, that denieth the Father and the Son" (1 John 2:22).

Christian theology has always maintained that Jesus of Nazareth was the Christ, the anointed Redeemer of God, very God himself (Isaiah 9:6; Micah 5:2; John 1:1, 14, 18; Colossians 2:9; Revelation 1:16–17; Isaiah 44:6; etc.). He is the second person of the Trinity, not the theosophical emanation from the impersonal essence they acknowledge as God. And this is why Theosophy is not Christian and is indeed the very antithesis of historic Christian theology.

The Vicarious Atonement

Theosophy is opposed to not only the true biblical teaching of God's personality and nature, as well as the deity of His Son, but it also vigorously denies Christ's substitutionary sacrifice for all sin (1 John 2:2).

One of the most concise statements concerning the views of Theosophy in this area comes from the pen of L. W. Rogers, who wrote,

Back of the ancient doctrine of the vicarious atonement is a profound and beautiful truth, but it has been degraded into a teaching that is as selfish as it is false. That natural truth is the sacrifice of the Solar Logos, the Deity of our system. Sacrifice consists of limiting himself in the manner of manifested worlds, and it is reflected in the sacrifice of the Christ and other great teachers. Not the sacrifice of life, but a voluntary returning to live in the confinement of material body. Nobody more than the Theosophist pays to the Christ the tribute of the most reverent gratitude; we also hold with St. Paul that each must work out his own salvation. Were it not for such sacrifice, the race would be very, very far below its present evolutionary level. The help that such great spiritual beings have given mankind is incalculable, and is undoubtedly altogether beyond what we were able to comprehend. But to assume that such sacrifice has relieved man from the necessity of developing his spiritual nature, or in any degree nullify his personal responsibility for any evil he has done, is false and dangerous doctrine. . . . And true, too, we know that any belief that is not in harmony with the facts of life is a wrong belief . . . the vital point against this plan of salvation is that it ignores the soul's personal responsibility, and teaches that whatever the offenses against God and man have been, they may be canceled by the simple process of believing that another suffered and died in order that those sins might be forgiven. It is the pernicious doctrine that wrongdoing by one can be set right by the sacrifice of another. It is simply astounding that such a belief could have survived the middle ages and should continue to find millions who accept it in these days of clearer thinking.

The man who is willing to purchase bliss by the agony of another is unfit for heaven, and could not recognize it if he were there.

A heaven that is populated with those who see in the vicarious atonement the happy arrangement letting them in pleasantly and easily, would not be worth having. It would be a realm of selfishness, and that would be no heaven at all. . . . The hypothesis of reincarnation shows our inherent divinity, and the method by which the latent becomes the actual. Instead of the ignoble belief that we can fling our sins upon another, it makes personal responsibility the keynote of life. It is the ethics of self-help. It is the moral code of self-reliance. It is the religion of self-respect.[14]

The inconsistency of Theosophists is eclipsed only by their apparent lack of concern for the validity of established terms in both philosophy and theology. Here is a classic example of what we mean. Rogers wants Christians to believe that "nobody more than the Theosophist pays to the

14. Besant, *Anti-Christian*, 201–206.

Christ the tribute of the most reverent gratitude." But he denies categorically the expressions of that very Christ and the prophecies concerning Him, which state that He came for the express purpose of paying the penalty for all sin.

The Theosophist wants no part of the vicarious sacrifice of Jesus; in fact, it is personally repugnant to him. By his own admission, he considers it "an ignoble belief" that we can fling our sins upon another. But this is exactly what we are called upon to do in the New Testament.

The Scriptures bear incontrovertible witness to the truth that "Christ died for the ungodly" (Romans 5:6), and that "The blood of Jesus Christ . . . cleanseth us from all sin" (1 John 1:7). There is no doctrine found within the pages of the Bible that is better supported or substantiated than that of the substitutionary death of Christ for the sins of the world. As far back in the biblical record as Exodus, Moses wrote of God's symbolic use of blood for purification and sacrifice. It will be recalled that Jehovah delivered the Israelites from Egypt by causing all the firstborn of the nation, including Pharaoh's own son, to fall under the shadow of sudden death (Exodus 12). The Jews were instructed in this instance to sprinkle the blood of the young lamb on the doorpost and lintels of their homes, and God promised, "When I see the blood, I will pass over you" (Exodus 12:13). The Lord also instituted the animal sacrifices of the Levitical era and expressly stated, "It is the blood that maketh an atonement for the soul" (Leviticus 17:11).

Following this typology through into the New Testament, we find that Jesus was called the Lamb of God, who takes away the sin of the world (John 1:29), and further, that His blood, shed upon the cross, is our atonement or covering for sin, even for the sins of all mankind (Matthew 26:28; Romans 5:6–8; Ephesians 1:7; Colossians 1:20).

The believer in Christ therefore is saved by grace alone through faith in His blood, and its efficacy for the cleansing of all sin (Romans 3:25). John, the beloved disciple, reminds us in his powerful epistle of this fact (1 John 1:7), and Peter declares, "[We] were not redeemed with corruptible things, as silver and gold . . . but with the precious blood of Christ, as of a lamb without blemish and without spot" (1 Peter 1:18–19).

The pages of the New Testament bear incontrovertible testimony that Jesus Christ on Calvary purchased the church with his own blood (Acts 20:28), and in the great message of Christ to John recorded in the book of Revelation, we are told that He "washed us from our sins in his own blood" (Revelation 1:5). This was not a pagan sacrifice to placate the wrath of a heathen god's justice. The sacrifice was offered through the Eternal Spirit, to free the sons of men from the curse of sin and to open the path to salvation, through which we now can have boldness to enter into the holiest by the blood of Jesus—a new and living way to the very throne of God our Father (Hebrews 10:19–20).

Theosophy refuses to accept the vicarious atonement of Jesus Christ for the forgiveness of all sin. Instead, Theosophy teaches the inexorable law of Karma (the accumulated weight of one's bad actions that can only be "atoned for" through personal and individual good actions during a succession of lives [reincarnation] and which is sometimes called "the Law of Cause and Effect"). Annie Besant described it as the "law of causation . . . bidding man . . . surrender all the fallacious ideas of forgiveness, vicarious atonement, divine mercy and the rest of the opiates that superstition offers to the sinner."[15]

Consequently, through the application of the law of Karma, the biblical doctrine of the Atonement is neatly supplanted and the authority of Scripture circumvented or negated. Mrs. Besant once wrote that "The atonement wrought by Christ lies not in the substitution of one individual for another."[16] As the daughter of an Anglican clergyman and the former wife of another, Mrs. Besant must have known better, but she never satisfactorily explained what the biblical doctrine of the Atonement *does* mean, if it does not mean what the Christian church has always maintained.

For Theosophists the redemptive love of a personal God as revealed in the substitutionary sacrifice of His most precious possession, His Son, Jesus Christ, is totally unnecessary and is not the way of salvation. This fact alone would remove Theosophy from any serious consideration of compatibility with Christianity, although its "chapters" or centers can be found in many major cities of the United States and throughout the world. Its rate of growth seems considerably slower than it was in the 1920s, and we can hope that its complexity and the involved vocabulary utilized to describe its mazelike theology may yet render it more ineffective in an age in which precision of definition is at last coming into its own.

In order to be Christian, one must conform to the Scriptures. Theosophy fails to meet this requirement and must be considered anti-Christian.

15. Annie Besant, *Karma* (London: The Theosophical Publishing Society, 1904), 23.
16. Besant, *Anti-Christian*, 11.

Biblical Perspective

Theosophy as a religion is opposed to virtually every cardinal doctrine of the Christian faith, and finds no support from Judaism, little from Islam, and certainly none from the majority of world religions, with the exceptions of Buddhism and Hinduism. Christianity, Judaism, and Islam all confess a personal God and all believe in a resurrection of the body and in the authority of the Old Testament. Theosophy, on the other hand, rejects *all* these doctrines. Yet it continues to claim qualification for the role as a "unifier and peacemaker in religion."

In fact, Theosophy claims that it is wrong to make any objective religious truth claim: We must only experience religious truth for ourselves in a subjective way.

> As beings rooted in divinity, we each have the ability to discover reality for ourselves. To do this we must learn to judge what is true and false, real and illusory; not blindly follow the dictates of authority, however high. . . . By following our own spiritual instincts and intuitions, we awaken our latent potentials. Trying to force others to adopt what we believe to be the "proper" avenue of thought may be harmful. Everyone follows his or her own unique path of unfoldment.[17]

It is an interesting fact that Theosophy speaks in glowing terms of the ancient cult of Gnosticism, which thrived in the first three centuries of the Christian era, and which almost succeeded in doing irreparable damage to historic Christian faith. Paul's epistle to the Colossians and the epistle of 1 John are recognized by all biblical scholars to be direct apologetic thrusts against the teachings that spawned this cult: spiritualizing the Old Testament, redefining contemporary Christian terminology, substituting an impersonal god for the God of revelation, and reducing Jesus Christ to a demigod, or a pantheistic emanation from the unknowable divine essence. The well-known theosophical writer L. W. Rogers, however, disdains the counsel of the Holy Spirit, not to mention the warnings of the Apostles Paul and John when he states,

> The antagonism between scientific and religious thought was the cause of great controversy that occurred in the intellectual world in the late nineteenth

17. "Some Basic Concepts of Theosophy," Theosophical Society, https://www.theosociety.org/pasadena/ts/h_tsideas.htm.

century. If the early teaching of the Christian Church had not been lost, the conflict could not have arisen. The Gnostic philosophers who were the intellect and heart of the Church had a knowledge of nature so true that it could not possibly come into collision with any fact of science; but unfortunately, they were enormously outnumbered by the ignorant, and the authority passed wholly into the hands of the latter. It was inevitable that misunderstanding followed.[18]

Theosophists are great admirers of the Gnostics, and this is not at all surprising, since they have adopted much of the terminology and vocabulary of ancient Gnosticism, which looked with disdain upon the material properties of both the world and man, depersonalized God, and created various planes of spiritual progression, culminating in universal salvation and reconciliation through reincarnation and the wheel concept of progression borrowed unblushingly from Buddhism.

Theosophy does not hesitate to declare that

> God and man are the two phases of the one eternal life and consciousness that constitutes our universe! The idea of the immanence of God is that He is the universe; although he is also more than it is; that the solar system is an emanation of the Supreme Being as clouds are an emanation of the sea. This conception makes man a part of God, having potentially within him all the attributes and powers of the Supreme Being. It is the idea that nothing exists except God, and that humanity is one portion of him—one phase of his Being.[19]

In the theology of Theosophy there are seven distinct planes in the universe. The Physical is the most dense of these planes; that which is next in the order is called the Astral Plane, and above it, the Mental. There are four higher spiritual planes, but to all except initiates and adepts they are as yet "mere names." Man, of course, has a physical body, a mental body, and an astral body. But at this particular stage of cosmic evolution, with but few exceptions, the so-called higher spiritual bodies are still awaiting organization.[20]

Sin, Salvation, and Prayer

The Christian concepts of sin, salvation, and prayer need but passing mention relative to the reinterpretation they receive at the hands of theo-

18. Rogers, *Elementary Theosophy*, 22.
19. Rogers, *Elementary Theosophy*, 23.
20. Blavatsky, *Theosophical Glossary*.

sophical writers. The teaching of Theosophy on these principal Christian doctrines is very definite and important and should be understood.

The Bible plainly states that all men have come under the divine indictment of sin (Romans 3:23). The divine remedy for sin, as we have seen, is the redemptive work of Jesus Christ who "died, the just for the unjust to bring us to God" (1 Peter 3:18). So hideous and degrading was human sin in the eyes of a Holy God that it required the God-man's death to satisfy the righteous judgment of His Father. Salvation from sin is full and complete by faith in Jesus Christ "once for all" (Hebrews 10:10). "For the wages of sin is death" (Romans 6:23). Since the Theosophist wants no part of the redeeming sacrifice of the Cross, and since he denies that personal sin must be atoned for by a power outside himself, like Petra of old, he is deceived by the pride of his heart (Obadiah 3).

There can be little doubt that Theosophists, like Unitarians, consider salvation gained by character and progression. Theirs must be a God of love who allows the penalty of sin to be worked out on the wheel of reincarnation and by infinite progression. He does not judge; He cannot, for the spectacle of an impersonal principle judging the actions of a personal being is too much for any serious student of the philosophy of religion, and Theosophists are no exception.

The biblical doctrine of prayer also suffers at the hand of Theosophy. In the biblical vocabulary, prayer is personal communion with a personal God, not an abstract force or a cosmic consciousness. Jesus Christ himself encouraged us to pray many times (see Matthew 5:44; 6:6–7, 9; 9:38). He repeatedly emphasized its virtues and benefits. For the Christian, then, prayer is the link with the Eternal by which man can come

> The divine remedy for sin, as we have seen, is the redemptive work of Jesus Christ.

to "the throne of grace" in the power of the Holy Spirit and find "grace to help in time of need" (Hebrews 4:16).

Salvation for the Christian is by grace and true faith in God's only method for making men holy and through the only "name under heaven given among men, whereby we must be saved" (Acts 4:12). Human sin makes it necessary for this grand redemption, and since Theosophy denies it, it follows of a necessity that redemption would also be negated. Since Theosophy rejects the God of the Bible or any concept of a personal God, prayer in the biblical sense becomes impossible, and the sinner's most desperate need, which is to "call upon the name of the Lord" that he might be saved, not from a wheel of incarnations, but from eternal, spiritual, and conscious separation from the life and fellowship of God himself, is ignored or denied.

Contrasted to this biblical picture of sin, salvation, and prayer, Theosophy equates God the Father with the pagan gods Buddha and Vishnu,[21] and defines prayer not as personal supplication for divine mercy and grace (Philippians 4:6–7), but as "concentrated thought."[22] Theosophists also believe that personal sin is removed only by suffering in Kamaloka, "the semi-material plane, to us subjective and invisible, where the disembodied 'personalities,' the astral forms . . . remain. . . . It is the Hades of the ancient Greeks and the Amenti of the Egyptians, the land of Silent Shadows."[23] Personal salvation is obtained through various reincarnations, ending in absorption of the individual ego. These cannot be viewed as pleasant alternatives to biblical revelation, but they are all that Theosophy offers.

Resurrection versus Reincarnation

It is necessary for the Christian to understand the one great doctrine that forever removes any possibility of realizing fellowship with Theosophists. The Apostle Paul, in his great and grand chapter on the resurrection of the body (1 Corinthians 15), cites the resurrection of Christ and its subsequent effect upon the bodies of all mankind as *the* proof that God exists, that Christ is His Son, and that the redemption of all believers is assured by His personal triumph over the grave.

Paul goes to great lengths in this chapter to show that "if Christ be not raised, your faith is vain; ye are yet in your sins" (v. 17). For the great apostle, our hope for physical immortality lies alone in the triumphant physical resurrection of Christ (v. 14), who visibly and tangibly presented himself alive "by many infallible proofs" (Acts 1:3) to over 500 persons who knew that it was indeed Jesus who had conquered the grave on their behalf.

Our risen Lord also promised that one day we should be physically and morally as He is, and that God the Father, through Him, would raise the

21. Annie Besant, *The Seven Principles of Man* (London: The Theosophical Publishing Society, 1902), 58.
22. Annie Besant, *The Changing World* (London: The Theosophical Publishing Society, 1901), 68.
23. Blavatsky, *Theosophical Glossary*, 171–172.

believing dead and clothe them with immortality at His second advent (1 Thessalonians 4).

The condition of the Christian in death, however, is not one of suffering or repeated reincarnations while atoning for sin, as Theosophy would have it, but one of cognizant personal joy, literally the state of being "at home with the Lord" (2 Corinthians 5:8).

The resurrection of Jesus Christ and, for that matter, the resurrection of all mankind, leaves no room for the Theosophical dogma of concurrent reincarnations. We indeed concur with the Apostle Paul that, "If in this life only we have hope in Christ, we are of all men most miserable" (1 Corinthians 15:19). The souls of the dead do not pass through various reincarnations as Theosophy contends; rather, these souls are either experiencing happiness in Christ's presence (Philippians 1:21), in which case, to die is gain; or they are suffering conscious separation from His presence (Luke 16:19–31). In any case, Scripture clearly shows that reincarnation is not man's destiny, nor is it God's revealed plan for perfecting the souls of men. The Bible tells us that Christ died to fully redeem (Romans 5:6; Hebrews 9:26; 10:12).

Let us not then be deceived by the veneer of the intellectual and metaphysical jargon the Theosophist has mastered, nor retreat before his attempt to belittle the preaching of the Cross as "foolishness." We need not defer to his alleged "deeper revelation," to his claims that Theosophy is a higher form of revelation for our age. We are informed in Scripture repeatedly that "the preaching of the cross is to them that perish foolishness; but unto us which are saved it is the power of God" (1 Corinthians 1:18). Theosophy is just another attempt to supplant the authority of Christ and Scripture with the "philosophy and empty deceit" of the world (Colossians 2:8).

Theosophy, in common with the other non-Christian religions of the world, offers no living redeemer, no freedom from the power of sin, and in the end no hope for the world to come. Jesus Christ, on the other hand, offers promises by the mouths of prophets and the God who cannot lie that those who trust in and serve Him shall "receive [for their faith] an hundredfold, and shall inherit everlasting life" (Matthew 19:29).

We must seek to win Theosophists to a saving knowledge of the Gospel, but we must not forget that their theology has many labyrinths, for "there is a way which seemeth right unto a man," in the words of Solomon, "but the end thereof are the ways of death" (Proverbs 14:12).

Explore

Gnosticism
Pantheism
Law of Causation
Infallible Proofs of the Resurrection

Discuss

1. Theosophy is mostly drawn from what three sources?

2. How did Madam Helena Blavatsky change the meaning of reincarnation?

3. What does the Bible teach about sowing and reaping, and how is this different from reincarnation?

4. What three beliefs do Christianity, Judaism, and Islam all confess?

Dig Deeper

See *The Kingdom of the Cults Study Guide* available at WalterMartin.com.

9

Buddhism—Classical and Zen

Quick Facts on Buddhism

- Siddhartha Gautama followed the paths of previous "buddhas," or enlightened ones, until he discovered the Middle Road, the Four Noble Truths, and the Eightfold Path, and achieved enlightenment.

- Buddhism shows a heavy influence of Brahmanism, gods, and goddesses in Buddha's history and teachings.

- The Pali Tripitaka text is considered the most reliable teachings of Buddha; Mahayana Buddhism and other sects add to it.

- Man suffers because his desires are fixated on the illusion of self; this confines him to non-permanence within the laws of karma and reincarnation. Reaching Nirvana is the ultimate goal, where the self becomes extinguished in the Void.

Historical Perspective

Although Classical Buddhism is one of the four major world religions and not a "cult" as defined in chapter 1 of this volume, it still birthed a cultic brood that was repackaged in many ways, including Scientology, Est, Forum, Lifespring, and its older forms of Zen and Nichiren Shoshu.[1]

1. Kurt Van Gorden commentary.

As of 2012, the worldwide estimate for followers of the Buddha stood at more than 488 million.[2] Buddhism—once a religion of the East—has become a popular faith in the West. It continues to impact Christianity in its direct challenge and reinterpretation of biblical teachings.

People from all walks of life are interested in various aspects of Buddhism's religious philosophy, and as we approach this study, it is important to understand why there has been such a penetration of Asian philosophy on American college campuses: People are pursuing Eastern religions in the United States because their message has been dressed up to meet our cultural needs—they are responding to it because there is a deep awareness of a need for spiritual reality.[3] A great many Christian churches are not presenting Jesus Christ's Gospel with a compelling relevancy. They are not attempting to come to grips with today's problems and issues. People are quite literally leaving the Church in droves because they have not truly heard the Gospel, and those with no background whatsoever in historic Christianity go after Eastern Religions en masse, because they cloak their Eastern philosophy or religion in Western terminology.

Classical Buddhism

To understand the core of Buddhism and its far-reaching impact on India and the world, one must first become a student of history. Twenty-five hundred years ago Hinduism reigned supreme in India, and the people were subject to and enslaved by it.[4]

J. Isamu Yamamoto explains the Indian history:

> Over three thousand years ago the Aryans (a powerful group of Indo-European-speaking people) . . . [conquered] the Indus valley, the Aryans instituted Brahmanism (today it has developed into Hinduism) and the caste system in the Indian culture, which enabled the invaders to maintain the purity of the Aryan race and establish themselves as spiritual and social masters over the native Indians.[5]

The enslaving caste system played an important part for Indian reformers, like Buddha, who sought liberation from Hinduism.

2. "Buddhists," *Pew Research Center*, 2012.
3. Walter Martin, *Zen Buddhism, Hare Krishna, and Meher Baba* (Santa Ana, CA: One Way Libraries, 1976), side one of audio.
4. Martin (1974), audio, side 1.
5. J. Isamu Yamamoto, "The Buddha," *Christian Research Journal* (Spring/Summer 1994): 11.

Another important aspect of modern Hindu life, the caste system, began to emerge during the Vedic period. The system of classifying individuals into castes is vocational and related to skin color. The Rig-Veda speaks of five social castes:

(1) the Brahmins—the priestly scholarly caste;
(2) the Kshatriyas—the warrior-soldier caste;
(3) the Vaishyas—the agricultural and merchant caste;
(4) the Sudras—the peasant and servant caste;
(5) the Harijan—the outcasts or "untouchables."

Over time these castes underwent thousands of subdivisions. The top of the social scale remains the Brahmins, while the very bottom is comprised of what became known as "untouchables."[6]

Under Hinduism, the lot of the masses was poverty and despair, and the wheel of reincarnation or *samsara* loomed constantly before them like a never-ending nightmare of suffering and death. Discontent grew among the people, and many searched for something to break the relentless hold of Hinduism:

As the vast majority of the people were illiterate and indescribably poor, the gap widened between the few literates and the host of illiterates, between the few princes and rulers and their millions of subjects, between the few privileged of high caste and the great underprivileged population that belonged to the lower castes and outcastes. This gap grew wider and wider. And from the hopelessness among the many arose despair.[7]

There seemed no escape from the fate of having to endure an endless succession of painful lives before one could be freed to merge for eternity with the "World-Soul"—a state known as *Nirvana*.[8] Into this religion of strict castes and oppression was born the son of a minor *raja* or king sometime between 490 and 410 BC.[9] His philosophy of life would impact the world for centuries to come.

6. George A. Mather and Larry A. Nichols, "Hinduism History," in *Dictionary of Cults, Sects, Religions and the Occult* (Grand Rapids: Zondervan, 1993), 117.
7. Joseph Gaer, *What Great Religions Believe* (Signet, The New American Library: New York, 1963), 40.
8. Gaer, *Great Religions*, 30.
9. This date is approximate as there are no written historical records from the time of the Buddha.

Gautama Buddha, founder of the Buddhist religion, was the son of Suddhodana, a chieftain reigning over a district near the Himalayas in what is known today as the country of Nepal. At an early age, Siddhartha Gautama,[10] his true name, observed the many contradictions and problems of life; he abandoned his wife and son when he felt he could no longer endure the life of a rich nobleman, and became a wandering ascetic in search of the truth about life. Buddhist historians tell us that after almost seven years of wandering, inquiring, meditating, and searching, he found "the true path," and "great enlightenment," under the legendary Bo[11] tree (tree of wisdom), and thus attained Nirvana. Classical Buddhism maintains that cycles of reincarnations are necessary in order to attain Nirvana. The teachings of the Buddha are concerned with the ramifications of the "Four Noble Truths" and the "Eightfold Path": (1) Suffering; (2) Its cause; (3) Its cessation; and (4) The Way which leads to this cessation:

In its shortest form Buddha's teaching may be summarized as follows: Birth is sorrow, age is sorrow, sickness is sorrow, death is sorrow, clinging to earthly things is sorrow. Birth and rebirth, the chain of reincarnation, result from the thirst of life together with passion and desire. The only escape from this thirst is to follow the Eightfold Path: Right belief, right resolve, right word, right act, right life, right effort, right thinking, right meditation. The goal of Buddhism is Nirvana. A definition of this term is almost impossible for the simple reason that Buddha himself gave no clear idea, and in all probability possessed none, of this state. He was indeed asked by more than one of his disciples whether Nirvana was post mundane or post celestial existence, or whether it was annihilation. To all these questions, however, he refused an answer, for it was characteristic of his teachings that they were practically confined to the present life, and concerned themselves but little either with problems of merely academic philosophy or with the unknowable. . . . the *summum bonum* is release from karma and reincarnation, a goal which is to be attained by knowledge, and which consists in absorption into or reunion with the Over-Soul. This involves the annihilation of individuality, and in this sense Nirvana is nihilism, so that

10. Siddhartha Gautama Buddha. Buddha is not his name, although today he is addressed as such; it is a title of enlightenment. The family name is Gautama (excellent cow or best cow) and his given name was Siddhartha (one who achieved his goal). Buddha is also known as *Sakyamuni*, "Sage of the Sakyas" (his tribal ethnicity, where his family dwelt in northern India near Nepal).

11. Also spelled Bodhi Tree (Wisdom Tree), which is a fig tree located at Uruvela (State of Bihar, India), under which Siddhartha Gautama meditated for forty-nine days until he attained enlightenment, or Nirvana.

with the tacit ignoring of any real conception of the divine in the teachings of Buddha, Nirvana seems to imply the annihilation of the soul rather than its absorption.[12]

It is important to remember that there is a common denominator to Zen, Buddhism, I Ching, and all Eastern religious or philosophical backgrounds—none of them believe in the existence of a personal God. None of them believe that we can address Him as "Father." All of these, however, are trying to establish a quest for truth or establish an identification with this unknowable essence. They cannot define God, since God is the great unknowable. They claim unity with some kind of unknowable nature. They use Hindu philosophical terms, because Buddhism was derived from Hinduism.[13]

> The common denominator in all Eastern religious or philosophical backgrounds is the belief that a personal God does not exist.

While frequently regarded as a new religion, it is, strictly speaking, only a reformation of Brahmanism [Hinduism], and can not be understood without some knowledge of the conditions preceding it. The religious system of India as outlined in its oldest religious books, the Vedas, had reached in the Brahmanas and Sutras a degree of ritualism such as, perhaps, never existed elsewhere. This formalism produced a revolt, and from time to time arose various teachers, philosophers, and reformers, of whom the most influential was . . . Buddha.[14]

We become lost in a maze of terminology when God is reduced to an unknowable essence. What do we mean when we talk about God? Can we talk about God as subject and object relationship? Do we talk about God as "I and Thou"?

No. These religions do not talk about God in this way. They do not talk about God as a person. They sometimes use personal terms, but God is not a person. They behold God when they behold themselves, because all creation shares in their understanding of God. Reality, to them, is grounded in

12. Samuel Macauley Jackson, ed., *The New Schaff-Herzog Encyclopedia of Religious Knowledge* (Grand Rapids, MI: Baker Book House, 1977 reprint, volume 2), 293, as quoted in Martin (1985), 262.
13. Martin, audio, 1976.
14. Jackson, 1977, 292.

us, as human beings. It is not grounded in God and certainly not grounded in His divine Revelation, the Bible.

Modern Buddhism

There are fragmentations of these Eastern world religions that have produced cultic structures, but they essentially say the same thing.[15] Professor Wing-Tsit Chan of Dartmouth College comments:

1. Mahayana and Hinayana Buddhism

It was but natural that divergent opinions should arise within the faith itself. These remained comparatively unimportant, however, until the schism [AD 100] into the Mahayana and Hinayana [Therevada], or the "Great Vehicle" and "Little Vehicle." The latter still adhered strictly in the main to the original tenets of Buddhism. The Mahayanists, on the contrary, who form by far the larger sect, devoted themselves to all manner of speculation, being influenced not only by Hinduism but at a later period by Shamanism as well. The Mahayana postulates the existence of a thousand Buddhas with a supreme god. . . .

Buddhism was introduced into Tibet about the seventh century A.D. . . . Here is evolved the . . . celestial types of the Buddhas which appear on earth as men . . . who are represented on earth by the Dalai-Lama at Lhassa, and is the type of the Bodhisatva Maitreya, the future earthly Buddha and the savior of the world.

Buddhism was introduced into China in its Mahayanistic form by the emperor Mingti in 61 AD, and . . . was carried to Japan, where numerous sects have arisen, although the results have been little more than a further departure from the original faith.[16]

2. Zen

The second oldest of all the cult systems considered in this book is a form of Buddhism with a following of many millions.

"Zen," as it is known in America, is derived from the Japanese branch of the "meditation" school of Buddhist philosophy. Today, Zen claims 9.6 million followers in Japan and millions more around the world.[17] Zen

15. Martin, 1977, audio side two.
16. Wing-Tsit Chan, "Buddhahood," Vergilius Ferm, ed., *An Encyclopedia of Religion* (New York: Philosophical Library, 1945), 95.
17. See "Zen," ReligionFacts.com, November 20, 2016, http://www.religionfacts.com/zen and "Buddhists," Pew Research Center, December 18, 2012, http://www.pewforum.org/2012/12/18/gl obal-religious-landscape-buddhist/.

cannot be taken lightly, especially when it receives favorable attention from magazines of the standing of *Time*, *Newsweek*, *Life*, *U.S. News & World Report*, and *Reader's Digest*, to name a few.

Zealous followers of Zen trace their origin to Buddha, who, they claim, imparted to one of his disciples, Mahakasyapa (or Kasyapa), what has become known as "the doctrine of the Buddha mind." Buddha, as the legend goes, merely picked the flower in silence, and thus communicated the mystical fragment of his mind, hence the emphasis upon the "Buddha mind" in Zen.

Theological Evaluation

When we come to the Zen variety of Buddhism, we find a strong emphasis on the present and on practical meditation. The late Alan Watts, American proponent of Zen, described it this way:

> Perhaps the special flavor of Zen is best described as a certain directness. In other schools of Buddhism, awakening or *bodhi* seems remote and almost superhuman, something to be reached only after many lives of patient effort. But in Zen there is always the feeling that awakening is something quite natural, something startlingly obvious, which may occur at any moment. If it involves a difficulty, it is just that it is much too simple. Zen is also direct in its way of teaching, for it points directly and openly to the truth, and does not trifle with symbolism.[18]

Zen is hence revolutionary, holding that enlightenment comes with clarification and simplification through acting out of old values of time and experience, and depending upon only the supreme experience, "now." One state of consciousness and the next cannot be measured by hours or miles, as the Master tries to say, in a *koan* . . . the standard advice of Zen, using one of the 1,700 traditional questions to highlight it. The snap of a finger can be a lesson . . . indicating that this very moment is the immediate experience of reality, past time and embracing all dimensions.

> Zen is brusque in its teachings, aimed at the roots of inconsistency. It demands action of a curious sort. This can only be achieved when it is simple, natural and totally correct. It finds truth through shrinking away from error, not discovering a way to truth.

18. Alan W. Watts, *The Way of Zen* (New York: The New American Library, 1957), 83.

Such a mystic philosophy, oddly enough, bears a kinship to primitive Christianity. Like the ardent fundamentalist awaiting the second coming which will bring heaven to earth, the Zen ideal is to achieve a Nirvanic state and a saintly condition on this earth. . . . The *koan*, which goes back to the twelfth century, when it was devised to test the students' understanding of the Zen spirit and shake his mind from conventional thinking, leaves most professed Zen followers in Japan uninterested today. And, of course, one can never achieve *satori*—the nonrational, clear and intuitive understanding of reality—until he understands the exercises of *koan*. . . .

> In Zen, reality is not objective correlative truth, but subjective, egocentric reflection, which becomes reality if they deign to participate in its manifestation.

Zen is a paradox within a paradox, a mystical doctrine which laughs at all doctrines and dogma, and becomes a doctrine and dogma in the doing.[19]

With a philosophy such as this, it is easy to understand how Zenists can sit cross-legged (*zazen* Japanese), meditating upon a flower petal or a rock thrown haphazard over a floor or on a garden path. For them, reality is not objective correlative truth, but subjective, egocentric reflection, which becomes reality if they deign to participate in its manifestation. The following quotations deal with the theology of Zen Buddhism in a general way, for if ever a system was devoid of a theology, except by implication and interpretation, it is Zen.

Zen Teachings

1. *The Nature of God (Pantheism) and Morality*

I see much common ground in Zen and the mysticism of Meister Eckhart, as he wrote: The eye by which I see God is the same as the eye by which God sees me. My eye and God's eye are one and the same—one in seeing, one in knowing, and one in loving. . . . When I have shut the doors of my five senses, earnestly desiring God, I find him in my soul as clearly and as joyful as he is in eternity. . . .[20]

19. Richard Mathison, *Faith, Cults and Sects of America* (New York: The Bobbs-Merrill Company, Inc., 1960), 365, 367–368.
20. Sohaku Ogata, *Zen for the West* (Westport, CN: Greenwood Press, Publishers, 1959), 17, 18.

Zen consciousness is a mind made one with life, and even at its lowest produces a sense of one-ness with all humanity. Who, having this, needs rules of morality?[21]

Is Zen a religion? It is not a religion in the sense that the term is popularly understood; for Zen has no God to worship, no ceremonial rites to observe, no future abode to which the dead are destined, and last of all, Zen has no soul whose welfare is to be looked after by somebody else and whose immortality is a matter of intense concern with some people. Zen is free from all these dogmatic and "religious" encumbrances.

When I say there is no God in Zen, the pious reader may be shocked, but this does not mean that Zen denies the existence of God; neither denial nor affirmation concerns Zen. When a thing is denied, the very denial involves something not denied. The same can be said of affirmation. This is inevitable in logic. Zen wants to rise above logic, Zen wants to find a higher affirmation where there are no antitheses. Therefore, in Zen, God is neither denied nor insisted upon; only there is in Zen no such God as has been conceived by Jewish and Christian minds. For the same reason Zen is not a philosophy, Zen is not a religion.[22]

2. Self-Salvation

. . . for is it not the life of the soul that lives in perfect freedom and in perfect unity? There is no freedom or unity in exclusion or in limitation. Zen is well aware of this. In accordance with the demands of our inner life, therefore, Zen takes us to an absolute realm wherein there are no antitheses of any sort. . . .

Therefore, Zen does not mean a mere escape from intellectual imprisonment, which sometimes ends in sheer wantonness. There is something in Zen that frees us from conditions and at the same time gives us a certain firm foothold, which, however, is not a foothold in a relative sense. The Zen master endeavours to take away all footholds from the disciple which he has ever had since his first appearance on earth, and then to supply him with one that is really no foothold.[23]

In Zen there are no miracles, supernatural interventions, ways nor refuges. We bear the whole responsibility for our actions and no Sage whomsoever he be has the right to encroach on our free will.

21. Christmas Humphreys, *Zen Buddhism* (London: George Allen and Unwin Ltd., 1957), 178.
22. Daisetz Teitaro Suzuki, *An Introduction to Zen Buddhism* (London: Rider and Company/ The Buddhist Society, n.d.), 39.
23. Suzuki, *Introduction to Zen*, 67, 68.

We are at the same time responsible for our slavery and our freedom; the chains of our enslavement have been forged by ourselves, and only we can break them. . . .[24]

3. Sin and Evil

The opposites (*dvandva*) of light and darkness, good and evil, pleasure and pain, are the essential elements of the game, for although the Godhead is identified with Truth (*sat*), Consciousness (*chit*), and Bliss (*ananda*), the dark side of life has its integral part in the game just as every drama must have its villain, to disrupt the *status quo*, and as the cards must be shuffled, thrown into chaos, in order that there may be a significant development of the play. For Hindu thought there is no Problem of Evil. The conventional, relative world is necessarily a world of opposites. Light is inconceivable apart from darkness; order is meaningless without disorder; and likewise, up without down, sound without silence, pleasure without pain.[25]

For this reason the masters talk about Zen as little as possible, and throw its concrete reality straight at us. This reality is the "suchness" *(tathata)* of our natural, nonverbal world. If we see this just as it is, there is nothing good, nothing bad, nothing inherently long or short, nothing subjective and nothing objective. There is no symbolic self to be forgotten, and no need for any idea of a concrete reality to be remembered.[26]

From the foregoing, the deep-seated philosophical mysticism of the Zen school of meditation of Buddhism is accurately reflected, revealing Zen to be a philosophy that negates a personal God. Secondly, it denies the reality of sin due to the absence of an absolute standard of revealed law and holiness. Thirdly, it rejects the necessity of personal redemption from the penalty of sin revealed in the Person of Jesus Christ, who *is the* Way.

Zenists have no antidote for the piercing analytical pronouncements of Scripture: "All have sinned and come short of the glory of God. There is none righteous, no not one" (Romans 3:23; 3:10). And the reality of divine judgment can be brought to bear upon them through proper use of the Scriptures and logic. As we have mentioned previously, one trip through

---

24. Robert Linssen, *Living Zen* (London: George Allen and Unwin, LTD., 1958), 74.
25. Watts, *Way of Zen*, 45, 46.
26. Watts, *Way of Zen*, 127.

the gas ovens of Dauchau, Belsen, Auschwitz, and Buchenwald is worth a thousand theological propositions, and Zenists ought to be reminded of the fact that those crimes were crimes against an absolute standard which is not subjective, but objective and universal, i.e., "Thou shalt not kill" (Exodus 20:13).

The true nature of Zen is, in reality, that of ego-absorption, to the extent that one becomes obsessed with self, not with sins and the desperate need for their erasure. The Zenist is a stranger to social responsibility also, which leaves little to justify his existence.

The Core of Zen

Zen Buddhism is one of the more philosophic and orientally flavored imports of cultism, peculiarly adapted to the Western mind in that it decidedly shuns outright supernaturalism but encourages a "Satori" (enlightenment) experience, "an awakening of our original inseparability with the universe." The ultimate goal of Zen Buddhism is "the freeing of the will," so that "all things bubble along in one interrelated continual." Those who would be disciples of Zen must allow their ego to be detached until "one's real self calmly floats over the world's confusion" like a ping-pong ball skimming over the turbulent rapids of life. In a world faced with deprivation, hunger, disease, death, and the ever-present shadow of nuclear warfare, the denial of such reality borders on the criminal. Zen Buddhism, in our opinion, is the most self-centered, selfish system of philosophy that the depraved soul of man can embrace, for it negates the two basic principles upon which all spiritual reality exists, "Thou shalt love the Lord thy God with all thy heart, with all thy soul and with all thy mind . . . and thy neighbor as thyself" (Matthew 22:37, 39).

For Zenists, it is love of self first, last, and always. This is the core of Zen, which releases one from spiritual responsibility and substitutes intellectual enlightenment for conversion, and the absence of concern for one's fellow man for peace with God. Historically, Buddhism has produced nothing but indescribable conditions under which its subjects live. For in almost every area of the world where Buddhism of any form holds sway, there stalks the specter of disease, hunger, and moral and spiritual decay. The peoples of the Orient are the slaves of their religions, and Buddhism, with its egocentricity and inherently selfish concept of life and of responsibility to society, is by all odds one of the greatest offenders. Let those who consider Zen as a superior form of religious philosophy look well at its history and its fruit, for "by their fruits ye shall know them" (Matthew 7:20).

Biblical Perspective[27]

Reincarnation can easily be refuted from the Bible by at least ten Old and New Testament doctrines, but for the sake of brevity we have elected to list only four, all of which those believing in Reincarnation deny automatically. These biblical doctrines are:

(A) The Personality of God, (B) The Atonement of Christ, (C) The Physical Resurrection, and (D) Divine Retribution.

(A) For some unknown reason, all Reincarnationists reject the Personality of God, that He is a personal cognizant Spirit, a Divine Ego (Exodus 3:14), capable of a subject-object relationship with man and within the Godhead.

All Reincarnationists, then, are committed to a pantheistic concept of the Deity—God is conceived of as being the fountain of all existence from the tiniest atom to the most gigantic forms of matter, and further, these things are all *part* of His Substance, which permeates every particle *of* existence.

This position that God is all and all is God, or a manifestation of Him, is thoroughly refuted by the following verses of Scripture, which teach incontrovertibly that God is a Personal Spirit possessed of Attributes only a personality has, imminent in creation but apart from it as Creator: Transcendent in that He does not share His spiritual substance (John 4:24; Hebrews 1:3) with the products of His creative will.

1) God "remembers." Isaiah 43:25; Jeremiah 31:20; Hosea 8:13.
2) God "speaks" (subject-object relationship). Exodus 3:12; Matthew 3:17; Luke 17:5.
3) God "hears," "sees," and "creates." Genesis 6:5; Exodus 2:24; Genesis 1:1.
4) God "knows" (has a mind). Jeremiah 21:11; 2 Timothy 2:19; 1 John 3:20.

27. Adapted from Walter Martin, *The Christian and the Cults* (Grand Rapids, MI: Zondervan, 1956), 123–127.

5) God is a personal Spirit. John 4:24; Hebrews 1:3.
6) God has a will. Matthew 6:10; Hebrews 10:7, 9; 1 John 2:17.
7) God will judge. Ezekiel 18:30; 34:20; 2 Corinthians 5:10.

(B) Reincarnation is refuted most decisively by the atonement of Jesus Christ, since the doctrine of the Atonement teaches that God, through Christ's sacrifice on the Cross, has "purged" believers from all their sins (Hebrews 1:3) and counted them righteous for the sake of His Son (2 Corinthians 5:21). Reincarnationists, on the other hand, claim that successive "rebirths" are the instrument of cleansing for the soul and thereby do away with not only the efficacy of the Atonement but the very necessity itself of Christ's dying at all for the sins of the world.

The Bible, however, clearly teaches that "without the shedding of blood is no remission" (Hebrews 9:22) of sin, and Christ purchased the church with His own blood which is not corruptible as silver or gold are (1 Peter 1:18,19) but which is "precious" and the price of the soul's redemption "for it is the blood that maketh an atonement by reason of the life" (see Leviticus 17:11 RSV).

For the adherent of the Reincarnation theory, then, almost endless cycles of rebirth are necessary to cleanse the soul from sin, but for the Christian "the blood of Jesus Christ his Son cleanseth us from all sin" (1 John 1:7). This is the message of the Bible from Genesis to Revelation, redemption by blood through the sacrifice of "him that loved us and washed us from our sins in his own blood" (Revelation 1:5). (For further Scripture references see Matthew 26:28; Romans 5:6–8; Ephesians 1:7; Colossians 1:20, etc.)

(C) The doctrine of the physical resurrection of both Jesus Christ (and all men for that matter) is the foundation stone upon which the validity of Christianity stands, for in the words of the Apostle Paul, "If Christ be not raised, your faith is vain; ye are yet in your sins" (1 Corinthians 15:17). The Bible plainly states that Jesus rose from the grave in a physical form (John 20:27), that He was not raised a spirit (Luke 24:39–44) and that Christ himself after He had risen rebuked His disciples for their unbelief in His physical resurrection (Mark 16:14). It is evident, therefore, that though Jesus Christ was raised physically He had what the Bible terms a "spiritual body" (1 Corinthians 15:44–49), not a spirit form but an immortal, incorruptible physical body possessed of spiritual characteristics forever exempt from death (Romans 6:9), a body the likes of which all believers shall at one day possess at His glorious return and our resurrection (Philippians 3:4; 1 Corinthians 15:52–54).

Reincarnationists, however, do away altogether with physical resurrection and even claim that Christ rose spiritually, not physically, pointing to the facts that Mary Magdalene (John 2:14,15) and the Emmaus disciples did not recognize their risen Lord until He revealed himself (Luke 24:16, 31), whereas if He had risen in His former body, it is claimed they would have known Him immediately. Further than this, such persons often refer to 1 Peter 3:18 where it states that Christ was "made alive in the Spirit," the inference being that His was a spiritual resurrection. These objections, though apparently valid, crumble under the relentless pressure of sound exegesis, for in no way does Christ's veiling His identity from some persons after His Resurrection "prove" that He was not physically raised, as any cursory study of the Greek at the respective texts clearly indicates. The key to understanding these veiled appearances is found in Luke 24:16 and 31, two texts Reincarnationists religiously avoid commenting upon for the obvious reason that a correct exegesis of them *decimates* their spiritual resurrection claims.

Luke 24:16 in the Greek states simply that the eyes of the disciples "were kept from recognizing Him" (Greek *ekratounto*), which proves conclusively that Christ willed that they should behold His features yet be incapable of knowing that it was He, not because His form had changed, but because His will had dictated otherwise!

The other text, Luke 24:31, fully substantiates the Greek of 24:16 by showing that although the disciples had been conversing with Christ, *the eyes of their understanding were closed* by His will so that they could not comprehend until He chose to reveal it, that the risen Christ was their companion (Greek—*dienoichthēsan*, opened).

In regard to 1 Peter 3:18, a word study of the Greek completely corroborates the testimony of Scripture that Christ was raised in a physical form by God the Father but *through* the agency of the Holy Spirit (Romans 8:11). Thus when Peter says "put to death in the flesh," he quickly announces the triumph of God the Father who raised His Son Jesus from the dead (Acts 17:31) "by the Spirit" (1 Peter 3:18). Going beyond this, we further see that Jesus Christ was not raised a Spirit (John 20:28) and that in the Bible a spiritual resurrection is never taught at all, for His body did not know corruption (Acts 2:31, 13:37) and on the third day His Spirit and soul returned to that same body and brought it to life (Matthew 28:9).

Henceforth, it was a glorified body (Philippians 3:21), model of all the bodies of the saints (1 John 3:2). It could pass through walls (John 20:19), but it could be handled and felt (Luke 24:36–39). It could ascend into heaven (Acts 1:9), but before it did so it could eat fish and honey (Luke 24:41–43). What is unmistakably asserted, then, is that while Christ died on Calvary, He was "made alive" in a spiritual body; thus we see that the eternal Word made flesh for the suffering of death ceased living a mortal, fleshly existence and began to live a resurrection life in a spiritual body. As Luther so succinctly stated it:

> . . . Christ by His suffering was taken from the life which is flesh and blood . . . and is now placed in another life and made alive according to the Spirit . . . He has now passed into a spiritual and supernatural life.

The great doctrine of the physical resurrection of all men, saved and unsaved (John 5:28, 29), therefore eliminates the necessity of concurrent reincarnations and proves once more the fallacy of the entire system.

(D) Reincarnation is further refuted by the biblical doctrine of Divine retribution for sin, a doctrine inseparably connected with the nature of man and the state of the dead.

The Bible unmistakably teaches that at the death of the physical form, the soul leaves the body (Genesis 35:18) and, if saved, is instantly transported to the presence of God (2 Corinthians 5:8; Philippians 1:21–23). Those who have rejected Jesus Christ, on the other hand, go instantaneously to hell, a place of conscious separation from God and spiritual torment of a terrible nature (Luke 16:19–31). In addition to this, the Bible further warns that at the last judgment (Matthew 25:31–46) the unsaved dead will be cast into "outer darkness," there to wander *forever* in conscious separation and the indescribable retribution of eternal fire, for the endless ages of eternity (Matthew 8:12; 25:41, 46; 2 Peter 2:17; Jude 13; Revelation 20:15).

> The Bible unmistakably teaches that at the death of the physical form, the soul leaves the body and, if saved, is instantly transported to the presence of God.

Such is the Divine Will, Scripture tells us, for those who have committed the infinite transgression of rejecting God's love as expressed in Jesus Christ (John 3:16, 36). To this eternal pronouncement, Reincarnationists can offer no refutation, only a denial, and the pretended mysticism that dictates cycles of reincarnations in a clever attempt to accomplish what the Lord in His Word has already ordained, perfect justice at the hands of God's Son, the perfect righteous Judge (John 5:22).

Christians do not look forward to reincarnation; we look forward to *resurrection*, when Christ will return and clothe us with glorified bodies so that we may eternally serve and worship God (1 Corinthians 15:5). Our glorification is not accomplished by our own efforts, but by the "victory though our Lord Jesus Christ" (1 Corinthians 15:57). Christians have the assurance from God's Word though the Holy Spirit that "He who raised up Christ from the dead will also give life to your mortal bodies through His Spirit, who lives in you" (Romans 8:11).

Explore

World Soul (or Cosmic Consciousness)
Enlightenment
Nirvana
Mysticism

Discuss

1. Why did Buddha decide to leave Hinduism?

2. Was Buddha influenced by Hinduism?

3. Who is God in Zen teachings?

4. What did Jesus say about Buddha?

_____

_____

Dig Deeper

See *The Kingdom of the Cults Study Guide* available at WalterMartin.com.

10

The Bahá'í Faith

Quick Facts on the Bahá'í Faith

- The Bible is only one of the many sacred texts in the world, but the final authority was the writings of Bahá'u'lláh.
- Bahá'u'lláh fulfilled a worldwide messianic calling, which equated him with other world religion leaders (i.e., Christ, Buddha, Mohammed).
- God is one person. The doctrine of the Trinity is denied.
- Salvation is based upon man's good works coupled with God's mercy. The blood of Jesus Christ is not efficacious to cleanse anyone of sin.

Historical Perspective

The Bahá'í Faith is a non-Christian cult of distinctly foreign origin that began in Iran in the nineteenth century with a young religious Iranian businessman known as Mírzá' Ali Muhammad, who came to believe himself to be a divine manifestation projected into the world of time and space as a "Bab" (Gate) leading to a new era for mankind.

As Christianity, almost since its inception, has had heretics and heresies within its fold, so Islam was destined to experience the same fragmenting forces. Mírzá' Ali Muhammad, alias the "Bab," thus became one of the sorest thorns in the flesh of Islamic orthodoxy, so much so that he was murdered by Islamic fanatics in 1850 at the age of thirty-one. He had derived much of his early encouragement and support from a small Islamic sect in Iran, and he was a prominent teacher among them for six years prior to his death. Though Christians have not been known historically for putting to death those who disagreed with them (notable exceptions are the Reformation and Counter-Reformation, the Inquisition, and certain phases of the Crusades), violence may generally be said to follow in the wake of "new" revelations in most other religions, and unfortunately, in the case of Mírzá' the pattern held true.

The history of the Bahá'í Faith began with the stupendous claims of Mirza Husayn' Ali, a young Iranian who "was not a scholar. He received little formal education while growing up."[1] Yet he took the name Bahá'u'lláh, "asserting that He [sic] is the Messenger of God for all humanity in this day. The cornerstone of His teaching is the establishment of spiritual unity of all humankind, which will be achieved by personal transformation and the application of clearly identified spiritual principles."[2] Apparently, all the other world religious leaders had "forgotten their common origin. . . . Moses, Jesus, and Mohammed were equal prophets, mirroring God's glory, messengers bearing the imprint of the Great Creator."[3]

Today, this still remains the basic tenet of the Bahá'í Faith, albeit with the addition of Abraham, Moses, Zoroaster, Buddha, Jesus, Muhammad, Krishna, an eighth unnamed prophet, and Bahá'u'lláh the last great manifestation of the Divine Being, whose name literally means "the glory of God." The focus of Bahá'ísm is often popularized as "The Oneness of God, The Oneness of Religion, and the Oneness of Humanity."[4]

Modern Bahá'í Faith

Interestingly, the world headquarters of the Bahá'í Faith is in Haifa, Israel, from whence are circulated the writings of Bahá'u'lláh and 'Abdu'l-Bahá. Bahá'u'lláh reputedly left behind him 200 books and tablets, which, along with the writings of his son, constitute the final authority for religious faith and conduct where members of the cult are concerned.

The Bahá'í Faith utilizes the calendar for observances designed by the Bab, which consists of nineteen months, each having nineteen days. New

1. Kenneth E. Bowers, *God Speaks Again: An Introduction to the Bahá'í Faith* (Wilmette, IL: Bahá'í Publishing, 2004), 89.
2. Bowers, *God Speaks Again*, 299.
3. Marcus Bach, *They Have Found a Faith* (Indianapolis, IN: Bobbs-Merrill Company, 1946), 193.
4. Bowers, *God Speaks Again*, 169.

Year's Day falls on March 21. There are no ministers, and no ecclesiastical machinery or organization. The Bahá'ís employ only teachers, who conduct discussion groups in homes or Bahá'í Centers, and who are willing to discuss with anyone the unity of all religion under Bahá'u'lláh.

Bahá'ísm seeks to bring together all faiths in a common world brotherhood, in effect giving men a right to agree to disagree on what the Bahá'ís consider peripheral issues—the main goal being unity on all the great central truths of the world religions, with Bahá'u'lláh as the messiah for our age. 'Abdu'l-Bahá did his work well, and when he died (in 1921) at the age of seventy-seven in what is now Haifa, Israel, he bequeathed a budding missionary arm of his father's faith to Shoghi Effendi (Guardian of the Faith), whose influence continues in and through the teaching hierarchy of the contemporary Bahá'í movement in America.

> Bahá'ísm seeks to bring together all faiths in a common world brotherhood.

Theological Evaluation

The Bahá'ís holy books are the collected writings the Bab, Bahá'u'lláh, 'Abdu'l-Bahá, and the Universal House of Justice, particularly the Kitáb-i-Aqdas (Most Holy Book) and the Kitáb-i-Íqán (Book of Certitude). In the last era, Bahá'u'lláh is "the living Book who proclaimeth the Truth" and his infallibility in Truth shall "not [be] overtaken by error."[5]

The Unity of Threeness is the very core of belief: "The Oneness of God, The Oneness of Religion, and the Oneness of Humanity," but it is also paraphrased as a Unity statement, The Unity of God, The Unity of Religion, and the Unity of Man.

The basic principles of the Bahá'í Faith include the oneness of the world of humanity; the foundation of all religions as one; religion must be the cause of unity; religion must be in accord with science and reason; one must pursue independent investigation of truth; equality between men and women; the abolition of all forms of prejudice; universal peace; universal education; a universal language; the spiritual solution of economic problems; and an international tribunal.

5. Bahá'u'lláh, *Tablets of Bahá'u'lláh Revealed after the Kitáb-i-Aqdas* (Haifa: Bahá'í World Centre, 1978), 8:17.

The laws and obligations of the Bahá'í Faith include to pray and read the Holy Writings (from various religions) daily; to observe the Bahá'í Fast from sunrise to sunset for nineteen days prior to the Bahá'í "New Year" on March 20–21; to teach the cause of God; to contribute to the Bahá'í financial fund; to observe Bahá'í Holy Days, including the Nineteen Day Feast (every nineteen days from New Year's Day); to consider work as worship; to avoid alcohol and other drug abuse; to observe sexual chastity; to obey the government of the land; and to avoid gossip.

The qualifications for becoming a Bahá'í differ from country to country, and it is primarily a matter of individual, private faith. However, when one "catches the spark of Faith," understands the identities of Bahá'u'lláh, the Bab, and 'Abdu'l-Bahá, respects the Bahá'í leadership, and learns and adopts the teachings and laws of Bahá'ísm, then one generally makes a public declaration of faith and is welcomed into his or her local Bahá'í community.[6]

An Interview with a Bahá'í Teacher

In the course of researching the history and theology of Bahá'ísm, this author conducted numerous interviews with authoritative spokespersons for the Bahá'í movement. The following is a transcription of relevant portions of an interview conducted with one well-prepared and candid Bahá'í teacher.[7]

Question: Do you in Bahá'ísm believe in the Holy Trinity?

Answer: If by the Trinity you mean the Christian concept that the three persons—Father, Son, and Holy Spirit—are all the one God, the answer is no.

6. "What Bahá'ís Believe," accessed May 14, 2018, http://www.bahai.org/beliefs.
7. Bahá'í writers have challenged this chapter in two main Internet reviews. Their misguided and irrational conclusions call for a reply because both reviews repeat the same kind of logical fallacies, the body of their argument is a "straw man" fallacy, where they attack a weaker argument instead of what was really written. One such straw-man argument criticized the Bahá'í chapter because they did not like Walter Martin's interview. This ignored Walter Martin's clear statement of purpose: "The above excerpt has much more impact than my analysis alone would have. From an authoritative Bahá'í spokesperson, it most clearly expresses what separates Bahá'ísm from historic Christianity." Both reviews appeal greatly to *ad hominem* arguments, which logical fallacy shows the weakness of their argument by attacking the person instead of the substance of his claim. Both reviews are loaded with vitriolic, mean-spirited, and anger-filled language, which shows their unprofessional attitudes in dealing with someone who disagrees with Bahá'ísm—yet they want us to believe that Bahá'ísm brings peace and unity. For those interested in hearing Dr. Martin's interview, a free Bahá'í audio is available upon request at www.waltermartin.com.

We believe that God is one person in agreement with Judaism and Islam. We cannot accept the idea that God is both three and one and find this foreign to the Bible, which Christianity claims as its source. Not a few Jewish scholars are in complete agreement with us on this point, as is the Koran.

Question: Is Jesus Christ the only manifestation of Deity, that is, is He to be believed when He said, "I am the way, the truth, and the life: no man cometh unto the Father, but by me" (John 14:6)?

Answer: No, we believe that Jesus was only one of nine manifestations of the divine being and appeared in His era of time to illumine those who lived at that time. Today, Bahá'u'lláh is the source of revelation. Jesus was the way, the truth, and the life for His time but certainly not for all time.

"Jesus was only one of nine manifestations of the divine being and appeared in His era of time to illumine those who lived at that time."

'Abdu'l-Bahá points out that we are to honor all the major prophetic voices, not just one of them. He said:

Christ was the prophet of the Christians, Moses of the Jews—why should not the followers of each prophet recognize and honor the other prophets?[8]

'Abdu'l-Bahá also occupied an exalted place in the thinking of Bahá'ís. It was he who said,

The revelation of Jesus was for His own dispensation, that of the Son, and now it is no longer the point of guidance to the world. Bahá'ís must be severed from all and everything that is past—things both good and bad—everything. . . . Now all is changed. All the teachings of the past are past.[9]

Question: Since you believe that Jesus spoke to His own dispensation, how do you account for the fact that in numerous places in the New Testament both He and His apostles and disciples asserted that He was the same "yesterday, and to day, and for ever" (Hebrews 13:8), and that His words were binding and "would never pass away"?

8. *The Wisdom of Baha'u'llah* (Wilmette, IL: Bahá'í Publishing Committee, n.d.), 43.
9. *Star of the West* (Wilmette, IL: Bahá'í Publishing Committee, December 31, 1913), brochure.

Answer: You must realize that many of the things written in the New Testament were written long after Jesus died, hence it is impossible to have absolute accuracy in everything. It would be natural for His followers to assert such things, but the revelation of Bahá'u'lláh supersedes such claims.

Question: The resurrection of Jesus Christ from the dead is the true foundation of Christian experience. Does Bahá'ísm accept His bodily resurrection and ascension into heaven, and do you believe that He is indeed a high priest after Melchizedek order as intercessor before the throne of God for all men?

Answer: The alleged resurrection of Jesus and His ascension into heaven may or may not be true depending upon your point of view. As I said before, we are concerned with Bahá'u'lláh and the new era or age, and while we reverence Jesus as we do the great prophets of other religions, we do not believe that it is necessarily important that the Bahá'í Faith recognize every tenet of a specific religion. We believe that Jesus conquered death, that He triumphed over the grave, but these are things that are in the realm of the spirit and must receive spiritual interpretation.

Question: Then you do not actually believe in the bodily resurrection of Christ?

Answer: Personally, no. But we do believe that resurrection is the destiny of all flesh.

Question: In Jewish theology and Christian theology, much stress is laid upon sacrificial atonement for sin. The theology of Christianity in particular emphasizes that Jesus Christ is the Lamb of God who takes away the sin of the world. It was John the Baptist who so identified Him, and the New Testament gives ample testimony to His substitutionary atonement for the sins of the world. If, as Christianity maintains, "He is the propitiation for our sins: and not for ours only, but also for the sins of the whole world" (1 John 2:2), why, then, is 'Abdu'l-Bahá, or, for that matter, Bahá'u'lláh, important? If God has revealed himself finally and fully as the New Testament teaches in Jesus Christ (Colossians 2:9), why should further manifestation be necessary?

Answer: But, you see, that is precisely our position. God has not finally and fully revealed himself in any of the great manifestations, but through all of them, culminating in Bahá'u'lláh. A Christian may find spiritual peace in believing in a substitutionary atonement. In Bahá'ísm this is unnecessary. That age is past. The new age of spiritual maturity has dawned through Bahá'u'lláh, and we are to listen to his words.

Question: If, as you say, Moses, Buddha, Zoroaster, Confucius, Christ, Mohammed, Krishna, Lowe, and Bahá'u'lláh are all equal manifestations of the divine mind, how do you account for the fact that they contradict each other, for we know that God is not the author of confusion, or is He?

Answer: While it is true that there are discrepancies between the teachings of the great prophets, all held to basic moral and spiritual values. So we would expect unity here, and in the light of man's perverse nature, variety of expression in the writings and teachings of their disciples.

The above excerpt has much more impact than my analysis alone would have. From an authoritative Bahá'í spokesperson, it most clearly expresses what separates Bahá'ísm from historic Christianity. The fact that the major prophets of Bahá'ísm contradict each other is paradoxically overlooked by Bahá'ísm, which in its quest for an ecumenical syncretism prefers to avoid rather than explain the great contradictions between the major faiths.

As do most cults, the Bahá'í Faith will pick and choose out of the Bible that which will best benefit the advancement of their own theology, irrespective of context or theological authority. The author was impressed during this interview with the fact that the Bahá'í teacher who granted it had been a disciple for more than fifty years and was certainly in a position to understand the historic views of Bahá'ísm. Throughout the course of the interview, which was held at a Bahá'í meeting in her home, we had the opportunity time and time again to present the claims of Jesus Christ, and it became apparent that her "god" was Bahá'u'lláh. The Bahá'í plan of salvation is faith in him plus their own good works. Their concept of hell is largely remedial, not punitive. Their eschatology, a combination of Islam, Judaism, and Christianity; and their authority, the writings of Bahá'u'lláh and 'Abdu'l-Bahá.

All of the thirty-some persons present took extreme pride in the fact that they had arrived at a faith that they felt was progressively superior to all other religions, and each was magnanimously willing to embrace the truth that was in every one of them to bring about the new era of which their leader had prophesied.

There was no virgin-born Son, there was only an Iranian student; there was no miraculous ministry, there was only the loneliness of exile; there was no power over demons, there were only demons of Islam; there was no redeeming Savior, there was only a dying old man; there was no risen Savior, there was only 'Abdu'l-Bahá; there was no Holy Spirit, there was only the memory of the prophet; there was no ascended High Priest, there were only the works of the flesh; and there was no coming King, there was only the promise of a new era. In that room the words of the Lord of Hosts were fulfilled with frightening accuracy:

> These people honor me with their lips, but their hearts are far from me. They worship me in vain; their teachings are but rules taught by men (Matthew 15:8–9 NIV).

All the Bahá'í temples in the world and all the quotations from sacred books cannot alter the fact that the heart of man is deceitful above everything and desperately wicked. Who can understand it? Bahá'u'lláh could not, but could his disciples today? Penned in the words of our Lord:

> If ye were blind, ye should have no sin: but now ye say, We see; therefore, your sin remaineth. . . . Ye are from beneath; I am from above: ye are of this world; I am not of this world. I said therefore unto you, that ye shall die in your sins: for if ye believe not that I am he, ye will die in your sins. . . . When ye have lifted up the Son of man, then shall ye know that I am he, and that I do nothing of myself; but as my Father hath taught me, I speak these things. . . . He that believeth on me, believeth not on me, but on him that sent me. . . . And if any man hear my words, and believe not, I judge him not: for I came not to judge the world, but to save the world. He that rejecteth me, and receiveth not my words, hath one that judgeth him: the word that I have spoken, the same shall judge him in the last day. For I have not spoken of myself; but the Father which sent me, he gave me a commandment, what I should say, and what I should speak. And I know that his commandment is life everlasting: whatsoever I speak therefore, even as the Father said unto me, so I speak (John 9:41; 8:23–24, 28; 12:44, 47–50).

Biblical Perspective

Looking back over our survey of Bahá'ísm, we can learn a number of things about this strange cult. First, we can discern that, although it is Islamic in its origin, Bahá'ísm has carefully cloaked itself in Western terminology and has imitated Christianity in forms and ceremonies wherever possible in order to become appealing to the Western mind. The Bible warns us about the imitation of false prophets who masquerade as God's servants—Matthew 24:24; 2 Corinthians 11:13–15; and 2 Peter 2:1.

Second, Bahá'ísm is eager not to come into conflict with the basic principles of the Gospel, and so Bahá'ís are perfectly willing that the Christians should maintain their faith in a nominal sense, just so long as they acknowledge Bahá'u'lláh and the general principles of the Bahá'í Faith. Your Christianity does not have mixed fruit; you cannot pick grapes of thorns or figs of thistles (Matthew 7:16; James 3:12). Mixture in Christianity has always been forbidden (Galatians 1:6–9), but also look at the number of rebukes by Jesus in Revelation 2–3 for compromising, particularly Revelation 2:6, 16–17.

Third, Bahá'ísm deliberately undercuts the foundational doctrines of the Christian faith by either denying them outright or by carefully manipulating terminology so as to "tone down" the doctrinal dogmatism that characterizes orthodox Christianity. All of our doctrines are found in the Bible and not extra-biblical works: "All scripture is given . . . for doctrine . . . correction . . . instruction" (2 Timothy 3:16). Jesus said, "Thy word is truth" (John 17:17), so truth is not found elsewhere.

Bahá'ísm has few of the credentials necessary to authenticate its claims to religious supremacy. An honest Bahá'í will freely admit that in not a few respects their system was patterned after many of the practices of Islam and Christianity.

Bahá'ís will quickly draw upon the scriptures of any religion of their sacred nine to defend the teachings of Bahá'u'lláh and 'Abdu'l-Bahá.[10] In this they have a distinct advantage over the nominal Christian, because not a few of them are well informed concerning the scriptures of the religions of the world, particularly the Old and New Testaments and the Koran. Thus, it is possible for a well-trained Bahá'í cultist literally to run the gamut of the theological quotations in an eclectic mosaic design to establish his

10. The Bahá'í use a nine-point star to represent the nine world religions—nine paths to god: Bahá'í, Buddhism, Christianity, Hinduism, Islam, Jainism, Judaism, Shinto, and Sikhism.

basic thesis, i.e., that all men are part of a great brotherhood revealed in this new era by the manifestation of Bahá'u'lláh.

The cardinal doctrines of the Christian faith, including the absolute authority of the Bible, the doctrines of the Trinity, the deity of Jesus Christ, His Virgin Birth, vicarious atonement, bodily resurrection, and Second Coming are all categorically rejected by Bahá'ísm. They maintain that Christ was *a* manifestation of God, but not the *only* manifestation of the Divine Being.

> An honest Bahá'í will freely admit that in not a few respects their system was patterned after many of the practices of Islam and Christianity.

We must never be ashamed to tell others that Jesus is the exclusive Savior who cannot be replaced. He said "I am *the* way," not *a* way (John 14:6). Luke tells us that there is no other name under heaven that can be given (Acts 4:12). Jesus said that anyone who climbs up by another way, outside of Him, is a thief and a robber (John 10:1–8).

There is very little indeed that a true Christian can have in common with the faith of Bahá'í. There is simply no common ground on which to meet or to talk once the affirmations have been made on both sides of Jesus Christ, as opposed to Bahá'u'lláh. Of course, there is the common ground of Scripture upon which we can meet all men to proclaim to them the indescribable gift of God in the person of Christ, but there can be no ground for fellowship with the Bahá'í Faith, which is, at its very core, anti-Christian theology.

Jesus gave us the basic principle that you cannot serve two masters (Matthew 6:24). Jesus rebuked the Samaritan woman for thinking that her worship was the same as His: "You worship what you do not know; we worship what we do know" (John 4:22 NASB), so not all faiths are the same and they do not lead to God. Friendship with the world is enmity against God (James 4:4).

Finally, as is always the case with non-Christian cults, the refutation of Bahá'ísm must come from a sound knowledge of doctrinal theology as it appears in the Scriptures. No Christian can refute the perversions of the Bahá'í Faith unless he is first aware of their existence and of their conflict with the doctrines of the Bible. We must therefore be prepared to understand the scope of the teachings of the Bahá'ís, their basic conflict with the Gospel, and the means by which we may refute them as we witness for Christ.

Explore

Islamic Heresy
Manifestations of the Divine
Doctrinal Dogmatism
Ecumenical Syncretism

Discuss

1. Who is Bahá'u'lláh?

2. What is the Unity of Threeness?

3. Who is the Jesus of the Bahá'í?

4. What did Jesus teach in John 4:4–26 that proves all faiths are not the same?

Dig Deeper

See *The Kingdom of the Cults Study Guide* available at WalterMartin.com.

11

The Unity School of Christianity

Quick Facts on the Unity School of Christianity

- The Bible is the greatest of many sacred texts. It is not inspired by a personal God and it is not infallible.

- The biblical Trinity is an allegory and does not exist.

- God is not a personal being but *infinite mind* that can be expressed in *matter*.

- Jesus was neither the "Christ" nor God the Son, Second Person of the biblical Trinity—he was a master teacher.

Historical Perspective

The Unity School of Christianity, incorporated in 1914, is perhaps better known under its business names, Unity, Unity Church, or Silent Unity. It remains one of the largest Gnostic cults in Christendom with a reported membership and mailing list of 1 million people and 2 million contacts annually to its Silent Unity division.[1] Since its inception it has also been, by far, the best advertised through the printed page, correspondence courses, and multiple publications that fueled its tremendous growth during the twentieth century—making it the largest mail-order

---

1. Zack Zavada, "Overview of the Association of Unity Churches and Unity School of Christianity," ThoughtCo.com, updated March 17, 2017, https://www.thoughtco.com/unity-church-700123.

religious concern in the world. Its utilization of Internet technology in the twenty-first century has attracted a younger audience with an emphasis on vegetarianism, health, and an inclusive message. Today, it continues its well-funded outreach through the Unity Worldwide Spiritual Institute and Unity.org.

Like other non-Christian cults, Unity adopts biblical language to portray its essentially anti-Christian theological propositions. But when its true theological teachings are projected against the backdrop of biblical revelation and stripped of their protective terminology camouflage, the entire system is revealed to be a Gnostic masquerade and a clever counterfeit of the genuine Gospel of Jesus Christ.

As Phineas P. Quimby was the father of Christian Science, New Thought and Unity, Myrtle Fillmore was the theological mother of Unity. She formed Unity into a system that today resembles all three, but which clings to the special designation, "School." Fillmore was raised a Methodist and earned her living as a schoolteacher. Her early New England background was reflected in the naming of her sons, Lowell and Waldo, after James Russell Lowell and Ralph Waldo Emerson. There is no doubt that she became interested in transcendental philosophy at an early age.

Mrs. Fillmore moved to Kansas City, Missouri, in 1884, and became a convert to Christian Science in 1887. Her conversion to Mary Baker Eddy's version of Phineas Quimby's theology came about when she realized that "I am a child of God and therefore I do not inherit sickness."

Mrs. Fillmore credits her own appropriation of this principle with her healing from a variety of physical problems. She then converted her husband, Charles, a former real estate salesman who had built a considerable fortune, only to lose both it and his health.

Charles Fillmore dabbled in Spiritism and later became interested in Hinduism, from which the Fillmores derived a concept of reincarnation, properly modified, of course, so as to appeal to the Western mind. Burning with zeal for their new religious discovery, Myrtle and Charles Fillmore rented a small hall in Kansas City. Thus began the great religious cult that today encircles the globe.

In April of 1889, the Fillmores published their first magazine, *Modern Thought*, which they changed in 1890 to *Christian Science Thought*. Mary Baker Eddy, however, strongly objected to the Fillmores apparently capitalizing upon the terminology she popularized. Therefore, in 1891 the title of the publication was changed to *Thought*.

The name Unity was adopted in 1891, and as Charles Fillmore stated, "devoted to the spiritualization of humanity from an independent standpoint . . . a religion which . . . took the best from all religions."[2] Unity was a member for many years of the International New Thought Alliance, from which they withdrew in 1922, having far outstripped in membership both New Thought and Christian Science.

During this period, notably, at the Columbian exposition in Chicago in 1893, the Fillmores became intensely interested in the philosophy of Hinduism and Yogaism as later popularized by Swami Vivekananda of India. Charles Fillmore, who was no stranger to the writings of Spiritualists and Theosophists, drew heavily upon this encounter, and became an admirer of Vivekananda, incorporating many of the concepts of Yogaism, reincarnation, diet (vegetarianism), etc., into the theology of the emerging Unity School.[3]

> Unity differs primarily from Christian Science in that it admits that God is expressed in matter as well as in mind or spirit, while Christian Science maintains that matter is illusory and has no real existence.

Unity differs primarily from Christian Science in that it admits that God is expressed in matter as well as in mind or spirit, while Christian Science maintains that matter is illusory and has no real existence.

In 1903 Unity established its own ordination machinery. The Unity Field Department was established in 1918, and in 1921 the Unity Statement of Faith was adopted. Three years after the adoption of the statement, the Fillmores established the Unity Church Universal, which became the Unity annual conference that ordains ministers, approves their standings on a yearly basis, and supervises the operation of Unity centers, radio and television broadcasts, literature, and lecturers.

Charles Fillmore ran Unity alone after Myrtle's death in 1931 until he married his longtime secretary, Cora Dedrick. Following their deaths, Charles' sons assumed control.

2. James Dillet Freeman, *The Story of Unity* (Lees Summit: Unity School of Christianity, 1954), 55, 61.

3. Myrtle Fillmore, as a result of her experience with Christian Science and Swami Vivekananda, went on to found centers throughout the South and Middle West, along with a publishing house from which poured multiple millions of copies of tracts, pamphlets, books and magazines, all propagating the theology of the Fillmores.

From the unusual union of a Methodist turned Christian Scientist and a religious agnostic turned reincarnationist, came the Unity School of Christianity, in which many well-meaning persons are today imprisoned—totally unaware of the great debt that Unity owes to Phineas Quimby, Warren Evans, and Mary Baker Eddy.

The history of Unity is one of unbounded success from humble beginnings, springing from a relatively small gathering of persons under the tutelage of Myrtle Fillmore, who held twice-weekly meetings, setting forth a redefinition of the theology of Phineas P. Quimby and the "love principle, as taught by Christ."

Theological Evaluation

The doctrinal teachings of Unity speak for themselves and must be examined in the light of the Word of God.

1. *The Authority of the Bible*

". . . spiritual principle is embodied in the sacred books of the world's living religions. Christians hold to the Bible as the supreme exponent of spiritual principle. They believe that the Bible is the greatest and most deeply spiritual of all the Scriptures, though they realize that other scriptures, such as the Zend-Avesta and the Upanishads, as well as the teachings of Buddha, the Koran, the Tao of Lao-tse and the writings of Confucius, contain expressions of eminent spiritual truths" (Elizabeth Taylor, *What Unity Teaches*, Lees Summit, MO: Unity School of Christianity, 1952, 4).

". . . Scripture may be a satisfactory authority for those who are not themselves in direct communion with the Lord" (*Unity*, October 1896, vol. 7, 400).

2. *The Triune God (the Trinity)*

"The Father is Principle, the Son is that Principle revealed in the creative plan, the Holy Spirit is the executive power of both Father and Son carrying out the plan" (*Metaphysical Bible Dictionary*, Lee's Summit, MO: Unity School of Christianity, 1931, 629).

"God is not loving. God is love, the great heart of the universe and of man, from which is drawn forth all feeling, sympathy, emotion, and all that goes to make the joys of existence" (Charles Fillmore, *Jesus Christ Heals*, Lee's Summit, MO: Unity School of Christianity, 1947, 27).

"The doctrine of the trinity is often a stumbling block, because we find it difficult to understand how three persons can be one. Three persons cannot be one. . . .

"God is the name of the all-encompassing Mind. Christ is the name of the all-loving Mind. Holy Spirit is the all-active manifestation. These three are one fundamental Mind in its three creative aspects" (Charles Fillmore, *The Revealed Word*, Lee's Summit, MO: Unity School of Christianity, 1959, 200).

3. *The Deity of Jesus Christ*

"Christ, meaning 'messiah' or 'anointed' designates one who had received a spiritual quickening from God, while Jesus is the name of the personality. To the metaphysical Christian—that is, to him who studies the spiritual man—Christ is the name of the supermind and Jesus is the name of the personal consciousness. The spiritual man is God's Son; the personal man is man's son" (Fillmore, *Jesus Christ Heals*, 10).

"Jesus Christ Himself was a parable, and his life an allegory of the experiences that man passes through in development from natural to spiritual consciousness" (Charles Fillmore, *Christian Healing*, Lee's Summit, MO: Unity School of Christianity, 1942, 68).

> "Jesus Christ Himself was a parable, and his life an allegory."

"Christ is the only begotten Son of God, the one complete idea of perfect man and divine Mind. This Christ or perfect-man idea existing eternally in divine Mind is the true, spiritual, higher-self of every individual" (Fillmore, *Metaphysical Bible Dictionary*, 150).

4. *The Resurrection*

"Eventually all souls reincarnate on the earth as babes and in due time take up their problems where they left off at death" (Fillmore, *Teach Us to Pray*, 50).

". . . Jesus demands of the Pharisees, 'What think ye of Christ? whose son is he?' They answered, not as one might ordinarily expect, 'The son of Joseph,' but *'The son* of David.' In other words He was the reincarnation of David" (Ernest C. Wilson, *Have We Lived Before?* Kansas City: Unity, 1936, 41).

Biblical Perspective

The theology of the Unity cult, as revealed in the previously quoted extracts from some of its standard publications, is far removed indeed from the Gospel of Jesus Christ as preached by the early apostles and as transmitted through the centuries by faithful witnesses of God in each age.

1. *The Bible*

Proof that Unity continues to spiritualize and allegorize all passages of the Bible that are in direct contradiction to their jumbled theological structure can be found in any edition of *Unity* magazine, where the International Sunday School Lessons (a biblical presentation) are reinterpreted in the framework of Unity theology.

In company with Mrs. Eddy and most other gnostic religious thinkers, Unity refuses the historic exegetical positions of the Bible, and deliberately shuns any controversy with informed Bible scholars, lest their shallow pretentions and fraudulent scholarship be exposed to the glaring light of biblical truth. The Christian faith is founded upon belief in the Bible as the Word of God or as Paul put it, "All Scripture is given by inspiration of God [God-breathed], and is profitable for doctrine, for reproof, for correction, for instruction in righteousness: That the man of God may be perfect, thoroughly furnished unto all good works" (2 Timothy 3:16–17).

The Lord Jesus Christ, in referring to the Word of His Father, said, "Sanctify them through thy truth: thy word is truth" (John 17:17); and it was the Psalmist who stated, "For ever, O Lord, thy word is settled in heaven" and "Thy word is very pure" (Psalm 119:89, 140).

It is a well-known fact that Christ, during His lifetime, recognized the threefold division of the Old Testament—the law, the prophets, and the writings, and referred to them in their proper order at various times during the course of His ministry. Therefore, it is inconceivable that the early church should not have held in great esteem the record of the Old Testament, as well as the then-forming record of the new covenant, for which many of them eventually were to pay with their very life's blood.

Christians of all denominations who confess the cardinal doctrines of the Scripture (the Trinity, the Deity of Christ, the Virgin Birth, the Sinless Nature of Christ, the Vicarious Atonement, the Physical Resurrection, the Second Coming of Christ, etc.), recognize the importance of accepting the Bible in its historic and linguistic framework. Only those with no concern for the testimony of history and the facts of sound exegesis allegorize and spiritualize texts that they know reinforce the foundational doctrines of historic Christianity.

The adherents of the Unity cult are guilty of allegorization and spiritualization of all the cardinal doctrines of the Christian faith, and rather than criticize outright the statements of Scripture, they subtly undercut the great pronouncements of the Word of God by reinterpreting them, allegorizing them, and spiritualizing them, until they have sapped all of the revealed power of the Word of God, twisted it into the mold of the Fillmore religion and, in effect, "wrested the Scriptures to their own destruction" (2 Peter 3:16).

> Unity allegorizes and spiritualizes all the cardinal doctrines of the Christian faith.

Let us keep in mind, then, that the members of the Unity cult speak devotedly of the Bible, but they utilize the Bible *only* insofar as it can be wielded as a successful tool to lure the unwary soul into the meshes of the Fillmore cult. But for the true Christian, the Bible in its proper context and framework of history must ever remain the Word of God, inviolate, the final authority for the Church of Jesus Christ and the individual Christian life.

2. *The Trinity*

It is the clear teaching of the Word of God that the nature of God is spirit (John 4:24), and further, that He has manifested himself in the Old Testament in different ways (the Angel of Jehovah—Exodus 23:20; Judges 6:12 and 13; Judges 13, etc.; the Son of God—Daniel 3:25; as Emmanuel, *God with us*—Isaiah 7:14, etc.). In the eighteenth chapter of Genesis, for instance, it is recorded that Abraham entertained three visitors on the plains of Mamre, two of whom were angels (Genesis 19:1), the other whom Abraham addressed fourteen times as Jehovah God!

To further clarify the picture where an understanding of the true nature of God is concerned, the Bible in the creation account (Genesis 1:26, 27) quotes the Lord as saying, "Let *us* make man in *our* image, after *our* likeness. . . . So God created man in his own image, in the image of God created he him; male and female created he them," utilizing the Hebrew plural "us" and "our" while at the same time returning to the singular "his" in verse 27, clearly a Trinitarian indication.

As we approach the New Testament revelation of God we also find something far beyond the Jewish interpretation of solitary unity (Deuteronomy 6:4), for both at the baptism of the Lord Jesus Christ and His last resurrection appearance (Matthew 3:16–17; cf. Matthew 28:19), three distinct Persons are viewed as the one God, and nothing could be clearer than Christ's command to baptize in this threefold name of the Deity, Jehovah!

The God of the Bible and Father of our Lord Jesus Christ is a personal Being, a personal Spirit. This Almighty Person performs acts that only a personality is capable of: God hears (Exodus 2:24); God sees (Genesis 1:4); God creates (Genesis 1:1); God knows (2 Timothy 2:19; Jeremiah 29:11); God has a will (1 John 2:17); God is a cognizant reflectable ego, i.e., a personal being "I AM THAT I AM" (Exodus 3:14; Genesis 17:11). This is the God of Christianity, an omnipotent, omniscient, and omnipresent Personality, who manifests every attribute of a personality. He is therefore definitely not the God of Unity theology, for Unity teaches that "belief" in a personal God has retarded the progress of the race![4]

According to the theology of Unity, "The Father is principle, the Son is that principle revealed in the creative plan, the Holy Spirit is the executive power of both Father and Son, carrying out the plan" (Fillmore, *Metaphysical Bible Dictionary*, 629). However, this description does not coincide with the biblical revelation of the character of God, for Unity is at its very core a pantheistic form of religion, maintaining that man is in effect, part of God; whereas the Scriptures clearly teach that man is the result of God's creative power and separate from Him, as every creation is by its very nature, separate from its creator.

Bear in mind that whenever the adherents of Unity speak of "God," they do not speak of the God of Christianity or of the Judeo-Christian heritage. They speak, instead, of an abstract Principle, a divine Mind, which in no sense has a personality, neither can "it" be addressed as a personal being.

Unity perverts the doctrine of the Trinity, spiritualizing the very terms used to describe the relationship between the members of the godhead (Father, Son, Holy Spirit), and this dishonest practice should be unmasked at every opportunity by those interested enough in the truth concerning the character of God as we find it within the pages of Scripture.

4. Sarah B. Scott, *The True Character of God* (Lee's Summit, MO: Unity School of Christianity, n.d.), 3.

3. *The Deity of Christ*

One needs only to peruse superficially the literature of the Unity cult to realize quickly that in the theology of Unity, Jesus Christ is not the God-man of the New Testament doctrine.

The New Testament, which is in reality the continuation or the unfolding of the expression of God's will under the old covenant, categorically teaches that Jesus Christ is the Eternal Word of God (John 1:1), that He took upon Himself the form of a man (John 1:14; Philippians 2:6, 7), and further, that He is the Redeemer of Israel and the Savior of the world (Matthew 1:21–24; Acts 4:12).

Unity, in company with Christian Science, New Thought, Religious Science, etc., divides Jesus and Christ, reducing the God-man of Scripture to a perfect man indwelt by the Christ-consciousness, a consciousness present in *every* human being that only needs to be cultivated and developed—or as the *Metaphysical Bible Dictionary* states, "Christ is the only begotten son of God with one complete idea of perfect man and divine Mind. This Christ, or perfect-man idea, existing eternally in divine Mind is the true spirit and higher self of every individual."[5] We see, then, that all men are miniature "christs" so to speak, and in no sense whatsoever does Unity teach the intrinsic Deity and uniqueness of the incarnate Word of God.

By subtly making a differentiation between the man Jesus and "the Christ, the spiritual identity of Jesus," Unity attempts to divest the Lord Jesus Christ of His true identity, which the Scriptures reveal to be that of incarnate Deity (see Isaiah 9:6; John 5:18; Colossians 1:15–18; 2:9; Revelation 1:7, 8, 17, 18).

Charles Fillmore, in *Christian Healing*, counsels the adherents of Unity that when in doubt "claim your Christ understanding at all times . . ." which in one short phrase sums up the position of Unity regarding the Lord Jesus Christ.[6] For Mr. Fillmore taught that "Christ" is in reality "the superconscious mind, Christ-conscious, or spiritual-consciousness. . . ." (*Metaphysical Bible Dictionary*, 155), a position which is directly opposed to the teaching of Scripture. There has been but one Christ, of whom Peter spoke when he said, "Neither is there salvation in any other: for there is none other name under heaven given among men, whereby we must be

5. Fillmore, *Metaphysical Bible Dictionary*, 150.
6. Fillmore, *Christian Healing*, 106, 107.

saved," and "this same Jesus, God hath made Lord and Christ" (Acts 4:12; 2:36).

Jesus Christ, then, was not Jesus and Christ as the Unity cultists would have us believe; rather, He was the biblical *God-man-two natures in one being*, "Jesus Christ the same, yesterday and to day and for ever" (Hebrews 13:8). The Lord Jesus Christ unmistakably identified himself with Jehovah (John 8:58) when He stated that "Before Abraham was, I AM" (cf. Exodus 3: 14). And it is this one fact that establishes the unity of Christ with the Eternal Trinity—Father, Son, and Holy Spirit—and establishes beyond question in the mind of any intelligent exegetical student of Scripture the identity and Deity of Jesus Christ. "This is the true God, and eternal life" (1 John 5:20).

4. *The Resurrection of Christ*

Unity, through its various publications and especially its *Statement of Faith*, Article 22, has gone on record as stating the following things relative to the Resurrection.

"We believe the dissolution of spirit, soul and body, caused by death, is annulled by rebirth of the same spirit and soul in another body here on earth. We believe the repeated reincarnations of man are the merciful provision of our loving Father to the end that all may come to obtain immortality through regeneration, as did Jesus."

In lieu of the great doctrine of the bodily resurrection as taught in both the Old and the New Testaments, the Unity cult teaches cycles of reincarnation until eventual perfection is reached. The true Christian position concerning death, however, is taught in numerous places in Scripture. For example, in 2 Corinthians 5:8, Paul emphatically states that "to be absent from the body is to be present with the Lord [or at home with the Lord]." And again, in Philippians 1:21–23, the great apostle anticipates his departure from this life to be with Christ, and certainly not to go through repeated lives.

To refute the Unity position, reincarnation vs. resurrection, the reader is referred to the fifteenth chapter of 1 Corinthians where the doctrine of the physical resurrection of the body to immortality is clearly stated. After reading this, the observant reader will immediately note the difference between the theology of Paul under the inspiration of the Holy Spirit, and the theology of the Fillmores and Unity, via the medium of the "great deceiver"!

In *Jesus Christ Heals*, Charles Fillmore wrote: "Salvation through Jesus Christ is not accomplished by looking forward to freedom but by realizing that we are now free through His freeing power, which we are using to cut the bonds with which our thoughts have bound us. Then we have only to establish ourselves in real life and strength by understanding that these attributes of Being are omnipresent and that our affirmations of that presence, will cause us to become conscious that we do now and here live, move, and have our being in eternal life and strength."[7] The Unity cult has not departed from this teaching of Fillmore, which directly contradicts the testimony of the Lord Jesus Christ when He said, "Let not your heart be troubled, ye believe in God, believe also in me. In my Father's house are many mansions: if it were not so I would have told you. I go to prepare a place for you. And if I go and prepare a place for you, I will come again and receive you unto myself; that where I am, there ye may be also" (John 14:1–3).

Contrary to the teachings of Unity then, "It is appointed unto men once to die, but after this the judgment" (Hebrews 9:27); and "It is a fearful thing to fall into the hands of the living God" (Hebrews 10:31) are pronouncements that, while they held no terror for the Fillmores during their long lives, doubtless are more meaningful today.

The Reincarnation Theory of Unity

The theory of reincarnation, transmigration, or rebirth is best described briefly as a process where at the death of the body, the soul passes into the bodies of lower animals or other human beings in an ever-rotating cycle (from body to body) until purification from sin is accomplished. When this sinless state has been attained, the soul passes thence to Nirvana (Buddhism) or the dwelling place of Brahma (Hinduism). These places consist of nothing more than "the eternal peace," reached by absorption of the soul and all vestiges of individual personality into the world soul or whatever philosophical abstraction it may constitute.

In Unity, as in Theosophy, humans reincarnate only as humans, not as lower forms of life. Both Helena Blavatsky and the Fillmores redefined reincarnation to make it more palatable to the Western mind. Blavatsky wrote, "Reincarnation means that this Ego will be furnished with a *new* body, a *new* brain, and a *new* memory."[8]

7. Fillmore, *Jesus Christ Heals*, 165.
8. H.P. Blavatsky, "Reincarnation and Karma," Blavatsky Study Center, *BlavatskyArchives. com*, http://blavatskyarchives.com/blavatskykarmareincarnation.htm.

In the case of Unity, reincarnation has been given a new façade. A good deal of "evidence" has been introduced by them to show that the Unity concept of reincarnation is not only logical and rational, but that it is the only "reasonable" solution to many so-called insoluble problems that orthodox Christianity cannot solve.

We shall consider at this time only those evidences most frequently submitted, the remainder being largely peripheral in character.

The Evidence

These four points in one form or another make up the basic premises upon which the theory of reincarnation is based:

(1) There are persons, places, and experiences that we already know—we do not have to become acquainted with them. Somehow, we feel we already recognize them. Have you ever felt that you have been to a place or known a person before you experienced the meeting? This is evidence of reincarnation.

(2) All men are not born equal in regard to either station in life, opportunity, or condition of health. Some babies are born blind, deaf, or diseased—many persons are cut down in the flower of youth. If God is just, He cannot allow such things to happen to the apparently innocent. Therefore, He must be punishing them for their previous sins while in another form, and this will continue on until all are purified of past mistakes. Reincarnation, then, is the only fair evidence of God's being perfectly just to all men.

(3) Unfinished thoughts and unfinished work abound in everyone's experience, and God could not justly waste these undeveloped talents. Rather, He gives us countless opportunities to utilize them by supplying concurrent rebirths in which to bring our thoughts and works to fruition.

(4) Many documented and verified cases of persons who have been able to recount their previous lives in detail are recorded in the files of reputable professional hypnotists, psychologists, and research organizations. These cases establish the fact of reincarnation beyond reasonable doubt and are available for evaluation.

Abundant "evidence" is also submitted from the "inspired" writings of numerous Eastern religions and Western cults, but the pattern is always uniformly the same. The Unity School, however, differs slightly from the more "orthodox" systems of transmigration in that Unity claims that reincarnation is a "Christian doctrine" and that the Bible fully teaches and supports it as such.[9] Some of the common texts cited are: Matthew 16:17; 17:11; 22:42; John 9:2; Revelation 5:5 and 22:16. We shall discuss these and their contextual meanings contrasted with the interpretation of Reincarnationists a little later on, but the fact remains that not a few have dared to claim support from the Scriptures for this pagan dogma.

The Biblical Position

Reincarnation can easily be refuted from the Bible by at least ten Old and New Testament doctrines, but for the sake of brevity, we have elected to list only four, all of which those believing in reincarnation, including the Unity School, deny automatically in accepting their transmigration hypothesis. These biblical doctrines are: (1) The Personality of God; (2) The Atonement of Christ; (3) The Physical Resurrection; and (4) Divine Retribution.

1. For some unknown reason, all Reincarnationists reject the Personality of God, that He is a personal cognizant Spirit, a divine Ego (Exodus 3:14) capable of a subject-object relationship with man and within the Godhead.

All Reincarnationists, then, are committed to a pantheistic concept of Deity—that God is conceived of as being the fountain of all existence from the tiniest atom to the most gigantic forms of matter, and further, these things are all part of His Substance, which permeates every particle of existence.

This position that God is all and all is God or a manifestation of Him, is thoroughly refuted by the following verses of Scripture, which teach incontrovertibly that God is a Personal Spirit possessed of attributes that only a personality has, immanent in creation, but apart from it as Creator. Transcendent in that He does not share His spiritual substance (John 4:24; Hebrews 1:3) with the products of His creative will.

A. God remembers. Isaiah 43:25; Jeremiah 31:20; Hosea 8:13.

B. God speaks (subject-object relationship). Exodus 3:12; Matthew 3:17; Luke 17:6.

9. Wilson, *Have We Lived Before?*, 28.

C. God sees, hears, and creates. Genesis 6:5; Exodus 2:24; Genesis 1:1.

D. God knows (has a mind). Jeremiah 29:11; 2 Timothy 2:19; 1 John 3:20.

E. God is a personal spirit. John 4:24; Hebrews 1:3.

F. God has a will. Matthew 6:10; Hebrews 10:7, 9; 1 John 2:17.

G. God will judge. Ezekiel 18:30; 34:20; 2 Corinthians 5:10.

2. Reincarnation is refuted most decisively by the atonement of Jesus Christ, since the doctrine of the Atonement teaches that God, through Christ's sacrifice on the cross, has "purged" believers from all their sins (Hebrews 1:3) and counted them righteous for the sake of His Son (2 Corinthians 5:21). Reincarnationists, on the other hand, claim that successive "rebirths" are the instrument of cleansing for the soul and thereby do away with not only the efficacy of the atonement, but the very necessity itself of Christ's dying at all for the sins of the world.

The Bible, however, clearly teaches that "without the shedding of blood is no remission" (Hebrews 9:22) of sin, and Christ purchased the church with His own blood which is not corruptible as silver or gold are (1 Peter 1:18, 19), but which is precious and the price of the soul's redemption.

For the Unity adherent of the reincarnation theory, the almost endless cycles of rebirth are necessary to cleanse the soul from sin. But for the Christian, the blood of Jesus Christ, God's Son, cleanses us from all sin (1 John 1:9). This is the message of the Bible from Genesis to Revelation, redemption by blood through the sacrifice of "him that loved us and washed us from our sins in his own blood" (Revelation 1:5). (For further Scriptures see Matthew 26:28; Romans 5:6–8; Ephesians 1:7; Colossians 1:20, etc.)

3. The doctrine of the physical resurrection of Jesus Christ (and all men, for that matter!) is the foundation stone upon which the validity of Christianity stands, for in the words of the Apostle Paul—"If Christ be not raised, your faith is vain; ye are yet in your sins" (1 Corinthians15:17). The Bible plainly states that Jesus arose from the grave in a physical form (John 20:27), that He was not raised a spirit (Luke 24:39–44) and that Christ Himself after He had risen, rebuked His disciples for their unbelief in His physical Resurrection (Mark 16:14). It is evident, therefore, that though Jesus Christ was raised physically, He had what the Bible terms a "spiritual body" (1 Corinthians 15:44–49), not a spirit form, but an immortal, incorruptible physical body possessed of spiritual characteristics forever

exempt from death (Romans 6:9), a body the like of which all believers shall one day possess at His glorious return and our resurrection (1 John 3:2; 1 Corinthians 15:52–54).

Unity does away altogether with physical resurrection, and even claims that Christ rose spiritually, not physically, pointing to the facts that Mary Magdalene (John 20:14, 15) and the Emmaus disciples did not recognize their risen Lord until He revealed Himself (Luke 24:16, 31). Unity claims they would have known Him immediately if His body had been a physical resurrection. Further than this, such persons often refer to 1 Peter 3:18, where it states that Christ was "made alive in the spirit," the inference being that His was a spiritual resurrection. These objections, though apparently valid, crumble under the relentless pressure of sound exegesis, for in no way does Christ's veiling His identity from some persons after His Resurrection prove that He was not physically raised, as any cursory study of the Greek at the respective texts clearly indicates. The key to understanding these veiled appearances is found in Luke 24:16 and 31, two texts Reincarnationists religiously avoid commenting upon for the obvious reason that a correct exegesis of them destroys their spiritual resurrection claims.

Luke 24:16 in the Greek states simply that the eyes of the disciples "were kept from recognizing Him" (Greek *ekratounto*), which proves conclusively that Christ willed that they should behold His features yet be incapable of knowing that it was He, not because His form had changed but because His will had dictated otherwise!

The other text, Luke 24:31, fully substantiates the Greek of 24:16 by showing that, although the disciples had been conversing with Christ, *the eyes of their understanding were closed* by His will, so that they could not comprehend until He chose to reveal it, that the risen Christ was their companion (Greek *dienoichthesan*—opened).

In regard to 1 Peter 3:18, a word study of the Greek completely corroborates the testimony of Scripture that Christ was raised in a physical form by God the Father but *through* the agency of the Holy Spirit (Romans 8:11). Thus, when Peter says "put to death in the flesh," he quickly announces the triumph of God the Father, who raised His Son Jesus from the dead (Acts 17:31) "by the Spirit" (1 Peter 3:18). Going beyond this, we further see that Jesus Christ was not raised *a* Spirit (John 20:28) and that in the Bible a spiritual resurrection is never taught at all, for His body did not know corruption (Acts 2:31; 13:37) and on the third day His Spirit and soul returned to that *same* body and brought it to life (Matthew

28:9). Henceforth, it was a glorified body (Philippians 3:21), a model of all the bodies of the saints (1 John 3:2). It could pass through walls (John 20:19), but it could be handled and felt (Luke 24:36–39). It could ascend into heaven (Acts 1:9), but before it did so, it could eat fish and honey (Luke 24:41–43). What is unmistakably asserted is that while Christ died on Calvary, He was "made alive" in a spiritual body; thus we see that the eternal Word made flesh for the suffering of death ceased living a mortal, fleshly existence, and began to live a resurrection life in a spiritual body. As Luther so succinctly stated,

> Christ by His suffering was taken from the life which is flesh and blood . . . and is now placed in another life and made alive according to the Spirit . . . He has now passed into a spiritual and supernatural life.[10]

The great doctrine of the physical resurrection of all men, saved and unsaved (John 5:28–29), eliminates the necessity of concurrent reincarnations and proves once more the fallacy of the entire system.

4. Reincarnation is further refuted by the biblical doctrine of divine retribution for sin, a doctrine inseparably connected with the nature of man and the state of the dead.

The Bible unmistakably teaches that at the death of the physical form, the soul leaves the body (Genesis 35:18) and if saved, is instantly transported to the Presence of God (2 Corinthians 5:8; Philippians 1:21–23). Those who have rejected Jesus Christ, on the other hand, go instantaneously to hell, a place of conscious separation from God and spiritual torment of a terrible nature (Luke 16:19–31). In addition to this, the Bible further warns that at the last judgment (Matthew 25:31–46) the unsaved dead will be cast into "outer darkness," there to be forever in conscious separation and the indescribable retribution of eternal fire for the endless ages of eternity (Matthew 8:12; 25:41, 46; 2 Peter 2:17; Jude 13; Revelation 20:15).

Such is the divine Will, Scripture tells us, for those who have committed the infinite transgression of rejecting God's love as expressed in Jesus Christ (John 3:16, 36). To this eternal pronouncement, reincarnationists can offer no refutation, only a denial and the pretended mysticism that dictates cycles of reincarnations—a clever attempt to accomplish what

10. Martin Luther, *Epistles of St. Peter & St. Jude Preached & Explained by Martin Luther*, 160.

the Lord in His Word has already ordained, perfect justice at the hands of God's Son, the perfect righteous Judge (John 5:22).

In order to join Unity, it must be understood that one would have to renounce every basic doctrine of the Christian faith—denying the Deity, physical resurrection and personal Second Coming of our Lord, and believing in the reincarnation of the soul as opposed to the doctrine of the physical resurrection of the body.

Let us not forget that under the apparent sugar-coated shell of tolerance and pseudo-love that characterizes Unity there lies a subtle, but firm, denial of the basic principles of the Gospel of Jesus Christ.

To those who would drink at this well of supposed spiritual refreshment, our warning must be clear and definite:

> Try the spirits whether they are of God: because many false prophets are gone out into the world (1 John 4:1).

Even in this brief study of the Unity cult, no objective student of Scripture can deny that Unity is distinctly within the boundaries of this warning, and we would be bereft of wisdom not to listen to this counsel from the Word of God.

Explore

Allegory
Terminology Camouflage
Exegetical
Western Reincarnation

Discuss

1. What is the principle Myrtle Fillmore embraced?

2. What is the all-encompassing mind?

3. According to the Bible, reincarnation cannot be part of the cycle of life. Why not?

4. Where in the Bible does it say that the physical body of Jesus was resurrected?

─────────────────── **Dig Deeper** ───────────────────

See *The Kingdom of the Cults Study Guide* available at WalterMartin.com.

12

Armstrongism, the Worldwide Church of God, and Grace Communion International

Quick Facts on Armstrongism, The Worldwide Church of God, and Grace Communion International

- Armstrongism teaches that the Bible is God's Word, but it is best interpreted by Herbert W. Armstrong—God's Apostle.
- Jesus and the Father are two gods of the "God Family."
- The Holy Spirit is not God and not a person within the nature of God.
- The resurrection of Jesus was spiritual, not physical.

Historical Perspective

Cults come and go, but rare indeed is the repentance of cult leadership that results in heresy being replaced with biblical Christianity. Such is the story of the Worldwide Church of God. Once known far and wide as the cult of Armstrongism, it chose, through repentance, to join hands with conservative Christians in heralding the Gospel.

The Worldwide Church of God, originally founded by Herbert W. Armstrong (1892–1986), was led through this remarkable change by his successor, Joseph W. Tkach (1927–1995). He reversed Armstrong's most damnable doctrines in full acceptance of the Trinity, Christ's divinity and humanity, the person and deity of the Holy Spirit, the bodily resurrection of Jesus, and salvation by grace through faith alone.

In 1991 Kurt Van Gorden, Senior Researcher for *The Kingdom of the Cults* and Dr. Alan Gomes of the Talbot School of Theology, met with the leadership of the Worldwide Church of God to discuss its transitioning doctrinal stance. At that time, the church still believed Herbert W. Armstrong's view that God comprised two persons, the Father and Son. This was prior to their embracing the Trinity.[1] They were rapidly admitted into the National Evangelical Association in 1997, and everything seemed positive.[2] Surmounting numerous hurdles, like shrinking membership, splinter groups, litigation, dropping finances, was not an easy task, but the steadfast leadership of Joseph Tkach, Jr. proved successful. To further distance the Worldwide Church of God from the erring splinter groups they officially changed their name to Grace Communion International (GCI) in 2009.

Based upon that foundation, we and other Evangelicals who met with the transitioning leadership, gave them a "clean bill of health." It was expected that they would grow from there, so the 1998 edition of *The Kingdom of the Cults* published a glowing commendation about their changes, which the church excerpted and kept on their website for several years. Moving from cultism to Christianity is not an easy task, which is why individuals and small groups of people who leave cults are encouraged to seek support for their transition, because we have seen multiple cases where it is too easy to slide back into error if there is insufficient grounding in the Bible and Christianity.

> They have embraced a host of new teachers who bring a mixed bag of truth and error.

The Worldwide Church of God hit the ground running in the mid-1990s and was surrounded by helpful theologians who guided their theological quest. In recent times, however, they have embraced a host of new teachers who bring a mixed bag of truth and error, particularly in a branch of universal reconciliation salvation. This mixture strays from the clean bill of health with which they began.

1. See Alan W. Gomes and Kurt Van Gorden, "Special Report: The Worldwide Church of God in Transition," *Christian Research Journal*, Spring 1992, 35. We were delighted when they fully accepted the historic Trinity position and renounced a number of Mr. Armstrong's false teachings.

2. In 1998 their official website stated, "Armstrong had many unusual doctrines. . . . After Armstrong died in 1986, church leaders began to realize that many of Armstrong's doctrines were not biblical. These doctrines were rejected" (http://www.wcg.org:80/lit/AboutUs/brieflist.htm).

The GCI is aware that these fringe beliefs compromise integrity. Numerous Christians wrote to them through their website to challenge their new doctrinal paradigms, but to no avail, except that the GCI published disclaimers to deny that they are outright Universalists, pantheists, or panentheists. If the statements of a Christian group are so unclear that it causes their members and outsiders to ask them if they have strayed, then that should sound an alarm that they are sailing in uncharted waters and danger lurks ahead.

Mystical Union and Variant Teachings

The GCI still holds commendable doctrinal positions that remain unaltered and are very clearly articulated, as on the Trinity (God is Father, Son, and Holy Spirit), salvation by grace, and Christ's bodily resurrection, and their denial of Armstrong's British-Israelism, the God-family, and legalism. Although far from erring to the point of being non-Christian, there still have been some recent misguided shifts on important doctrines.

In distinguishing God's essential nature from his economy and relationship with man, the first remains the same, but the latter has shifted somewhat by adopting a mystical or esoteric explanation of our future relationship to God. They describe this in terms of "Incarnational Trinity," "participation" or "union" *in* the Trinity," and "the great dance" of the Trinity. They express this by quoting Dr. C. Baxter Kruger: "The Spirit's passion is to bring his anointing of Jesus to full and personal and abiding expression in us as unique persons, and not only in us personally, but in our relationship with the Father in Jesus, and in our relationships with one another, and indeed with all creation, *until the whole cosmos is a living sacrament of the great dance of the Triune God.*"[3]

The article's accompanying artwork depicts three overlapping colored circles to represent the Trinity (which is a common visual aid for articles about God), but what is uncommon is that the website adds two human figures standing inside the Son's circle within the Trinity, thus placing mankind in mystical union in the Trinity. Kruger is careful in another article to state that we do not lose our personal identity, as in pantheism, for this incarnational dance, which he calls "The Great Dance," that we have with

3. Ted Johnson, "What Is Incarnational Trinitarian Theology?," *The Surprising God*, GCI. org, accessed May 1, 2018, http://thesurprisinggodblog.gci.org/p/what-is-trinitarian-incarnational .html. Emphasis added.

God. This kind of language is quite unfortunate and it too closely resembles the Hindi language about Shiva—the cosmic dancing god of Hinduism.[4]

In one GCI video, Kruger is mindful that he is echoing error, so he clarified his position so listeners would not think that he promotes "pantheism." Similarly, the GCI theologian, Dr. Gary Deddo, published an article to make sure readers also do not mistake the GCI message as a similar heresy, "panentheism."[5] Apparently not all dances with God are good, either, because Deddo labeled the new book *Divine Dance* (Whitaker House, 2017), by the Emerging Church writer Richard Rohr, as a "panentheist" example. Yet Deddo also failed to tell his readers that the GCI video-celebrity, William Paul Young (*The Shack*), endorsed Rohr's panentheistic book by writing its foreword. That incongruity remains unresolved.

Since the GCI is not Eastern Orthodox, it seems out of step that they would place so much emphasis on the Orthodox concept of *theosis* (deification of divinity of man) that surfaces on their website. Even though they explain it in different terms than Orthodoxy, its apparent purpose is to explore the mystical "union" language used by their associated teachers (Young, Kruger, and others) concerning how humans "participate" in the Triune God. For example, their theologian, Michael Morrison, states this about the divinity doctrine, *theosis*: "Just because Eastern mystics used the term doesn't mean that they've got the corner on it."[6] But in this interview, Myk Habets clarified it: "We can't become God. God purposed in Christ that we could have the next-best thing. We can be in Christ, who is God, and he calls us children, not slaves. We can participate." This is the rub. When attempting to blend Evangelical teachings with the terminology of "Eastern mystics" or Emerging Church teachers, we will end up with a bad mixture. But what is also surprising here is that the GCI already left a false

4. Kruger, Young, Rohr, and others describe the Christian God as if he were the Hindu god Shiva, who is the cosmic ecstatic dancer, as often seen in Hindu artwork. Such language is found nowhere in the Bible and was totally foreign to Christianity until these recent writers surfaced. The GCI places disclaimers on some of their web pages stating, "Though GCI embraces the theology discussed here, blog posts are not official denominational statements." Ibid. However, this is a two-edged sword; if you put something false, for example, on your website without refutation, then you have given tacit approval of its content and teaching. Simply stating that you *may* disagree does not state *where* you disagree and the potential of spiritual harm to your readers makes you responsible.

5. Gary Deddo, "Avoiding the Pitfall of Panentheism," updated November 30, 2016, https://update.gci.org/2016/11/beware-panentheistic-teachings.

6. Michael Morrison, "Theosis: Participation in the Divine Nature—An Interview with Myk Habets," accessed May 1, 2018, https://www.gci.org/yi/habtes4. See also https://www.gci.org/articles/theosis-participation-in-the-divine-nature-an-interview-with-myk-habets.

teaching that tried to make man into God, from Mr. Armstrong's "God is a family" and "we become God" tenants.[7] That should have safeguarded them from the attraction of similar language used by mystics or Emerging Church adherents in their union, deification, and *theosis*.

That is the quagmire of error and false teachings—it eventually becomes a tangled web. The GCI is testing so many new ideas that they end up publishing disclaimers to their own position, stating that they are not "pantheists," "panentheists," "universalists," "neoorthodox," or that they embrace both sides of "soul sleep," "evolution," hell and annihilation. James warns us that when our speech has a conflicting message, then we risk being double-minded, and unstable in all of our ways (James 1:8). It is time to reassess what theologians you are in company with, if you sound so much like your opponent that you have to state that you are not in that camp.

Embracing neoorthodoxy is another problem for GCI. Karl Barth, the father of neoorthodoxy, is often quoted by the GCI theologians (nearly 1,000 hits on their website). Barth was somewhat reactionary to the extremely liberal theologians of his day and attempted to swing the pendulum back toward Jesus Christ, which is noble, but he erred along the way and was challenged broadly by twentieth-century Evangelical writers. On Barthian neoorthodoxy, Dr. Walter Martin quoted from J. Oliver Buswell's systematic theology in his seminary classes to demonstrate that Barth's view of God was essentially modalistic.[8] This is where GCI needs to be careful, because of their affinity with Barthian theologians like C. Baxter Kruger, T. F. Torrence, J. P. Torrence, and other neoorthodox teachers. The departure from conservative Evangelicalism to neoorthodoxy has pitfalls.

Universalism Controversy

Traditional universalism is divided into two extremely different camps, the Trinitarian Universalists and the Unitarian Universalists. The modern

---

7. Herbert W. Armstrong, "Why Must Man Suffer?" *The Plain Truth*, October 1983, 21. Armstrong wrote, "God is the family name. The fact that God is a family is very significant. . . . God's purpose is to make us immortal like God, until we become God as he is God."

8. James Oliver Buswell Jr., *A Systematic Theology of the Christian Religion* (Grand Rapids: Zondervan, 1962), 1:123–124. Buswell wrote, "In a brief conversation with Karl Barth in Switzerland in August 1950, I referred to his *Dogmatics in Outline* and asked if his view of the Persons of the Trinity, as there expressed, was not Sabellianism. 'Well, you could call it Sabellianism,' he frankly replied. Barth sometimes denied that he is a 'modalist.' But my esteemed colleague, Dr. Alan Killen, who is a specialist and critic in the field of the Barthian type of theology, tells me that a careful analysis of Barth's views shows that he really is a modalist, or Sabellian."

American movement claims John Murray as the founder of Trinitarian Unitarianism, and Hosea Ballou is credited with the Unitarian branch.

The new universalism movement is different in several respects. They try to sound Evangelical while holding a very liberal doctrine, so they renamed their position as "evangelical universalism, hopeful universalism, inclusion universalism, universal reconciliation," and other new labels. This repackaged theory is based upon two axioms: The new expression argues the *possibility* that all humanity will be saved, while traditional universalism simply states that *all will* be saved. The corollary is that the new expression argues the *possibility* that *some may* go to hell, while classic universalism simply states that *nobody* goes to hell. If someone goes to hell, then a third axiom applies to the GCI. Both Herbert W. Armstrong and the GCI teach that someone in hell may get out of hell through repentance or a "reeducation" about Jesus. This is a preposterous "Get out of hell free" message.

This creates a twofold problem. The GCI has returned to a doctrine taught by Herbert W. Armstrong that is unbiblical and surrounded with universalism teachers, like William Paul Young (*The Shack*), C. Baxter Kruger (Perichoresis), T. F. Torrance, J. P. Torrence, Robin Parry, Rob Bell, John Crowder, Ray Anderson, Steve McVey, Elmer Colyer, Michael Jinkins, Trevor Hart, Miroslav Volf, Colin Gunton, Robert Capon, Darrel Johnson, and John Jefferson Davis. All of these people teach either by video or written material for the GCI, which fosters a multifaceted universalism quandary, because as with the dancing-god precept above, not all universalists teach exactly the same way. A book that thoroughly examines and refutes the modern universal reconciliation movement, including some GCI teachers, is *Exposing Universalism: A Comprehensive Guide to the Faulty Appeals Made by Universalists Paul Young, Brian McLaren, Rob Bell, and Others Past and Present to Promote a New Kind of Christianity*, by the Western Seminary senior professor of New Testament languages, James B. De Young (Eugene: Wipf and Stock Publishers, 2018). Professor De Young employs the early church Fathers and biblical refutations for this growing heresy.

Herbert W. Armstrong's type of universal reconciliation was different, because he placed the reconciliation between the second resurrection and God's final judgement. As with all universalism, he makes it a broad way to salvation. Armstrong wrote, ". . . in the Great White Throne Judgment after the millennium, Old Testament Israel will be resurrected . . . they will come to know that Christ the Savior had come and died for them. And upon repentance they shall receive the Holy Spirit and with it salvation and eternal life."[9] This offers salvation and eternal life after death of which it is assumed that most will accept Christ in the hereafter. Similarly, the GCI published a popular article that teaches universal reconciling: "We believe that in Christ the Lord makes gracious and just provision for all, even for those who at death appear not to have believed the gospel."[10]

The Problem of Universal Reconciliation

Unfortunately, the error of universal reconciliation is growing in popularity:

> The danger of Universalism or Universal Reconciliation is that one may be led to believe that if God intends to save everyone, then we can afford to be lax both in our Christian lives and in our zeal to proclaim the riches of the gospel. . . .
>
> We ought always to fix in our minds these three facts: (1) the grammar of the New Testament teaches that there will be everlasting bliss for those who accept Jesus Christ as Lord and Savior (John 5:24, 6:47, etc.); (2) this same grammar teaches, with the same words, in the same syntactical form, and many times in the same context, that there will be everlasting punishment for those who willfully reject Jesus Christ as Lord and Savior (John 3:36; Matt 25:32,33; Rev 20:10; etc.); and (3) salvation from sin has been provided for all men through the blood of the Cross (1 John 2:2), and whosoever will may come, according to the will of God, who orders all things after the counsel of His own will. But that God knows and has declared in His Word that many will not accept His provision of redemption and will in fact, trample underfoot the blood of Jesus, no qualified scholar denies. These are the persons clearly described in Scripture, those "whose end is destruction, whose God is their belly" (Phil 3:19), "raging waves of the sea, foaming out their own shame; wandering stars, to whom is reserved the blackness of darkness forever" (Jude 13).
>
> If we keep these three cardinal points before us, recognizing that the Scriptures as a unit teach these truths whether or not we can accept them on a rationalistic basis or whether or not we can understand the character of God this side of eternity, we shall protect ourselves from the error of

---

9. Herbert W. Armstrong, *The Mystery of the Ages* (Pasadena: Worldwide Church of God, 1985), 354.

10. Michael Feazell, "Only One Name," GCI.org, accessed May 1, 2018, https://www.gci.org/gospel/onlyone. See also https://www.gci.org/articles/only-one-name/.

universal reconciliation and of Universalism itself. This is the error which has plagued the Christian church since the days of Origen, and which has laid the groundwork for many more heresies, since this form of theology has the tendency to lead the unwary further into fields of doctrinal deviation.

Let us, then, heed the Apostle Paul, and faithfully "put on the whole armor of God, that ye may be able to stand against the wiles of the devil" (Eph 6:11).[11]

Prior to the breakup of the Worldwide Church of God, some fifty splinter groups separated from Herbert W. Armstrong during his lifetime. Armstrong's teaching bred a hundred factions of which ninety presently remain. The founder's son, Garner Ted Armstrong, even took thousands of followers away from the founding church and established the Church of God, International, in Tyler, Texas. His playboy lifestyle followed him in the 1990s with new charges of sexual misconduct, again forcing a temporary step-down from his new church (*Los Angeles Times*, November 23, 1995). In spite of that, faithful Church of God, International members, reinstated him as their iconic representative on 315 cable stations in North America. His espoused doctrines follow those of his father, namely, denial of the Trinity, denial of the bodily resurrection, and denial of biblical salvation.

Among the groups that broke away during the 1990s, the largest is led by Gerald Flurry at The Philadelphia Church of God in Edmond, Oklahoma. *The Philadelphia Trumpet*, their official magazine, is a constant reminder of Herbert W. Armstrong's old doctrines. Most of the splinter cults of Armstrongism retain the name "Church of God" somewhere in their title. They mix legalism, including strict Sabbatarianism, with a variety of Armstrong's leading doctrines. Two other noteworthy groups among these are the Global Church of God, located in San Diego, California, and the United Church of God in Arcadia, California.

The largest and main body, Grace Communion International, now with headquarters in Charlotte, North Carolina, is the only branch that rejected Armstrongism and turned to Christianity. Joseph Tkach Jr., son of the former president, Joseph W. Tkach, led the GCI until his retirement on January 1, 2019. Greg Williams is now president. The CGI has 50,000 members in 900 congregations spanning 70 countries, with mission work in another 20 countries.

11. Walter R. Martin, *Essential Christianity* (Santa Ana, CA: Vision House, 1980), ebook edition, chapter 11.

Theological Evaluation

The Armstrong cults believe that Armstrong was God's sole channel of divine truth. Armstrong believed that biblical truth had been lost from the first century until rediscovered by him in 1927. He wrote about himself as the "Elijah" who would preach before the second advent of Jesus Christ. He also taught that he was unique in the human race as Christ's new "apostle" and that he had "restored" essential truths to Christianity. He championed his work in gloating terms, as when he introduced the *Mystery of the Ages* in 1985, saying, "I candidly feel it may be the most important book since the Bible!"[12]

Such self-glorifying sentiments are not uncommon to Armstrong. He had previously announced in January 1979 that his book *The Incredible Human Potential* had Jesus Christ as the author and Mr. Armstrong as the stenographer! "Actually," he wrote, "I feel with deep conviction that I myself did not author this book—that the living Jesus Christ is its real author. I was merely like a stenographer writing it down. And with that understanding, I feel I may say that this is the most important—the most tremendously revealing—book since the Bible!"[13]

> Armstrong claimed his writings were more than mere interpretation or commentary.

Two of Armstrong's books mediate between humanity and the Bible. He claimed his writings were more than mere interpretation or commentary by ruling out all others as equal, second only to the Bible. "I am not writing foolishly," he boldly stated, "but very soberly, on *authority* of the *living Christ!*"[14] These stupendous claims either need to be upheld or exposed as fraudulent. Under the spotlight of God's Word, we will discover the indeed fraudulent nature of Armstrong's twisted biblical texts.

Of his mission, Armstrong said,

I know of no other who has ever become founder of a religion, or a religious leader of any kind, who ever came into the truth in the way God brought me into it. . . . God brought me through a process that erased former misknowledge—and, as it were, gave me a clear start from "scratch." I wonder if you realize that every truth of God, accepted as truth doctrine

12. As quoted by Gerald Flurry, "Personal," *The Philadelphia Trumpet*, February 1997, 1.
13. Herbert W. Armstrong, "Personal from . . . ," *The Plain Truth*, January 1979, 45.
14. Herbert W. Armstrong, "End Vietnam War Now!" *The Plain Truth*, February 1967, 47.

and belief in the Worldwide Church of God, came from Christ through me, or was finally approved and made official through me. . . . I was appointed by Jesus Christ, the head of the Church.[15]

Others had less of the Holy Spirit than he did, he affirmed:

The Holy Spirit is given to us by degrees. . . . I firmly believe that God by His grace granted me a much fuller portion of His Spirit at the very beginning than is the average experience.[16]

Uniquely, he is Christ's apostle, "His one apostle for this twentieth century."[17] He revealed that he was the "Elijah" type who precedes the return of Jesus Christ.[18] He claims special privileges during the millennial reign of Christ. According to Armstrong, he will also run the "Headquarters Church" himself under Jesus Christ for the entire planet earth.

His parallels for Elijah, John the Baptist, and himself break down because the Bible speaks of one messenger like Elijah, not two messengers. Both Isaiah 40:3 and Malachi 3:1–5 speak singularly of one messenger, which ample New Testament evidence reveals to be John the Baptist (Luke 1:17). Armstrong hangs his premise upon Matthew 17:11, that John the Baptist did not "restore all things."[19] However, the verses following this (Matthew 17:12–13) make it clear from the mouth of Jesus Christ that John indeed fulfilled Malachi's prophecy. Simply because Armstrong does not know how John fulfilled the prophecy gives no justification for claiming that he did not do so, nor that there should be another futuristic "Elijah" type. Anyone who believes in Jesus can rest assured that Jesus knew more on the subject than Armstrong. Furthermore, Matthew 17:13 finalizes the subject in saying, "Then the disciples understood that he was talking to them about John the Baptist." Notice the missing element for Armstrong's theory. It is not John the Baptist and some future figure in the twentieth century, but John the Baptist alone.

In 1958 Mr. Armstrong wrote a letter to Robert Sumner, a writer on cults and false religions. "First," he wrote, "let me say—this may sound

15. Herbert W. Armstrong, "Personal from . . . ," *The Plain Truth*, February 1977, 17.
16. Herbert W. Armstrong, "The True Facts of My Own Conversion," *The Plain Truth*, June 1977, 9.
17. *The Plain Truth*, July 1977, 1; and February 1978, 43.
18. Herbert W. Armstrong, *Mystery of the Ages* (Pasadena: Worldwide Church of God, 1985), 8:284–286.
19. Armstrong, *Mystery*, 285.

incredible, but it's true—*Jesus Christ foretold this very work—it is, itself the fulfillment of his prophecy* (Matthew 24:14 and Mark 13:10). . . . Astounding as it may seem, there is no other work on earth proclaiming to the whole world this very *same gospel* that Jesus taught and proclaimed!"[20]

Throughout the years Armstrong continually maintained that his organization alone truly represented Christianity, while all others were false. Since 1933, he credited himself with restoring "at least eighteen basic essential truths . . . to the true Church."[21] In order to combat the obvious representation of Christianity during the last two millennia, Armstrong referred to the true church as an "underground" remnant called the "little flock." Armstrong's lofty pedestal crashes to the ground in the face of Jesus' words in Matthew 16:18, where He said that the gates of hell shall not prevail against His church. This demonstration of the church of Christ as a perpetually visible entity destroys Armstrong's notion. What went out in the first century was never lost and continually grew. The undeniable fact is that the church of Jesus Christ has always been visible and remains so until His return, as Paul said, "throughout all generations" (Ephesians 3:21). The church is built upon the foundation of the apostles and prophets with Jesus Christ as the chief cornerstone (Ephesians 2:20).

In specific reference to the "little flock" statement of Jesus in Luke 12:32, it was never intended as a description of the church for two millennia. It was spoken to the twelve before Christ's crucifixion. The conversion of 3,000 souls in Acts, chapter two, began the rapid church expansion and dispels such folly. Armstrong was not the first to appeal to the "little flock" quotation in support of his small following, but to claim this represents the entire story of the church through nineteen centuries makes the commission of Christ (Matthew 28:19 and Mark 16:15) positively absurd. Christ commissioned his followers to go into the entire world not for a "little flock," but that "a great multitude that no one could count, from every nation, tribe, people and language" (Revelation 7:9) could be reached.

Biblical Perspective

The Bible, according to Mr. Armstrong, was not properly understood since the first century because it was a coded jigsaw puzzle. He claimed

20. Personal letter to Robert Sumner, November 27, 1958.
21. Armstrong, *Mystery*, 207.

special anointing to decode it and put the puzzle together. The story went that God purposefully hid the biblical message from the world until the second Elijah (Armstrong) preached in the final days preceding Christ's return.

On the Bible, Armstrong said, "It is like a jigsaw puzzle which must be assembled piece by biblical piece . . . and since before AD 70, it has been entirely *suppressed*."[22] Further, he wrote, "The Bible was a coded book, not intended to be understood until our day in this latter half of the twentieth century. . . . I learned that the Bible is like a jigsaw puzzle—thousands of pieces that need putting together."[23]

> The most damaging blow to Armstrong's theory is found in 1 John 2:27 where it states, "You do not need anyone to teach you."

Imagine that God hid his Word for 1,900 years awaiting the arrival of Armstrong! In blatant contrast, Jesus told us "Thy word is truth" (John 17:17), thus expressing God's intention for all mankind to find plainly stated, uncoded, unsuppressed truth upon examination. It would have been easier for Armstrong if Jesus had said, "Thy word is a coded jigsaw puzzle," but no such thought exists. The most damaging blow to Armstrong's theory is found in 1 John 2:27 where it states, "You do not need anyone to teach you." Here, the Apostle John clearly tells the church that the Holy Spirit teaches us beyond dependency upon Armstrong. So much does God expect the common Christian, led by His Spirit, to understand what they read that the Bible is replete with such references (Psalm 119:4, 104; Luke 11:28; Revelation 1:3).

New Revelations

The introduction to *Mystery of the Ages* states, "The final crystal-clear reason that impelled me to write this book did not fully reveal itself to my mind until December of 1984. It was a mind-boggling realization—a pivotal truth."[24] Again, "All these mysteries were . . . a coded message not allowed to be revealed and decoded until our time."[25] At times Armstrong

22. Herbert W. Armstrong, "How Far Can You Get from Being 'A Prophet of Doom'?" *The Plain Truth*, October/November 1977, 3.
23. Armstrong, *Mystery*, xii.
24. Armstrong, *Mystery*, x.
25. Armstrong, *Mystery*, xiii.

claimed his writings are "a last warning from the *Eternal God!*"[26] New revelation outside of Scripture is a mark of all of the cults.

The Trinity of God and the Divinity of Man

Armstrong was an outspoken anti-Trinitarian, as revealed in these quotations:

> But the theologians and "Higher Critics" have blindly accepted the heretical and false doctrine introduced by *pagan* false prophets who crept in, that the *Holy Spirit* is a *third person*—the heresy of the *"Trinity."* This limits God to "Three Persons."[27]
>
> The false Trinity teaching does limit God to three persons. But God is not limited. As God repeatedly reveals, his purpose is to reproduce himself into what well may become billions of God persons. It is the false Trinity teaching that limits God, denies God's purpose and has palpably deceived the whole Christian world.[28]

Armstrong's denial of the Trinity was superseded by his "binitarian" (two persons in the Godhead) view. He held to the deity of Jesus, correctly calling Him Jehovah from the Old Testament. His denial of the deity of the Holy Spirit left him with two persons as God (binitarian), instead of three persons (Trinitarian). Within this scope, however, he diverges into "ditheism" (two god Beings). We have seen in a previous quotation his address of "two Superbeings" and "Superpersonages." He speaks elsewhere: "In the very beginning, before all else, there existed two living Beings composed of Spirit. . . . One was named the Word. . . . The other was named God . . ."[29] When Armstrong calls the Father and Son two beings, then it is difficult to maintain monotheism, since two beings require ditheism, a form of polytheism.

The nature of God is spirit, according to Armstrong, but His shape, form, and stature is that of a man! In their correspondence course, he asks, "Does the Father therefore appear like a man? Comment: Christ clearly indicated that the Father has the general form and stature of a

26. Armstrong, *Vietnam*, 47.
27. Herbert W. Armstrong, *Just What Do You Mean—Born Again!* (Pasadena: Radio Church of God, 1962), 19.
28. Armstrong, *Mystery*, 37.
29. Herbert W. Armstrong, "World Peace Just around the Corner," *The Plain Truth*, November/December 1984, 4.

mortal man!"[30] *The Plain Truth* reveals, "We are made of material flesh, but in the form and shape of God . . ."[31] And, "Now notice once again Genesis 1:26: 'God (*Elohim*) said, Let us make man in our image, after our likeness (form and shape).' . . . God is described in the Bible as having eyes, ears, nose, mouth, hair, arms, legs, fingers, toes."[32] Still, "Man was made in the form and shape of God. For example, notice the human hand. God has hands (2 Chronicles 6:4)."[33] Finally, in *Mystery of the Ages*, he reveals,

> Perhaps it will make God more real to you when you realize he is in the same form and shape as a human being. . . . God is invisible to human eyes. . . . But even though God is composed of spirit and not visible matter, God nonetheless does have form and shape. . . . In various parts of the Bible, it is revealed that God has a face, eyes, a nose, mouth and ears. He has hair on his head. It is revealed God has arms and legs. And God has hands and fingers. . . . God has feet and toes and a body. . . . If you know what a man looks like, you know what is the form and shape of God, for he made man in his image, after his very likeness.[34]

In this section we cannot sidestep his "God Family" doctrine. He taught that "God" was a family name for two beings, the Father and Son. The God Family will soon become billions of God Beings comprised of those "born again." The quotations are numerous because he equivocated the terms "immortal," "resurrection," "saved," "born again," "Church of God," "God Family," and "Kingdom of God."[35]

His God Family doctrine projects a future divine human race. He expressed the future divinity of mankind: "God's purpose is to make us immortal like God, until we become God as he is God."[36] Elsewhere he wrote, "That is, once born again, one is born not of a human father in mortal physical human flesh, but of god, impregnated by God's Spirit, in immortal *spirit composition*, as a God Being! *Born of God!* . . . But he is *born again* only in the immortal spirit life to come—at the time of the resurrection.

30. Herbert W. Armstrong, ed., *Ambassador College Bible Correspondence Course* (Lesson 9) (Pasadena: Ambassador College, 1966): 8.
31. Armstrong, "Just What Do You Mean: Born Again?" *The Plain Truth*, February 1977, 28.
32. Armstrong, *The Plain Truth*, February 1979, 42.
33. Armstrong, "Never Before Understood," *The Plain Truth*, September 1981, 26.
34. Armstrong, "Never Before Understood," 26.
35. Armstrong, *Mystery*, 37–39.
36. Herbert W. Armstrong, "Why Must Man Suffer?" *The Plain Truth*, October 1983, 21.

When born again, he will be spirit—no longer mortal flesh and blood."[37] Once again, "You and I potentially may *become God!* For *God* is a collective *Family*—the *Divine Family*—into which *the Church* is to be born!"[38] And, "By a resurrection, we become *born* God personages—personages just as are God the Father and Christ the Son! We shall have the entire *universe* put under our feet (Hebrews 2:8)."[39]

The repentant, Christian branch, GCI, embraced the Trinity and they refute the heresies of Armstrong. They state, "God, by the testimony of Scripture, is one divine Being in three eternal, coessential, yet distinct Persons—Father, Son, and Holy Spirit."[40] We add to this the scriptural support that there can exist but one God (Deuteronomy 4:39; 6:4; Isaiah 44:6–8; 45:21–22; and Mark 12:32). Yet the Bible also shows us the three distinct Persons within God's nature (Father, Romans 1:7; Son, John 20:28; and Holy Spirit, Acts 5:3–4). All three persons are coequal in the nature of God (Matthew 28:19; Isaiah 48:16). For the avid student of God's Word, we recommend a more thorough study of the Trinity found in a number of reliable Bible encyclopedias. (See also Index: Trinity.)

Isaiah 43:10 plays an important role in refutation of Armstrong, for God unequivocally states that "Before me no god was formed, nor will there be one after me." The "God family," "Born Gods," "God personages," and "God Beings" are dealt a deathblow in the face of Isaiah 43:10. None preceded Him, and absolutely none will follow. Armstrong's idea of two God Beings coexisting in eternity is answered well by Isaiah 44:8, where God tells us He knows of no others beside himself. No other beings existed with Him.

Isaiah succinctly deals with Armstrong's concept that God the Father is in the form, stature, and shape of man. Rhetorically, he asks, "To whom then will you liken God? Or what likeness will you compare to Him?" (Isaiah 40:18 NKJV). Here, Isaiah tells us nothing is likened to God, but Armstrong believes God had parts in comparison to man's likeness. Any number of biblical passages on the omnipresence of God destroy this view. When the Bible states that the "heaven and the heaven of heavens cannot contain You" (1 Kings 8:27 NKJV), then how does Armstrong purpose that

37. Herbert W. Armstrong, "This Is the Worldwide Church of God," *The Plain Truth,* January 1979, 3.

38. Herbert W. Armstrong, "A Voice Cries Out Amid Religious Confusion," *The Plain Truth,* December 1980, 40.

39. Armstrong, *The Plain Truth,* September 1980, 30.

40. *Statement,* 2.

he is limited to the form, shape, and stature of man? Scripture answers this well (2 Chronicles 2:6; 6:18; Jeremiah 23:24).

The Nature of Christ

Armstrongism taught that Jesus was Jehovah, but not the Son, before His birth through Mary. We must understand that his view of the incarnate Christ destroys the very foundation of God's eternal nature! For example, God cannot lie (Hebrews 6:18) because it is against the nature of One who is pure holiness and truth. Armstrong made the immutable, eternal, immortal God contradict His essence by giving up His immortality while on earth and converting His spirit-essence into flesh. He made Jehovah divest himself totally of immortal spirit, convert into flesh, then reconvert His mortal flesh back to immortal spirit at His resurrection, making him the first "born again" saved person. He stopped being "very God" and then became "very God" again. While He was dead, the other God Being, the Father, ran the universe, since the immortality of Jesus was temporarily dysfunctional. Then, when Jesus raised from the dead, He raised in a spirit-body, but not the physical body that had died.

Armstrong wrote:

> Jesus did not become the Son of God until about 4 BC, when born in human flesh of the virgin Mary.[41]
>
> Christ was converted into flesh . . . he who had existed from eternity . . . he who was *God*—he *was made flesh*—converted *into* flesh, until he *became* flesh; and then he *was* flesh! . . . He divested himself of inherent immortality for the time being. He gave up immortality for us—that he might *die* for us . . . that he, even as we, might be resurrected from the *dead*, and given by the Father immortal life—that is, converted back into spiritual immortality so that he by the resurrection once again *became* divine Spirit—or very *God*!
>
> Jesus was also *God*—he was both human and divine. But he was not *God* inside of, yet separate from, the body of flesh—he, God, *was made flesh*, until he, still *God*—God *with us*—became God *in* (*not* inside of) the human flesh—God manifest *in the flesh* (1 Timothy 3:16). . . . Jesus *died*! Jesus *was dead*! . . . If there were no other Person in the Godhead, then the Giver of all life was dead and all hope was at an end! . . . But the Father still reigned in high heaven!

41. Armstrong, *The Plain Truth*, February 1979, 41.

> Not Resurrected in Same Body. . . . Now notice carefully, God the Father did not cause Jesus Christ to get back into the body that had died. . . . And the resurrected body was no longer human—it was the Christ resurrected *immortal*, once again *changed*! As he had been changed, converted *into* mortal human flesh and blood, subject to death, and for the *purpose of dying for our sins*, now by a *resurrection from the dead, he was again changed, converted into immortality.*[42]

> Because they knew what Jesus had looked like—and in his born-again, resurrected body he looked the same, except he now was composed of spirit instead of matter! . . . He was born in a spirit body, which was manifested to his apostles in the same apparent size and shape as when he died.[43]

The main branch of the Worldwide Church of God, the GCI, rejected Armstrong's Christology and states, "When the Word came in the flesh, though he was fully human and fully divine, he voluntarily set aside the prerogatives of divinity."[44] They also state that he was "two natures in one Person" and "raised bodily from the dead."[45] These statements, written in agreement with historic creeds of Christianity, stand in biblical opposition to Armstrong's fallacy. Add to that these supportive verses on Christ's immutability: "Jesus Christ the same yesterday, and to day, and for ever" (Hebrews 13:8). And, "Before Abraham was, I am" (John 8:58). Jesus, the eternal I AM, could not stop being who He is and then regain an unchangeable nature. That would be a contradiction of terms. Philippians 2:6–8 answers the contrived story of Armstrongism. Jesus had two natures, that of eternal God, and that of a servant, man. Neither nature (*morphe* in Greek) was altered during the incarnation. His deity was not altered by His humanity, and His humanity was unaltered by His being God. This shows that His deity was distinct from His humanity. One did not merge or convert into the other.

According to Colossians 2:9, all the fullness of Deity dwells in Him bodily, which means nothing was lacking in His deity, it was the fullness. Had He given up immortality, then He would not have the fullness of Deity—Colossians corrects Armstrongism here. See also John 1:1; 1:18; 5:18; 20:28; Acts 20:28; and Revelation 1:8.

42. Armstrong, "Why Christ Died and Rose Again," *The Plain Truth*, abbreviated version, April 1982, 20.
43. Armstrong, "Personal from . . . ," *The Plain Truth*, January 1978, 44.
44. Anonymous, *God Is . . .* (Pasadena: Worldwide Church of God, 1992), 30.
45. Anonymous, *God Is*, 30.

Was Jesus referred to as the Son previous to His incarnation? We find an affirmative answer in the Psalms: "Kiss the Son, lest he be angry" (Psalm 2:12). Also, in Proverbs 30:4 (NKJV), the question is asked, "Who has established all the ends of the earth? What is His name, and what is His Son's name?" We must also remember that Jesus was the "sent Son" (John 3:16) into the world, which agrees with these Old Testament passages that He was the Son before His incarnation.

The physical resurrection of the same body that Jesus had died with on the cross is central to Christianity. It cannot be some non-material spirit-body that only looked similar to the one that died. Paul reminds us that if the Resurrection did not happen, our faith is in vain (1 Corinthians 15:14).

When Jesus made His post-resurrection appearances He offered the print of the nails in His hands (John 20:27) as proof that it was the same crucified body. Otherwise, Jesus would have been deceiving His disciples with imitation prints. He offered His hands and feet as evidence (Luke 24:39). Of utmost importance, He denied that He was other than "flesh and bones, as ye see me have" (Luke 24:39). He proved His physical body by eating with His disciples (Luke 24:42; John 21:12–13). This is how Luke can assuredly tell us that He showed himself alive with many infallible proofs (Acts 1:3).

The Personality of the Holy Spirit

The teaching of Armstrong on the Holy Spirit is twofold. First, he believes that the Holy Spirit was not God, nor a person within the nature of God. Second, he believed the Holy Spirit impregnates the believer (begotten) in Jesus as a down payment for salvation. In this his purpose was to name the Holy Spirit a "divine sperm" and "sperm" impregnating the believer. Once the Holy Spirit leads a person through a faithful life, then the "begotten" person is finally "born again" at the resurrection to become a member of the God Family.

Armstrong specifically focused upon the person and deity of the Holy Spirit. He wrote, "He [Simon the sorcerer] taught, and his false church later (AD 321) made official, the 'Trinity' doctrine, saying the Holy Spirit of God is a *ghost*—a third spirit *person*—thereby doing away with the fact that we can be begotten by God's Spirit."[46] Further, he says, "The theologians . . .

46. Armstrong, "Foundation, History, Authority, and Doctrine of the Worldwide Church of God," *The Plain Truth* (February 1978): 41.

have blindly accepted the false doctrine introduced by *pagan* false prophets who crept in, that the Holy Spirit is a third person."[47]

About the Holy Spirit impregnating the repentant person, he said, "The Holy Spirit also is the divine 'spiritual sperm' that impregnates with immortal God-life!"[48] And, "If 'fertilized' by the male divine sperm of God (his Holy Spirit—actually God-life), he would have been begotten, but not yet born as God."[49]

The Christian doctrine of the Holy Spirit is guarded as precious in the sight of believers. Therefore, denial of His person is an assault upon the very nature of God. The Bible shows us that the Holy Spirit acts only as a person can act or respond (John 14–16; Matthew 12:31; Romans 8:26–27; Ephesians 4:30; and Hebrews 10:29). The Holy Spirit has the attributes that belong only to God (Luke 1:35–37; Isaiah 40:13; Hebrews 9:14). The Holy Spirit is also called God (2 Samuel 23:2–3; Acts 5:1–4; 1 Corinthians 6:19–20).

There are many other errors in Armstrong's theology that could easily fill a small volume. Let it be said, however, that the theology of Armstrongism contains just enough truth to make it attractive to the listener who is unaware of the multiple sources of heretical doctrine he has drawn upon for the balance of his theological system.

Armstrongism is dangerous as it makes profuse use of the Bible and professes to swear allegiance to only "the plain truth of the Scripture," while, in reality, its allegiance is to the interpretations of the Scripture propagated by Herbert W. Armstrong, whom one author has aptly described as "Mr. Confusion."

Since "God is not the author of confusion" (1 Corinthians 14:33), there is one sure remedy to the problem of the spread of Armstrongism. Turn off the television and radio wherever it is promoted and open your Bible, for within its pages God is always broadcasting the eternal message of the Gospel of grace impregnated by the Spirit of God in every essential necessary to the redemption of the soul and re-creation and living of the Christian life. When this is supplemented by attendance in a truly Christian church where that Gospel is preached, there is no need to listen to the Herbert Armstrongs of our day, for as the psalmist so beautifully described it, "The entrance of thy words giveth light."

47. Armstrong, *Born Again?* 19.
48. Armstrong, "Confusion," 6.
49. Armstrong, "Captive," 42.

Explore

Pantheist vs. Panentheist
Modalism
Anglo-Israelism
Universalism

Discuss

1. What restores us to healthy Christianity?

2. How does Armstrongism redefine the nature of God?

3. Was Jesus referred to as the Son previous to His incarnation?

4. How did Jesus prove He was alive?

Dig Deeper

See *The Kingdom of the Cults Study Guide* available at WalterMartin.com.

13

The Unification Church

Quick Facts on the Unification Church

- The Unification Church believes that the Bible is untrustworthy in its reliability.

- God is dualistic in his nature, like the yin and yang of Taoism.

- The crucifixion of Jesus was an alternative plan and it only saved mankind halfway. Sun Myung Moon is the Messiah and true salvation comes by being a member of the Unification Church.

- The Trinity was an invention of Jesus and there have been many "trinities" through the ages, including a satanic trinity.

Historical Perspective

The Unification Church, founded and led by Korean-born Rev. Sun Myung Moon (1920–2012), demonstrates the growing trend toward New Age beliefs worldwide.[1] The distinctive features of this kind of cult include (1) its special appeal to educated young people from the middle class; (2) its habit of conducting business, especially recruiting, under multiple pseudonyms or anonymously; (3) its Westernization of Eastern religious ideas; and (4) its misinterpretations of Scripture to persuade outsiders that its Eastern religious orientation is compatible with and, indeed, is the fulfillment of, biblical Christianity. Such groups as the Unification

---

1. Frederick Sontang, *Sun Myung Moon and the Unification Church* (Nashville: Abingdon, 1977), 133. See also chapter Appendix B: New Age Spirituality for further information on the New Age movement.

Church are further characterized by what appears to be obvious, widespread, and forceful psychological pressure on members to conform and remain loyal to the group at all costs. This psychological pressure is present in all the cults, as we noted in the opening chapters of this book. It is perhaps more obvious with groups newly arrived in America whose converts are mainly young people whose families have had little or no previous exposure to the group.

Misinterpretations of Scripture are used to persuade outsiders that its Eastern religious orientation is the fulfillment of biblical Christianity.

On January 6, 1920, Yong Myung Moon (Shining Dragon Moon) was born of Confucian parents, humble farmers, in the town of Dok A, Jung-Juin, the providence of Pyongyang Buk-do, in North Korea. The family converted to the Presbyterian Church in 1930, but the youthful Yong Myung Moon retained ancestral veneration common to Confucianism. According to Unification writer Kwang-Yol Yoo, Moon experimented in contacting ancestors in the spirit world during his early teenage years, and his spiritual quest was likened to that of Buddha.[2]

Shortly following the Second World War, Moon drifted from one "Pentecostal" group to another. Yoo's history reveals that most of these untrained Pentecostal Christian groups blended séances, spiritism, ancestral spirit guidance, and a host of occult practices with their Christianity. Mingling indigenous beliefs with Christianity is a problem in foreign missions, especially when it involves occult practices like necromancy, which is strictly forbidden in Scripture (Deuteronomy 18:10–11).

Moon wrote *Divine Principle* in 1951–1952 under postwar hardships in Pusan. By virtue of his strong will, he trekked onward and established the Unification Church on May 1, 1954, in Seoul, South Korea. One year after founding his church, he was arrested (July 4, 1955) for irresponsible sexual activity that caused a scandal at Ewha Women's (Methodist) University in Seoul. Several Korean newspapers covered the story.[3] Moon was released October 4, 1955, because the eighty women involved in the incident exercised their right of silence in court. It was also reported by the Church of the Nazarene

2. Kwang-Yol Yoo (in a five-part series), "Unification Church History from the Early Days," *New Hope News*, Washington, DC: The Unification Church, 1:9–10, 12–13; 2:1.
3. Some of the newspaper accounts can be seen at https://tragedyofthesixmarys.com/ewha-as-told-in-1955-newspapers.

Korea Mission that Moon's church was involved in an unusual sexual "blood cleansing" rite (*pikareum*) in which a woman was to have sexual intercourse with Sun Myung Moon three times to cleanse her blood from Satan's lineage. The "cleansed" woman could then cleanse her husband through sexual union with him. This ritual was based upon the Unification doctrine that Eve fell by having intercourse with Satan; therefore, a woman having intercourse with Moon, who is Lord of the Second Advent, would be cleansed. Just as Eve passed Satan's tainted blood lineage on to Adam, likewise the cleansed Unification member passes purification of blood on to her spouse.[4]

Sun Myung Moon died in South Korea of pneumonia at age 92 on September 2, 2012. Almost immediately there was a family power grab for leadership, much of it by underhanded schemes. What rocked the UC hard was the late disclosure of Rev. Moon's secret illegitimate children while he preached the opposite, which caused many to become disillusioned and leave. But the repetitive scandals caused one True Child, Un-Jin Moon, to defect and join with Nansook Hong, a former daughter-in-law, in renouncing Moon as a "con man" and "false Messiah" on CBS's *60 Minutes*. Mother Moon has taken the control, but not without first stepping over several True Children who were in her way.

The Unification Church is not much larger today than it was in the mid–1970s. They still claim about 3 million people worldwide.[5] Since the death of Sun Myung Moon in 2012, membership and activity in America has suffered. Moon was driven to reform America politically and religiously, but his surviving wife, Hak Ja Han Moon, who now leads the organization from South Korea, does not share his passion. She has removed much of their American presence, selling off a few properties, and withdrawing programs that once thrived. Their largest following is in Japan and South Korea. There are over 900 worship centers in Korea and 55 in the United States.

There are at least seventy-five front groups that were created by the UC to promote their agenda. A few of the larger ones owned and operated by the UC, to which patrons unwittingly give homage, are:

American Clergy Leadership Conference (ACLC)
CAUSA International

---

4. The major points of this ritual were confirmed by a Korean government cable, February 1963, and sent to the United States Central Intelligence Agency. See James Coates, "Moon Church Traced from Sex Cult," *Chicago Tribune Press Service*, March 27, 1978.
5. Statistics derived from Religionfacts.com/unification-church

Collegiate Association for the Research of Principles (CARP)
International Coalition for Religious Freedom
International Conference on the Unity of the Sciences
Little Angels Children's Folk Ballet of Korea
The *Washington Times* newspaper
Universal Peace Federation
Women's Federation for World Peace

Theological Evaluation

It was not until Moon was released from prison in Danbury that he publicly called himself "Lord of the Second Advent." In his unedited speech, he said, "I am now in the position of Lord of the Second Advent to the world. . . . But with my emergence as the victorious Lord of the Second Advent for the world, a new order has come into being."[6]

In Sun Myung Moon's sermons, he leaves little doubt that he proclaims himself as the new messiah. It is not difficult for any reasonable person to draw the only conclusion he allows. If the messiah is the Lord of the Second Advent, and the Lord of the Second Advent includes the True Parents, then Moon is claiming all titles for himself by claiming to be the True Parent. In the last two decades of his life, Moon more frequently called himself the Messiah, the Lord of the Second Advent. But this was taught early on as well; as one example, Dr. Kim Sudo's *120-Day Training Manual* states, "if only they can understand the fall of man they can understand that Father is the Messiah."[7] Again he writes, "Unless people can understand Father is Messiah, then they cannot move in."[8]

Unification theology blends Taoist philosophy and the Bible. The church publishes a number of books to explain this concept, but the most authoritative is the *Divine Principle*. All spiritual and physical entities are described in dualistic terms in Unification theology. Moon believes that God has a "key," called "new truth," which will unlock "all these difficult biblical

6. Sun Myung Moon, *CAUSA Seminar Speech*, August 29, 1985, 7–8. Other subsequent published versions have edited these lines out.
7. Dr. Kim Sudo, *120-Day Training Manual* (The Holy Spirit Association of the Unification of World Christianity, n.d.): 222.
8. Sudo, *Training Manual*, 400.

mysteries."[9] That key is later revealed as the Taoist *Book of Changes* (*I Ching*), through which Moon interprets the Bible and history.[10]

Nothing is exempt from dualism, whether in its essential nature or its relationship to other things. "God," Moon revealed, "consists of dual characteristics."[11]

Although the Bible is considered a scripture, its authority is replaced by Moon's *Divine Principle*. Moon taught that the Bible was not a trustworthy text. He stated, "The Bible, however, is not the truth itself, but contains the truth."[12] To say that the Bible is not truth, but only contains truth, opens the door for textual, historical, and doctrinal error. Jesus, in direct opposition to Moon's teaching, spoke in the highest terms about biblical authority when he said, "Thy Word is truth" (John 17:17). We are also reminded of Psalm 119:151, which states, "Thou art near, O Lord; and all thy commandments are truth."

> Unification theology blends Taoist philosophy and the Bible.

Moon held the opinion that science outdates the Bible. He counts it "impossible" in this "modern scientific civilization" to use "the same method of expressing the truth" as found in the New Testament.[13] Therefore, he reasons, a "new truth must appear."[14] And, like other cult leaders before him, Moon proclaims himself as the sole source for this new truth. The introduction of *Divine Principle* summarizes the matter: "This truth must appear as a revelation from God himself. This new truth has already appeared! God has sent His messenger. . . . His name is Sun Myung Moon."[15]

We have already seen that Moon's revelations depend upon spiritism. He makes spiritism a replacement or a substitute for the Holy Spirit. He taught, "Spirit men pour out spiritual fire. . . . They enable earthly men to see many facts in the spirit world in a state of trance, give them the gift of prophecy, and inspire them spiritually. Through such activities,

---

9. Dr. Young Oon Kim, *Divine Principle* (San Francisco: The Holy Spirit Association for the Unification of World Christianity, 1960, third edition, 1963), 15. The original title of this work was *Divine Principles*. However, since it is much more widely known by its later title, *Divine Principle*, this text uniformly refers to it as such. If the original edition is referred to, that is indicated in the text or footnote.

10. Kim, *Principle*, 26.
11. Kim, *Principle*, 26.
12. Kim, *Principle*, 9.
13. Kim, *Principle*, 131.
14. Kim, *Principle*, 131.
15. Kim, *Principle*, 16.

substituting for the Holy Spirit, they cooperate with earthly men to fulfill the will of God."[16]

It is no wonder, then, that Moon's "new truth" disagrees with the Bible, since he admits that his insight comes from spirits and not from the Holy Spirit. The Holy Spirit inspires the true Word of God (2 Peter 1:21). Jesus tells us that the Holy Spirit brings His words to the remembrance of the disciples (John 14:26) as the divine protector from error in Scripture. He also speaks only what is truth (John 16:13), which prevents any distortion in God's message. There cannot be any substitution for the Holy Spirit; such is the warning of Paul (2 Corinthians 11:4).

Contact with departed sprits becomes the test for authenticity in the *Divine Principle*. It states, "Any Christian who, in spiritual communication, can see John the Baptist directly in the spirit world will be able to understand the authenticity of all these things."[17] The idea that proof for revelation is grounded in spiritism is in direct violation of God's Word. A reading of Deuteronomy 18:10–12 or Isaiah 8:19–20 shows us that God counts all such activity as abominable.

Revelation for Moon carries an unusual dispensational motif. He believes in three "testaments": the Old Testament, the New Testament, and the Complete Testament. The Complete Testament is the *Divine Principle*. Even though the Complete Testament was given by Moon, he indicates that further revelation is yet to come. The "Complete" Testament evidently lacks completeness. A quarter of a century ago Moon promised an additional revelation called "Book Two,"[18] which is yet to surface. Its content, according to Moon, will irresistibly turn the heart of the most stubborn person toward him. A book with such powerful influence seemingly should have been released some years ago, since his church has suffered a loss of about one million people from its highest membership.

Biblical Perspective

God

God is described in dualistic characteristics by Moon. God's internal essence is both male and female, positive and negative (yang and yin). God's

16. Kim, *Principle*, 182.
17. Kim, *Principle*, 163.
18. Sun Myung Moon, *Master Speaks*, March 16, 1972, 4.

external relationship is subject and object, male and female (yang and yin). Our discussion begins with the essence of God—what is His nature in Unification theology?

Unification teachers have met with theologians from all walks of life and, by that, they have adopted Christian theological terminology and added it to their doctrines with a slight twist. When the definitions are examined, then the semantical changes emerge that alter the true meaning. Such words as *trinity, omnipresent, omnipotent, omniscient,* and *immutable* are commonly used in Unification thinking, but with entirely different meanings than Christian theology. The god presented by Moon is not the Trinity: He changes and he has needs, without which he would literally cease to exist.

Beginning with God's essence, Moon teaches that God "exists with His dual characteristics of positivity and negativity."[19] The standard symbol representing Taoism is a circle with a curved "s" division through the middle. The left side is white and the right side black. Each side contains its opposite color represented by a small circle. This symbol also underlies the Unification thesis for God. God is white and black simultaneously. He is positive and negative, male and female, subject and object, yang and yin. The god of Unification theology is dualistic.[20]

In expressing his view of God, Moon teaches, "The *Book of Changes (I Ching)* . . . emphasizes that the foundation of the universe is Taeguk (ultimacy) and from this comes Yang and Yin." He adds, "Taeguk . . . represents God, the subject who contains dual essentialities."[21] The original *Divine Principle,* translated by Dr. Young Oon Kim, explains the relationship: "Though there are dual characteristics in God's nature, namely, true fatherhood and motherhood, He appears as a masculine character [subject] to His creation [object]."[22] Moon expounds upon this dual nature, "A man can be divided into two identical halves. Because God is like that He made man the same so He could interact with him. God created everything to resemble himself, especially man."[23]

Rev. Moon apparently has no understanding of the eternal, undivided essence of God. As often stated in creedal form, we do not confuse the

19. Kim, *Principle,* 24.
20. Anon., *Outline of The Principle: Level 4* (New York: The Holy Spirit Association of the Unification of World Christianity, 1980): 4–6.
21. Kim, *Principle,* 25–26.
22. Kim, *Principle,* 3.
23. Moon, *Master Speaks,* March 19, 1978, 10.

persons of the Trinity (Father, Son, and Holy Spirit), nor do we divide the substance (one eternal, omnipotent, omniscient God).

Jesus

In the case of the second person of the Trinity, the Son, the creeds additionally summarize the scriptural teaching that He was one divine *person* who, from the incarnation and forward, possesses two *natures*, His eternal divine nature and His human nature. His human body came into being at His conception by the power of the Holy Spirit "overshadowing" the virgin Mary. The personal unity of Christ is indisputable throughout Scripture, as Christ said, for example, "Before Abraham was, *I* am" (John 8:58). Paul affirmed, "There is *one* Lord, Jesus Christ" (1 Corinthians 8:6). The Apostle John declares, "The Word was God" (John 1:1) and "The Word became flesh" (John 1:14), so that we "beheld *his* glory" (John 1:14). Moon's illustration that God is divisible, the same as man, fails. God does not even divide His attributes with another: "I am the Lord: that is my name: and my glory will I not give to another" (Isaiah 42:8). Had the dualism of Moon been true, the Bible would be false, and we would have to deny the clear statement of Scripture: "Thus saith the Lord the King of Israel . . . I am the first, and I am the last; beside me there is no God" (Isaiah 44:6). Rev. Moon tried to correct the Holy Spirit here by saying that God is dualistic, but the Holy Spirit's record of truthfulness is spotless.

> Jesus was one divine **person** who, from the incarnation and forward, possesses two **natures**—His eternal divine nature and His human nature.

The Unification Church denies the historic Christian doctrine of the Trinity. Although they use the term *trinity* at times, they have redefined it into any group of three beings. The word *Trinity* is used to summarize what we see of God's nature in the Bible. Therein we find one God and no others (Isaiah 43:10). God is personal as the Father (Matthew 6:9). God is personal as the Son (Matthew 3:17). God is personal as the Holy Spirit (Acts 5:3). And together the three persons are uniquely one God in Scripture (Isaiah 48:16; Matthew 28:19).

Dr. Kim apparently misunderstood this biblical doctrine, because she erroneously attaches polytheism to its definition. She said, "Many

Christians seem to worship three Gods: Father, Son, and Holy Spirit. . . . We believe the doctrine of the Trinity is mistaken, if it means the Father, Son, and Holy Spirit are three personal Gods."[24] Is it any surprise that Moonies reject the Trinity when one of their best theologians incorrectly defines it? Moon also redefines the Trinity: "Jesus and the Holy Spirit become one body centered on God; this is called 'Trinity.'"[25] Even more clearly, in the original *Divine Principle*, Moon teaches, "By uniting with the Holy Spirit, Jesus established the Holy Trinity for the first time—but spiritually."[26] Now Rev. Moon informs us that the Trinity had a beginning! Only after Jesus united with the Holy Spirit the first time did the Trinity begin. It is impossible, by any biblical standard, to arrive at Moon's conclusion without forsaking every Scripture that speaks about God's nature. The Bible speaks consistently about the tri-personal nature of God. Beginning in Genesis 1:26–27; 3:22; 11:7–8, to Isaiah 6:8, God uses the plural pronouns "us" and "our" in speaking of himself. Throughout the Old Testament we find God speaking of another person who shares His nature, showing more than one person (Isaiah 48:16; Jeremiah 50:40; Zechariah 2:8–11; 10:12). In the New Testament the relationship and equality of the persons of God is well established (Matthew 28:19; 2 Corinthians 13:14; and John 15:26).

The word "trinity" for Moon was God's ideal family of Adam and Eve, centered (foundationally) upon God. These three were to become the original trinity, but the fall of man truncated this hope. What occurred in Eden was a satanic trinity, which Moon believes was passed on to humanity. He teaches, "Due to the Fall, Adam and Eve . . . centered on Satan, thus resulting in a trinity centered on Satan. Therefore, their descendants have also formed trinities centered on Satan."[27]

All created entities are in a dualistic subject/object relationship with God, according to Moon. Creation is actually God's "second self, the visible God."[28] Moon describes God's nature, "We cannot see God because God exists as a spiritual force."[29] God is "the center," the "internal

24. Young Oon Kim, *Speeches on Unification Teaching* (Barrytown, NY: Unification Theological Seminary, 1986), 4–7.

25. Kim, *Principle*, 217.

26. Kim, *Principle*, 68.

27. Kim, *Principle*, 217.

28. Sun Myung Moon, *God's Warning to the World* (New York: The Holy Spirit Association of the Unification of World Christianity, 1985), 18.

29. Moon, *Master Speaks*, March 16, 1972, 1.

character" of the physical universe.[30] The universe "is the substantial manifestation of the invisible God."[31] The original *Divine Principle* states, "God is energy itself."[32]

Unification theology is immediately recognized as panentheism; that is, God is said to be invisibly "in" everything, but they distinguish him from the material atoms. Panentheism is superbly dealt with and refuted by Dr. Norman L. Geisler in *Christian Apologetics*.[33] Biblically, if God existed before creation (Moonies admit this), then for creation to become his "visible second self" it requires a change in his nature. In the Bible, God is unchangeable and immutable as we find in Psalm 102:26–27 or Malachi 3:6.

Another interesting aspect of creation in Unification theology is that apparently Lucifer and angels assisted God in creating all things. Moon said, "The archangel [Lucifer] had worked with God to create all the things in the universe; he knew everything."[34] Moon also explains, "God created the angels as servants who were to assist in the creation of the universe."[35] Yet nobody can produce a single line from the Bible that makes Lucifer or angels co-creators with God. Instead, we find that Jesus Christ is revealed as the Creator in His preexistence as second person of the Trinity (John 1:3, 10; 1 Corinthians 8:6; Colossians 1:16–17; and Hebrews 1:2, 10). The biblical fact is that Jesus created all things and Lucifer did none of it.

The god portrayed by Moon is weak, needful, and is limited in power. Moon speaks of God as one who is destructible. He says, "Since God must live in everything that is created, God himself must have these two separate elements [Sung Sang and Hyung Sang]. God must have the same nature as the rest of His creation, for without having such characteristics, He would eventually be destroyed by trying to exist in such a world."[36] Again, he wrote, "If man did not exist then God would vanish."[37] Even the *Divine Principle* carries this theme, "In order for God to exist externally,

30. Kim, *Principle*, 25.
31. Kim, *Principle*, 40.
32. Kim, *Principle*, 4.
33. Norman L. Geisler, *Christian Apologetics* (Grand Rapids, MI: Baker Book House, 1976), 193–213.
34. Moon, *Master Speaks*, March 16, 1972, 8.
35. Kim, *Principle*, 76.
36. Moon, *Master Speaks*, March 19, 1978, 9.
37. Moon, *Master Speaks*, May 22, 1977, 6.

God has dual essentialities."[38] It is inconceivable that God is dependent upon creation for His existence. The biblical doctrines about His eternality demonstrate that He exists independent of creation (1 Chronicles 16:36; Job 36:26; Psalm 41:13; 90:1–4; 93:2; 102:24–27; Isaiah 40:28). God speaks in exacting terms, "God is not a man" (Numbers 23:19); "I am God, and not man" (Hosea 11:9), which refutes His dependency upon man.

The Holy Spirit

Even though the Unification Church puts the "Holy Spirit" in its official name, The Holy Spirit Association for the Unification of World Christianity (HSAUWC), its followers know little about the third person of the Trinity. As quoted earlier, Moon teaches that disincarnate spirits are a valid substitute for the Holy Spirit, which is abominable doctrine and blasphemous. Moon informs us that the Holy Spirit is the female aspect of God and became the spiritual bride of Jesus—in fact, his spiritual wife! Moon stated, "The Holy Spirit is a female spirit, this is because she came as the True Mother, that is, the second Eve."[39] He elaborates, "In Christianity we have only spiritual parents. The Holy Spirit is the mother spirit; and with Jesus Christ and the Holy Spirit working together we cleanse our sins and are given rebirth on the spiritual level."[40] Green auras, according to Moon, represent the Holy Spirit.[41] Dr. Kim adds, "Unification Theology portrays the Holy Spirit not as an individual person, but rather as divine energy. . . . Like God himself, the Spirit is invisible and incorporeal—a bright light or a field of magnetic energy, so to speak."[42]

The biblical understanding of the genuine person and deity of the Holy Spirit is evident in many places (2 Samuel 23:2–3; John 14:26; 15:26; 16:5–15; Acts 5:3–4; and 1 Corinthians 6:19–20). From all of the above Unification theology, one need not go much further than 2 Corinthians 11:4 for refutation. It says, "For if he that cometh preacheth another Jesus, whom we have not preached, or if ye receive another spirit, which ye have

38. Kim, *Principle*, 40.
39. Kim, *Principle*, 215.
40. Moon, *Master Speaks*, September 22, 1974.
41. Moon, *Master Speaks*, March 16, 1972, 7.
42. Kim, *Speeches*, 5.

not received, or another gospel, which ye have not accepted, ye might well bear with him." Failure in any single point disqualifies one from fellowship, but Moon has succeeded in violation of all three.

Jesus' warning in Matthew 24 about false christs and false prophets hit the mark with Sun Myung Moon. Furthermore, Moon cannot make a genuine claim to Jesus' messianic office, because Jesus said himself, "salvation is *from* the Jews" (John 4:22), therefore, being Korean born prevents him from being the true Messiah.

Explore

Dualism

Refuting Tao

Disincarnate Spirits

The Second Eve

Discuss

1. What is Tao?

2. What replaces the authority of the Bible in Unification?

3. How does the Bible describe the Messiah?

4. Who is the biblical Holy Spirit?

_____

_____

——————————————— **Dig Deeper** ———————————————

See *The Kingdom of the Cults Study Guide* available at WalterMartin.com.

14

Scientology

Quick Facts on Scientology

- Scientology teaches that the Bible is a byproduct of Hindu scriptures.
- God or gods may exist, but the individual must decide for himself.
- Christ is a legend that preexisted earth-life on other planets and was implanted into humans on earth. Jesus was just a shade above "clear" and was no greater than Buddha or Moses.
- Reincarnation sufficiently explains man's existence, but Scientology is the freedom from reincarnation.

Historical Perspective

The Church of Scientology[1] is the most litigious religion in the history of churches founded in the United States. They have been the plaintiffs in an enormous number of lawsuits compared with most churches and/or religions. A few of their court battles have benefited others' rights. In that regard, Scientology's legal claims have occasionally helped stay the erosion of religious liberty. On the other hand, critics of Scientology allege that many of their lawsuits are malicious vendettas against ex-members and

1. Scientology, Dianetics, Hubbard, and E-Meter are trademarks and service marks of the Religious Technology Center.

perceived enemies of the church. This aggressive conduct has produced the counterproductive effect of souring outsiders' view of Scientology.

Christians historically cherished free speech and religious freedom as God's gift; however, an important part of our freedom is to label unbiblical conduct as sinful and heretical doctrine as false or cultic.

Several articles, both pro and con, have been written about Scientology's religious nature. In our observation, it has all the marks of a religion. It has its own set of scripture, it holds a worldview, and it seeks spiritual enlightenment. By biblical standards we justifiably call it a false religion. We define any religion as false whenever and wherever it departs from the biblical God and His plan of salvation as understood and proclaimed by the historical orthodox Christian church. Scientology is positively a religion sincerely followed by numerous people, but it is a false religion by biblical standards.

We must categorically separate denial of rights from proper examination and analysis by Scripture. Jesus also rebuked false teachers of His day without denying their freedom to believe what is wrong. Consider His "woes" to the Pharisees as an example (Matthew 23:13–30). Religions that deny Christ's deity, atonement, resurrection, and grace lead to an eternal hell and separation from God (John 10:1, 8; Matthew 5:29–30; 10:28; 18:9).

While the bulk of this chapter focuses on the theological aspects of Scientology, we will also examine its history to see how it came about. If their founder, L. Ron Hubbard, fabricated parts of his history and exaggerated his research as a substitute for truth, then it warrants examination by Scripture. In 1 Thessalonians 5:22 we are warned to abstain from all appearance of evil. Ephesians 5:11 counsels us, "Have no fellowship with the unfruitful works of darkness, but rather reprove them." We expect the same criterion for those who examine Jesus Christ, but in his life we do not find clandestine schemes or misconduct. Jesus, being sinless and God incarnate, has no equal and cannot be superseded by any other (John 1:1; 8:46; 18:20).

The Dianetics movement was once seen as a 1950s fad, which some commentators thought would fade away as many fads do.[2] Other writers perceived Dianetics as a cult from the beginning.[3] Under our earlier theological definition of cultism, the Church of Scientology is a non-Christian cult.

2. See Martin Gardner, *Fads and Fallacies in the Name of Science* (New York: Dover Publishing, 1957), 263, and Paul Sann, *Fads, Fallacies, and Delusions* (New York: Crown Publishing, 1967), 113ff.

3. *Time*, July 24, 1950, 64; *Newsweek*, October 16, 1950, 59; *American Mercury*, August 1951, 76; and *Time*, September 3, 1951.

Hubbard believed that he was the fulfillment of a 2,500-year-old Buddhist prediction about the Maitreya—a second Buddha. He sealed this sentiment with his book *The Hymn of Asia*, where it predicted a "red-haired or golden-haired" Maitreya would "arise in the West to complete the job Buddha began."[4] A Scientology magazine, *Advance!*, promoted Hubbard as the Buddhist Maitreya and unwittingly labeled themselves as a cult by stating, "In Buddhist lands Mettaya [Maitreya] became a great favorite [second Buddha]. Various cults devoted to him arose."[5] The Maitreya-cult exists in their church, where they are devoted to L. Ron Hubbard as the figurehead. Hubbard embraced devotion to himself in *The Hymn of Asia*, "Everywhere you are I can be addressed, But in our temples best, Address me and you address Lord Buddha, Address Lord Buddha, And you then address Metteyya."[6]

> L. Ron Hubbard believed that he was the fulfillment of a 2,500-year-old Buddhist prediction about the Maitreya—a second Buddha.

What is this movement called Scientology? It claims to be a "church" and an "applied religious philosophy." How do its teachings compare with the teachings of the Bible? What is L. Ron Hubbard's qualification for developing a system that claims to be "the most vital movement on Earth today"?[7] In this analysis of a complex religious and philosophical system, we will explore some answers to these questions. We will provide a survey of Scientology and, by contrast, show the major points at which statements in Scientology materials contradict biblical teaching.

L. Ron Hubbard

The founder of Scientology, Lafayette Ronald Hubbard (L. Ron Hubbard, affectionately called "Ron" by Scientologists), was born on March 13, 1911, in Tilden, Nebraska. Hubbard, a popular science fiction writer of the 1930s and 1940s, made a career change by allegedly announcing at a New Jersey science fiction convention, "Writing for a penny a word is ridiculous. If a man really wanted to make a million dollars, the best way

---

4. L. Ron Hubbard, *The Hymn of Asia* (Los Angeles: Church of Scientology of California Publications Organization, 1974), no numbered pages.
5. *Advance!*, December 1974, 5.
6. Hubbard, *Hymn of Asia*.
7. L. Ron Hubbard, "The Aims of Scientology" (Hollywood: The Church of Scientology Celebrity Center, 1974, 1977), one-page flyer.

would be to start his own religion."[8] The following year, in May 1950, Hubbard released *Dianetics: A Modern Science of Mental Health*,[9] which has become an entry-level reading for converts to Scientology. Hubbard's overnight success with *Dianetics* virtually gave him a new career in writing self-help and religious books. His first book on Scientology was published in 1951, and the Church of Scientology was first incorporated in Camden, New Jersey, on December 22, 1953.[10]

Hubbard spent his final years in seclusion from the public eye. Top Scientologists isolated him from most family and church members until his death in Creston, California (a small town north of San Luis Obispo). According to a copy of his death certificate, he succumbed to a cerebral vascular accident (stroke) on January 24, 1986. In their refusal to believe that such a great "science of the mind" master could die a horrific death, the word "dead" or "died" was never used at his eulogy. Instead, the new president of Scientology, David Miscavige, announced that L. Ron Hubbard decisively "discarded the body" to move on to the next level of research, outside his body.[11] How or when this new extra-terrestrial research would become available to planet earth is left unsaid.

Hubbard himself apparently encouraged an examination of his belief system such as that undertaken in this volume. The seventh article of the Creed of Scientology states, "All men have the inalienable rights to think freely, to talk freely, to write freely on their own opinions and to counter or utter or write upon the opinion of others." If they hold faithful to their creed, they should expect counter writings. With this, we counter the opinions of L. Ron Hubbard.

The Dianetics Movement

As an accomplished science fiction writer, Hubbard had no difficulty coining new terms. This talent became the bedrock for new terminology

8. *Time*, April 5, 1976, 57.
9. Unless otherwise noted, all quotations from the 1986 edition: L. Ron Hubbard, *Dianetics: The Modern Science of Mental Health* (Los Angeles: Bridge Publications, Inc., 1986).
10. In actuality, it was a subordinate corporation under the parent corporation, the Church of American Science, incorporated on the same date. The purpose for the Church of Scientology was to "train and indoctrinate ministers and brothers in the principles and teachings of the Church of American Science," and, "this corporation shall be under the direction and subordinate to The Church of American Science." The first Church of Scientology that was an independent entity was incorporated in California on February 18, 1954.
11. Bent Corydon, *L. Ron Hubbard, Messiah or Madman?* (Fort Lee, NJ: Barricade Books, 1992), 17.

in Dianetics and Scientology. Church publications often contain glossaries of the new terms. They also publish a technical dictionary with 3,000 new terms and definitions. It is interesting, however, that the word *Scientology* was originally used in 1934 by a German social psychologist, Dr. A. Nordenholz.[12] A French physiologist, Richard Semon, coined "engram" in 1904.[13] *Engram* is one of the most commonly used words in Dianetics and Scientology.

Dianetics means "through thought" or "through the soul." Hubbard promoted Dianetics by publishing three long excerpts of his theory in the periodical *Astounding Science Fiction*, May 1950, October 1950, and January 1951. According to *Publisher's Weekly*, *Dianetics* sold 55,000 copies in the first two months and more than 750 Dianetics groups started nationwide.[14] They advertised its readership a year later as 150,000 people with 2.5 million followers. Dianetics swept college campuses and blazed through middle-class America with a faddish appeal that evolved into a cultic structure.

The glowing benefits of Dianetics seemed virtually unlimited as Hubbard promoted his new "science of the mind."[15] Mankind, according to Hubbard, "is basically good."[16] The basic instinct for all people is survival.[17] Man's environmental conditions and painful experiences result in failure. If a man changes his circumstances and eliminates pain, then his condition improves. The two most important factors for man's survival, then, are avoiding pain and gaining pleasure.[18]

The structure of man's mind is simplified by dividing the mind into three main categories: the analytical mind, reactive mind, and somatic mind.[19] The analytical mind works like a "perfect computer, it never makes a mistake."[20] It is also the "I" of a person.[21] The reactive mind works on a "totally stimulus/response basis."[22] The reactive mind holds mental picture

12. George Malko, *Scientology: The Now Religion* (New York: Dell Publishing, 1970), 64. Malko parallels Hubbard's and Nordenholz's models, which reveals some scant hypothetical resemblance (116–119).

13. Daniel L. Schacter, *Stranger Behind the Engram* (Hillsdale, NJ: Lawrence Erlbaum Associates, Publishers, 1982), 186.

14. *Publisher's Weekly*, September 16, 1950, 1124.

15. Hubbard, *Dianetics*, 7.

16. Hubbard, *Dianetics*, 26.

17. Hubbard, *Dianetics*, 29.

18. Hubbard, *Dianetics*, 44.

19. Hubbard, *Dianetics*, 61.

20. Hubbard, *Dianetics*, 62.

21. Hubbard, *Dianetics*, 61.

22. Hubbard, *Dianetics*, 577.

images of past experiences called "engrams," which are apparently the "single source of aberrations and psychosomatic ills."[23] Some liken the reactive mind to the subconscious mind. The analytical and reactive minds direct the somatic mind and "place solutions into effect on the physical level."[24] This mind keeps the body regulated and functioning.

Humanity's problem is that the reactive mind frequently interrupts the analytical mind. The analytical mind, which essentially "*is* the person,"[25] could flawlessly run a person's life (being a perfect computer) except for the interference from the reactive mind.[26]

It appears that this villain of the analytical mind causes it to shut off. Scientology calls this a moment of unconsciousness, though often the body is awake and animated. Hubbard explains, "When the individual is 'unconscious' in full or in part, the reactive mind is cut in, in full or in part. When he is fully conscious, his analytical mind is fully in command of the organism."[27] During these unconscious moments, the reactive mind takes in a detailed recording from the sensory organs. This recording is not a "memory," but an image, like a motion picture, called an "engram."[28] Everything said, seen, touched, or sensed is recorded by the reactive mind as the "engram." The reactive mind stores this engram, which works to stimulate the person to react to the stimuli.

The example is given: "Suppose as an example of an engram and its effects on the Spirit, Mr. A has a tonsillectomy under anesthetic. During the operation, the surgeon, who wears glasses, comments angrily to a clumsy nurse, 'You don't know what you are doing.' Mr. A recovers. A few months later, Mr. A, a bit tired during a hard day at the office, has an argument with his employer (who happens to also wear glasses), who says, 'You don't know what you are doing.' Mr. A suddenly feels dizzy, stupid, and gets a pain in his throat. There is installed a kind of conditioned semantic response which affects the Thetan [man's spirit in Scientology]."[29] These engrams make man react insanely in society, in fact, they make man "mad, inefficient, and ill."[30]

23. Hubbard, *Dianetics*, 577.
24. Hubbard, *Dianetics*, 56.
25. Hubbard, *Dianetics*, 61.
26. Hubbard, *Dianetics*, 66.
27. Hubbard, *Dianetics*, 82.
28. Hubbard, *Dianetics*, 83.
29. Staff of Scientology, *Scientology: A World Religion Emerges in the Space Age* (Los Angeles: Church of Scientology Information Service, 1974), 28.
30. Hubbard, *Dianetics*, 84.

The solution to the reactive mind interrupting the analytical mind is to rid the reactive mind of all engrams. Once this is accomplished, the person is called "clear." The clear person has no reaction to the same situation because no engram stimulates it. The goal of Dianetics is to clear the individual of all engrams of his past.[31] At first, Dianetics only dealt with engrams in this lifetime. After more probing, Scientologists claim that they carry engrams from past lives (reincarnation), which also need to be cleared.

The "clear" person is on the evolutionary journey to the next stage of man, a godlike being called *homo novis*. Hubbard informs us that a clear individual

> . . . can be tested for all psychoses, neuroses, compulsions, and repressions (all aberrations) and can be examined for any autogenetic (self-generated) diseases referred to as psychosomatic ills. These tests confirm the clear to be entirely without such ills or aberrations. Additional tests of his intelligence indicate it to be high above the current norm.[32]

Hubbard continues listing the potential benefits for the clear person. It improves eyesight, stops ear-ringing, increases the IQ, cures the common cold, speeds thinking computations 120 times faster than normal, and saves marriages.[33]

The application of Hubbard's hypothesis is to vanquish the engrams through "Dianetic therapy." This is accomplished by an "auditor" who "audits" the engram through a form of counseling. After *Dianetics* was published, Hubbard introduced an electronic galvanometer, the E-meter, to help in auditing. The "pre-clear" (the person not yet clear) holds two tin cans connected by wires to the E-meter, while the auditor sits opposite him watching the needle on the E-meter. As the auditor gives "commands" to the pre-clear, the needle's fluctuation determines if they have detected a possible engram. The auditor tracks the engram by questioning the pre-clear with the goal of erasing it. That may only be the beginning of problems for the pre-clear, though. They may detect other engrams in connection with the first, producing a chain of engrams. It may take years of auditing for a person to become finally clear.

31. Hubbard, *Dianetics*, 14.
32. Hubbard, *Dianetics*, 14.
33. Hubbard, *Dianetics*, 17–18, 122, 125, 228, 411.

Hubbard claims that his results are scientifically valid and are based upon clinical study. Critics, however, renounced it from the start. *Publisher's Weekly*[34] reported that the American Psychological Association initiated the "first concerted action against" Dianetics at their September 1950 meeting. A resolution, adopted unanimously by the organization's 8,000 members, said that Hubbard's claims for Dianetics "are not supported by empirical evidence of the sort required for the establishment of scientific generalizations."

Dr. Morris Fishbeck, former editor of the *Journal of the American Medical Association*, went on record warning people about "mind-healing cults . . . like Dianetics."[35] Psychologist Eric Fromm aimed his comments at Hubbard's techniques. "Dianetics," he said, "has no respect for and no understanding of the complexities of personality." Dr. Fromm revealed that Hubbard had saturated Dianetics in "oversimplified truths, half-truths, and plain absurdities."[36]

One other problem that seemed to face Hubbard was that no "clears" could be found until February 1966, when John McMaster was called the world's first clear. It troubled critics that Hubbard never claimed to be clear himself until some years after *Dianetics* was published. Still, a little known story of an earlier clear is found in several newspapers of 1950.

On August 10, 1950, Hubbard rented the Shrine Auditorium in Los Angeles. An estimated crowd of 4,000 came to see the world's first clear, Miss Sonya Bianca, a physics student from Boston. Fitting with the Dianetic theory, Hubbard announced that she had perfect recall and could remember every moment of her life. When members of the audience questioned her, she could not remember basic physics formulas nor the color of Hubbard's necktie, which she had seen moments before. People began leaving the auditorium as they threw more taunting questions at Bianca. Hubbard quickly explained that he had accidentally placed her in the "now" by calling her to "come out now." Therefore, Hubbard reasoned, she could only remember the present "now" and nothing past. No reporters seemed convinced of his explanation, and on that note the Bianca debacle ended.

Although most Scientologists still claim that the world's first clear came in 1966, this is apparently not true according to Hubbard. In *The Journal*

34. *Publisher's Weekly*, September 16, 1950, 1124.
35. *Newsweek*, October 16, 1950, 59.
36. Sann, *Delusions*, 114.

of Scientology (January 15, 1954), Hubbard wrote of how he had cleared fifty people. He added that auditors had cleared many times that number.

The Church of Scientology

The first nonprofit organization Hubbard set up was the Hubbard Dianetic Research Foundation. By November 1950, they had developed three courses in Dianetics. In 1953, the Church of Scientology was founded as a nonprofit corporation. The meaning of Scientology, Hubbard says, is "knowing about knowing, or science of knowledge."[37]

The Church of Scientology uses a cross similar to the historical cross (*crux immissa*) of Christianity, with the exception that it has four shorter sunburst points protruding from the center. The *Technical Dictionary* tells us that Hubbard borrowed the cross from Christianity. It states, "The model of the cross came from a very ancient Spanish mission in Arizona, a sand casting, which was dug up by Ron."[38] Ministers of Scientology often dress in black clergy garments and a white collar with a three-inch cross hanging from the neck. Since they also use the title "Reverend," they could easily be mistaken for Christian ministers, but their theology tells a different story.

Hubbard's "discovery" of the "Thetan" contributed to the religious nature of Scientology. The Thetan is likened to man's spirit. In Scientology, the Thetan is a timeless entity, which reincarnates in interplanetary life-forms. Once reaching earth, it goes through various life forms until it reaches manhood. The Thetan's goal is freedom from the cycle of birth and rebirth, which is why Scientology is necessary to the member.

Most people who join the church do so after reading *Dianetics*. They follow this with advanced levels and the hope of obtaining "clear" in one lifetime. Additional courses are offered for survival through the eight dynamics of life: self, sex, group, mankind, other life-forms, MEST, spirits, and a Supreme Being. The cleared Thetan must learn to gain control over his environment and become an "Operating Thetan" (OT).

Matter, energy, space, and time (MEST) compose the physical universe. Everything but the Thetan is MEST. A Thetan can potentially control MEST by operating independently of his body.[39] Since the OT no longer

37. L. Ron Hubbard, *Dianetics and Scientology Technical Dictionary* (Los Angeles: American St. Hill Organization, 1975), 369.
38. Hubbard, *Technical Dictionary*, 371.
39. Hubbard, *Technical Dictionary*, 279.

needs his body, he can leave it at will through the act of "exterioriza-tion," similar to astral projection.[40] OTs climb fifteen levels, but the highest courses are obtainable by only a few members.

The church often reminds Scientologists in publications that "Scientol-ogy works." However, Scientologists, whose goal is to make the world a better place, were caught in deep criminal activity that runs contrary to their religion and philosophy. More than 5,000 Scientologists were involved in one of the most clandestine covert spying operations ever aimed at the United States government. Evidently, none of the 5,000 Scientologists had the moral character or ethical integrity to compel them to expose the criminal activity as it was planned and perpetrated. Quite accidentally, two Scientologists working undercover with phony IRS badges to gain entrance to the Assistant U.S. Attorney's office made a grave mistake and the cover was blown. They failed to sign in a second time with the night-time librarian, arousing his suspicion. He phoned the FBI, who instructed him to contact them should the two men return. They returned and the FBI caught them. The three-year operation came to a screeching halt.

These illegal activities were publicized when eleven top Scientologists were indicted in 1977. They named Mary Sue Hubbard, wife of the founder and director of the operation, among those charged with crimes. Court evidence, numbering approximately 33,000 documents, connected Scien-tologists to the infiltration of governmental offices, burglarizing, bugging, wiretapping, and stealing classified information. The operation targeted "the Federal Trade and Atomic Energy Commissions; the National Security Defense Intelligence Agencies; the Departments of Labor, Army, and Navy; the US Customs Service; Interpol, and numerous US police departments."[41] All eleven charged Scientologists originally pleaded innocent to the 28-count grand jury indictment. After much plea bargaining and examining the mountain of evidence against them, they pleaded guilty to one charge instead of a trial and a heavier sentence. Nine Scientologists (two of the eleven were in England) were sentenced on October 26, 1979. L. Ron Hub-bard and twenty-four other Scientologists were named as coconspirators, but not indicted.[42] Mary Sue Hubbard and four top Scientologists were given five-year prison terms and fined $10,000 each.

40. Hubbard, *Dianetics*, 115. Exteriorization is an act performed also by Pre-Clears and Clears, but often under the direction of an Auditor. OTs perform this at will.
41. *People's Weekly*, August 14, 1978, 23. See also *Christianity Today*, December 7, 1979.
42. *Reader's Digest*, May 1980, 91.

The Church of Scientology argues that it has long been oppressed by the American government. Even if we grant their argument, still, criminal activity is not the correct solution. The religious benefits of Scientology waned at this junction, because a "clear" person, especially an OT, should not be committing crimes. In these cases, Scientology did not work. This is a dark shadow for Operating Thetans, who are supposedly "cleared of all wrong answers or useless answers that keep them from living or thinking."[43]

The world headquarters for the Church of Scientology is in Clearwater, Florida. For several years, L. Ron Hubbard conducted business outside of governmental reach aboard a floating headquarters, the *Apollo*, part of a fleet of ships in international waters called the Sea Org. Today's leadership as another floating office, the *Freewinds*, a former cruise ship that wealthy Scientologists pay up to $15,000 for a week-long Caribbean cruise. It does double duty as a high-level decision-making office for top Scientologists.[44] So prized are Hubbard's writings that Scientology has built a multimillion-dollar nuclear bomb-proof vault tunneled into Walker Mountain, near Eureka, California, to store his writings.

The arm of Scientology reaches into several areas of life. People often point to the success stories of Scientology's anti-drug program. It apparently has a successful drug-rehabilitation program, Narcanon. It has a criminal rehabilitation program, Criminon. And it has a "non-religious" moral education program, The Way to Happiness. (Contrary to their claim, it has Hubbard's religion sprinkled throughout the text.) Scientology's Celebrity Center caters to renowned figures, often using their endorsements for programs. Those lending their notoriety to Scientology programs include actresses Karen Black, Priscilla Presley, Laura Prepon, Jenna Elfman, Nancy Cartwright, and Kirstie Alley; singers Lou Rawls and Beck; actors John Travolta and Tom Cruise; and jazz musicians Chick Corea and Stanley Clarke.

These programs are steppingstones to lead the unaware person into the false teachings of the church. Scientologists will point out many who have been helped without joining; however, the testimony of rehabilitation is not to be confused with biblical salvation. It is admirable when anybody leaves an addictive past, but they remain destitute of salvation without

---

43. Hubbard, *Technical Dictionary*, 75.
44. *The Cult Observer*, Vol. 9, No. 4 (1992), 9.

Jesus Christ. Scientology's false theology will lead people into an eternal hell without Christ. Recovered alcoholics and drug addicts still need to find a genuine and personal relationship with the Lord Jesus Christ, who alone regenerates man through the work of the Holy Spirit (Acts 4:12; Hebrews 1:2; Titus 3:5).

Theological Evaluation

The source of authority in any religion quickly tells the reader his or her world-view. Much of Scientology's literature never mentions God, Jesus Christ, the Holy Spirit, the Bible, salvation, or other theological terms associated with Christianity. All of L. Ron Hubbard's Scientology writings since *Dianetics* are considered "scripture" by the church. If his writings are scripture, then we must compare them with God's genuine Scripture, the Bible. Jesus reminds us that we do not gather grapes of thorns nor figs of thistle plants (Matthew 7:16). We have seen the bad fruit of Scientology's leadership, but another fruit to examine is its scripture, the writings of L. Ron Hubbard. We will also draw from their 1954 Articles of Incorporation California, which have a systematic outline of their tenets not found in other writings.

They described their "Holy Book" in their California Articles of Incorporation (2.i.14) as "a collection of the works of and about the Great Teachers, including the work, St. Luke." Yet, strangely, references to Luke's gospel in Scientology writings are virtually nonexistent. On the contrary, Hubbard revealed his other sources in his *Phoenix Lectures* (1954). He stated, "The [Hindu] Veda . . . is best read in a literal translation from the Sanskrit. . . . A great deal of our material in Scientology is discovered right back there. Tao means knowingness," he wrote. "In other words, it's an ancestor to Scientology, the study of 'knowing how to know.'" Furthermore, "The Veda, the Tao, the Dharma, all mean knowingness. . . . We first find this Buddha called actually *Bodhi*. . . . This probably would be a Dianetic Release. . . . Another level has been mentioned to me—Arhat, with which I am not particularly familiar, said to be more comparable to our idea of Theta Clear." And, "Dhyana . . . could be literally translated as 'Indian for Scientology,' if you wished to do that."[45] From this we see the eclectic nature of Hubbard's theological authorities. He was partial to a Buddhist prophetic

45. L. Ron Hubbard, *The Phoenix Lectures* (Los Angeles: The Church of Scientology of California Publications Organization United States, 1969), 12, 16, 18, 19.

interpretation and believed it applied to his life: "The truth of the matter is that you are studying an extension of the work of Gautama Siddhartha, begun about 2,500 years ago. . . . Buddha predicted that in 2,500 years the entire job would be finished in the West. . . . Well, we finished it!"[46]

Scientology claims its church "does not conflict with other religions or religious practices as it clarifies them and brings understanding of the spiritual nature of Man"[47] But Hubbard questioned the origin of the Bible, saying, "It is no wonder why we look into the Christian bible and find ourselves reading the Egyptian *Book of the Dead*." And, "The parables that are discovered today in the New Testament were earlier discovered, the same parables, elsewhere in many places. One of these was the Egyptian *Book of the Dead*, which predates the New Testament considerably."[48] Typical of Hubbard's writings, no evidence or source is provided in support of his claim.

There are important contradictions between the Bible and Hubbard's underlying sources for Scientology. Jesus, as the unique Son of God, gave no credence to other scriptures or to any distortions about God's nature. One example of Jesus distinguishing

> **Hubbard questioned the origin of the Bible.**

between truth and error is the account of the Samaritan woman (John 4). The Samaritans are closely related to Judaism, yet he told the Samaritan woman, in John 4:22 that Samaritans do not know whom they worship. If Jesus differentiated between the Samaritan god and the Jewish God, then we should also distinguish between Mr. Hubbard's synthesizing of religions and Christianity. Jesus also challenged world teachers in John 10:8, "All that ever came before me are thieves and robbers." Since the Vedas, Confucius, Lao-tzu (Taoism), the Buddha, and the Egyptian *Book of the Dead* all came before Christ, He openly renounces them as "thieves and robbers." Rather than attempting homogenization, as Hubbard did, Jesus isolated His teachings from all others. Jesus singled himself out as man's only hope (Matthew 7:22–23; John 8:24; 14:6).

Truth for the individual in Scientology is often subjective and existential. To quote Hubbard, "Know thyself . . . and the truth shall set you free." In

---

46. *Advance!*, December 1974, 5, as quoted from L. Ron Hubbard's 1966 taped lecture, Scientology, Definitions III.

47. L. Ron Hubbard, *Volunteer Minister's Handbook* (Los Angeles: Church of Scientology, 1976), xiv.

48. Hubbard, *Phoenix Lectures*, 9, 27.

contrast, Jesus said, "If ye continue in my word, then are ye my disciples indeed; and ye shall know the truth, and the truth shall make you free" (John 8:31–32). Jesus gave an objective standard for truth: himself (John 14:6) and the Word of God (John 17:17). Never is man called "truth" in the Bible; neither is man's inner self. God is called truth (Deuteronomy 32:4; Isaiah 65:16), as is Jesus (John 14:6), the Holy Spirit (1 John 5:6), the Word of God (John 17:17), and the Gospel (Galatians 2:5, 14). Never is man or knowledge of "thyself" called truth.

The subjective nature of truth in Scientology allows variation on some items. Hubbard wrote, "What is true for you is what you have observed yourself."[49] What one person perceives as truth may not be what another person perceives. So, what by normative standards would be called a contradiction outside of Scientology can be synthesized within the organization. An example found in Hubbard's book *Axioms and Logics*, Axiom 31, states, "Goodness and badness, beautifulness and ugliness are alike considerations and have no other basis than opinion."[50] We would biblically challenge the first proposition on the basis that goodness and badness are moral terms, not merely synthesized opinions. By biblical standards, the absolutes of God's moral law provide a basis for determining the value of human conduct.

In our following study, Hubbard can apparently state two contradictory and opposing propositions without determining which is true. Hubbard at times can speak of one God (monotheism) and at other times of many gods (polytheism), without denial of either and while affirming truth in both statements. Hubbard also taught that "Truth is relative to environments, experience, and truth."[51] If truth is relative, in Hubbard's thinking, then he can apparently justify holding two opposing propositions without contradiction. This is how he writes equally about the existence of one God and many gods existing simultaneously.

Biblical Perspective

Scientology describes deity in three ways: a Supreme Being, God, and gods. Members are free to choose (or not choose) their concept of God. *The Scientology Catechism* (as found in *What is Scientology?*) states, "What is the

49. L. Ron Hubbard, *Technical Bulletins* (Los Angeles: Scientology Publications, 1976), 4:203.
50. L. Ron Hubbard, *Axioms and Logics* (Los Angeles: American St. Hill Organization, 1973), 5.
51. Hubbard, *Axioms and Logics*, 12.

Scientology concept of God? We have no dogma in Scientology and each person's concept is different. . . . Each person attains his own certainty as to who God is and exactly what God means to him. The author of the universe exists. How this is symbolized is dictated by your early training and conscience."[52] This affirmation declares that some kind of deity exists, but there is no further definition. The most organized statement of Scientology's catechism is found in *What is Scientology?* on pages 197–220. [53] They further teach, "although the existence of the Supreme Being is affirmed in Scientology, His precise nature is not delineated, since the Church holds that each person must seek and know the Divine Nature in and for himself."[54] They address God in the monotheistic sense in many places, yet Hubbard also speaks of the activity of gods elsewhere. In their Articles of Incorporation (California, 1954, section 2.h) we even find a pantheistic or perhaps panentheistic concept: "Believing that Man's best evidence of God is the God he finds within himself . . . the Church of Scientology is formed to espouse such evidence of the Supreme Being and Spirit as may be knowable to Men."

Hubbard appears to embrace nearly every form of deity: deism, theism, polytheism, pantheism, panentheism, and even the lack of deity, atheism. By definition, these are opposed to one another, but Hubbard finds no contradiction in promulgating monotheism and polytheism together. In his *Phoenix Lectures*, he indiscriminately allowed for both concepts: "Let us take up what amounts to probably ten thousand years of study on the part of Man, on the identity of God or gods."[55]

He also exposes false gods commingled with true gods. "There are gods above all other gods," he wrote. "There is not argument here against the existence of a Supreme Being or any devaluation intended. It is that amongst the gods, there are many false gods elected to power and position. . . . There are gods above other gods, and gods beyond the gods of the universes."[56] Furthermore, he wrote in the Hymn of Asia, "There can be love for Gods." And, "Behave[,] Obey[,] Be Courteous[,] To gods[,] Lord Buddha[,] And myself[,] And to your leaders."[57]

52. Staff of Scientology, "The Scientology Catechism," *What Is Scientology?* (Los Angeles: Church of Scientology of California, 1979), 200.

53. Staff, "The Scientology Catechism," 197–220.

54. Staff of Scientology, *Scientology: A World Religion Emerges in the Space Age* (Los Angeles: Church of Scientology Information Service, 1974), 17.

55. Hubbard, *Phoenix Lectures*, 3.

56. L. Ron Hubbard, Scientology 8–8008 (Los Angeles: ASHO, 1967), 73.

57. L. Ron Hubbard, *Hymn of Asia* (Los Angeles: Church of Scientology of California Publications Organization, 1974), 227, 241.

Their book on world religion leaves little doubt that the Hindu Brahman is closely paralleled with Scientology's understanding of the Supreme Being. Here God is spoken of in terms of pantheism and Hinduism.[58]

Though Hubbard provides no strict definition of the Supreme Being, his descriptive characteristics are enough for the Christian reader to see its unbiblical nature. Hubbard rejects the Christian doctrine of the Trinity. His *Phoenix Lectures* state, "The Christian god is actually much better characterized in the Vedic Hymns [Hinduism] than in any subsequent publication, including the Old Testament."[59] Again, he said, "The god the Christians worshipped is certainly not the Hebrew god. He looks *much* more like the one talked about in the Veda."[60]

What he mistakenly assumed is that the Hindu "triad" is the basis for the Christian "Trinity." This is not historical or biblical. The Trinity is based solely upon the revelation of God's Word. Hubbard also wrote, "For a long while, some people have been cross with me for my lack of cooperation in believing in a Christian Heaven, God, and Christ. I have never said I didn't disbelieve in a Big Thetan but there was certainly something very corny about Heaven *et al*."[61]

Scientologists are taught by Hubbard that man is part God and can attain a "godlike" nature. He wrote, "A pre-clear is a precise thing, part animal, part pictures, and part God."[62] In Hubbard's evolutionary development of Homo sapiens, he teaches that man will evolve into "*homo novis*," described as "very high and godlike."[63]

Scripture denies the possibility of other gods besides the true God. There is but one God (Deuteronomy 4:39; 6:4; Isaiah 43:10; 44:8; Mark 12:32; Ephesians 4:6; 1 Timothy 2:5; and James 2:19).

The Bible always presents a sharp distinction between God and man. Scripture reminds us in Numbers 23:19, "God is not a man, that he should lie." Hosea 11:9 says, "I am God, and not man, the Holy One in the midst of thee." A study of God's omnipotence, omnipresence, and omniscience truncates the words of Hubbard (1 Samuel 2:3; 1 Kings 8:27; Job 42:2; Jeremiah 23:24; 32:17; Romans 11:33).

58. Staff, *A World Religion*, 5.
59. Hubbard, *Phoenix Lectures*, 31.
60. Hubbard, *Phoenix Lectures*, 27.
61. L. Ron Hubbard, "Heaven," *Hubbard Communication Office Bulletin* (hereafter *HCOB*) (May 11, 1963), one page, as quoted by Kevin Anderson, *Report of the Board of Inquiry into Scientology* (Melbourne: Australia Parliament Government Printer, 1965), 150.
62. L. Ron Hubbard, *Scientology Clear Procedure, Issue One* (Los Angeles: ASHO, 1969), 21.
63. L. Ron Hubbard, *History of Man* (Los Angeles: ASHO, 1968), 38.

Jesus

When L. Ron Hubbard mentions Jesus Christ, it is rarely in reverence and mostly with disparagement. A few lines previously, we saw that Mr. Hubbard refused to believe in the Christian Christ. Implants are false concepts forced upon a Thetan, and Scientology chalks up "Christ" as an implant more than a million years ago. He wrote, "You will find . . . the Christ legend as an implant in pre-clears a million years ago."[64] He taught interplanetary travel for the Thetan. Certain planets have implant stations for Thetans where the Thetan goes after the animal or human body dies. The Thetan is then shot down from that planet into a new body (reincarnation) on earth or elsewhere just before birth. It is from these implant stations that Hubbard is claiming that the Christ implant was forced into Thetans a million years ago.

Mr. Hubbard casts doubt upon the uniqueness of Jesus as the Messiah. His *Phoenix Lectures* state, "Now the Hebrew definition of Messiah is one Who Brings Wisdom—a Teacher. Messiah is from 'messenger'. . . . Now here we have a great teacher in Moses. We have other Messiahs, and we then arrive with Christ, and the words of Christ were a lesson in compassion and they set a very fine example to the Western world."[65] It does not take a great deal of biblical knowledge to refute Hubbard here, for many young students in Christian churches are aware that the Hebrew definition for Messiah is "anointed." It does not come from "messenger," but from "to rub" or "anoint." Hubbard proves his ignorance of Hebrew and Christian terminology. Had Mr. Hubbard fairly investigated and understood the biblical claims about Jesus, then perhaps he would not have so carelessly criticized Christ as an implanted legend.

The Church of Scientology teaches that Jesus Christ may have believed in reincarnation: "There is much speculation on the part of religious historians as to the early education of Jesus of Nazareth. It is believed by many authorities that Jesus was a member of the cult of the Essenes, who believed in reincarnation."[66] Hubbard attributes Hindu teachings to Jesus. "Christ," he wrote, "was a bringer of information. He never announced his sources. He spoke of them as coming from God. But they might just as well have come from the god talked about in the Hymn to the Dawn Child

---

64. L. Ron Hubbard, *Professional Auditor's Bulletin 31*, quoted by Anderson, *Report*, 150.
65. Hubbard, *Phoenix Lectures*, 27–28.
66. Staff, *A World Religion*, 15.

. . . the Veda."[67] Hubbard looks down upon Jesus from his OT VIII position, claiming, "Neither Lord Buddha nor Jesus Christ were OT, according to the evidence. They were just a shade above clear."[68]

Let us remember that the Apostle Peter dealt with Hubbardian theories long ago. Peter, denying any mythology or legend to Christ, said, "We have not followed cunningly devised fables, when we made known unto you the power and coming of our Lord Jesus Christ, but were eyewitnesses of his majesty" (2 Peter 1:16). Jesus also denied anyone could be the Messiah other than himself (Matthew 24:3–5, 11). He unashamedly said, "No man cometh unto the Father, but by me" (John 14:6). Luke settles the idea of multiple ways of salvation in Acts 4:12, "For there is none other name under heaven given among men, whereby we must be saved."

Jesus was not a man looking for salvation with the rest of humanity. He was sinless (John 8:46; 1 Peter 2:22) and had no need to be "a shade above clear." He fully announced His sources (Luke 24:44), which have nothing to do with the Essenes nor the Vedas. In the Bible He is seen as an eternal, active person (Micah 5:2) who is one with the Father (John 10:30) and the second person of the Trinity (Matthew 28:19).

Salvation

Scientologists prefer to use the term *rebirth* instead of *reincarnation*, although the term *reincarnation* is found in their writings. Hubbard emphasized that salvation is to be free from the endless cycle of birth and rebirth. The way to salvation is to erase engrams through auditing. The proof to many Scientologists that they release engrams through auditing is the accompanying sign. "When one releases an engram," Hubbard wrote, "the erasure is accompanied by yawns." (Tears, sweat, odor, panting, urine, vomiting, and excreta might also indicate a released engram.)[69]

Scientology's view of reincarnation includes extraterrestrial life, evolution on other planets, evolution on earth, implant stations, forgetter implants, and engrams that keep people trapped in reincarnation. The OT III, section three, material was entered into court cases, from which we find Hubbard's journey of the Thetan. He claims this discovery was in December 1967:

67. Hubbard, *Phoenix Lectures*, 27.
68. L. Ron Hubbard, *Certainty Magazine*, 5:10, as quoted by Anderson, *Report*, 150.
69. L. Ron Hubbard, *Science of Survival* (Los Angeles: AHOS, 1973), 2:255.

The head of the Galactic Confederation (76 planets . . . 95,000,000 years ago) solved overpopulation (250 billion or so per planet) by mass implanting. He caused people to be brought to Teegeeack (Earth) and put an H-bomb on the principal volcanoes . . . and then the Pacific area ones were taken in boxes to Hawaii and the Atlantic ones to Las Palmas and there "packaged." His name was Xenu.

[The result of Hubbard's investigation into this formerly undiscovered data was that] one's body is a mass of individual Thetans stuck to oneself or to the body. . . . Thetans believed they were one. This is the primary error . . . by [a] BODY THETAN is meant a Thetan who is stuck to another Thetan or body but is not in control. . . . A CLUSTER is a group of body Thetans crushed or held together by some mutual bad experience.[70]

Scientologists thought they only needed to clear their Thetan, but now Hubbard tells them they have body Thetans and clusters to be rid of. This keeps them bound to the church for longer periods trying to achieve salvation.

Hubbard tells them that some of these body Thetans have been asleep on their Thetan for seventy-five million years. Ridding it makes the body Thetan as sort of a cleared being. Hubbard also believes he went back four quadrillion years ago (give or take a few years).

These incarnations and reincarnations are the supposed dilemma of the Scientologist. Reincarnation is answered in Hebrews 9:27: "It is appointed unto men once to die, but after this the judgment." Biblically, we live and die once. We have no preexistence in other bodies and we did not come from outer space. Jesus denied preexistent souls for people. "Ye are from beneath; I am from above: you are of this world; I am not of this world" (John 8:23). We find that reincarnation does not fit into God's plan of salvation. Jesus' death upon the cross would be unnecessary if reincarnation were true. Nevertheless, we find that Jesus was fore-ordained as the "Lamb slain from the foundation of the world" (Revelation 13:8). Jesus' sermons on heaven and hell would be a lie if reincarnation were true. But we find that Jesus always spoke the truth (Hebrews 4:15).

> Jesus' bodily resurrection from the tomb refutes reincarnation, since He resurrected to the same body.

70. Church of Scientology International v. Steven Fishman and Uwe Geertz, United States District Court, Central District of California, case 91-6426HLH(Tx), 76–100.

Jesus' bodily resurrection from the tomb refutes reincarnation, since He resurrected to the same body (John 20:27). "He showed himself alive after his passion by many infallible proofs, being seen of them forty days, and speaking of the things pertaining to the kingdom of God" (Acts 1:3; see also 1 Corinthians 15:1–8). The resurrection of Jesus is proof that His grace will save us who place our trust in Him for our salvation. Every Christian has what every Scientologist is looking for—that is, salvation.

Scientology is undoubtedly a religion, and deserving of the same freedom of belief and expression as any other religion in the United States, including biblical Christianity. It is also open to the same kind of critical evaluation by the Bible that responsible Christians put their own teachings to on a regular basis (Acts 17:11). When the teachings of Scientology are compared to biblical truth, Scientology is illuminated as the empty façade of biblical imitation it truly is.

Explore

Maitreya (a Second Buddha)
Dianetics History
The Reactive Mind
Thetan
Enneagram

Discuss

1. Who is the Jesus of Scientology?

2. What is *homo novis*?

3. How is truth defined in Scientology?

_____

_____

4. How does Jesus refute reincarnation?

_____

_____

─────────────── **Dig Deeper** ───────────────

See *The Kingdom of the Cults Study Guide* available at WalterMartin.com.

15

Eastern Religions

Quick Facts on Eastern Religions

- There is no single Hindu idea of God.
- All souls are eternal and accountable for their own actions.
- Karma is the debt of one's bad actions for which one must atone.
- Hinduism denies the Trinity, the Deity of Christ, the Atonement, sin, and salvation by grace through the sacrifice of Jesus Christ.
- Hinduism replaces resurrection with reincarnation, and both grace and faith with human works.

Historical Perspective

This book has undertaken to survey some of the major cults that exist and are active in the United States today. During my ministry of more than thirty years in this field of apologetics, I have seen hundreds of smaller cults come and go. During this time, I have observed trends in cultic structures. Often, the fads of society are reflected in the fads of cults or cultic belief. Nowhere is this more evident than in the general American culture's strange preoccupation with anything Eastern or Asian. This "fad" traces its roots to the appearance of a Hindu guru at the Chicago World's Fair at the turn of the century, although popular interest in Eastern things did not explode in American society until the 1960s and 1970s. From Nehru jackets in the 1960s to Tao and the new physics in the 1980s, Eastern influence has pervaded Western society.

The last few decades have seen the explosive growth of New Age (or occultic) religious cults with their roots in classic Hindu thought. Today, there are literally hundreds of large and small cults in America with Eastern ideas and practices. In this short summary, we will survey the Hindu roots of these cults and then present a quick look at three well-known imports: Rajneeshism, the International Society for Krishna Consciousness (ISKCON or Hare Krishnas), and Transcendental Meditation (TM).

Hinduism

Hinduism today is not the same as Hinduism five thousand years ago. The Hindu religion has evolved over the past five millennia of Indian religious history. Hinduism seeks to be a synthesis of the various religious ideas and influences from throughout the Indian subcontinent, representing hundreds of separate cultural, social, and tribal groups. The term *Hindu* itself is not indigenous to India. It comes from the Persian designation of the Indus River. Yogi Ramacharaka notes,

> Hinduism today is not the same as Hinduism five thousand years ago.

> The different Hindu sects, while practically appearing as different religions, in reality regard themselves as but different sects and divisions of the One Eternal Religion of India, of which each, of course, considers itself the best and most favored channel of expression and interpretation.[1]

- Hinduism claims the oldest form of karma, but little evidence exists to support dates and authors of Hindu scriptures.
- The original word *karma* meant a "religious act" or "animal sacrifice."
- *Karma*'s meaning changed to "cause and effect" about 800 to 400 BC. This change could reflect Buddha's influence.

Hindu Scripture

The Hindu scriptures were collected over hundreds of years, beginning with the writing of the oral traditions around the last half of the second

1. Yogi Ramacharaka, *The Philosophies and Religions of India* (Chicago, IL: The Yogi Publication Society, 1930), 271, 272.

millennium BC. These scriptures are known as the *Vedas* ("wisdom" or "knowledge"). The concluding portions of the Vedas are called the *Upanishads*, which are a synthesis of Vedic teachings. The general assumptions of the Upanishads include a belief in pantheism, karmic retribution, and reincarnation. Perhaps the most well-known section of the Vedas is the Hindu epic called the *Bhagavad-Gita*, which tells the story of the warrior-prince Arjuna, and his charioteer, Krishna, who is actually the disguised incarnation of the Hindu god Vishnu. The Gita was written down and subsequently modified between 200 BC and AD 200.

An illustration of the pluralism or contradictory nature of Hinduism is found by comparing the god of the Gita with the god of earlier Vedic literature. God, as described by the Gita, is personal and often sounds even monotheistic (only one God who is personal and not a part of creation exists). However, when one reads earlier Vedic scripture, God is presented as being definitely pantheistic (all of existence is, in some way, divine) and perhaps even monistic (all of existence is one, whether any divinity exists at all). The monotheistic characteristics of the Gita were appropriated by the founder of ISKCON, and consequently ISKCON teaches a more monotheistic rather than pantheistic idea of God today.

Contemporary Hinduism

There are three basic classifications into which the hundreds of Hindu sects can be divided: (1) the abstract monists, who stress the philosophical oneness of the universe instead of religious or theistic ideas; (2) the Vishnuites, who are devoted to the worship (in many different manners) of the god Vishnu (in many different manifestations) as the supreme form of divinity; and (3) the Shivaites, who are devoted to the worship of the god Shiva as the highest manifestation of divinity. TM, with its philosophical concentration, relates to the monistic classification, while ISKCON believes that Krishna, the supreme God, is also known as Vishnu and so they are identified with the Vishnuites. Rajneesh differed from them both in that he was philosophically agnostic and pragmatically Hindu. He had no inhibitions about subjecting Hinduism to any interpretation that fit his presuppositions, particularly in the realm of morality.

World religion expert Professor Ninan Smart notes the problems of the varieties of contemporary Hindu systems:

It might be asked, by way of conclusion, What is the essence of Hinduism? A hard question. There are orthodox Hindus who deny the existence of God. There are others who while not denying God, relegate him to a second place, as a secondary or illusory phase of the Absolute. Amid such a variety of theological views, what remains as necessary to Hindu belief? Certainly the doctrines of rebirth and that of an eternal soul. The picture of the world as a place where the immortal spirit within man is virtually endlessly implicated in the round of reincarnation has dominated the Indian imagination for about three millennia. In addition, a complex social system has given shape to the actual religion of the subcontinent over a long period.[2]

ISKCON (Hare Krishnas)

A major Hindu sect is the International Society for Krishna Consciousness, or ISKCON, a modern school of Vishnu Hinduism that developed from the fifteenth-century teachings of a man named Chaitanya, who instituted worship of Vishnu as God against the prevailing local worship of Shiva. Chaitanya taught that Krishna was the supreme personality of the Godhead.

ISKCON itself began in the 1960s in New York City, founded by the Vishnu yogi His Divine Grace Abhay Charan De Bhaktivedanta Swami Prabhupada, born in Calcutta, India, in 1896. It was officially incorporated in July 1966. Shortly afterward, Prabhupada traveled to San Francisco and found a ready audience of enthusiastic followers among the hippies of Haight-Ashbury. Hare Krishnas, the followers of ISKCON, are well-known today in America for their fund-raising activities through public solicitation, their public *sankirtanas* or spiritual chanting, their community vegetarian "feasts," and their often public ceremonies honoring their idols. One of the most well-known such ceremonies takes place annually on the beach west of Los Angeles and involves elaborate feasting, a parade as the devotees take their idols to the ocean for "spiritual" bathing, and a mini-festival to which thousands of Southern Californians flock as though it were a country carnival.

Prabhupada received his "calling" to preach the gospel of Krishna to English-speaking people in 1922, from his spiritual master, Srila Bhak-

2. Ninan H. Smart, *The Religious Experience of Mankind* (New York: Charles Scribner's Sons, 1976), 155, 156.

tisiddhanta Sarasvati Thakur. However, it was not until 1936 that he finally assumed the responsibility on the death of his master.[3]

The ISKCON magazine, *Back to Godhead*, began publication in 1944, and continues today as the best-known publication of the ISKCON publishing company, the Bhaktivedanta Book Trust.

Prabhupada died in 1977. At the time of his death, there were 108 ISKCON centers worldwide, fifty-one volumes of literature published in English, and more than 5,000 full-time communal members, or disciples. His most well-known book is *Bhagavad-Gita As It Is*.

After the death of Prabhupada, inner turmoil and public suspicions threatened to dismantle the international organization. ISKCON went through a series of leadership changes, resulting from inner power struggles, competing claims of succession to Prabhupada, the resignation and/or defection of numerous leaders, the indictment and eventual conviction of various leaders for crimes ranging from tax evasion through drug dealing to murder, and charges by family members of false recruitment and deliberate concealment of underage converts from their parents and authorities.

Once the dust settled, the current leadership structure was instituted. ISKCON is led by a Governing Body Commission, which consists of thirty top leaders worldwide. Day-to-day operations are handled by the various GBC members in their respective areas of authority, and general policy changes are decided upon during the annual GBC meeting in Mayapur.

ISKCON places of worship (called temples), preaching centers, housing complexes, and other operations work independently of one another but under the direction of the area GBC member. A Temple President runs each temple, assisted by a Treasurer, Secretary, and Temple Commander. In areas where there are not sufficient numbers of full-time practicing, initiated devotees for a temple, there might be a preaching center servicing the interested but not-yet-initiated community. All temples, preaching centers, restaurants, shops, etc., must be officially designated ISKCON and cannot use trademarked names of ISKCON, Hare Krishna, or Govinda's ("healthy" stores and restaurants) without permission.

3. As his following grew, he was elevated to a higher spiritual position, and in 1950, chose the full renunciation of material life.

TM (Transcendental Meditation)

TM is a spiritual practice, or yoga, which was first introduced to the Western world by its founder, Maharishi Mahesh Yogi, as a religious exercise or philosophy. Encountering skepticism from nonreligious Westerners, Maharishi revamped his TM program. In the 1970s, he promoted the movement as a scientifically sound, nonreligious psychological exercise designed to relieve stress, to bring peace to the inner man, thereby having a positive effect on society, and to enable the advanced practitioner to participate in astral projection (his soul leaving his body) and levitation.

TM still wears its secular label in its own promotions today, and most Westerners are unaware of its religious presuppositions and nature.

Theological Evaluation

Hindu Beliefs

God. There is no single Hindu idea of God. Hindu concepts of deity can include any of the following: monism (all existence is one substance); pantheism (all existence is divine); panentheism (God is in creation as a soul is in a body); animism (God or gods live in nonhuman objects such as trees, rocks, animals, etc.); polytheism (there are many gods); henotheism (there is one god we worship among the many that exist); and monotheism (there is only one God).

> Yoga is referred to as "Hindu Evangelism" by Hindu Yogis.

Karma and Samsara. Fundamental to Hindu thought is the idea that all souls are eternal and accountable for their own actions throughout time. Karma refers to the debt of one's bad actions, which must be atoned for (through various Hindu systems) in order for one to escape the wheel of samsara or reincarnation (the soul inhabits successive human bodies) or transmigration (the soul inhabits successive bodies—human, animal, or even plants or inanimate objects).

Salvation. The three major paths to Hindu "salvation" include *karma marga* (method), the way of disinterested action; *bhakti marga*, the way of devotion; and *Jnana marga*, the path of knowledge or mystical insight. Jnana marga achieves self-realization through intuitive awareness and mystical insight. Bhakti marga achieves self-realization through ritualistic sacrifice and discipline.

Yoga. Meaning "yoke together," Yoga is fundamental to Hinduism and cannot be divorced from it. Individual positions in Yoga are designed as worship poses—a worship directed to Hindu gods and goddesses. The chant "Om" begins the awakening of the Kundalini or serpent spirit that has led some to experience severe depression and even demonic possession. A Christian who is walking with Jesus Christ should be aware of the deeper meaning behind Yoga or "Hindu Evangelism" as it is called by Hindu Yogis. Although Christians cannot be possessed by a demon, they can open themselves up to life-threatening oppression by these spirits and endanger their families.

Dr. Kurt Koch, noted German authority on the occult, states the following about the occultic side of yoga and his interviews with those who practiced it: "This technique of relaxation and these 'emptying exercises,' so highly spoken of by the yogis lead to the inflowing of another spirit—other spirits. The students of yoga did not notice it."[4] Similarly, Dr. Koch, who has compiled volumes of case studies on people involved in the occult, wrote the following about meditation: "My counseling work in East and West has given me insight into the nature and practice of meditation. I am totally opposed to meditation in the Far Eastern pattern. . . . We cannot empty ourselves by means of techniques and postures—then other powers flood in."[5] Dr. Koch's warning is clear—if one empties the mind it becomes an open vessel for other spirits.

It is important to note what Jesus said concerning spirits, particularly demonic spirits that invade human bodies.

> When an unclean spirit goes out of a man, he goes through dry places, seeking rest, and finds none. Then he says, "I will return to my house from which I came." And when he comes, he finds it empty, swept, and put in order. Then he goes and takes with him seven other spirits more wicked than himself, and they enter and dwell there; and the last state of that man is worse than the first (Matthew 12:43–45 NKJV).

From Jesus we learn about the motivation of demons. They wander the *dry places* in another dimension and are looking for *rest.* They desire a *home* and aggressively pursue it, even returning after exorcism if the person has remained *empty* inside. Demonic spirits prefer to inhabit human

4. Kurt E. Koch, *Occult ABC* (Germany: Literature Mission Aglasterhausen, 1978), 257–258.
5. Koch, *Occult ABC,* 243, 244, 246.

beings. Once they are successful, they destroy lives because they cannot be anything other than what their nature is—evil. Rather than experimenting with the occult practice of Yoga, where the person unwittingly opens the soul to demons, it is much better to close the door and refuse participation.[6]

ISKCON Beliefs

God. Although the bulk of Hindu scripture is pantheistic (everything is a part of God), portions of the Hindu scripture, notably the Bhagavad-Gita, are basically monotheistic presentations of Hinduism. Hinduism, in seeking to be a synthesis of a variety of Indian thought and belief, contains within its vast scriptural tradition a variety of beliefs about God, even though those beliefs may contradict one another. Since the Bhagavad-Gita, which implies a form of monotheism, is the most sacred scripture to ISKCON, we find that the ISKCON belief in God is essentially monotheistic, and Krishna is said to be the supreme personality of the Godhead. Any incarnation of the one God is an incarnation of Krishna: "ALL the lists of the incarnations of Godhead are either plenary expansions or parts of the plenary expansions of the Lord, but Lord Sri Krsna is the original Personality of Godhead Himself."[7]

Christ. To ISKCON, Jesus Christ is Krishna's Son, but in a position no more unique to God than any other man could strive to attain. To the Hare Krishna, then, Jesus Christ is not the unique Son of God, God manifest in the flesh. He is not an incarnation of Krishna.

Salvation. Salvation in ISKCON is obtained by removing one's karmic debt through devotion to Krishna and right actions through multiple incarnations: "All these performers who know the meaning of sacrifice become cleansed of sinful reactions, and, having tasted the nectar of the remnants of such sacrifices, they go to the supreme eternal atmosphere."[8] ISKCON also says, "From the body of any person who claps and dances before the Deity, showing manifestations of ecstasy, all the birds of sinful activities fly away upwards."[9] ISKCON salvation comes to those initiates

6. Walter Martin, Jill Martin Rische, Kurt Van Gorden, *The Kingdom of the Occult*, Thomas Nelson, 2008, 8–9.
7. Siddha Swarup Ananda Goswami, *Jesus Loves KRSNA* (Vedic Christian Committee and Life Force, Krsna Yoga Viewpoint, 1975), 14.
8. A. C. Bhaktivedanta Swami Prabhupada, *Bhagavad-Gita As It Is* (New York: The Bhaktivedanta Book Trust, 1968), 81.
9. A. C. Bhaktivedanta Swami Prabhupada, *The Nectar of Devotion* (New York: The Bhaktivedanta Book Trust, 1970), 75.

who "follow the four regulative principles, chant sixteen rounds of the Hare Krishna mantra on neck beads every day, and follow all the regulated temple programs."[10]

TM Beliefs

God. TM concentrates on those Hindu scriptures that present a pantheistic view of God. Therefore, God in TM is pantheistic, and one's goal is to lose his own personality in the oneness of God. This also, of course, takes away from the unique and separate personality of God: "Being is the living presence of God, the reality of life. It is eternal truth. It is the absolute in eternal freedom."[11]

Jesus Christ. TM ignores Jesus Christ almost entirely, although Maharishi teaches that anyone can become as enlightened as Jesus Christ through the application of TM techniques. It is clear from his neglect of Jesus Christ and from his worldview that he does not consider Jesus Christ to be the unique Son of God, God manifest in the flesh.[12]

Salvation. Salvation in TM is accomplished by realizing that one is in union with the Creative Intelligence: "The answer to every problem is that there is no problem. Let a man perceive this truth and then he is without problems."[13] This realization comes through practicing the meditations of TM: "A huge mountain of sins extending for miles is destroyed by Union brought about through transcendental meditation, without which there is no way out."[14] Salvation is almost a misnomer, since one is not truly a sinner, but just forgetful of his oneness with the divine.

Today, Transcendental Meditation has gained unprecedented popularity, finding its way into schools, social programs, and military Post Traumatic Stress Disorder (PTSD) therapies. It is enthusiastically promoted by many media celebrities and enjoys the unofficial designation of a "religion free" form of meditation.[15] There are hundreds of other Eastern groups

10. Anon., The Structure, 1.

11. Maharishi Mahesh Yogi, *The Science of Being and the Art of Living* (New York: The New American Library, 1968), 22.

12. See, for example, Maharishi Mahesh Yogi, *Meditation of Maharishi Mahesh Yogi*, 123, 124.

13. Maharishi Mahesh Yogi, *Maharishi Mahesh Yogi on the Bhagavad-Gita* (New York: Penguin Books, 1967), 257.

14. Mahesh Yogi, *Bhagavad-Gita*, 299.

15. For more information on the influence of modern-day TM, see the David Lynch Foundation for Consciousness-Based Education and World Peace, and tm.org.

embracing the unwary—ISKCON and TM are just two examples of pervasive Eastern thought.

Biblical Perspective

In conclusion, Hinduism, for all of its diversity and contradictions, is not compatible with Christianity. In all its forms, Hinduism denies the biblical Trinity, the deity of Christ, and the doctrines of the Atonement, sin, and salvation by grace through the sacrifice of Jesus Christ. It replaces resurrection with reincarnation, and both grace and faith with human works. One cannot, then, achieve peace with God through Hinduism or any of its sects.

> The foundational doctrine of Hinduism—reincarnation—is clearly contradicted by the Bible.

The foundational doctrine of Hinduism—reincarnation—is clearly contradicted by the Bible. Hebrews 9:27 teaches us that we live only one lifetime, after which comes the judgment of our souls. Scripture further points out that those who have come to faith in Christ will be in God's presence immediately after death, not reincarnated (Philippians 1:21–23; 2 Corinthians 5:8). Those who do not know Christ likewise will not be reincarnated, but go to a place of punishment (Job 21:30–34; Matthew 26:41; 2 Peter 2:9).

The most effective precursor to evangelism of those caught in this web of deceit is prayer. The Bible tells us that we do not struggle against flesh and blood, but against spiritual forces of darkness that blind men's minds (Ephesians 6:12; 2 Corinthians 4:4).

The doctrines of Hinduism, like those found in all other world religions, promote beliefs that guide people into a Christless eternity. Christians must share the grace and peace of Jesus Christ, lovingly and gently: "In meekness instructing those that oppose themselves; if God peradventure will give them repentance to the acknowledging of the truth; and that they may recover themselves out of the snare of the devil, who are taken captive by him at his will" (2 Timothy 2:25–26).

C. S. Lewis wisely observed that at the end of all religious quests one must choose between Hinduism and Christianity; the former absorbs all others and the latter excludes them. Peace with God is not achieved by looking inside oneself but by looking up to Him of whom Moses and the prophets did write—Jesus of Nazareth, the Christ and Son of God.

/——————————————— **Explore** ———————————————\

Pantheism
Wheel of Samsara
Karmic Debt
Roots of Yoga

/——————————————— **Discuss** ———————————————\

1. How many gods and goddesses are there in Hindu theology?

_____

_____

2. Give an illustration of the contradictory nature of Hinduism.

_____

_____

3. Who is Jesus in Hinduism?

_____

_____

4. Is Transcendental Meditation secular?

_____

_____

/——————————————— **Dig Deeper** ———————————————\

See *The Kingdom of the Cults Study Guide* available at WalterMartin.com.

16

Islam—The Message of Muhammad

Historical Perspective

Islam is the second largest religion in the world, next to Christianity. Although Islam is a world religion and not technically a "cult" as defined in this book, it is a religion that originated approximately 500 years *after* the birth of Christ, and directly contradicts His teachings. Its place in the religious historical record, relative to Christianity; its growing presence in the United States; and its anti-biblical theology requires a response.

According to Scripture, the ancestors of modern Arabs can be traced back to Shem and are properly known as Semites. Shem's descendant Eber gave rise to two lines: Peleg's line, from which Abraham is descended, and Joktan's line, which contains the names of many Arab groups. However, many Arab tribes trace their ancestry to Ishmael, the firstborn son of Abraham.[1] The word *Arab* refers to nomads or bedouins and may be connected with the word for desert or wilderness.[2] The original meaning expanded to refer to Arabic speakers and those living in Arabia. "Arabness" seems to be inherited through the male since intermarriage with non-Arab women was common and is still permitted by the Koran. The Spanish Umayyad Caliph Abd-er Rahman III (ruled 929–961), who was proud of his ancestry from the former ruling clan of Mecca before Muhammad, was actually only 0.93 percent Arab.[3]

The Koran mentions these pagan deities in Sura 53:19–20: "Have ye seen *Lat*, and *'Uzza*, and another, the third (goddess), *Manat?*"[4] This is followed by an assertion (vv. 21–23) that these goddesses, the daughters of Allah—the moon god—according to pre-Islamic Arab theology,[5] are mere human creations that divide God into parts. These deities were popular at Mecca at the time of Muhammad's birth. *Lat*, or *al-Lat* ("the goddess"), was the sun god; *Uzza* or *al-'Uzza* ("the mighty one"), the planet Venus; and *Man'amat*, the god of good fortune. Other gods mentioned in the Qur'an include *Wadd* (another moon god, mentioned above), *Suw'a*, *Ya-ghuth*, and *Nasr* (Sura 71:23). Of these gods, *al-'Uzza* appears to be the supreme deity in Mecca.

It is believed by some scholars that *Allah*, or *al-Ilah* ("the god"), can be traced to *Ilah*, the South Arabian moon god. Henotheism, or the worship of only one god while not denying the existence of other gods, may have existed in pre-Islamic society. The Koran speaks of *hanifs*, pre-Islamic Arab monotheists who were neither Christian nor Jewish. Extant evidence shows that Allah meant "the (one) God" for the many Christians, Jews, monophysites, and Nestorians who lived throughout the Arabian Peninsula.[6]

1. See Louis Bahjat Hamada, *Understanding the Arab World* (Nashville: Thomas Nelson, 1990), 40–59.
2. A. K. Irvine, "The Arabs and Ethiopians," in D. J. Wiseman, ed., *Peoples of Old Testament Times* (Oxford University Press, 1973), 289–290.
3. Cited in Peter Mansfield, *The Arabs* (New York: Penguin Books, 1978), 46.
4. From the translation of A. Yusuf Ali, *The Holy Koran: Translation and Commentary* (Brentwood, MD: Amana Corp., 1983 [1934]), 1445.
5. See Alfred Guillaume, *Islam* (London: Penguin Books, 1954), 6.
6. Guillaume, *Islam*. *Monophysitism* is the belief that Christ has a single divine nature that inhabits a fleshly body, which has a different nature than other human bodies, or that the human and divine natures were mixed. It may be traced to Apollinaris (c. 310–390) and Eutychius (c. 378–454) and presently continues in some Armenian, Coptic, Ethiopian, and Syrian Jacobite churches. *Nestorianism* is a heresy that was falsely attributed to Nestorius (d. c. 451), Patriarch of Constantinople; namely, that Christ had two persons and two natures. He actually taught that Mary was the *Christotokos* ("Christ-bearer"). Christ possessed a common *prosopoón* (literally "face," but used here metaphorically for "person," especially for one's innermost being). See Peter

Muhammad

Muhammad was born in Mecca, near the Middle Western coastal region of Arabia, about AD 570, to Abdullah (or Abd Allah), who died two months after he was born, and Aminah, his mother, who died when he was six. Mecca was a large commercial city known for the Ka'aba ("cube"), a building famous for its 360 idols containing images of the moon god *Hubal, al-Lat, al-'Uzza, and Manat,* and the Black Stone. Muhammad's family was of the relatively poor Hashemite clan of the Quraysh tribe, and it is the patriarch of that tribe, Fihr (known as *qirsh* or "shark") of the Kinnah tribe, who Muslims claim to be a descendant of Ishmael and an inheritor of God's promise to Hagar in Genesis 21:18.[7] After the death of his mother, he was sent to live with his grandfather, Abd-al-Muttalib, who provided a Bedouin foster mother for him, Halimah, and was raised in the desert. After the death of his grandfather when Muhammad was eight, he returned to Mecca to live with his uncle, Abu Talib. At twenty-five, Muhammad married a wealthy forty-year-old widow, Khadijah, after she proposed to him. Muhammad remained with Khadijah for twenty-five years and had two sons, who died in infancy, and four daughters. After Khadijah died in 619 or 620, Muhammad married a widow of a disciple and a six-year-old (who moved in with him when she was nine), Aisha. His seventh wife was his ex-daughter-in-law; by the time of his death he had twelve wives and two concubines (including Maryam, an Egyptian Coptic slave).[8]

Toon, "Nestorianism; Nestorius" in J.D. Douglas, ed., *The New Dictionary of the Christian Church* (Grand Rapids, MI: Zondervan, 1978), 699–700.

7. A divine promise is given regarding Ishmael's descendants in verse 16:10 (also 17:20; 21:13, 18): they are to make a great nation. According to 16:11–12, Ishmael will be "a wild ass of a man," which may mean "unrestrained," but can also mean "lawless" since he will be constantly fighting with all men while "he shall dwell in (or preferably *against* [see Derek Kidner, *Genesis: An Interpretation and Commentary*, Tyndale Old Testament Commentaries (Downers Grove, IL: InterVarsity Press, 1967), 127], or *in defiance of*, Victor P. Hamilton, *The Book of Genesis, Chapters 1–17*, The New International Commentary on the New Testament [Grand Rapids, MI: Eerdmans, 1990], 454–455) the presence of his brethren" (v. 12). Ishmael and his mother, Hagar the Egyptian (Genesis 16; 21:9), left Abraham after Sarah found Ishmael to be mocking during or after the feast given for the weaning of Isaac (Genesis 21:9–12). They wandered to Beersheba in southern Canaan (v. 14) and later to Paran in the southern Sinai region (v. 21). His twelve children ruled as princes from Havilah (central or northern Arabia) to Shur (northern Sinai), according to Genesis 25:12–18. Muhammad, according to Muslim historians, is descended from either Nebajoth, Ishmael's firstborn, or Kedar, his second son. Many authorities, however, are dubious of an Ishmaelite ancestry for Muhammad, noting that the issue was first brought up only after Meccan Jews refused to convert to Islam.

8. Ali Dashti believes that he had sixteen wives, two concubines, and four "lovers"; see *Twenty-Three Years: A Study of the Prophetic Career of Mohammed* (London: George Allen & Unwin, 1985), 120–138.

Interestingly, Sura 4:3 limits the number of wives to four, and in Sura 4:31 marriage to one's daughter-in-law was prohibited. But in Sura 33:36–40, Muhammad was conveniently given a new revelation from God that ordered Zaid, Muhammad's adopted son, to divorce his wife so Muhammad could marry her by God's command. This is called abrogation.

According to extra-Koranic sources, Muhammad's first mystical experience was allegedly being attacked by two men who cut his belly open in search of something. His foster mother thought he was demon-possessed after finding him standing and not having appeared to be the victim of any violence. He later claimed his nonexistent attackers to be angels who cleansed his heart. In AD 610, he claimed to have received his first of a series of revelations of the Koran from God through the angel Gabriel. His first disciple was his wife, then his cousin Ali, then his slave, and then his friend Abu Bakr. His wife and his uncle, who was his protector, both died in 619 or 620. The following year he was offered protection from powerful families in Yathrib, north of Mecca.

After his uncle Abu Talib died, the leaders of the various Meccan tribes and clans vowed to assassinate him. The angel Gabriel warned him of this, and he and his friend Abu Bakr fled to Yathrib, renamed Medina. This migration is known as the *hijra* and marks the beginning of the Islamic calendar. Yathrib was a town dominated by Jewish groups but was at that time without a stable government, primarily consisting of feuding Arab factions and mediating Jewish tribes. Muhammad soon established the *umma*, a theocracy (or dictatorship) under his authority, and held complete control of the town.

Badr was conquered in 626, and in 627 a Meccan army 10,000 strong arrived to attack Medina, but Muhammad and his 3,000 men had prepared by digging a trench around the city. The Meccans later gave up and turned back. The Medinans retaliated by attacking a Jewish tribe, the Banu Qurayza, for allegedly conspiring with the Meccans, and Muhammad ordered the death of hundreds of Jewish males by beheading. The women and children of the tribe were sold into slavery. Two other Medinan Jewish tribes, the Banu Qaynuqa and the Banu Nadir, were driven from their homes and had all of their property confiscated. In 628 they conquered another group of Jews at Khaybar, who paid the *jizya*[9] to be left alone.

9. A special poll tax non-Muslim "People of the Book" paid in order to have legal rights and protection. They were also to be excluded from military service.

Finally, in 630, Muhammad and his army conquered Mecca. On June 8, 632, Muhammad died.

His successors soon wrested Palestine (Israel and its capital, Jerusalem) and Syria away from the Jewish inhabitants and the Byzantines (629–641), conquered Iraq and Persia (633–643), Egypt (639), Tripoli (644), Toledo in Spain and western India (712), Crete (825), and Sicily (899). In West Africa, Muslims under Almoravid rulers pillaged the capital of Ghana (1076). Nubia, in East Africa, survived, as did a few small Christian nations until the 1500s.

Arab domination of conquered lands did not last forever, and soon many Muslim states declared their independence. In the early 1000s, the Seljuk Turks, who had only recently embraced Islam, began taking over territory previously held by Arab Muslims. By 1055, Tughrul Beg, leader of the Seljuk Turks, took control of Baghdad. Eventually, under the Ottoman Turks, who supplanted the Seljuks, Muslims went far into Europe, conquering Serbia (1459), Greece (1461), Bosnia (1463), Herzegovina (1483), Montenegro (1499), parts of Hungary (1526–1547) and Poland (1676). Although there were wars with European countries in the interim, many countries did not regain independence until the 1800s. Many Middle Eastern areas held by the Turks were lost under Napoleon Bonaparte, and later held by the British and French.

Several modern Middle Eastern countries did not come into existence as we know them until the early twentieth century. Iraq became independent in 1921, Egypt in 1937, Lebanon in 1945, Syria in 1946, Jordan in 1946, and Kuwait in 1961.

Since the September 11, 2001, terrorist attacks and the rise of ISIS (Islamic State in Iraq and Syria), there is an unprecedented interest in Islam and worldwide debate on its long-range goals. Islam in America is growing rapidly, despite deep concern and confusion surrounding its core beliefs, Sharia law, and the high-profile brutality of ISIS. Today, the open-borders policy of America and most of the world spreads the hidden culture of *Jihad*, and for the first time in history, Americans now expect and fear foreign terrorist attacks on American soil.

Unfortunately, most Christians still understand little about Islamic theology, confusing the identity of *Jehovah*, the God of Israel and the Christian church, with the Muslims' *Allah*. There is a pressing need to address these theological differences—an urgency for Christians to study the heritage that is ours in Christ and resist confusion and error—in order to share biblical truth effectively with Muslim friends and neighbors.

"There is no God but Allah, and Muhammad is the prophet (or messenger) of Allah" is the great *Shahada* or "confession," which faithful Muslims around the world declare daily. This declaration of faith effectively distinguishes Muslims from every other world religion, including Christianity and Judaism. More than 1.8 billion people worldwide worship *Allah* and revere Muhammad as his prophet.[10]

Jehovah, the God of Israel and the Christian church, is not Allah.

Islam is a powerful global religious, social, and political force. Every Christian should recognize the implications of this, equip themselves with an active defense of the biblical faith, and share the Gospel of Jesus Christ in love with the followers of Muhammad.

Definitions

Islam, like many religions, has its own vocabulary to describe its beliefs. A quick look at some of the most important religious terms in Islam will provide a basis for further discussion of Islamic history and belief:

Allah is the Arabic term for "God" and cannot be translated easily into English. One Muslim writer defined it thus: "The word means the unique God who possesses all the attributes of perfection and beauty in their infinitude. Muslims feel strongly that the English word 'God' does not convey the real meaning of the word 'Allah.'"[11]

Imam is Arabic for "leader"—literally meaning "one who goes before."

Islam, the Arabic term for "submission," is the name of the religion that came out of the revelations and teachings of Muhammad.[12]

Mahdi, the redeemer of Islam who will come at the end of the world before the day of judgment.

10. Curiously, the 2015 Pew Research Center report quotes 1.8 billion Muslims worldwide, a number *unchanged* since the adherents.com statistic referred to in the 2003 edition of *The Kingdom of the Cults*. Michael Lipka, "Muslims and Islam: Key findings," Pew Research Center, 2015, http://www.pewresearch.org/fact-tank/2017/08/09/muslims-and-islam-key-findings-in-the-u-s-and-around-the-world/.

11. Badru D. Kateregga, *Islam and Christianity* (Grand Rapids: Eerdmans, 1980), 1.

12. Since there is no standardized method of transliterating Arabic script into Roman script, Islamic terms are often spelled in a variety of ways (e.g., Muhammad, Mohammed; Moslem, Muslim, etc.). We have chosen to use the spelling most popular with Muslims who write in English.

Muslim is the name given to one who adheres to the religion of Islam. *Muslim* is a synonym of *Islam* and means "one who submits." The Muslim submits to the will of Allah as revealed by Muhammad.[13]

Koran (or Qur'an) is Arabic for "the recitation," and refers to the collection of revelations supposedly given by Allah through his archangel to Muhammad and preserved as the Islamic scripture. Muslims believe in the Law of Moses, the Psalms of David, and the Injil, or gospel of Jesus (Isa). However, they believe that those scriptures were superseded by the scripture given through Muhammad, and that the Bible used by Christians and Jews is a distorted version of those other scriptures (even though the Bible predates the Qur'an). Wherever the Bible contradicts Islam, the Muslim says the Bible is incorrect.

Sharia means "the path" in Arabic and is every rule or principle (found in the Qur'an and Hadith) that Allah has "legislated" or divinely revealed that must be done to achieve salvation.

Schools of Islam[14]

Out of 1.8 billion Muslims worldwide, the greatest number by far are members of the Sunnite school. They accept the first four caliphs in direct succession from Muhammad and no others. Ninety percent of the Muslims in the Middle East and most parts of the Muslim world are Sunnis. Wahhabism is a literal, puritanical form of Sunni Islam held by the Saudi rulers.

The second largest school of Islam is the Shi'ite school. The name Shi'ite refers to those early Muslims who chose to follow Ali, the son-in-law of the prophet, as the prophet's heir to the leadership of Islam. For the Twelver Shi'ites, there followed a line of twelve *Imams* or spiritual heads[15] who claimed Ali as an ancestor. Most of them were killed, and the twelfth and final Imam, Muhammad, disappeared as a child in AD 878. It is believed that eventually he will miraculously return to his people as the *Mahdi*, in a manner not altogether unlike the Judeo-Christian Messiah. He is the

---

13. In the modern world of PC (politically correct) culture, it is incorrect to refer to a Muslim as a "Mohammedan," even though Western culture commonly used this term up to and throughout most of the twentieth century. Another possible reason for this change is the perception that Muslims today have a strong aversion to anything resembling idol worship, and if a Muslim would accept the appellation "Mohammedan," he might think that he could be accused of worshiping Muhammad.

14. "School" as used here means "school of thought"—comparable to denominations in Christianity.

15. In Sunni Islam, "imam" refers only to the leader of a congregation.

hidden *Imam* who will bring about a golden age before the end of the world. Although much smaller than the Sunnite school, the Shi'ites gained international attention when the Ayatollah Khomeini, the radical Shia leader, took control of Iran in 1979. Ninety-five percent of Iran's Muslims are Shi'ites, and today Iran is a Shi'ite Islamic republic. Azerbaijan, Bahrain, Iraq, and Yemen also have large numbers of Shi'ites. Shi'ites are especially strong in Iran, Iraq, Afghanistan, and Pakistan.

A third school that has now penetrated the United States government, some state and city governments, and even school districts, is known as the Muslim Brotherhood, or *Ikhwan*, a xenophobic Egyptian fundamentalist group that strongly believes that Islamic civil law, *Sharia*, should be the law of the state. Members of this group are known for their terrorist activities, and a member's offshoot was responsible for the death of Egyptian president Anwar El-Sadat.[16]

Islam also has its sects, and it is interesting to note that President Hafez Assad of Syria is an Alawite. They are most populous in Syria, although still a minority (such as the esoteric Druze, who are not considered Muslims by orthodox Sunnis and believe in ten Imams, similar to the Shi'ites). They live primarily in Israel and Lebanon. Finally, two very high-profile Muslim groups that continue to promote hatred, war, and the killing of innocent civilians are Hezbollah (Party of God) and Hamas, both devoted to the destruction of Israel.

Theological Evaluation

At first glance, Islamic belief appears to be almost compatible with Christianity and/or Judaism. Often people claim that the Muslims believe in the same God as Christians: "They just don't accept Jesus Christ." However, as we shall see, the Muslim God is not like the Christian God.

Islam rejects the biblical doctrines of the Trinity and the deity of Christ, so much so that written within and *all over* the inner walls of the Dome of the Rock mosque in Jerusalem (built AD 692) are specific theological arguments and warnings to all Muslims that *Allah has no son* and is "one" in nature, not "three."[17]

16. Caesar E. Farah, *Islam* (New York: Barron's Educational Services, 1994), 185.
17. "Inscription from the Dome of the Rock," Islamic Awareness, http://www.islamic-aware ness.org/History/Islam/Inscriptions/DoTR.html.

God

For the Muslim, Allah is the only true God. There is no such blasphemous thing as the "Trinity." The Muslim God is unapproachable by sinful man, and the Muslim's desire is to submit to the point where he can hold back the judging arm of Allah and inherit eternal life in a heavenly paradise, often pictured in terms of food, wine, and sexual pleasure.

But Allah is not only a harsh, wrathful God, although the overwhelming teaching in the Koran is that he is sovereign, distant, and angry. Muslims also believe he is loving and forgiving, as Sura 11:90 says, "Ask forgiveness of your Lord, then repent to Him; surely my Lord is All-compassionate, All-loving" and 85:14 says, "He is the All-forgiving, the All-loving." The Koran is clear that Allah is merciful. But unlike Christians, Muslims do not emphasize a *personal* relationship with God. Scripture tells us that those who trust in Christ do the Father's will, and have been redeemed and adopted as sons (Romans 8:14–15; Galatians 3:26). We are heirs of God (Galatians 4:7) and the Father loves and treats us as His children (Matthew 12:47; Mark 3:35; Hebrews 12:5, 7). We can even be called His friends (John 15:13–15; James 2:23). On the other hand, those who deny the Son have the devil for their father (John 8:44).

> For Muslims, Allah is the only true God. There is no such blasphemous thing as the "Trinity."

To Muslims, God has no likeness (Sura 42:11), is transcendent (Sura 4:171), is unknowable (apart from revelation), and is wholly other and totally different. He is neither physical nor spirit. The Bible, contradicting the Koran, tells us that we have been created in God's image and likeness (Genesis 1:26–27) and that we have knowledge of God in our hearts (Romans 1:19–20). Moreover, Scripture tells us that God is Spirit (John 4:24).

Currently, there are two schools of thought in Islam that offer varying interpretations of who God is. According to the orthodox school, God is said to have a "face, hand, and soul, but it is not legitimate to inquire how, for these belong to his qualities; God has no body."[18] Guillaume adds that in the Fiqh Akbar, a creed compiled around the year 1000 and representative of orthodoxy, "Allah is absolute in his decrees of good and evil. He does not resemble his creatures in any respect. He has existed from eternity with his qualities, those belonging to his essence and those pertaining to

18. Guillaume, *Islam*, 135.

his activity."[19] The Qur'an is the eternal speech of God, the angel Gabriel to Muhammad. The Qur'an contains terms that attribute qualities to God, and the orthodox Muslim believes that God has attributes, but is not sure what they mean.

Nevertheless, many Muslims believe that God is neither physical nor spirit. God is a totally unique being that has no similarity in any sense to any other being. This view is based on the assumption that to believe otherwise would mean that God somehow shares his attributes and by implication leads to the grave sin of assigning partners to God (called *shirk*) (Sura 4:116; 5:72; 9:31).

Jesus Christ

To the Muslim, Jesus Christ is merely one of the many prophets of Allah (Sura 4:171; 5:74). According to Islam, the prophet Muhammad supersedes Jesus Christ. Jesus Christ is not the Son of God or a part of any Trinity (Sura 5:17; 5:116; 19:35).[20] We are told that He was nothing but a slave on whom God showed favor (Sura 43:59); yet elsewhere we are told the Messiah is not a slave (Sura 4:172). Jesus Christ did not atone for anyone's sins, although He was himself sinless (Sura 3:46) and is one of those who are near to God (Sura 3:45). Positively, the Koran says that Jesus Christ performed miracles (Sura 3:49; 5:110) and was the Messiah (Sura 3:45; 4:157, 171). But Jesus Christ did not die on the cross. Various Muslim traditions say that He either miraculously substituted Judas Iscariot for himself on the cross, or that God miraculously delivered Him from the hands of the Romans and Jews before He could be crucified. Most Muslims believe that Jesus Christ was taken bodily into heaven without having died (Sura 4:157). However, Sura 199:33 says He died and would be resurrected.

It is interesting to compare Jesus and Muhammad according to the Koran:

Jesus did miracles (Sura 3:49; 5:110), but Muhammad did not (Sura 13:8: "thou art a warner [of coming divine judgment] only"; also 6:37; 6:109; 17:59 and 17:90–93).

19. Guillaume, *Islam*, 135.

20. It is possible, as Geoffrey Parrinder argues, that Muhammad was not refuting Christianity, but early pseudo-Christian cults. The Islamic "trinity" referred to may be related to the Collyridian heresy previously mentioned. The Nestorians would have agreed that to say "God is Christ" would be misleading since to them it would imply that *all* of God is Christ. This is the reason they objected to the term *theotokos* ("God bearer"), preferring instead *Christotokos*, or if *theotokos* were to be used it would be in combination with *anthrotokos* ("man bearer"). It is known that there were many Nestorian missions to Arabia in Muhammad's day.

Jesus was sinless (Sura 3:46), but Muhammad sinned and needed forgiveness (Sura 40:55: "ask forgiveness of thy sin"; 42:5: "ask forgiveness for those on the Earth"; 47:19: "ask forgiveness for thy sin"; 48:2: "that Allah may forgive thee of thy sin").

Jesus was called "the Messiah" and was even born of a virgin (3:45–57)! Yet Muhammad is supposed to be the greatest of the prophets.

Sin and Salvation

The Qur'an teaches that all have sinned—"If God were to take mankind to task for their wrongdoing, he would not leave here one living creature" (Sura 16:61a; see also 42:5)—and were created weak (Sura 4:28). We are even told that Muhammad sinned (Sura 40:55; 47:19; 48:2). Every Muslim who hopes to escape the judgment of Allah must fulfill the works of the Five Pillars of the Faith (Sura 10:109):

1. Recitation of the *Shahada* ("There is no God but Allah, and Muhammad is the prophet of Allah");

2. Five daily prescribed prayers (*Salat* or *Namaz*) in Arabic. These prayers include genuflection and prostration in the direction of the holy city, Mecca;

3. Almsgiving (*Zakat*), which involves the duty to give a certain percentage of one's total income to help others. This is not considered charity but an obligation arising out of the realities of a world where there is poverty, inequality, injustice, and suffering. Generally, performing *zakat* is to be done privately unless there is a pressing reason for the giving to be made known publicly.

4. Fasting (*Saum* or *Ruzeh*) during the entire month of Ramadan, when Muslims are supposed to fast from all food and drink from sunrise to sunset in atonement for their own sins over the previous year. Muslims are allowed to eat and drink after sunset, and some get up before sunrise to eat before the fast begins again.

5. A pilgrimage (*Hajj*) to Mecca, the holy city, at least once in a Muslim's lifetime. The *hajj* takes place after Ramadan. The Muslim pilgrims engage in elaborate rituals both at the famous mosque in Mecca that holds the Kaba and in areas surrounding their most sacred city.

Jihad is sometimes referred to as a sixth pillar of Islam. Since 9/11 there has been constant debate about the meaning of the term. Many Muslims and some secular experts on Islam have tried to say that *jihad* only refers to personal spiritual struggle. *Jihad* can and often does mean one's individual efforts to be righteous but it is often used by Muslims both past and present to refer to actual military struggle or "holy war." Saying that *jihad* is simply spiritual struggle ignores Islamic history and the actions of contemporary Muslims, including militants like Osama bin Laden, who used it to refer to acts of killing in the name of Allah.

Biblical Perspective

The three key topics of discussion between a Christian and a Muslim should be the nature of God, the identity and deity of Jesus Christ, and salvation by grace alone apart from works. Christians can share with Muslims that the Christian God transcends man's finitude and sinfulness because He cares about people individually, and He loves individuals.

Divine love is a concept often missing from Islam, and yet it is essential to human peace and happiness with God. A powerful witness of Scripture to God's love is John 3:16: "For God so loved the world, that He gave His only begotten Son, that whosoever believeth in him should not perish, but have everlasting life." When told about Jesus, many Muslims will refuse to listen, claiming that our Scriptures are distorted and untrustworthy. The Christian can refer the interested Muslim to the many fine volumes available showing the inerrancy and inspiration of the Bible, both Old and New Testaments. This can provide a foundation for the Christian to present the New Testament teaching that Jesus Christ is truly God and is the only way to salvation (see chapter 5 on Jehovah's Witnesses for a thorough discussion of the deity of Christ).

Divine love is a concept often missing from Islam.

A second approach would be to show how the Muslim view of a God who can change the scriptures of Judaism, Christianity, and Islam prevents any system of morality and ethics from ever existing. Such a God is self-contradictory and prevents us from ever knowing anything for certain, especially our salvation. The Christian can also share how the Qur'an holds to a high view of Scripture (Sura 4:47; 4:54) and that believers should check the Qur'an against the Bible (Sura 5:44–49; 10:95). The Muslim may charge that Jews and Christians have mistranslated the Bible, but the Qur'an says that they only *misinterpret* and *disbelieve* it (Sura 3:70–71). According to the Qur'an, only Jews have mistranslated Scripture (Sura 2:75–79; 4:46). Textually, all variations of the Qur'an were destroyed by Caliph Uthman (ruled 646–656), and his version is the only version in existence.

The Old Testament has several extant versions that were around many years before Muhammad was even born, such as the Septuagint, the Syrian Peshitta, and the Targums. The New Testament has at least 9,000 manuscript copies existing before Muhammad, as well as over 36,000 quotations in the writings of the early church Fathers. The Koran cites its elegance as evidence for its inspiration (Sura 17:88), but many eloquent books have been written throughout history, from the *Iliad* and the *Odyssey* to *Paradise Lost* and *Moby Dick*. Does their eloquence also make them divine revelation? Obviously eloquence, even if true (and it is debatable that the Koran is stylistically elegant), is totally irrelevant.

The evidence clearly shows that the Bible we have is very close to the original and that it has not been tampered with. Moreover, there are multiple discrepancies in the Koran as well as many places where it contradicts Scripture. Sura 11:42–43 contradicts Genesis 6–7 by saying that Noah had a son who died in the flood and Sura 3:41 contradicts Luke when it says that Zechariah was speechless for three days (Luke 1:18–20). Sura 61:6 claims that Muhammad fulfills prophecy both in the Torah and in the Gospels.

The Koran claims to fulfill prophecies in Deuteronomy 18:15–18 and John 14:16. Deuteronomy 18:15–18 is a portion of a speech given by Moses to the Israelites, beginning at Deuteronomy 5:1, in which Moses prophesied that God would raise up a prophet like him from their midst. The meaning of this prophecy is partially explained in verse 34:10: "And there arose not a prophet since in Israel like unto Moses, *whom the Lord knew face to face*" (italics added). Yet the Koran was revealed to Muhammad by the angel Gabriel, not directly by God, and Muhammad never claimed to be a descendant of Israel, but of Ishmael. If the Koran is to fulfill the Torah and the Gospels as it claims, the Muslim should read Acts 3:22–23, in which Peter speaks of Jesus as the prophet spoken of by Moses.

John 14:16 reports that Jesus said that the Father will give the Helper to His disciples and that He would abide with them forever. Verse 17 adds that He would dwell with them and be in them. The Greek word for "Helper," or more properly "Advocate," *parakletos* is claimed by Muslim apologists to be *periclytos* "renowned." Somehow this word, which is not found anywhere in the New Testament, is understood by Muslims to mean "praised one," since the Sura claims that Jesus prophesied that he was sending the "good tidings of the Messenger who comes after me, whose name shall be Ahmad ["Praised One"]." To add to their claim, Muslim apologists argue that the verse has been tampered with by Christians (contradicting Sura 2:73–79). But there is not a single manuscript copy that has *periclytos* nor is there any contextual sense where Muhammad could somehow be fitted into the verse. Muhammad, being human, could not abide with Christ's disciples forever, dwell with them over 500 years before he was born, nor live in them. If he could, he would be a much greater prophet than he claimed! On the other hand, there is ample evidence to suggest that Sura 61:6 was interpolated after Muhammad's death. W. Montgomery Watt cogently shows that *"it is impossible to prove that any Muslim child was called Ahmad after the Prophet before about the year 125."*[21]

At any rate, John 14:26 specifically identifies the parakletos with the Holy Spirit.[22] Sometimes the Muslim will argue that the rapid spread of Islam shows the truth of the religion (Sura 41:53), but several empires have spread faster than Islam, such as the empires under Alexander the Great and Genghis Khan. One could also counter that the rapid spread of communism was evidence of its truthfulness. Their argument is simply an appeal to irrelevancy.

It is important to begin any discussion by *defining your terms*, and then sharing the good news that Jehovah—the God of the Bible and Creator of all—gave salvation as a free gift through the death and resurrection of His only Son, Jesus Christ. Peace with God does not depend on human, insufficient efforts, but on the grace of God displayed through the atonement of Jesus Christ on the cross.

No one can work his way to heaven (or Muslim paradise). The Muslim will agree that Allah could justly choose to bar all men from paradise since

21. *Early Islam: Collected Articles* (Edinburgh: Edinburgh University Press, 1990), 43–50. Italics his. The year 125 means 125 years after the Hijra according to the Muslim dating system (ca. AD 755). For additional evidence that this is a later insertion, see Parrinder, *Jesus*, 96–100.
22. For more on the meaning of *parakletos*, see Leon Morris, *The Gospel According to John*, The New International Commentary on the New Testament (Grand Rapids, MI: Eerdmans, 1971), 662–666. For more contradictions between the Bible and the Quran, see Gleason L. Archer Jr., *A Survey of Old Testament Introduction* (Chicago: Moody Press, 1964), 498–500, as well as the previously mentioned works by Parrinder and Dashti.

no man is perfect as Allah is perfect. However, *biblical* salvation does not depend on man's imperfections. Biblical salvation depends on the work and love of God. "For by grace are ye saved through faith; and that not of yourselves; it is the gift of God: not of works, lest any man should boast" (Ephesians 2:8–10).

Finally, Christians should love Muslims and point them consistently to the Bible as the only source of truth. Muslims have a definite zeal for Allah. They desire to follow him and express their worship of him through their lives. The Christian should respect the Muslim's sincere intentions and share with them the life-changing Gospel of Jesus Christ.

Christians believe the God of the Bible is great. When a Christian can demonstrate the power of the Word of God through the Holy Spirit, and use his own life as an example of the joy and peace possible to those who love Jesus Christ, he becomes an effective example of God's love for all—including Muslims. The Holy Spirit is able to touch the hearts of all human beings and a kind, respectful, and *prayer-filled* approach may provide the opportunity for Muslims to recognize Muhammad's distorted concepts of God, and to come to know and worship the One, true God, and His Son Jesus—Second Person of the Trinity, and Savior of the world.

Explore

Jehovah's Identity vs. Allah's Identity
The Dome of the Rock Inscriptions
Five Pillars of Islam
Abrogation

Discuss

1. Who is Allah?

2. Compare Jesus and Muhammad according to the Koran.

   _____

   _____

3. Why do Muslims need to celebrate Ramadan?

   _____

   _____

4. Does the rapid spread of Islam prove it is of God? (Review Gamaliel's argument in chapter 1.)

   _____

   _____

Dig Deeper

See *The Kingdom of the Cults Study Guide* available at WalterMartin.com.

17

The Jesus of the Cults

Quick Facts on the Jesus of the Cults

- Understand the nature of the "other Jesus".

- Give biblical reasons *why* Christians must identify him as counterfeit and refute his "other gospel."

- Remember that the message of the Cross itself is offensive and controversial by nature.

- Defend the faith and evangelize because Christ commanded it.

Historical Perspective

Since the earliest days of Christianity, both apostle and disciple alike have been confronted with the perversion of the revelation God has given us in the person of Jesus Christ. Historically, this perversion has extended not only to the teaching of our Lord but, more importantly, to the person of Christ; for it is axiomatic that if the doctrine of Christ himself, i.e., His person, nature, and work are perverted so that the identity of the life-giver is altered, then the life that He came to give is correspondingly negated.

It is at precisely this juncture that in this day and age we come face to face with the phenomenon that the Apostle Paul described in 2 Corinthians, chapter 11, as "the other Jesus."

The problem is twofold, in that we must understand the nature of the "other Jesus" and then give the biblical reasons why it is the obligation of Christians to identify him as a counterfeit and refute his other gospel.

There can be little doubt that the Christian of today can expect to encounter the very same or, at least, similar errors and perversions of the gospel message that his ancestors before him did. He should not be discouraged when they appear to have more success in twisting the truth of God than the Christian has in presenting it.

The epistle to the Galatians reminds us that there are those who would "pervert the Gospel of Christ," and who represent "another gospel," which in reality is not another but a counterfeit of the original, designed by the master craftsman of all evils, our adversary, the devil.

> We must understand the nature of the "other Jesus" and identify him as counterfeit.

It may seem like oversimplification and naiveté to some people to suggest that Satan is the prime mover and architect of the major cult systems, but a careful consideration of the biblical evidence will allow no other conclusion.

In his Second Corinthian epistle, Paul penned one of the most solemn warnings recorded anywhere in the Bible, to which we have made previous reference. He addressed this warning to Christians who were in great danger of having their minds (not their soul's salvation) corrupted from the simplicity that is in Christ Jesus. He was afraid, he said, that if someone should come to Corinth preaching "another Jesus, another Spirit, and another gospel," the Corinthians might well be swept along with it to the sterilization of their Christian life and witness for Christ. Paul went on to underscore this point by drawing a deadly parallel between true Christianity and pseudo-Christianity that he likened to a carefully designed copy of the original revelation of God in Christ.

After revealing the existence of a counterfeit Jesus, Holy Spirit, and gospel, Paul completed the parallel by showing that there are also counterfeit "apostles" and counterfeit "disciples" (workers) who transform themselves in appearance and demeanor to appear as ministers of Christ, but in reality, Paul states, they are representatives of Satan (2 Corinthians 11:13). He further informs us that this is not to be considered fantastic, unbelievable, and incredible, for Satan himself is often manifested as "an angel of light." So we are not to be surprised when his ministers emulate their master and disguise themselves as ministers of righteousness (2 Corinthians 11:14–15).

Now, of course, Paul was speaking of those who could be readily identified as spiritual wolves in sheep's clothing the moment their teachings were compared with the true gospel (Galatians 1:8–9), not just anyone with whom we have a disagreement in the realm of theology.

Simply because Christians disagree on certain peripheral issues cannot be taken as a valid reason for asserting that such are dissenters and ministers of Satan, unless that dissent involves the person and work of our Lord, in which case their unbelief would automatically invoke the apostolic judgment.

Theological Evaluation

The person and work of Christ is indeed the very foundation of Christian faith. And if it is redefined and interpreted out of context and therefore contrary to its biblical content, the whole message of the Gospel is radically altered and its value correspondingly diminished. The early apostles clearly saw this, including John and Jude; hence, their repeated emphasis upon maintaining the identity and ministry of the historical Jesus over against the counterfeits of that Person already beginning to arise in their own era.

The "other Jesus" of the false cults of that day (Gnosticism and Galatianism, or Legalism) threatened the churches at Colosse, Ephesus, and Crete, and invoked powerful apostolic condemnation and warning in the epistles of First John, Galatians, and Colossians.

In order that we may better understand precisely how these Scriptures may be applied in our own day, we need only cite some contemporary illustrations of the "other Jesus" the Bible so graphically warns against, and the entire issue will come into clear perspective.

1. The Jesus of Christian Science

In the theological structure of the Christian Science religion, as we have already seen, Gnosticism was revived and Mrs. Eddy became its twentieth-century exponent. Mrs. Eddy declared concerning *her* Jesus:

> The Christian who believes in the First Commandment is a monotheist. Thus he virtually unites with the Jew's belief in one God and recognizes that Jesus Christ is not God as Jesus Christ himself declared, but is the Son of God (*Science and Health*, 152).

Mrs. Eddy spelled out her view so that no one could possibly misinterpret her when she wrote:

> The spiritual Christ was infallible; Jesus, as material manhood, was not Christ (*Misc. Writings*, 84).

Now, a careful study of Matthew, chapter 16, will reveal that Jesus Christ acknowledged the confession of Peter to the effect that He was Jesus the Christ, the Son of the living God. And it would be foolish to maintain that Jesus was not material manhood in the light of the New Testament record that He was born of woman, subject to the limitations of our nature apart from sin, and physically expired upon the cross in our place. The Jesus of Mrs. Eddy is a divine ideal or principle, inherent within every man, and Jesus was its supreme manifestation. Since Mrs. Eddy denied the existence of the physical universe, she also denied the reality of human flesh and blood, maintaining that it was an illusion of mortal mind. Hence, neither Christ, nor any man, for that matter, possesses a real body of flesh and bones and, for her, Jesus Christ has not come in the flesh.

> Jesus acknowledged in Matthew 16 that He was Jesus the Christ, the Son of the living God.

It seems almost unnecessary to refer to the fact that our Lord acknowledged the reality of flesh and blood when He declared to Peter: "Blessed art thou, Simon Bar-jona: for flesh and blood hath not revealed it unto thee, but my Father which is in heaven" (Matthew 16:17).

At this particular juncture, the words of the Apostle John take on new meaning when he declares:

> Every spirit that confesseth not that Jesus Christ is come in the flesh is not of God: and this is that spirit of antichrist, whereof ye have heard that it should come; and even now already is it in the world (1 John 4:3).

John's previous words then apply with great force to the Jesus of Christian Science and its "prophetess," Mrs. Eddy:

> Who is a liar but he that denieth that Jesus is the Christ? He is antichrist, that denieth the Father and the Son (1 John 2:22).

We need not emphasize the point, for it is quite evident that the "other" Jesus of Christian Science is a Gnostic Jesus, an idea, a principle—but not

God incarnate (John 1:14). Because of this, although Mrs. Eddy, her literature, and Christian Scientists utilize the name of Jesus, theirs is not the Christ of the Scriptures, but an extremely clever counterfeit about whom the Holy Spirit graciously saw fit to warn the church.

2. The Jesus of Jehovah's Witnesses

The next example is quite different from the Jesus of Christian Science, but another Jesus nonetheless. According to the theology of the Watchtower,

> The true Scriptures speak of God's Son, the Word, as "a god." He is a "mighty god," but not the Almighty God who is Jehovah (*The Truth Shall Make You Free*, 47).
>
> In other words, he was the first and direct creation of Jehovah God (*The Kingdom Is at Hand*, 46–47, 49).

The founder of Jehovah's Witnesses, Charles Taze Russell, described this Jesus as having been Michael the Archangel prior to his divesting himself of his angelic nature and appearing in the world as a perfect man (*Studies in the Scriptures*, 5:84). For Jehovah's Witnesses, their Jesus is an angel who became a man; he is a god, but he is not God the Son, second person of the Holy Trinity.

As the chapter on Jehovah's Witnesses amply demonstrates, the Scriptures refute this and flatly controvert the Watchtower's theology by teaching that Jesus Christ is the Word, God the only begotten one (John 1:18, from the Greek), and no less than the great "I AM" of Exodus 3:14 (compare John 8:58) and the First and the Last of the apocalyptic-Isaiah contrast, well-known to any informed student of the Scriptures (compare Revelation 1:16–17 with Isaiah 44:6).

Just as Mrs. Eddy's Christ is an abstract idea, the Christ of Jehovah's Witnesses is a second god with an angelic background. He, too, qualifies as "another Jesus" in the context of the Pauline prophecy.

3. The Jesus of the Mormons

The teachings of the Mormon religion, which differ from both Christian Science and Jehovah's Witnesses, claim that their god is one among many gods, as evidenced by their own literature:

> Each of these gods, including Jesus Christ and his Father, being in possession of not merely an organized spirit, but a glorious body of flesh and bones

(Parley P. Pratt, *Key to the Science of Theology* [1973 ed.], 44; see also, *Doctrine and Covenants*, 130:22).

Theologian Pratt held no unique view where Mormonism was concerned; in fact, the Mormons have a full pantheon of gods. Jesus, who before his incarnation was the spirit-brother of Lucifer, was also a polygamist, the husband of the Marys and Martha, who was rewarded for his faithfulness by becoming the ruler of this earth (see chapter 6—Mormonism).

The Apostle Paul reminds us in his epistle to the Galatians that "God is one" (Galatians 3:20). Numerous passages from the Old Testament, previously cited in the chapter on Mormonism, demonstrate the absolute falsity of the idea that there are a multiplicity of gods and an exaltation to godhood to which men can aspire. As for the concept of Jesus as a polygamist and a brother of Lucifer, this need not be dignified by further comment.

The Jesus of the Mormons is quite obviously "another Jesus" with whom truly redeemed men have nothing in common, even though he be arrayed as an angel of light and with all the credentials of the angel Moroni's angelic proclamation to Joseph Smith, the prophet of the restored Christian religion!

It would be possible to go on listing the other cult systems, but it is apparent that further comment would be superfluous; the evidence is overpowering.

The Jesus of the Christian Scientists, the Mormons, the Jehovah's Witnesses, and of all the cult systems is but a subtle caricature of the Christ of divine revelation. In cult theology, He becomes an abstraction (Christian Science, Unity, Metaphysics, New Thought), a second god (Jehovah's Witnesses, Mormonism, Theosophy, Rosicrucianism, Baha'ism), a pantheistic manifestation of deity (Spiritism, The Great I Am); but he is still incontrovertibly "another Jesus," who represents another gospel and imparts another spirit, which by no conceivable stretch of the imagination could be called holy.

Herein lies the problem that Christians must face and come to grips with, and there are excellent reasons why it is not only our responsibility but our duty.

Biblical Perspective

In the course of delivering numerous lectures on the subject of non-Christian cults and their relationship to the Christian church, one of the most frequently asked questions has been, "Why should Christians oppose and criticize the beliefs of others whether they be cults or other world religions?"

To answer this question we must first recognize that to oppose and criticize is neither unethical, bigoted, nor unchristian; rather, it is the epitome of proper Christian conduct where a very vital part of the Christian witness is concerned. There are some good people who feel that it is beneath their dignity to engage in the criticism of the beliefs of others, and the society in which we live has done much to foster this belief. "Live and let live" is the motto of our civilization; don't buck the tide of uncritical tolerance or, as the saying goes, "bend with the wind or be broken." In addition to this type of reasoning there also has been promulgated a distinctly non-controversial spirit mirrored in the fact that leading newspapers and periodicals, not to mention the mass media of communication, radio and TV, refuse to carry advertisements for debates on religious issues for fear of being thought un-American, since it is now fashionable to equate criticism of another's religion with an un-American spirit!

We must remember, however, that controversy in itself has always been a stimulus to thought and in our own great country has provoked many needed reforms in numerous instances. We might also observe that there is the easily verifiable fact that the criticism of another's religious beliefs does not necessarily postulate personal antagonism toward those who entertain such beliefs. Hence it is possible for a Protestant to criticize Roman Catholicism or Judaism, for example, without being in the least antagonistic to members of either faith. Let us not forget that honest criticism, debate, and the exploration of controversial issues involves the basic right of freedom of speech within constitutional limits; and the New Testament itself, the very cradle of Christianity, reflects in a startling way the fact that the faith of Jesus Christ was built and nourished

> The message of the Cross itself is offensive and controversial by nature.

upon the controversy that it provoked. It was said of the early Christians that they "turned the world upside down" (Acts 17:6); indeed the message of the Cross itself is offensive and controversial by nature. Robert Ingersoll, the late great agnostic and renowned antagonist of Christianity, was wise enough to recognize this fact and stated in his famous lectures, "If this religion is true, then there is only one Savior, only one narrow path to life. Christianity cannot live in peace with any other religion."

There are many reasons why books and chapters like this should be written, but we shall turn to the Bible itself for the basic reasons—believing that in God's Word, the source of our faith, will be found the evidence that its defense is very much His will.

Let us begin by noting the historical fact that Jesus Christ and His apostles warned repeatedly of false prophets and teachers.

Throughout His entire ministry, our Lord was constantly on guard against those who attempted to ensnare Him with trick questions and supposed contradictions between what He taught and the teachings of Moses and the prophets. Added to this, these professional interrogators masqueraded as religious, pious, and even tolerant zealots and professed that they were the descendants of Abraham, heirs to the covenant, and the servants of God. To these people our Lord addressed His most scathing denunciations, calling them, among other things, "whited sepulchers," "children of the devil," "dishonorers of God," "liars," "murderers," and "wolves." Since our Lord was both God and man, He alone could gaze through the centuries and see those who would arise following in the train of His contemporary antagonists, and at least two very graphic prophecies of their characters and objectives are to be found in His discourses.

In the seventh chapter of the gospel according to Matthew, Christ enunciated a very definite warning:

> Beware of false prophets, which come to you in sheep's clothing, but inwardly they are ravening wolves. Ye shall know them by their fruits. Do men gather grapes of thorns, or figs of thistles? Even so, every good tree bringeth forth good fruit; but a corrupt tree bringeth forth evil fruit. A good tree cannot bring forth evil fruit, neither can a corrupt tree bring forth good fruit. Every tree that bringeth not forth good fruit is hewn down, and cast into the fire. Wherefore by their fruits ye shall know them. Not every one that saith unto me, Lord, Lord, shall enter into the kingdom of heaven; but he that doeth the will of my Father which is in heaven. Many will say to me in that day, Lord, Lord, have we not prophesied in thy name? and in thy name have cast out devils? and in thy name done many wonderful works? And then will I profess unto them, I never knew you: depart from me, ye that work iniquity (Matthew 7:15–23).

From this discourse we learn some very important things. We learn that there shall be false prophets, that they shall appear in sheep's clothing, and that their inward or spiritual nature is that of wolves (v. 15). We are further told that we shall be able to recognize them by their fruits. We are informed that they will prophesy in His name; in His name cast out devils, and in His name perform miracles (v. 22). With the full knowledge that they would do these things, our Lord adds "then will I profess unto them, I never knew you . . . ye that work iniquity" (v. 23). There can be little doubt that He intended this as a warning, for He prefaces His statements with a very strong Greek term "beware," literally, "be wary of or take care, because of" false prophets. The designation "wolves in sheep's clothing" is therefore not that of some misguided and overzealous Christian apologist, but one that finds its authority in the words of God the Son, and this is the reason why Christians are to listen to it.

Our Lord supplemented His discussion of these individuals when in the twenty-fourth chapter of Matthew, while speaking of the circumstances surrounding His Second Advent, Christ declared: "For there shall arise false Christs and false prophets, and shall show great signs and wonders; insomuch that, if it were possible, they shall deceive the very elect" (v. 24).

Further comment on this point is not necessary; He designated them "false Christs" and "false prophets"; it was He who prophesied that they would show great signs and wonders, and it was He who warned that if it were possible, the subtlety of their evil would deceive the very elect, or the church. Apparently our Savior thought it important enough to repeat, for in verse twenty-five He says, "Behold, I have told you before."

The Apostle Paul, utilizing the identical language of the Lord Jesus Christ, succinctly phrases a divine warning concerning these same people.

> For I have not shunned to declare unto you all the counsel of God. Take heed therefore unto yourselves, and to all the flock, over which the Holy Spirit hath made you overseers, to feed the church of God, which he hath purchased with his own blood. For I know this, that after my departing shall grievous wolves enter in among you, not sparing the flock. Also of your own selves shall men arise, speaking perverse things, to draw away disciples after them. Therefore watch, and remember, that by the space of three years I ceased not to warn every one night and day with tears (Acts 20:27–31).

It appears from this very pointed statement that Paul was not afraid "to declare unto you all the counsel of God." Indeed, the greatest of the apostles warns us to "take heed," and this is to involve not only ourselves but all Christians; and though it is addressed principally to pastors, it underlines the existence of "grievous wolves" about whom Paul says, "I ceased not to warn every one night and day with tears." Should not that which was important to him be as important to us for whom he intended it? It is of no small interest and importance that this charge of Paul to the Ephesian elders was taken very seriously by them, for in Revelation, chapter 2, Christ commends the church at Ephesus for heeding Paul, in that he "tried them which say they are apostles, and are not, and hast found them liars" (v. 2).

Paul, of course, made much mention of such persons elsewhere, describing them as "enemies of the cross of Christ" (Philippians 3:18) and "false apostles, deceitful workers, transforming themselves into the apostles of Christ" (2 Corinthians 11:13). He does not even hesitate to describe them as "Satan's ministers" (2 Corinthians 11:14–15). The first and second epistles to Timothy, also of Pauline authorship, reflect the same attitude: "Now the Spirit speaketh expressly, that in the latter times some shall depart from the faith, giving heed to seducing spirits, and doctrines of devils; speaking lies in hypocrisy; having their conscience seared with a hot iron" (1 Timothy 4:1–2).

The express speaking of the Spirit, of course, underscores the importance of the counsel given, and it is significant to observe that it is to take place in the "latter times," when men shall "depart from the faith," listen to "seducing spirits," and become captives of "the doctrines of demons." This is tremendously strong language in the original Greek and is followed by his counsel in the second epistle to "preach the Word" and to "reprove, rebuke, and exhort with all longsuffering and doctrine" those who in the time to come "will not endure sound doctrine; but after their own lusts shall heap to themselves teachers who shall tickle their ears; and the truth shall be turned into fables" (2 Timothy 4:3–4, from the Greek).

It is more than a casual coincidence that the Apostle Peter acknowledges the authority of Christ and Paul by utilizing their very language: "But there were false prophets also among the people, even as there shall be false teachers among you, who privily shall bring in damnable heresies, even denying the Lord that bought them, and bring upon themselves swift destruction" (2 Peter 2:1).

For Peter, it appears "false prophets" were a distinct reality, "false teachers" not figments of overwrought fundamentalist imaginations, and "destructive heresies," which "denied the Lord that bought them," vivid dangers to be guarded against. As we approach the end of the New Testament, we find John, always noted for his doctrine of love, balancing that doctrine magnificently with the teaching of divine judgment upon those whom he describes as "false prophets . . . gone out into the world" (1 John 4:1) and "deceivers . . . entered into the world, who confess not that Jesus Christ is come in the flesh. This is a deceiver and an antichrist" (2 John 7).

The next to the last book in the Bible, the comparatively small epistle of Jude, is likewise in full agreement with the verdict of our Lord and the other apostles:

> Certain men crept in unawares, who were before of old ordained to this condemnation, ungodly men, turning the grace of our God into lasciviousness, and denying the only Lord God, and our Lord Jesus Christ. . . . These are spots in your feasts of charity . . . clouds they are without water, carried about of winds; trees whose fruit withereth, without fruit, twice dead, plucked up by the roots; raging waves of the sea, foaming out their own shame; wandering stars, to whom is reserved the blackness of darkness for ever (vv. 4, 12–13).

As we have noted, all of the quotations are in context, refer to the same individuals, and characterize them in an identical manner. The description is not pleasant, but it is a biblical one originating with God the Holy Spirit, not with the so-called interpretational fancies or bigoted intolerances of uninformed extremists. God used these terms for people He describes in His Word; God warns the church of Christ about their existence, their methods, their teachings, their subtleties, and their final judgment. The church neglects, at her peril, such divine counsel.

There are naturally some who will not agree with this position; they will quote the advice of Gamaliel, which he addressed to the Jews in the book of Acts (5:38–39). They, too, will say, "Let them alone: for if this counsel or this work be of men, it will come to nought: But if it be of God, ye cannot overthrow it; lest haply ye be found even to fight against God." The only difficulty, as we have noted earlier, is that the context clearly indicates the advice was given by Gamaliel to the Jews, and Gamaliel was not an inspired writer, an apostle, or even a Christian. If his advice is to be followed and his criterion to be recognized, then the thriving growth of the various non-Christian cults, all of which deny the fundamentals of the Christian faith, must be acknowledged as the work of God! No consistent thinker of Christian orientation could long entertain such a warped conclusion without doing violence to a great portion of the New Testament.

There are also others who, in their attempt to excuse themselves from meeting the challenge of the Jesus of the cults, will refer to the ninth verse of Jude where Michael the archangel, when contending with the devil, refused to argue with him but rather referred him to the Lord for rebuke. Once again, however, the context reveals that Michael did not keep silence by choice but by necessity because as the Greek so clearly reveals, "He did not dare bring against Satan a blasphemous judgment," for the simple reason that Satan was his superior in authority. The Greek word translated "durst" in our King James Bible carries the meaning of not doing something for fear of retaliation by a superior power (Greek: *etolmese*), so this line of reasoning also fails.

The reasons why we must answer as well as be prepared to evangelize such people are quite clear. The church must do it because Christ and the apostles commanded her to do so, unpopular though it may be, and to this all true Christians should be unequivocally committed, for no other reason than out of respect for our Lord. Certainly if our mothers, wives, children, or country were attacked and misrepresented, our love for them would *compel us* to defend them. How much more then should love for our Redeemer so motivate us in the defense of Him and His Gospel.

The Jesus of the cults is a poor substitute for the incarnate God of the New Testament. Along with the equally important imperative of cult evangelism stands the very real need to give to everyone that asks of us "a reason for the hope that is within us" (1 Peter 3:15). That hope is the Jesus of biblical theology and of history, and once we understand the true nature of the Jesus of the cults we can discharge our duty faithfully and by contrast unmask him and his creator for all to see. We may sum this up with the thought-provoking words of our Lord when with absolute finality He declared: "Behold, I have told you before" (Matthew 24:25).

Explore

Simplicity in Christ
Spiritual Wolves
Peripheral Issues
Destructive Heresies

——————————————— **Discuss** ———————————————

1. What is the foundation of the Christian faith?

   _____

   _____

2. Should Christians oppose and criticize the beliefs of others? What is Christ's example?

   _____

   _____

3. Some use Gamaliel to argue against evangelism and the defense of the faith. Why is this a false argument?

   _____

   _____

4. What is the true nature of Jesus?

   _____

   _____

——————————————— **Dig Deeper** ———————————————

See *The Kingdom of the Cults Study Guide* available at WalterMartin.com.

Cult Evangelism—Mission Field on Your Doorstep

Historical Perspective

The last one hundred years of American history have seen the evangelization of large segments of the American populace to a degree never imagined by any evangelist in the history of Christianity.

Beginning with the evangelical emphasis of Charles G. Finney, through the massive impact of D. L. Moody, Gypsy Smith, Billy Sunday, culminating in Billy Graham, and now the enormous "Harvest" crusades, American Christianity has enjoyed great spiritual privileges withheld from the world since the days of the Reformation and the Knox, Wesley, and Whitefield revivals so dear to the memory of church historians.

Yet there are many people today, in both the clergy and the ranks of the laity, who are seriously reevaluating the meaning of evangelism and its importance, if not to the church, at least to themselves. More and more, Christians are beginning to think in terms of *personal* evangelism as opposed to mass evangelism, primarily because all *successful* evangelism of enduring worth—since the earliest days of Christianity—has been of a personal nature. While it is true that great evangelists draw crowds and preach to multitudes of people, they, too, are dependent upon the so-called "personal touch," as evidenced by the fact that Billy Graham has more than once attempted to remove the "tag line" from his *Hour of Decision* radio program, "The Lord bless you real good," only to have such attempts reversed by the constituency that, despite its size, still desires the feeling of a personal relationship.

We must consider carefully the pattern of evangelism laid out for us in the New Testament.

The follow-up work of every major evangelical crusade must be on a personal basis to be effective. A stamped envelope and a short memory course are no substitute for the personal workers, whose on-the-spot faithfulness, patience, and perseverance build up and edify young converts after the first warm glow of the conversion experience has begun to abate.

This, of course, brings us to a consideration of the all-important question: What is evangelism? Is it merely mass rallies where so-called "wholesale" decisions for Christ are made? Is it, on the other hand, just the task of the local church to shoulder the responsibility of having a week or two of meetings for revival and evangelistic purposes each year? By evangelism, do we mean massive emphasis upon radio and television to communicate the good news of redemption? Or, is evangelism somehow or other bound up with *all* of these forms of expression, and yet, in essence, none of them? Is it perhaps possible that evangelism was intended, in its primary purpose, to be personal and individualistic to the degree that each Christian feels the responsibility to evangelize his neighbor, and that this is really the root of the whole matter from which the tree of church evangelism and mass evangelism, both in crusades and the mass media, are to draw their strength and spiritual stamina? To answer these questions, and to place evangelism in its proper perspective where the challenge of non-Christian cults is concerned, we must consider carefully the pattern laid out for us in the New Testament.

Theological Evaluation

If anything proceeds from the pages of the New Testament, it is the message that the early Christian church labored under the magnificent obsession of the divine paradox. They were separate as individuals in each congregation, whether it was Ephesus, Corinth, Crete, or Philippi. But in some mysterious sense, they were "one body" in Christ (Ephesians 4:4). Through acceptance of the divine Redeemer, God had shattered and broken down the walls of race, color, and social status. They were no longer "Barbarian, Scythian, bond nor free: but Christ is all, and in all" (Colossians 3:11).

Each of these New Testament Christians was admonished by the Holy Spirit to be an ambassador or representative for his Savior (2 Corinthians 5:20). The Apostle Paul set the supreme example of this in the New Testament church by declaring that the primary responsibility of the Christian was to preach the Gospel (1 Corinthians 15:1–4), and it is precisely at this juncture that, if we are willing, we can understand the meaning of New Testament evangelism.

The Greek word translated *gospel* literally means "good news," as most Christians well know. But what many do not know is that the word translated *preach* comes from the Greek *evangelizomai,* which means "to publish" the Gospel or declare it abroad for all the world to hear.

The early Christians considered themselves evangelists in that sense (1 Corinthians 1:17), and in the writings of Paul, Peter, John, and others, this great unalterable truth shines through. Christianity was not something entrusted only to clergymen, pastors, teachers, or professional evangelists, it was a personal message entrusted to those who had experienced the power of its transforming properties in their own lives, and who went literally from house to house and turned the world upside down because they were not ashamed to proclaim it. The early Christians went forth two by two. They went forth in the power of the resurrected Christ. They went forth with a message—a message based upon experience shared by all and an experience that strengthened and comforted all. These were not people who were preoccupied with the things of the world, with contemporary political intrigues or the reigns of the Caesars, with

> Each New Testament Christian was admonished by the Holy Spirit to be an ambassador or representative for his Savior.

the showplaces of Ephesus and the coliseums of Rome. These were people who were possessed by a Spirit totally removed from the spirit of the age in which they lived—a Spirit who commanded them to convict the world of sin, because though they had been its victims they had now become its conquerors because of the Redeemer.

The incredible zeal with which they proclaimed this message of the living Christ, the Gospel of the Resurrection, the certainty of sins forgiven, the present possession of peace with God, exerted an awesome influence and power over the minds of those with whom they came in contact, almost without exception. The Philippian jailer abused Paul and Silas until he experienced the presence of their Master. Then he, too, with his whole house, believed the incredible. Sergius Paulus, beset though he was by a demonic medium who sought to pervert the Gospel and turn him away from the faith of Christ, was stunned by the authority of a man filled with the Holy Spirit. Saul, who was also called Paul, and whose amazement turned to faith and life eternal. Even those who resisted the magnificence of New Testament evangelism were frightened by its clarity and power and felt even as Festus, who raved at the apostle, "Paul, thou art beside thyself; much learning doth make thee mad" (Acts 26:24). Agrippa the king could not be dissuaded even by the remarks of Festus, but withdrew from the presence of the Holy Spirit with the trembling admission, "Almost thou persuadest me to be a Christian" (Acts 26:28).

All of these evangelists had three things in common. First, they had experienced the person of the risen Christ and had passed out of death into life. Second, they were dominated by the Holy Spirit, alien to this world because the world does not know Him and cannot receive Him, because the world is evil and He is God. Third, they obeyed the injunction of the apostles and as ambassadors for Christ fearlessly published the Good News that Light had come into the world, and that God had indeed appointed a day in which He would judge the world in righteousness by the man whom He had ordained and given assurance to all men by raising Him from among the dead.

It is not difficult to see why the Christians of the first century were able to spread Christianity throughout the earth without the aid of radio, television, traveling caravan, precision crusades, or yearly evangelistic and revival meetings. Every day was an evangelistic campaign for them; every service a revival meeting; every road a path to someone who needed Christ; every house a dwelling place for those for whom He died. These were people who were evangelists in the full meaning of the term as God had intended and commanded it. They rose to the challenge with a supreme confidence and conviction born of experience and faith, which, despite their limitations and human frailties, made them worthy of the name "saints." They could do all this because they had truly found Him "of whom Moses in the law, and in the prophets, did write, Jesus of Nazareth" (John 1:45), and they had believed Him that "where two or three are gathered together in my name, there am I in the midst of them" (Matthew 18:20).

If we want to have evangelism in the true biblical sense of the term, we must return to the *content* of the evangel and to the *methods* of the New Testament church. We must utilize every modern method possible, but we must not allow them to overshadow or interfere with the great personal responsibility that rests upon every Christian. For in that very real and personal sense, it is true of us as it was of the Apostle Paul, "For Christ sent me not to baptize, but to preach the gospel" (1 Corinthians 1:17).

The Philippian Christians were admonished by the Apostle Paul to "shine as lights in the world; holding forth the word of life" (2:15–16). This they could do only by being willing to shine in contrast to the darkness that surrounded them and by being willing to stand in the defense of the Gospel as they held forth the Word of Life.

We are told in the simplest terms that the Gospel is God's power unto salvation (Romans 1:16), but what *is* that Gospel?

The Apostle Paul states it for us in what might be called a capsule version. When writing to the Corinthians he said:

> For I delivered unto you first of all that which I received, how that Christ died for our sins according to the scriptures; and that he was buried, and that he rose again the third day according to the scriptures (1 Corinthians 15:3–4).

The very usage of the word *Christ* in the Pauline theology identifies the office of the Anointed One with that of the second Person of the Trinity, He who is God "over all, God blessed for ever. Amen" (Romans 9:5, from the Greek).

Paul does not, however, stop at this, but goes on to point out that Christ died for our sins, that is, *in place of our sins*, a clear statement of the substitutionary atonement of the Cross. Then he concludes with "He rose again the third day," which in the context of 1 Corinthians 15 can *only* refer to a bodily resurrection (Luke 24:39ff.).

We can see then that the content of the Gospel is, at its very minimum, the Deity of Christ, the substitutionary atonement of the Cross, and His bodily resurrection from the grave. This Good News, when enunciated and published fearlessly by believers, has the effect of convicting men of their sins and leading them to true repentance toward God and faith in the Lord Jesus Christ. James Packer, in his stimulating book *Evangelism and the Sovereignty of God*, has put it this way:

> What was this Good News Paul preached? It was the news about Jesus of Nazareth. It was the news of the incarnation, the atonement, the kingdom, the cradle, the cross and the crown of the Son of God. It was the news of how God glorified His Servant, Jesus, by making Him Christ, the world's long-awaited Prince and Saviour. It was the news of how God made His Son man, and how as man, God made Him Priest and Prophet and King, and how as Priest, God also made Him a sacrifice for sins, and how as a Prophet, God also made Him a law-giver to His people, and how as King, God has also made Him judge of all the world, and given Him prerogatives which in the Old Testament are exclusively Jehovah's own—namely to reign until every knee bows before Him, and to save all who call on His Name. In short, the good news was just this, that God has executed His eternal intention of glorifying His Son by exalting Him as the great Saviour for great sinners. Such was the Gospel which Paul was sent to preach; it was a message of some complexity, needing to be learned before it could be lived by, understood before it could be applied and needed therefore to be taught. Hence Paul as a preacher of it, had to become a teacher. He saw this as part of his calling; he speaks of "the Gospel whereunto I am appointed a preacher . . . and a teacher" (2 Timothy 1:10ff.).[1]

Evangelism then has content, as well as zeal, courage, and an attitude of constant prayer—distinct methods of propagation.

Biblical Response

Techniques of Cult Evangelism

It is the testimony of the Word of God that He has raised up the Gentile nations and made available to them the Gospel of the Kingdom and

1. James I. Packer, *Evangelism and the Sovereignty of God* (Downers Grove, IL: InterVarsity Press, 1975), 47.

its Messianic King, which Israel rejected because of unbelief. The Scriptures declare that the purpose of God in doing this is to "provoke them to jealousy" (Romans 11:11) that they may perceive what they have lost and repent, that the natural olive branch may be grafted in again, whereas now, only the wild branch (Gentiles) shares the blessing of Messiah's covenant and coming Kingdom.

In the kingdom of the cults today, we are witnessing something akin to this and yet, despite its corrupt purposes, progressing at an alarming rate of speed. We see the various cult systems, specifically Jehovah's Witnesses, Mormonism, Unity, and others, utilizing the methods of Christianity and of New Testament propagation of the Christian message, wooing converts from professing Christian fellowships—Protestant as well as Roman Catholic! This bewildering proselytizing has caused consternation in many congregations and parishes across America and abroad, and it is accelerating, not slowing down.

We see the strange, but just, judgment of God upon the Christian church because of her *lethargy* in that He is allowing the forces of darkness to succeed with the methods of light while denying the *source* of light and life, the Gospel of Jesus Christ. In order that we may offset the ever-widening circle of cultic influence, Christians must first of all face the fact that we have been woefully delinquent in the exercise of our responsibility of personal evangelism. Second, many Christians have taken for granted the great doctrines of the Bible they learned and accepted at their conversion and have not studied to show themselves "approved unto God, a workman that needeth not to be ashamed, rightly dividing the word of truth" (2 Timothy 2:15). Third, the average Christian knows *what* he believes, but is unable to articulate *why* he believes, insofar as being able to document the *why* of his belief from the Scriptures, which he frequently finds a frustrating and exasperating task. The clergy is largely at fault in this respect because they do not always emphasize the teaching ministry of the pulpit, but rather, settle for an evangelistic emphasis with very little doctrinal depth.

A survey was taken in the Department of Biblical Studies at King's College. Of some three hundred students polled, fewer than ten had heard a sermon in the last four years in their respective churches on the doctrines of the Trinity, the Deity and Humanity of Jesus Christ, or the relationship of grace and faith to works. Similar surveys have been conducted in colleges, seminaries, and Bible institutes in many major cities throughout the country. The result has been almost identical. There *must* be something fundamentally wrong when important areas of doctrine such as these are neglected or glossed over lightly.

The various cult systems, particularly Jehovah's Witnesses and the Mormons, capitalize on conditions such as this. Many an embarrassed Christian rushes to the telephone when he has a Jehovah's Witness "minister" or Mormon "elder" in his living room to get answers from a generally overworked pastor, when a little consistent study of the Scriptures would have given him a tremendous sense of security and more important, provided him an opportunity to preach Christ in the true sense of personal evangelism to the cultists.

Throughout the world today, Christian missionaries are faced with proclaiming the unsearchable riches of the Gospel. And due to the tremendous amount of funds made available for world missions in the last one hundred years in the United States, a good many Christians have become lethargic and apathetic as to their own personal responsibility toward proclaiming the Gospel of Christ here at home. Ministers are constantly discovering that their congregations are dwindling at prayer meetings, that even their Sunday evening services have been winnowed considerably by television and other extracurricular social activities. Yet many don't see evangelism in the United States as a *pressing* need. Given the postmodern spirituality of American culture—openly hostile to Christianity—the growth of a variety of new religions, and a resurgence of Paganism, the time has come for mission strategists and denominations to view the United States as a fertile mission field in desperate need of trained missionaries, finances, and resources. Here then, lies part of the problem.

> We must return to positive Christian evangelism on the fiercely personal basis of door-to-door and neighbor-to-neighbor effort.

As we have shown in the preceding chapters, the non-Christian cult systems in America have grown tremendously in the last one hundred years. By a subtle utilization of a redefined terminology coupled with a surface knowledge of the Bible, and encouraged by the fact that a great many Christians are unable to answer their perversions (a fact that serves to confirm them even more definitely in those deviations), the zeal and missionary activities of the cults have tremendously increased. The only way to offset this is by a return to positive Christian evangelism on the fiercely personal basis of door-to-door and neighbor-to-neighbor effort whenever the opportunity presents itself. But over and beyond this, it is time that the Church of Jesus Christ begins to consider the cults themselves as a mission field—a mission field on the doorstep of the Church wherever she exists in the world, both at home and abroad.

This is by no means an impossible task. The last thirty years of the writer's life has been spent largely in this field and has confirmed his opinion that cultists too can be reached with the Gospel. They are part of the world that God so loved that He sent His only begotten Son to redeem.

Precisely how we may implement the evangelization of cultists is an important and vital subject about which nothing has been written, comparatively speaking, in the last century and which today presents an ever-expanding challenge to the Christian. We, too, must obey, as did the Apostle Paul, the command to publish the Good News and to pick up our credentials as ambassadors for Christ and present them to those who would evangelize *us* with a gospel other than that which the New Testament proclaims.

The following techniques and observations would be useful in any genuine Christian effort to evangelize cultists, when they are offered not as a panacea to the problem but as a tested means toward the end of bringing cultists to personal faith in Jesus Christ. This is the object of all true evangelism in any century.

1. The Human Element

One of the first things that confronts a Christian as he attempts to evangelize a cultist is the *psychological barrier* that exists in the minds of a great many persons, to the effect that cultists must be a special breed of individuals impervious to standard techniques of evangelism and generally well enough versed in the Bible to confuse, if not convince, the average Christian.

While there is an element of truth in both of these statements, it is generally traceable to experiences the Christian has had personally, either directly or indirectly, with cultists, or to those encounters with cultists in which the Christians did not fare too well. In fact, in not a few instances, they have been routed, frustrated, and embarrassed. This generally tends toward reticence, lest there be a repeat performance.

The second explanation for this phenomenon is the seemingly implanted fear that cultists should not be permitted to enter the Christian's home, in the light of 2 John 10:

If there come any unto you, and bring not this doctrine, receive him not into your house, neither bid him God speed.

Now, in context, this passage is a sentence in a letter to the Elect Lady, in whose home a Christian church quite obviously met, as the early church was prone to do, there being no cathedrals or modern churches such as we know them today. In this connection, a very common one (see Philemon 2), John warns her not to allow anyone to preach in church meetings or teach doctrines that do not honor Christ in every aspect of His Person, Nature and Work. It is clear that he is referring to false teachers being given a voice in the church, not to a cultist sitting in your living room! That the passage cannot be taken literally in that connection is quite evident, because if a twentieth-century Christian's plumbing froze when the weather was twenty degrees below zero and his cellar was rapidly flooding with water, he would not dream of asking the plumber who came over at 2:00 A.M. to fix the pipes whether he "brought the doctrine of Christ" to his home. Rather, such a question would never enter his mind. Yet the plumber might be a Unitarian, Mormon, or a Jehovah's Witness! Doubtless, Christians have had them in their homes, fixing their plumbing, electricity, or furnaces and never once inquired of their views concerning the doctrine of Christ. Yet some Christians who utilize 2 John 10 as an excuse for not evangelizing cultists would never dream of using it if the cultist were a plumber!

Many pastors have instructed their flocks on the basis of this passage and other out-of-context quotations to close the doors in the faces of cultists rather than to invite them in and, in the tradition of Christian evangelism, confront them with the claims of Christ. There is no authority in the Word of God for neglecting one's responsibility as an ambassador of Christ, and the cults do not constitute a special category of evangelism.

The Christian is probably right in assuming that the average cultist does have a working knowledge of the Bible. Most of them are quite diligent in their study, both of their own literature and that of the Scriptures. And it may be true that the well-trained cultist may appear to be impervious to the proclamation of the Gospel and its defense (when necessary). But that he is some special species of unbeliever in whose presence the Christian must remain mute and the Holy Spirit impotent is a gross misconception and should be abandoned by all thinking Christians.

We *must* strive to keep foremost in our minds that cultists are precious souls for whom Jesus Christ offered himself, and that they are human beings who have homes, families, friends, emotions, needs, ambitions, fears, and frustrations, which all men have in common. The cultist is special in only one sense, that he is already "deeply religious," and therefore, probably one of the most difficult persons in the world to reach with the Gospel of Christ. He has rejected historical Christianity and entertains in most cases hostility, if not active antagonism, to its message. The cultist, therefore, considers evangelical Christians his greatest potential, if not actual, adversaries. Hence, an attitude of tolerance and love should always be manifested by the Christian to relieve, where possible, this tension and the hostile feelings of the cult adherent.

The technique of "setting the cultist at ease" does indeed take a great deal of patience, for the individual cultist firmly believes that he has found "the truth," and as such, often considers the Christian message to be inferior to his own revelation. This fact is generally reflected in his attitude of superiority and even genuine resentment when the Gospel is presented. This resentment may take many forms, but it always conforms to the general thrust that since he has found the truth, how can the Christian dare to attempt to convert *him*? Cultists believe they already have progressed far beyond the evangelical Christian stage or station on the "religious railroad track" through their special revelations and superior experiences with God.

According to one psychologist, cultists also transfer their antagonism for the theology of historical Christianity to those who propagate its message, thus identifying the belief with the individual and personalizing the controversy. If the Christian who is interested in evangelizing cultists would realize this fact at the outset of his conversation with cult adherents, he could then make a careful distinction between the theology of Christianity, which is the real source of the antagonism, and the personality of the individual Christian, thereby allowing the cultist to see the Christian as a redeemed personality, independent of his theological structure. This would make possible a form of objective discussion of biblical truth, subject to the categories of analysis, logical consistency, context, and exegesis.

While this may not necessarily undercut any portion of the cultist's theological system, it will break down or assist in breaking down the psychological conditioning of the cultist to the attitude that any person who disagrees with *his* interpretation of Christianity is automatically an object of antagonism.

In approaching the problem of cult evangelism, it must be remembered that cultists, in their respective systems of theology, are almost always by nature dependent upon either forms, ceremonies, rituals, good works, right living, or self-sacrifice as a means of pleasing God and obtaining justification. Fundamentally then, cultism is a form of *self-salvation*, emphasizing deliverance from sin through human effort or merit in cooperation with their concept of the personality of the Deity.

The Christian must therefore, in the light of this fact, point out from Scripture (since most cults recognize it as authoritative or at least partially binding), the folly of self-justification, righteousness, or human effort as a means of obtaining redemption. We should always remember that repentance, atonement, regeneration, resurrection, and retribution in the biblical sense is seldom part of the cultist's vocabulary, and *never* of his personal experience. The Christian must *define*, *apply*, and *defend* the historical meanings of these terms, before it is possible to effectively proclaim the Gospel. In a word, one must begin at the beginning, repeat, emphasize, and repeat. This is the sowing of seed that one day, by God's grace alone, will bear fruit to eternal life.

Adherents of the cults are constituted, psychologically speaking, so that they are, almost always, victims of what might be termed a mass delusion of grandeur coupled with a dogged sense of personal pride. The Scripture records that Satan fell from his first estate through measureless pride (Isaiah 14:12–14), so also today, he uses the same weaknesses of the human character as a tool in shaping cult adherents to his own ends. This pride is evident in most cultists, and contributes to the delusion that they are the possessors of the true faith that saves, guardians and defenders of that which is alone holy, and administrators of divine revelation to the mass of mankind who are enmeshed in a Christianity that all cultists agree has been perverted by theologians and philosophers, thus necessitating the true restoration of the gospel through their efforts.

It has been the writer's experience that almost all cultists suffer from the concept that his or her group will at last emerge victorious over all its adversaries, inherit an eternal kingdom, and have the pleasure of viewing its enemies being either tormented or destroyed. Such cultists cling to an illusion of impending and imminent majesty or greatness, which, when linked with their intrinsic concepts of human ability and supposed merit before God, leads to mass delusion and spiritual darkness of the most terrible nature imaginable.

The task of the Christian evangelist, then, is to reveal tactfully the true nature of man as Scripture portrays him. And in a spirit of deep concern with the practice of earnest prayer, reveal to the cultist God's view of fallen man and the certain destiny of those who follow in the pride-filled footsteps of Lucifer, "the god of this world" (2 Corinthians 4:4).

The nature of cultists is to be on the defensive, for they are acutely aware of the lack of unity and brotherly love clearly evidenced in many reputedly evangelical movements. They know that evangelicals are united, insofar as the cultist is concerned, only in their opposition to *him*. They, therefore, lay much stress upon the various divisions in orthodox circles, not to mention the lack of clarity where the cardinal doctrines of the Christian faith are concerned. They apparently never tire of stating, "At least we are united; you are divided, even in your own groups." It is this type of accusation that cuts the true Christian deeply. He must answer this charge by admitting differences of opinion on minor issues, but emphasizing solidarity on the fundamentals of the Gospel, which all cultists deny in one form or another.

The Christian must never forget that a well-trained cultist can be a powerful opponent, adept at text-lifting, term-switching, and surprise interpretations of "proof texts." He should be on guard constantly lest he be deceived into admitting something that will later be utilized against him and to the detriment of both the Gospel and his personal witness.

2. Common Ground

Before attempting to evangelize a cultist, the Christian should, whenever possible, find a common ground of understanding (preferably the inspiration and authority of the Scriptures or the Personality of God), and work from that point onward. Christian workers must, in effect, become all things to all men that we might by all means save some (1 Corinthians 9:22). The Christian cannot afford to have a superiority complex or reflect the idea that he is redeemed and the cultist is lost. Redemption of the soul is a priceless gift from God and should be coveted in all humility, not superiority, as just that—a gift—unearned and unmerited, and solely the result of sovereign grace.

The necessity of a common ground cannot be overemphasized for any sane approach to the problem of cult evangelism Unless some place of agreement, some starting point be mutually accepted by both parties, the discussion can only lead to argument, charges, counter-charges, rank bitterness and, in the end, the loss of opportunity for further witness; and the soul of the cultist could be forfeited! Friendliness then—open and free manifestation of Christian love and a willingness to talk over the points of diversions—will go a long way toward allaying the suspicion of the average cultist and open further vistas for profitable and effective witnessing.

Throughout all of this, the Christian should be governed by increased activity in his prayer life, praying wherever possible in the presence of, and with, cultists, so that through the prayers that are uttered, the cultist may sense the relationship of the Christian to Him who is the Father of spirits, and our Father by faith in Jesus Christ.

3. Subliminal Seeding

The advertising industry of America has pioneered in motivational research and has taught us that ideas may be implanted in our minds beneath the level of consciousness or conscious awareness, and that they are dutifully recorded and do in no small measure influence our thinking and actions. Jingles sung on the radio and on television quite often motivate people to purchase the product about which the jingle chants.

Christians who wish to evangelize cultists can profit from the findings of such motivational research into subliminal suggestion to an amazing degree.

It is the conviction of this writer that the Word of God and prayer, addressed to Him through the Holy Spirit, is the most powerful motivating force in the universe, and can be subliminally utilized in cult evangelism by the implantation of seed thoughts about the Gospel of Christ, as well as the Gospel itself.

How this may be done is best illustrated by examples drawn from the writer's own experiences.

Jehovah's Witnesses are probably the most active and zealous of all the missionaries of cultism in America today. When called upon by Jehovah's Witnesses, the writer for many years employed the following approach with great success.

I would invite the Watchtower adherent or adherents into the living room, but before they had opportunity to speak concerning their literature, I would state that I never discussed religion or the Bible unless such a discussion was preceded by prayer, to which all present agreed. I would then quickly bow my head and address the Lord as Jehovah God. One must be particularly careful in dealing with Jehovah's Witnesses, to always address the Deity by the name Jehovah, or else the Witnesses may not pray or bow their heads. Instead, they will admire the bric-a-brac, thumb through their Bibles, reach for their briefcases, and generally keep occupied until you have completed your prayer. Should the reader be interested in knowing how I learned this, I must confess that on occasion—I peeked!

When the name of Jehovah is being used, the average Watchtower adherent will immediately bow his head, and after you have finished praying and *before* they can pray, begin the conversation by saying, "Now what was it that you wanted to discuss?"

Always keep in mind in dealing with Jehovah's Witnesses that they come equipped with a portable arsenal in the form of a briefcase that contains the major publications of the Watchtower Society for their handy reference. At the outset you must insist that they use nothing but the Scriptures and that it must be a recognized translation (King James, Revised Standard Version, New International, New American Standard, etc.). You must further insist upon a discussion of cardinal doctrines, particularly concerning the person, nature, and work of Jesus Christ. Thus deprived of his Watchtower material and his Watchtower translations and circumscribed to the person of Christ in discussion, even the best trained Jehovah's Witness is at a distinct disadvantage. On the other hand, the Christian who is indwelt by the Holy Spirit then has a definite advantage.

After the discussion had gone on for some time, and I had listened to as much of "Pastor" Russell's theology as I could tolerate for one evening, I would remind the Witnesses of the lateness of the hour and asked if we couldn't close with a word of prayer. I would then immediately bow my head and begin praying again.

Now what I have mentioned is, by itself, only an outline of how to conduct one's self in the presence of Jehovah's Witnesses, with one important exception. During my opening and closing prayers I would totally preach the Gospel, emphasizing the Deity of Christ, His death for our sins, the certainty of knowing that we have eternal life *now*, by faith in Him, and that salvation comes by grace alone, independent of human works. I would profusely quote the Scriptures, and in actuality be preaching a three-minute sermonette, subliminally implanting the true Gospel of Jesus Christ and, I might add, blissfully uninterrupted. For no one, not even the most zealous disciple of "Pastor" Russell, Joseph Smith, or Brigham Young, can interrupt a prayer. I have seen such a methodology or technique of evangelism make a tremendous impact upon Jehovah's Witnesses and other cultists, because, for six minutes of the evening at least, the Christian has the opportunity to present the true Gospel of Christ without interruption.

We must believe that God's Word will not return unto Him void, but will accomplish what He pleases and prosper in the thing whereto He has sent it (Isaiah 55:11).

4. The Vocabulary of Redemption

Non-Christian cultists of all varieties are prone to one psychological and spiritual insecurity: They are all aware of the fact that they do not *now* possess eternal life or peace with God. In fact, it is toward this end that they are vigorously pursuing the theology and practices of their respective systems.

There can never be a substitute, therefore, for an individual Christian's personal witness to what Christ has done for him. A word of caution, however, must be inserted at this juncture. As we know, cultists have their own vocabulary, so it will be necessary for the Christian to define carefully his terms when he speaks of conversion—its means and its effect upon his spirit, mind, and life. The only really unanswerable argument is the argument of a transformed life, properly grounded in the authority of the Scriptures and motivated by love for God and for one's fellow man. Key terms that must be carefully defined are: the new birth or "born again"; justification; atonement; Deity and resurrection of Christ; resurrection; forgiveness; grace; and faith. It is inevitable that eternal retribution be discussed, because this is the very thing from which Christ died to save us.

The Scriptures admonish us to be "His witnesses," and in order to do this we must be willing to endure all things and be governed by patience, temperance, grace, and love. Then regardless of how the truth of God be assailed, perverted, or distorted, and no matter how much our own characters and motives are attacked, Christ will be honored by our conduct.

The vocabulary of redemption involves personal involvement, testimony to the effect of Christ's power both to redeem the soul and to transform the individual, his morals, his ethics, his life. And most of all, it involves the power to impart to him the peace of God that passes all understanding, the peace that Christ said would come only to those who made peace with God (Philippians 4:7).

5. *The Secret of Perseverance*

One of the most important techniques of cult evangelism is that of perseverance with cultists. Anyone who has ever worked extensively in the field of cults will readily testify that this takes a great deal of grace and understanding on the part of the Christian. Many times cultists will deliberately "bait" Christians (particularly Jehovah's Witnesses and the Mormons) in an attempt to provoke the Christian into losing his patience, thus justifying their own teachings. In order to avoid such pitfalls and to be able to endure the many forms of abuse and persecution, which will come about when a Christian penetrates the theology of the cultist with the Sword of the Spirit, one must have discovered a secret that, when prayerfully understood and applied, can make the endurance of *anything*, for the sake of Christ, possible.

If one were attacked, severely assaulted, and abused by a frightened blind man, it would be possible not only to forgive him, but even persevere to the end of loving him, despite his actions. For after all, both reason and logic argue, he *is* blind, and in a sense, not responsible for his actions.

We are forever in debt to the Apostle Paul, who pointed out in his second letter to the Corinthians that those who are outside of Christ have indeed been spiritually blinded by the god of this age. Satan has caused a cloak of *delusion* to descend over their minds and understandings, so that Christ's Gospel, which is the light of the world, cannot penetrate to them. The secret of perseverance is to know and to understand, regardless of what a cultist says or does, that he is doing it out of spiritual blindness. Since our warfare as Christians is not against flesh and blood (the cultist), but against the spiritual forces of darkness that rule this world (Satan and his emissaries), it is possible to love the cultist, endure his abuses, perversions, and recriminations, while at the same time faithfully bearing witness for Christ.

This technique of cult evangelism should never be minimized. And once it is properly appreciated, it can become a great asset to the Christian.

There are doubtless many, many more things that could be mentioned in connection with cult evangelism, such as the important fact that when dealing with the Gnostic cults (Christian Science, Unity, New Thought, etc.), distinct emphasis must be placed upon personal sin, which they all negate or deny; also the certainty of retribution as taught by the Lord Jesus Christ should be emphasized. We might also profitably note that in dealing with religions that have had their origin outside the United States (Baha'ism, Theosophy, Zen, etc.), the Christian ought to have a working knowledge of what the doctrines of these cults are in relation to the historical Christian revelation. It is foolish to attempt to discuss Christian doctrines with those who do not accept the authority of the Scriptures, which is most certainly the case in regard to the three cults just mentioned.

Finally, evangelism, particularly cult evangelism, must never fail to emphasize that Christ and the disciples taught certain irrevocable doctrines as well as consistent ethics and morality.

It has been the experience of the author, based upon numerous personal contacts with cultists of all varieties, that there has yet to be born a cultist who can confuse, confound, or in any way refute a Christian who has made doctrinal theology an integral part of his study of the Scriptures. Cults thrive upon ignorance and confusion where the doctrines of the Scriptures are concerned, but are powerless to shake Christians in their faith or effectively proselytize them when the Christian is well grounded in the basic teachings of the Bible and given over to a study of the great doctrinal truths of the Word of God. These mighty buttresses of Christian theology must no longer be taken for granted by Christian believers nor should pastors and teachers assume that the average Christian has sound knowledge concerning them. The rise of cultism to its present proportions indicates a great dearth of knowledge where doctrine is involved, and is a decided weakness in the battlements of orthodox theology, which the Church ignores at the risk of innumerable souls.

Accepting then the fact that the poison of cultism can be effectively combated only by the antidote of sound doctrine, the next problem is the immunization of Christians against the teachings of the cults. The answer to this problem lies within the pages of God's Word; it involves study (2 Timothy 2:15) on the part of Christians, instruction on the part of the pastor and teacher (1 Timothy 4:1–6), coupled with a willingness to start at the beginning where sound doctrine is concerned, even as the risen Christ did with the doubting disciples, and to reexamine the reason *why* Christians believe what they believe. Particularly recommended for intensive study are the doctrines of biblical inspiration, the Trinity, Deity of Christ, Personality and Work of the Holy Spirit, the Atonement, justification by faith, works, the Bodily Resurrection of Christ, and the resurrection of all mankind.

The great and true Trinitarian doctrine of God and the Deity of Jesus Christ should be inculcated ceaselessly in Christian minds so that the Lord's people may never forget that Jesus Christ is the core of God's plan for the ages. The fact that He vicariously died and bodily arose, thus vindicating His claim to Deity through obedience to the righteous character of both His Father's will and law, both of which He perfectly fulfilled at Calvary, must be perpetually emphasized.

It is a well-known fact that no antidote for poison is effective unless it is administered in time and in the proper dosage prescribed by a competent physician. In like manner, Christian doctrine should not be taught in a dry, matter-of-fact way, as it so often is, but should be given in small doses over a long period. The treatment should begin at once, from the Sunday school level right through college and seminary where the need is urgent.

Christians must realize while the opportunity is yet ours that the teaching of sound doctrine does not predicate a dead orthodoxy. When properly understood, a living acceptance of and familiarity with doctrine form the giant pillars of truth upon which our faith rests, a familiarity that has always produced great leaders and effective workers for the proclamation of the Gospel of grace.

The evangelization of cultists is the task of the Christian church of which each Christian is a member, a part of the Body of Christ. Until this is recognized, and Christians are urged and encouraged by their pastors and leaders to forsake the portals of Hollywood and the domain of the great gods, Television, etc., for door-to-door publishing of the Good News of God's love in Jesus Christ for a lost world, the evangelization of cultists will continue to be one of the great tragedies of the Christian church in our day. It is excellent that we support foreign missions and send the light of God's Gospel around the globe, but it is quite another thing for us to begin here, where the demand is personal, challenging, and equally rewarding. This challenge is cult evangelism, the mission field on *your* doorstep.

Explore

Mass Delusion
Common Ground
Spiritual Blindness
Doctrine

Discuss

1. Why is a cultist hostile?

2. Why is it important to quote Scripture?

3. What is prayer methodology?

4. What does God say about His Word?

Dig Deeper

See *The Kingdom of the Cults Study Guide* available at WalterMartin.com.

Appendix A

The Satanic Temple (TST)

Historical Perspective

If there is one thing modern history has proved time and time again it's that evil sells consistently well. The Satanic Temple, or TST, founded by former Church of Satan High Priest Shane Bugbee and kindred spirit Douglas Misicko (alias Lucien Greaves), is no exception to the rule. This latest commercial repackaging was launched in 2013 as a small-scale movie project by Spectacle Films, who put out a casting call for the newborn Satanic Temple as part of a media stunt mocking Florida Governor Rick Scott.[1] According to *Fox News*:

1. "In a 2014 Village Voice article 'Malcolm Jerry' [sic] is outed as the filmmaker Cevin Soling, owner of Spectacle Films. (villagevoice.com)," according to the Church of Satan's "The Satanic Temple Fact Sheet" by Joel Ethan, https://www.churchofsatan.com/the-satanic-temple-fact-sheet/.

The spokesman, Lucien Greaves of Cambridge, Mass., earlier this month had been listed on the Actors Access website as the casting director in an ad seeking unpaid, nonunion actors in Tallahassee. They were wanted to perform in a "mockumentary" titled "The Satanic Temple."

Greaves insisted it wasn't all a hoax, although a smile creased his face as he said it.[2]

> The primary purpose behind the founding of The Satanic Temple was a political attack against people of faith.

The shock value of the satanic name brought instant media curiosity, and the positive press triggered an outpouring of financial support. A new satanic star was born in the photogenic Misicko, with Bugbee relegated to relating his encounters with Misicko in a revealing 2013 article from *Vice* magazine. It seems the pair had originally decided to pay homage to a real live Satan in their new belief system, but later reneged on the deal in favor of a more politically correct skepticism.[3]

Determined to undermine George W. Bush's Faith Initiative, Bugbee confirmed the commitment to political activism, revealing that the primary purpose of The Satanic Temple was a political attack against people of faith:

The first conception was in response to George W. Bush's creation of the White House Office of Faith-Based and Community Initiatives," said Mr. Jarry [aka Bugbee], who was raised by irreligious Jews. "I thought, 'There should be some kind of counter.'" He hit on the idea of starting a faith-based organization that met all the Bush administration's criteria for receiving funds, but was repugnant to them.[4]

Bugbee and Misicko hit the national spotlight riding an enormous current of American cynicism, and their new brand of satanism morphed quickly from two-guys-and-a-movie-script to a satirical political crusade aimed at challenging Judeo-Christian beliefs in court. Today, legal letters

2. Associated Press, "Florida 'Satanists' Praise Governor for Prayer Bill," *Fox News* January 26, 2013, https://www.foxnews.com/us/florida-satanists-praise-governor-for-prayer-bill. See also https://www.huffingtonpost.com/2013/01/14/satanists-rally-for-rick-scott_n_2471328.html.
3. Joel Ethan, Church of Satan, "The Satanic Temple Fact Sheet," https://www.churchofsatan.com/the-satanic-temple-fact-sheet/.
4. Mark Oppenheimer, "A Mischievous Thorn in the Side of Conservative Christianity," *The New York Times*, July 10, 2015, https://www.nytimes.com/2015/07/11/us/a-mischievous-thorn-in-the-side-of-conservative-christianity.html.

and lawsuits are the modus operandi of The Satanic Temple, whose aggressive atheistic/agnostic brand of satanism continues to troll Christians, and in the name of "free inquiry, rationalism, and scientific understanding" erase the "loathsome stink" of them whenever possible.[5] This passion for the satanic spotlight extends to the evangelism of kids, although they deny any intent to evangelize. TST is actively confronting the Christian Good News Clubs in schools across America, enthusiastically marketing their After School Satan Clubs as "Educatin' With Satan."[6] The curriculum amounts to arguments that, in essence, portray science as the beginning and end of knowledge, and rational humanism as a reasonable alternative to Christian "stink."[7]

Douglas Misicko is now the official spokesman for the well-funded Satanic Temple, with headquarters located in Salem, Massachusetts. According to the Church of Satan (CoS), **"The Satanic Temple" is a registered Trademark** of United Federation of Churches LLC, which is listed as **registered to Douglas Misicko. . . . Reason Alliance LTD is a religious non-profit also registered to Douglas Misicko** at the same address."[8]

It follows the pattern of many newborn cults in announcing a set of fluid "tenets" to live by that, in this case, appear to evolve in answer to TST's ongoing doctrinal war with Anton LaVey's *Church of Satan*. LaVey's Satanists do not appreciate Bugbee and Greaves' redefinition of Satan and a satanic movement they consider their own. It is ironic that the devil, who spends much of his time causing division, is stuck with it in his own "churches" and almost surreal to hear the Church of Satan argue that, "As Satanism is a recognized 'New Religious Movement,' it's important for an understanding of what is and what is not Satanism to be maintained."[9] This is exactly what the Christian church has been saying about its definitions and doctrine for centuries.

One look at a video released by former Satanic Temple High Priest Brian Werner is enough to reveal the infighting and power struggles in the TST, as does the recent defection of another high-profile Satanist, Emma Story, who points out that TST members are bound by the dictates of Lucien Greaves (Misicko):

5. The Satanic Temple, "Educatin' With Satan," After School Satan Clubs, https://afterschoolsatan.com/.
6. The Satanic Temple, "Educatin' With Satan."
7. The Satanic Temple, "Educatin' With Satan."
8. Ethan, "Satanic Temple Fact Sheet."
9. Ethan, "Satanic Temple Fact Sheet."

It's become increasingly clear to me over the past year or so that the personal opinions of Lucien Greaves are the organizational opinions of The Satanic Temple, and I was naive to think otherwise. Though they haven't been formally declared canon, Greaves's Patreon posts generally end up being treated as organizational policy—Patreon content is routinely cited in internal TST discussions as evidence of what TST's stance is on any given issue.[10]

The emphasis on the influence of one person in a hierarchy of an organization follows the pattern of cult development in the long history of the kingdom of the cults, with TST's "interpretation" based on an absence of Satanic canon or precedent.

This agnostic/atheistic Satanism, along with the distribution of titles like *high priest* and *reverend* to people with no education or training in Satanism, has caused multiple splits in the Satanic ranks.[11] The hardcore Satanists abhor the fact that many TST members don't know or care about Anton LaVey or his *Satanic Bible*. They categorize The Satanic Temple as "a political organization that has nothing to do with Satanism," posting a detailed listing of the errors of Douglas Misicko and The Satanic Temple on their website.[12]

Misicko aka Greaves responded to the Satanic Church's fact sheet with one of his own, arguing point by point with the underlying premise that the Church of Satan does not have a corner on the market of Satanism simply because they think they do. He goes on to redefine, once again, the role of TST. "We wanted an active and relevant Satanism, one that would do exactly the things that TST are doing presently. We didn't need an organization to tell us how to think, how to properly be 'true' Satanists, or as a mere social club in which we could construct ourselves into the highest ranks of a false hierarchy."[13]

Former spokesperson for The Satanic Temple Jex Blackmore disputes the legitimacy of TST's public persona as an organization committed to justice. Blackmore, who labels herself a performance artist and who blogged

10. Emma Story, "Why I'm Leaving the Satanic Temple," August 7, 2018, https://medium.com/@emmastory/why-im-leaving-the-satanic-temple-528bbc06432b, August 7, 2018.

11. Brian Werner, *High Priest Brian Werner Resigns from The Satanic Temple*, https://www.youtube.com/watch?v=ZIN4aZ8IMz0.

12. Ethan, "Satanic Temple Fact Sheet."

13. Lucien Greaves, "Correcting the Church of Satan Fact Sheet," *The Satanic Temple Arizona Blog*, October 11, 2017, satanictemplearizona.com, https://thesatanictemplearizona.com/correcting-the-church-of-satan-fact-sheet/.

her abortion while part of TST, created a performance piece that "called on people to sabotage and execute 'the president.'" She claims the disapproval this piece generated among the leadership of TST was the main reason for her resignation:

> My departure was mutually agreed upon, but it was also business as usual—a small group of individuals with no accountability to the organization they represent asserting a paternalistic need to put a woman in her place, gain control, and undermine her autonomous power. I will not compromise the content of my creative work to satisfy the fears and complacency of others. The Satanic Temple that I joined years ago, when it was full of potential and courage, no longer exists and I cannot allow my voice, however controversial, to be silenced.[14]

Political Strategy

In its short incarnation, The Satanic Temple has established a reputation for suing those who violate its perception of the separation of church and state. Their successful use of legal demands usually results in the installation of a modern satanic *Baphomet* statue (or monument of their choice) next to whatever religious object caused the offense. The state of Oklahoma and the city of Belle Plaine, Minnesota, are two examples of this litigious approach. Belle Plaine is currently responding to a TST lawsuit based on the fact that the city allowed a veterans' monument of a soldier kneeling to the cross on public grounds. When challenged by TST, the city removed the monument, but TST considered the removal a violation of their civil rights, and is now suing Belle Plaine anyway.[15]

A lawsuit was also filed against Netflix and Warner Bros. for copyright infringement of a Baphomet statue that TST claims was used without permission throughout the new *Sabrina* Netflix series. "The lawsuit seeks 'at least' $50 million. To make matters even juicier, the Church of Satan has also responded to news of the lawsuit."[16]

14. Jex Blackmore, *The Struggle for Justice is Ongoing*, Medium.com, August 6, 2018, https://medium.com/@JexBlackmore/the-struggle-for-justice-is-ongoing-6df38f8893db.

15. Casey Ek, "Satanic Temple Moves to Sue City," *Belle Plaine Herald*, October 24, 2018, http://www.belleplaineherald.com/news/satanic-temple-moves-to-sue-city/article_0d992726-d7 3b-11e8-bf1a-4b2d154d0314.html.

16. Stephan Horbelt, "The Satanic Temple and the Church of Satan Are Butting Heads over Netflix's Sabrina," *Hornet*, November 14, 2018, https://hornet.com/stories/satanic-temple-church-of-satan-sabrina/.

In a letter written by Reverend Joel Ethan of the Church of Satan last week regarding the Sabrina lawsuit, he refers to the Satanic Temple as being "known for childish PR stunts" and describes the Temple as "not in any way representative of the apolitical, individualistic and atheistic religion of Satanism."[17]

Three weeks after the suit was filed, Netflix settled with The Satanic Temple. The terms of the agreement were not made public except for the fact that TST's ownership of Baphomet will now be acknowledged in all Sabrina credits.[18]

Activist and aggressive in their approach, TST recently added Twitter to its court docket—suing them over what they claim are freedom of speech issues. Although sympathy for Twitter is hard to come by due to their censorship of Christians and conservatives, the irony of the situation is once again impossible to miss. By taking on the social media giant, TST may inadvertently be fighting a battle for the Christians whose "stink" they despise.

Baphomet

Baphomet is a name that some argue appeared after a historical incident related to the torture of several Knights Templar members (c. AD 1312). Their subsequent confessions to worshiping a name similar to Mahomet (Muhammad)—the prophet of their Muslim enemy—began the centuries-long semantics argument between Baphomet and Mahomet, but there is little primary evidence to support the event or the name derived from it.

In essence, the Satanic Temple's statue of Baphomet is a modern artist's image of Satan that appears to have borrowed much of its design from a drawing by a Catholic priest turned occultist, Eliphas Levi (c. 1830), and the Rider-Waite Tarot card deck published about 1910.[19] The image known

17. Horbelt, "Butting Heads Over Netflix's Sabrina."

18. Anders Bylund, "Netflix Settles Lawsuit with The Satanic Temple," *The Motley Fool*, November 23, 2018, Fool.com, https://www.fool.com/investing/2018/11/23/netflix-settles-law suit-with-the-satanic-temple.aspx.

19. Tarot.com reflects Levi's influence on the design of the 1909-1910 "The Devil" taro card, https://www.tarot.com/tarot/cards/the-devil/rider. According to Samuel Taylor's comprehensive history on the origin and development of ancient card games, individual "Taro Card" occult meanings are historically linked to India, with a steady stream of evidence documenting its European emergence as "Tarocchi Cards" c. AD 1500. For comprehensive documentation of the origin and development of Taro, see Rev. Ed. S. Taylor, *The History of Playing Cards: Anecdotes of*

THE SATANIC TEMPLE (TST)

as "The Goat of Mendes" first appeared in 1854 as part of Levi's work on the occult, and was also the cover for his book on occult philosophy entitled *Transcendental Magic, Its Doctrine and Ritual*.[20] Historically, he has long been accepted as the artist who created it.[21]

The earliest available version of The Satanic Temple's website (January 13, 2013) includes the image of *The Devil* from the Rider-Waite deck, while the second version a few days later (January 15, 2013) replaces the Rider-Waite image with the Eliphas Levi drawing.[22] The card depicts a winged, half-human, half-goat devil with long horns, hooves, and a prominent pentagram. It also includes a naked man and woman— replaced by a young boy and girl in The Satanic Temple version of Baphomet.

A credible historical trail for this half-goat creature can be traced to the Greek god Pan, who was revered by a rural people known as Arcadians (c. 600 BC). He was the god of shepherds and goat-herders, and received very little attention from sophisticated, urban Greeks until the Battle of Marathon about 490 BC.[23] The earliest image of Pan is as a goat standing on its hind legs and can be traced to the caves of Attica during the same time period. "In Attica, Pan represents an uncivilized and savage nature which is contrary to the order of the polis."[24]

Throughout history, the Greek mythology of Pan varies depending on which ancient personality is discussing him. His parentage and identity remain—at best—debatable, and his appearance and personality interchangeable with the god Dionysus, or Bacchus in the Roman pantheon of gods. As time passed, images similar to the ancient sculptures of Pan

Their Use in Conjuring, Fortune-Telling & Card Sharping, Google Books, https://play.google.com /books/reader?id=HQNVAAAAcAAJ&hl=en&pg=GBS.PA224.

20. Debbie Elliot, "Eliphas Levi, Baphomet and the Sign for Peace," *The Sunday Tribune*, February 6, 2019, https://www.thesundaytribune.com/2019/02/06/eliphas-levi-baphomet-and -the-sign-for-peace/.

21. "The drawing was originally published in the first livraisons of Lévi's famous Dogme de la haute magie, published by Guiraudet et Jouaust in 1854, and featured as the frontispiece for the two-volume edition of Dogme et rituel de la haute magie, published by Germer Baillière in 1855–1856, and for the extended second edition of 1861." Julian Strube, *The "Baphomet" of Eliphas Lévi: Its Meaning and Historical Context*, Correspondences 4 (2016) 1–43, https://corres pondencesjournal.com/wpcontent/uploads/2016/12/15303_20537158_strube.pdf.

22. See The Wayback Machine, January 13, 2013, and January 15, 2013, https://web.archive .org/web/20130113023103/http://www.thesatanictemple.com/.

23. W. Watkiss Lloyd, "The Battle of Marathon: 490 B.C.," *The Journal of Hellenic Studies*, 380–395, 1881, https://www.jstor.org/stable/623580?seq=1/subjects.

24. Nadine Pierce, *The Archaeology of Sacred Caves in Attica*, https://macsphere.mcmaster .ca/bitstream/11375/10306/1/fulltext.pdf.

made their way into medieval card games, and finally to pagan illustrations used for Tarot cards and other occult paraphernalia in the late 19th and early 20th centuries.[25]

Whether intentional or not, The Satanic Temple managed to design their version of a historical Pan, and have been using it in lawsuits with the intent to either remove Christian symbols from public places or force cities to allow a satanic Baphomet statue to be built on the same site as a Christian symbol. They claim to represent American ideals such as freedom of speech, equality, and justice while ignoring entirely the biblical roots of American history, where Satan's ancient identity is clearly defined as a personal, evil being.[26] A version of their early Tenets redefines both God and Satan in the distorted image of TST.[27] Early American settlers were largely Puritans and Huguenots who crafted laws rooted in the Ten Commandments and rejected Satan in any form. They viewed God as the omnipotent, omniscient, and omnipresent Creator, and Satan as His far weaker creation.[28]

The Puritans recognized the reality of the devil as a personal evil being, and were not inclined to welcome him. That TST is now doing its best to incorporate various biblical principles into their Tenets would be humorous if it were not so successful. Satan continues to portray himself as an angel of light.

TST has an agenda to redefine Satan as a misunderstood force for good, and to normalize satanism whenever and wherever they can. We should remember their assessment of God and plan accordingly: "Even though we see it metaphorically, we see the Biblical God as a tyrannical force."[29]

25. *Aphrodite, Pan and Eros* Statue c. 100 BC. Nikos E. Kaltsas, Nikolaos Kaltsas, Ethnikon Archaiologikon Mouseion (Greece), David Hardy, *Aphrodite, Pan and Eros*, Sculpture in the National Archaeological Museum, Athens, J. Paul Getty Museum, 2003, 29.

26. Satan's identity can be traced from antiquity. See *The Kingdom of the Cults*, chapter 1.

27. Earliest known posting of TST's definition of God and Satan, later removed from The Satanic Temple website May 11, 2014. See The Wayback Machine, June 20, 2013, https://web.archive.org/web/20130620172850/ http://www.thesatanictemple.com/ and May 11, 2014, https://web.archive.org/web/20140511220756/http://thesatanictemple.com/

28. God created Lucifer as a righteous being with free choice. Lucifer said, "I will ascend above the heights of the clouds; I will make myself like the Most High" (Isaiah 14:14). God said, "You were blameless in your ways from the day you were created, till unrighteousness was found in you" (Ezekiel 28:15). So God created Lucifer *blameless* but his free choice was rebellion.

29. Wesley Baines, "Inside The Satanic Temple: An Interview with Lucien Greaves, Founder of The Satanic Temple," Beliefnet.com, n.d., https://www.beliefnet.com/faiths/inside-the-satanic-temple.aspx?p=3#9DFyUlQL2vCEFCOk.99.

Theological Evaluation

Today, the Satanic Temple has effectively shed the puerile image of a satanic theater stunt, evolving into a well-funded, pseudo-religious entity. Its latest incarnation of beliefs is labeled the *7 Tenets* and they reveal the political and atheistic agenda behind the pentagrams and Baphomets.

> There are seven fundamental tenets.
> - One should strive to act with compassion and empathy toward all creatures in accordance with reason.
> - The struggle for justice is an ongoing and necessary pursuit that should prevail over laws and institutions.
> - One's body is inviolable, subject to one's own will alone.
> - The freedoms of others should be respected, including the freedom to offend. To willfully and unjustly encroach upon the freedoms of another is to forgo one's own.
> - Beliefs should conform to one's best scientific understanding of the world. One should take care never to distort scientific facts to fit one's beliefs.
> - People are fallible. If one makes a mistake, one should do one's best to rectify it and resolve any harm that might have been caused.
> - Every tenet is a guiding principle designed to inspire nobility in action and thought. The spirit of compassion, wisdom, and justice should always prevail over the written or spoken word.[30]

This latest version of TST's Tenets is quite different in content and approach from the original Beliefs posted on their website in 2013:

> The Satanic Temple seeks to separate Religion from Superstition by acknowledging religious belief as a metaphorical framework with which we construct a narrative context for our goals and works. Satan stands as the ultimate icon for the selfless revolt against tyranny, free & rational inquiry, and the responsible pursuit of happiness.
>
> In theological terms, the mythology translates thus:
> *God is supernatural and thus outside of the sphere of the physical. God's perfection means that he cannot interact with the imperfect corporeal realm. Because God cannot intervene in the material world, He created Satan to preside over the universe as His proxy.*[31] Satan has the compassion and

30. The Satanic Temple, *Tenets*, https://thesatanictemple.com/pages/tenets.
31. TST's original definition of Satan as "God's proxy" and a misunderstood force for good parallels an ancient belief taught by the Arab Yezidi tribe, who worship Tawsi Melek—the peacock angel—whose identity matches the biblical Satan. http://www.yeziditruth.org/the_peacock_angel.

wisdom of an angel. Although Satan is subordinate to God, he is mankind's only conduit to the dominion beyond the physical. In addition, only Satan can hear our prayers and only Satan can respond. While God is beyond human comprehension, Satan desires to be known and knowable. Only in this way can there be justice and can life have meaning.

The Satanist harbors reasonable agnosticism in all things, holding fast only to that which is demonstrably true.[32]

Clearly, Satan is represented as an actual spirit being here, and "God" is acknowledged as a limited supernatural being who exists in perfection "outside the sphere of the material." This attempt at logic runs headlong into the unavoidable conclusion that if God is not subject to the material and Satan is "subordinate" to him, then God must be *superior.*

TST tackles the supremacy puzzle with another illogical argument that God's supremacy limits him, preventing him from interacting with the "material world." No mention is made of how *supremacy* makes God weak or how a "subordinate" or inferior Satan is chosen as the only "conduit" to a perfect God. This missing foundation of basic logic in TST's first attempt at theology may explain why it was eventually deleted from The Satanic Temple's website.

By May 11, 2014, TST had introduced a new set of Tenets, with the focus on an agnostic/atheistic philosophy. God was gone, and Satan as a spirit being was gone, with Lucien Greaves claiming, "We reject supernaturalism and strive to approach all things with reasonable agnosticism."[33] This agnostic philosophy was, in fact, a revamped atheistic philosophy wrapped in the ancient biblical values of compassion, justice, wisdom, and freedom—all divorced from anything Divine. Logic was, once again, nowhere to be found and its absence did not seem to deter Greaves or TST.

See *The Kingdom of the Occult* for more information. "There are further indications that Melek Taus is 'the Devil'. The parallels between the story of the peacock angel's rebellion, and the story of Lucifer, cast into Hell by the Christian God, are surely too close to be coincidence. The very word 'Melek' is cognate with 'Moloch', the name of a Biblical demon—who demanded human sacrifice." Sean Thomas, Telegraph, *The Devil Worshippers of Iraq*, https://www.telegraph.co.uk/news/worldnews/1560714/The-Devil-worshippers-of-Iraq.html.

32. See The Wayback Machine, June 20, 2013, The Satanic Temple Website, https://web.archive.org/web/20130620172850/http://www.thesatanictemple.com/.

33. Hemant Mehta, "The Satanic Temple Wants to Place a Monument Outside Oklahoma's Capitol Building. What Could Go Possibly Wrong?" *Friendly Atheist*, Patheos.com, https://friendlyatheist.patheos.com/2013/12/04/the-satanic-temple-wants-to-place-a-monument-outside-oklahomas-capitol-building-what-could-possibly-go-wrong/#ixzz34kqVJ9pV.

Redefining Satan

Although today most people familiar with religious movements equate the names of Aleister Crowley, Anton Szandor LaVey, or the Church of Satan with Satanism, its origin is far older and more extensive than any of these. Two main schools of thought that emerged during the twentieth century in religious Satanism became known as Traditional Satanism and Modern Satanism.[34] Traditional Satanism teaches that Satan is a personal spirit being, and Modern Satanism teaches an impersonal entity or corporate evil embodied under the name of Satan.[35] Historically, Traditional Satanism can be traced back to the roots of Judaism and from there to the New Testament age through the writings of the Christian church, which defines it as a belief system that reveres Lucifer, in direct contrast to the gospel portrayal of Jesus Christ as God Incarnate.

The idea of an impersonal Satan was essentially unknown in past centuries—it exists today as a product of twentieth-century philosophical trends that redefined all biblical terms, including Satan. As a direct result of this liberal interpretation of Scripture, Satanists now have flexible definitions for who or what Satan is, and in what manner he or it exists.[36]

"The idea of an impersonal Satan was essentially unknown in past centuries—it exists today as a product of twentieth century philosophical trends that redefined all biblical terms."

This redefinition has made its way into the twenty-first century, with TST's new take on the old Satanic image. Satanic philosophy is now the

34. Paraphrased from Walter Martin, Jill Martin Rische, Kurt Van Gorden, *The Kingdom of the Occult* (Nashville: Thomas Nelson, 2008), 385. "The analysis here of Satanism as a religion uses 'traditional Satanism' and 'modern Satanism' to divide theological categories. Traditional, in this work, refers to the first century through to the present time, as running concurrently with 'modern Satanism' from the nineteenth century forward. Other scholars, such as J. Gordon Melton (1992), use 'traditional Satanism' to mean sixteenth century through the twenty-first century, but this leaves the first- to fifteenth-century Satanists in a historical limbo. Massimo Intorvigne [2006] uses 'organized Satanism' in reference to the sixteenth century through modern times, ignoring anything prior to that date. James R. Lewis's [2001] usage of 'traditional Satanism' and 'modern Satanism' [2002] corresponds to our usage." Martin, Rische, Van Gorden, *The Kingdom of the Occult*, 385n6.

35. "Minor subsets exist, such as a dualism, where God and Satan are equal powers, other Satanists may claim that an unnamed power permeates the universe that they can harness, and some are pantheists, where Satan is one god among many." Martin, Rische, Van Gorden, *The Kingdom of the Occult*, 385n7.

36. Martin, Rische, Van Gorden, *The Kingdom of the Occult*, 385–386.

bringer of light, the purveyor of all that is good, and the new face of "reasonable" thought. What they cannot change, though, is the existence of the being behind the philosophy, his historical presence in archaeo-logical and cultural evidence, and his pattern of attacking God and His people. They cannot change his nature or control it, and he cannot hide it. His nature is evil and he cannot be other than what he is. Nowhere is this truth more obvious than in TST's first public battles, and in the language used to describe God and Christians. Although claiming to be free of any supernatural affiliation, they have in reality been taken captive to do Satan's will.

Biblical Perspective

The Bible tells us that Satan is real—an angel who fell like lightning from heaven; that he is a fallen leader, a failure, and a creature limited by his created nature (Luke 10:18; John 8:44).[37] Although brilliant and a master strategist, he is not omniscient, not omnipresent, and not omnipotent. In essence, he is the ultimate loser who rejected perfect love and was forced to flee the beauty of heaven for the temporary asylum of a doomed earth. Yes, he is powerful—so powerful that "even the archangel Michael, when he disputed with the devil over the body of Moses, did not presume to bring a slanderous judgment against him, but said, 'The Lord rebuke you!'" (Jude 1:9 BSB). But Satan is a constructed being, with a beginning and an end, originally made without sin by the hand of the architect and designer of all. It is ironic that this *one fact* automatically disqualifies him for divin-ity, and reveals a cosmic level of delusion in the satanic persona. He is a creature who has fought for centuries to be divine—something that by nature, he can never be.

That he is an enemy to be feared and respected is simply common sense, but the ancient, absolute truth is that there is no equality between good and evil. Our culture works to instill this false narrative in us from birth, but it is a lie. God's power far surpasses that of Satan. When Jesus was tempted in the wilderness, Satan could only offer Jesus things that God had already created like bread or the kingdoms of this world (Luke 4:1). He must ask God for permission to do things here on earth (Job 1:9; 2:6;

---

37. For a detailed analysis of Satan's nature, history and purpose, see Martin, Rische, Van Gorden, *The Kingdom of the Occult*, chapter 1.

Luke 22:31–32). He specializes in illusion and lies, always working to hide his true nature as he did with Eve in the Garden. "But the serpent said to the woman, 'You will not surely die. For God knows that when you eat of it your eyes will be opened, and you will be like God, knowing good and evil'" (Genesis 3:4–5 ESV).

He has masqueraded as an angel of light ever since his arrival on earth—working against God from the beginning—and it will not end until he is physically removed from this earth. History records the truth of his identity. Nineteenth-century records of séances have the demonic manifestations actually appearing and pointing to a verse in a Bible sitting in the middle of a séance table! This is the strategy of Satan—to present himself as an angel of light who is somehow always greater than the God who made him. To deny his historical identity, as The Satanic Temple has chosen to do, does not *erase* it or change the truth of it.

> Satan has masqueraded as an angel of light ever since his arrival on earth . . . and it will not end until he is physically removed from it.

The Bible teaches he is, in reality, the archenemy of God and man:

Jesus said that he is a murderer, liar, and the father of all lies (John 8:44), the ruler of the world (John 16:11), and the wicked one (Matt. 13:38). John called him the dragon, the old serpent, and the Devil (Rev. 20:2), he is the "accuser" of the brethren both day and night (Rev. 12:10) and he is the angel of the bottomless pit (Rev. 9:11). Paul called him the prince of the power of the air (Eph. 2:2), the ruler of darkness (Eph. 6:12), the god of this world (2 Cor. 4:4), and one who masquerades as an angel of light (2 Cor. 11:14). Peter wrote that he is the adversary of the Christian (1 Peter 5:8). This is Satan, a being whose goal it is to destroy as many humans as possible before his final confrontation with Jesus Christ where he will be cast into the lake of eternal fire (Rev. 20:10).[38]

All of this is denied by The Satanic Temple, which divorced its personal definition of Satan from cultural, historical, and biblical roots, and embraced a theater construct of him—like a monstrous statue on a movie set—impressive and empty.

38. Martin, Rische, Van Gorden, *The Kingdom of the Occult*, 395.

Answering Agnosticism and Atheism

Today we are faced with this aggressive agnostic spirit, presented under the guise of the scientific method—and The Satanic Temple is one of many embracing it. It is even being fostered in seminaries across America! They can't say there is no God or that they believe there is no God. They have to say they don't *know* if there is a God. This is the idea that we can never really know anything with finality; we must continually experiment.

A friend, who is a scientist, exemplifies this spirit. He honestly believes that as a scientist, he can never know anything with an absolute degree of certainty. If you bring up the law of gravity, his answer is that every time we demonstrate the law of gravity it is true, but it's only a statistical probability. He argues that it's very possible that the 450 billionth time we drop a cube of gold to the ground it may be suspended in the air—it's a statistical probability. As a scientist, he could never say the law of gravity is irreversible; it would always be subject to advancing knowledge.

But when you put this argument under the proverbial microscope, a new picture emerges. Suppose you were to see a man who passed through the physical experience that we call death. There was no respiration. The heart stopped. In fact, he was dead for about 72 hours, and rigor mortis set in. You examined him completely and to your satisfaction, and according to the physicians who examined him, he was dead. And then within a few hours, you saw the same man resuscitate completely, and a few days after that, ascend up—contrary to the laws of gravity—and disappear out of your sight. What would you think?

The answer he gave was that, granting the fact that I was sane and that the event occurred under all these conditions, he would assume that something had taken place that was, for the moment, beyond the realm of our scientific understanding. But that a time may well come when we would understand perfectly the power that enabled this man to resuscitate himself and to rise up against the laws of gravity. But my friend wouldn't admit that the person was divine, because science recognizes no divinity.

In other words, the resurrection of Jesus Christ, to which I was alluding, could never in the vocabulary of science be miraculous, because science recognizes the non-existence of the miraculous. Whatever appears to be miraculous could be explained if we had further data.

You can never win an argument with a person who reasons like this. No matter how much data you produce, they have a basic premise that

THE SATANIC TEMPLE (TST)

operates against you. The basic premise is this: *I'm not going to believe it.* I'm not going to believe in the supernatural event. I'm going to believe in a natural event. Everything is natural.

It is an age-old argument, and today we confront this same basic philosophy. Starting with David Hume, the great British philosopher and empiricist who first instituted the systemization of this kind of thinking, right through Bertrand Russell to Richard Dawkins.[39] This is why a scientist can say there is nothing miraculous. This is why an agnostic can say, "I don't really know because no matter how much I learned, there is so much more that I don't know, and it may throw out everything that I do know." And this is the type of skepticism and the type of agnosticism we find in the world today.

An atheist, like a Christian, holds that we can *know* whether or not there is a God. The Christian holds that we can know there *is* a God; the atheist, that we can know there is *not*. The agnostic suspends judgment and says he doesn't know. He says that there are not sufficient grounds either for affirmation or for denial. At the same time, an agnostic may hold that the existence of God, though not impossible, is very improbable. He may even hold it so improbable that it is not worth considering in practice. In that case, he is not far removed from atheism. They are two peas in a pod, split by a semantic hair.

How does an agnostic regard the virgin birth of Jesus and the Holy Trinity? Since an agnostic does not believe in God, he cannot think that Jesus was God! People who reason like this tell you they are not atheists. They claim to be *broadminded*, open to the scientific method of inquiry. They wish you to accept that they are logical, scientific, and rational. This is not something new—this thinking has been around for centuries. And this is the foundation for the revamped philosophy of The Satanic Temple.

But the truth is that most of the people who claim to be agnostic are 99 percent of the time really atheists. They use science as a cover for their atheism, while claiming to be reasonable and open-minded. But the fact is that they act, from the very first moment of conversation, as if God does not exist. This is a very careful form of quasi-atheism. It sounds like

39. Some may debate the geographical roots of Hume as either Scottish or British, but the Stanford Encyclopedia of philosophy states that he was "generally regarded as one of the most important philosophers to write in English." Walter Martin characterizes him as British based on this academic criteria and the fact that he spent a great deal of his life in Great Britain. See https://plato.stanford.edu/entries/hume/.

agnosticism, but it isn't. A true agnostic is an honest person who says I just don't know. He doesn't say I believe one way or the other—he just doesn't know. In the case of The Satanic Temple, their Tenets reveal that they began with an acceptance of the reality of a supernatural world, God, and Satan, and regressed to an agnostic and atheistic philosophy.

Language is a very deceptive thing. The Satanic Temple is adept at using it to redefine biblical and historical terms in their quest to craft a new political Satanism, and that is why context is the key to refutation. Words in context mean exactly what they say. When Christians face agnosticism and atheism, we must face it within the context of Scripture.

Evil is biblically and historically satanic in origin and it cannot be divorced from him (Isaiah 14:14). In virtually every ancient culture, Satan or a devil or the evil one is present. His plan to ruin the children of God and separate them forever from their Father came to fruition in Eden, and man became infected with evil too—in need of a Savior who most would reject (Genesis 3:1–14). "And this is the judgment: the light has come into the world, and people loved the darkness rather than the light because their works were evil" (John 3:19 ESV).

The Satanic Temple, David Hume, Bertrand Russell, Christopher Hitchens, Richard Dawkins—all must answer for deeds that are evil. The deeds of all mankind literally reek with evil and rebellion against the throne of God. And all of this pious agnostic, scientific, methodological double-talk will never for a moment suffice to explain the man who says that he's an agnostic yet lives like the devil, professing he's agnostic about morality or agnostic about life. He's open-minded on everything and usually 99 percent of the time, he lives an open morality, too—open to everything. For once you abandon the foundations, it takes very little time for the building itself to collapse.

Today, we are facing a carefully defined form of unbelief. Abraham Lincoln characterized it very well when he said,

> We have been the recipients of the choicest bounties of Heaven. We have been preserved, these many years, in peace and prosperity. We have grown in numbers, wealth and power, as no other nation has ever grown. But we have forgotten God. We have forgotten the gracious hand which preserved us in peace, and multiplied and enriched and strengthened us; and we have vainly imagined, in the deceitfulness of our hearts, that all these blessings were produced by some superior wisdom and virtue of our own. Intoxicated with

unbroken success, we have become too self-sufficient to feel the necessity of redeeming and preserving grace, too proud to pray to the God that made us![40]

For where there is no vision the people perish (Proverbs 29:18). You don't have to say "I don't believe in God" to go to hell; all you have to do is ignore Him. You don't have to be anti-God or anti-Christ—all you have to do is *ignore* Christ. "How shall we escape if we neglect so great a salvation?" (Hebrews 2:3 NKJV).

This is the horror of our age. It is not always what is said that is so evil; it is what is *ignored* that is evil. It is the caricature of religion subtly done in entertainment. It is the domination of our media by ecumenical theologians who stand up and say that what Dr. So and So believes is really not too bad. He's trying to give us a new dimension of Christianity—and this man denies the deity of Jesus Christ! It is the domination of our seminaries and the domination of our educational institutions. It is the subtle creeping or perversion of deadly agnosticism, which has seeped into the moral fiber of a nation that built its foundations upon the proclamation of a non-agnostic premise: that our government rests upon the existence and the worship of the God who gave us that freedom. To forget it—to ignore Him—is to imperil everything.

Rome did not fall in one day; she fell in steps well marked by history. The first step was her utter abandon to paganism, which finally resulted in skepticism and agnosticism, so that Roman consuls and the fathers of Rome could write on their tombstones, "I was not. I was. I am not. I care not." Our reply must be with the words of our Lord Jesus, "I came that they may have life and have it abundantly" (John 10:10 ESV).

A few years ago, an elderly pastor made this observation: "In my years of witnessing for Christ and of pastoring the needs of thousands of people, I have noted one important truth never controverted—Satan has no happy old people." *Satan has no happy old people.* But Christ does, for the person who faces the grave can face it in the glory of the Resurrection. "Because I live, you will live also" (John 14:19 NKJV).

As the facts are concerned, it is evident as a matter of logic that since the religions of the world all disagree, and all claim to be the true religion, that only one of them *can* be true. That is the inexorable law of logic—one

40. Abraham Lincoln, "Proclamation Appointing a National Fast Day," March 30, 1963, Speeches & Writings, *Abraham Lincoln Online*, http://www.abrahamlincolnonline.org/lincoln/speeches/fast.htm.

of them has to be true. All religions of the world contradict each other, so it's obvious that one of them is telling the truth and the rest are not.

But society today will not accept that—all religions must be right—no matter how much they contradict each other. All of them are right at the same time. This isn't logical or rational, but we are living in the age of the revolt *against* reason. We are living in the age of the abandonment of logic. We are living in the age when people are not dominated by thought, when they are not dominated by principle, by ethic, or by control; when their minds do not function as they functioned many times in the past. We are living in an age of apathy when a living baby can be murdered minutes after birth and people don't want to get involved. Something has eaten like the proverbial canker into the moral fiber of a nation. It is only when men forget they are men that they begin to live like animals.

We cannot forget. We dare not forget that the philosophy of agnosticism 1) has never produced an enduring civilization; 2) has never contributed markedly to the development of mankind; 3) has been the father of at least two major systems of world disaster: Communism and Nazism. So often agnosticism and its parallel philosophy, atheism, argue that religion has been the greatest deterrent to progress in the world. They cite the fact that millions of people have been burned as witches and tortured in the name of religion. But let us not forget that true Christians follow the teachings of Christ. "A new commandment I give to you, that you love one another, even as I have loved you, that you also love one another" (John 13:34 NASB). The true church, with all her faults, does not kill. Many of the people who were doing the persecuting long ago were not Christians.

The Church has been in the forefront fighting for the freedom, dignity, and development of mankind and civilization. It was the missionary force of the Christian church that made it possible for people to colonize lands, build empires, and bring about the civilization of this world. It was the missionary cross of Jesus Christ that turned the cannibals into Christians. Churches build hospitals and care centers. Churches distribute food and clothing worldwide, and manage millions of charitable organizations. When you stop to examine the premise of the argument that Christianity has slowed progress, it is false. The people allegedly killed by the tares living in the wheat field of Christianity number fewer than 115 million in two millennia. Today the atheistic philosophies of Nietzsche, Marx, and Engels have destroyed more than 100 million human beings in *60 years*. Atheism and agnosticism produce nothing but bitter fruit—sour grapes.

They contribute nothing to mankind but remain the ever-present critics of everyone else.

What is it, then, that the richest nation in the world is cursed with? She is cursed with agnosticism. She has turned a deaf ear to the God of the Bible, to the foundations of a republic that God has laid out for us. And she has pursued the pathway that can culminate only in destruction. If God spared not the angels that sinned but hurled them down to hell in judgment until the last day; if He annihilated Sodom and Gomorrah with fire from heaven and if He brought Germany and Japan to the brink of annihilation because they turned themselves from the Living God, He will not hesitate with Russia or the United States. We are fools indeed if we think for one moment that a flag in a church is a deterrent against Divine judgment.

The real root of our problem is that which Jesus Christ recognized long ago, "you refuse to come to me that you may have life" (John 5:40 ESV). The root of the problem is that the heart of man "is deceitful above all things, and desperately sick; who can understand it?" (Jeremiah 17:9 ESV).

What must come from the church is a loud, clear, intelligent sound that will call the young people in our schools and our colleges to an appreciation of the value of Christianity. What is needed in the church is a voice of conviction and power from the Word of God that Jesus Christ, the living Savior, can change the lives of men and women. A voice raised against the philosophies and false theologies of our day, against the terrible pharisee-ism of segments of our own communities—a voice calling for the desperate need of revival in our time.

The church is at the crossroads. In the face of Satan's power, may God give us a great burden for our nation, for our universities, and for our seminaries. We must shine as lights in this world, for the night is indeed coming when no one can work (John 9:4).

Explore

Rational Humanism
Material World
Supernaturalism
Ecumenical

Discuss

1. Why do organizations like The Satanic Temple redefine historical personalities like Satan?

   _____

   _____

2. What is the biblical and historical identity of Satan, and what has he always wanted?

   _____

   _____

3. What do Christians and atheists have in common?

   _____

   _____

4. What is Truth? God's Word is truth (John 17:17). Jesus is truth (John 14:6).

   _____

   _____

Dig Deeper

See *The Kingdom of the Cults Study Guide* available at WalterMartin.com.

Appendix B

New Age Spirituality—
The Age of Aquarius[1]

> **Quick Facts on New Age Spirituality**
>
> - All things are divine, including earth; humans are not more valuable than other creatures.
> - All is one and all is God. God is an impersonal consciousness and power— "the Universe."
> - Jesus was an enlightened teacher.
> - There is no absolute truth, only *personal* truth for each individual.

Historical Perspective

So many people, Christian and non-Christian alike, know so little about the evils of New Age thinking. The advent of the nineteenth century brought with it a new stirring of occult power, and since that time, it has insidiously infected Western culture and theology. "In the late '60s and early '70s, Yogi Bhajan—who brought Kundalini Yoga to the West—began speaking about the Age of Aquarius, and said that the transition to the new era would

1. Material for this chapter was excerpted from Walter Martin, *The New Age Cult* (Minneapolis: Bethany House Publishers, 1989).

begin in November 1991 and end on November 11, 2011. Then humankind would remain in the Aquarian Age for roughly 2,000 years."[2]

During the late 1950s and into the mid-1960s, New Age spirituality was like a great iceberg, nine-tenths below the surface. But in the 1960s, it began to grow bold—surfacing in full force by the 1980s. The Church by and large did not respond to it until the iceberg had surfaced, and even then we only halfheartedly attacked the problem.

Theosophy, the Unity School of Christianity, Christian Science, Spiritism, Baha'ism, and Rosicrucianism, all were spearheads of current New Age teachings, and as founder and director of Zondervan Publishing House's Division of Cult Apologetics (1955–65), and founder and director of Christian Research Institute since 1960, I urged Christian publishers to distribute books and tracts on these cults and the occult, that were even then a growing threat to the Church.[3] I delivered thousands of lectures, crisscrossing America and the world for more than 38 years trying to get the message across. Sometimes, I felt like a frustrated Paul Revere calling out, *"The cults are coming, the cults are coming!"* That sounded to many like a litany of impending disaster. But so it has proved to be.

The rise of the New Age Movement boomed with the Swamis of the Beatles, spreading worldwide their *gospel of the second chance*—reincarnation. Driven by a captivated media and a technology revolution, it resulted in a world so saturated with Hinduism that we are now living in the post-Christian era.

Today, though Christianity remains the largest religious group worldwide, hundreds of millions of people are involved in cults and New Age practices or occultic thinking.[4] Over the last 60 years, national magazines, newspapers, and radio and television programs have proclaimed and trumpeted an ever-changing New Age cult or spirituality.

Dusty old occult bookstores and virtually unknown publishers have given way to Amazon, Target, Walmart, and countless online outlets—purveyors of everything occult. There can be little doubt now that in the

2. Karena Virgina, "Kundalini 101: What Is the Aquarian Age, Anyway?," *Yoga Journal*, April 24, 2018, https://www.yogajournal.com/yoga-101/kundalini-yoga-what-is-aquarian-age.
3. Walter Martin passed away in 1989.
4. See worldwide statistics at Conrad Hackett and David McClendon, "Christians Remain World's Largest Religious Group, But They Are Declining in Europe," April 5, 2017, *Pew Research Center*, http://www.pewresearch.org/fact-tank/2017/04/05/christians-remain-worlds-largest-religious-group-but-they-are-declining-in-europe/.

wake of the Aquarian Age holocaust, we *must* act and we must be prepared to "give an answer to every man that asketh you a reason of the hope that is in you" (1 Peter 3:15).

We have had *enough* of hearing, "Just be positive and preach the Gospel" and "Don't offend people by defending your Christian faith or criticizing false teachings; God will protect the church." Throughout history, every time the Church has failed to defend the faith, false doctrines and heretical teachings have plagued us. Only the church militant can become the church triumphant. The challenge is here; the time is now!

By Divine grace, we still have time to confront and evangelize those practicing New Age spirituality, for this is the world of occultic darkness and spiritual danger beyond belief.

The World of the Occult and the New Age

The turbulent sixties provided the perfect atmosphere for the rebirth of what we now recognize as New Age Spirituality or the New Age Cult. The word *occult* is derived from the Latin and basically means "hidden/ secret" things. The term is used to describe practices such as astrology, numerology, witchcraft, crystal gazing, necromancy (communication with the dead), magic, and palm reading, which according to the Bible are forbidden to man and cursed by God (Leviticus 20:6; Deuteronomy 18:9–11; Acts 19:19). These satanically energized methods of obtaining otherwise unobtainable knowledge comprise the very heart and soul of New Age spirituality because they are the primary means through which New Age teachings are proclaimed. They may have modern-sounding names (e.g., astral projection, psychometry, radiance therapy, channeling), but they are the same practices the church of Jesus Christ has been standing against for more than nineteen centuries.

The neoorthodox theologian Nels Ferré correctly predicted the influx of Eastern and Indian philosophy and theology that characterized the sixties and concluded that the imported ideas would be a major challenge to historic Christianity.

The great English apologist and writer C. S. Lewis saw the battle lines clearly drawn. He noted that in the final conflict between religions, Hinduism and Christianity would offer the only viable options because Hinduism absorbs all religious systems, and Christianity excludes all others, maintaining the supremacy of the claims of Jesus Christ.

Occult Roots

To understand New Age spirituality, it is necessary that we recognize its ancient roots in the occult. The Bible forbids occultic practices, stating that they draw on satanic power. It describes several different dimensions or realms of reality such as heaven, hell, and the visible universe. And there is still another dimension that commands our attention. In Ephesians 2 and 6, the Apostle Paul speaks of this dimension as the realm of "the prince of the power of the air, the spirit that now worketh in the children of disobedience" (Ephesians 2:2). He declares that the Christian is engaged in spiritual combat against the forces that dominate that realm. In Paul's words, "our struggle is not against flesh and blood, but against the rulers, against the authorities, against the powers of this dark world and against the spiritual forces of evil in the heavenly realms" (Ephesians 6:12 NIV). The apostle goes to great lengths in his writings to warn us against "the devil's schemes" (Ephesians 6:11 NIV), echoing the words of Moses to the Israelites in the Old Testament. Moses communicated God's extreme displeasure with the inhabitants of the land of Canaan, who practiced abominable things and were, in effect, Satan worshipers:

> When you enter the land which the LORD your God gives you, you shall not learn to imitate the detestable things of those nations. There shall not be found among you anyone who makes his son or his daughter pass through the fire, one who uses divination, one who practices witchcraft, or one who interprets omens, or a sorcerer, or one who casts a spell, or a medium, or a spiritist, or one who calls up the dead. For whoever does these things is detestable to the LORD; and because of these detestable things the LORD your God will drive them out before you. You shall be blameless before the LORD your God. For those nations, which you shall dispossess, listen to those who practice witchcraft and to diviners, but as for you, the LORD your God has not allowed you *to do* so. (Deuteronomy 18:9–14 NASB)

This glossary of the occult warned Israel of impending wrath if they followed in the footsteps of the inhabitants of the land that God had chosen to give them.

The occult might be called a substitute faith that is found throughout the history of world religions—including that of the Hebrews themselves—as seen in their esoteric and occultic book *The Kabbalah*. The Bible speaks repeatedly against all occultic practices, giving special attention to astrologers (Isaiah 47) and those who were called "sorcerers" or "magicians" as recorded in the book of Daniel. There can be little doubt after reading 2 Kings 21 that God's judgment did come upon Israel for her failure to obey His commands concerning the occult. King Manassah violated all the prohibitions against the occult, bringing about the exile of the Jews, which eventually led to their repentance and restoration.

New Age spirituality is a revival of this ancient occultism. It holds historical ties to Sumerian, Indian, Egyptian, Chaldean, Babylonian, and Persian religious practices. *New Age* is a fresh title but, as *Time* magazine pointed out, the occult is nothing new: "So here we are in the New Age, a combination of spirituality and superstition, fad and farce, about which the only thing certain is that it is not new."[5]

The Theosophical Connection

For all practical purposes, the New Age Cult can be equated with the transplantation of Hindu philosophy through the Theosophical Society founded by Helena Blavatsky in the latter part of the nineteenth century in the United States. Madame Blavatsky, as she was known, promoted spiritism, séances, and basic Hindu philosophy while manifesting a distinct antagonism to biblical Christianity.

Marilyn Ferguson, in her book *The Aquarian Conspiracy*, notes that the "Age of Aquarius" occupies a center seat in the arena of New Age thought, and when coupled with the emphasis of such cults as Christian Science, New Thought, Unitarian Universalism, Rosicrucianism, and Science of Mind, or Religious Science, it becomes a formidable vehicle for New Age thinking.

The theology of New Age spirituality assumes an evolutionary process. The world is waiting for more revealers of truth (*avatars*), such as Buddha, Mohammed, Confucius, Zoroaster, Moses, Krishna, and ultimately one designated as the Lord Maitreya, an incarnation of the Buddha, the Enlightened One. The Lord Jesus Christ is relegated to the role of a demigod or "one of many equally good ways." He's most surely not *the way*, *the* truth, and *the* life, as He taught in John 14:6.

A tremendously significant figure in the history of the development of the New Age thinking is Alice Bailey, who was involved with Madame Blavatsky in the Theosophical Society. She wrote more than 20 books,

5. *Time* magazine, Dec. 7, 1987, 62.

allegedly influenced by a spirit guide who communicated with her telepathically. According to Bailey, "In 2025 the date in all probability will be set for the first stage of the externalization [bodily appearances] of the Hierarchy." We also discover that "if these steps prove successful, other and more important reappearances will be possible, beginning with the return of Christ."[6]

If Bailey is right about the significance of the year 1975 in spreading the message of Theosophy, then the "christ" cannot appear until some time after 2025. In context, 1975 represents only a beginning, a stepping up of preparatory activity for a 50-year period.

In *Problems of Humanity* by Alice Bailey, we also find another interesting observation relative to the event that is called "the festival of humanity":

> [The festival of humanity] will be preeminently [the day] on which the divine nature of man will be recognized and his power to express goodwill and establish human rights relations [because of his divinity] will be stressed. On this festival we are told that Christ has for nearly 2,000 years represented humanity and has stood before the Hierarchy as the god-man, the leader of his people and the eldest in the great family of brothers (*PH*, 164).

Important as Alice Bailey's writings are, they obviously cannot be held as an infallible guide for New Age evolution. But the Theosophical Society did fuel the emerging New Age movement, and through the activities of Madame Blavatsky and Annie Besant, the society planned for the Lord Maitreya to appear in the person of Mrs. Besant's protégé, Krishnamurti. However, Krishnamurti declined the honor of Mrs. Besant's anointing due largely to the death of his brother and his subsequent disillusionment with the claims of Theosophy—and so the search and the anticipation continued.

Theological Evaluation

In 1982, newspapers across the country displayed full-page advertisements boldly stating: "The world has had enough . . . of hunger, injustice, and war. There is an answer to our call for help, a world teacher for all humanity. THE CHRIST IS NOW HERE."

6. Alice Bailey, *The Externalization of the Hierarchy* (New York: Lucis Publishing Companies, 1957), 530, 559.

This ad campaign was sponsored by the Tara Foundation under the leadership of Benjamin Creme, and asked such interesting questions as "Who Is the Christ?," "What Is He Saying?," and "When Will We See Him?" The ad ended in a call for peace: "Without sharing there can be no justice, without justice there can be no peace, without peace there can be no future."

Three other New Age groups joined the Tara Foundation, but the nebulous ad inevitably failed to attract the kind of attention Creme had anticipated. The "christ" of whom the Tara Foundation was speaking was not the Christ of biblical revelation, but an Indian guru who had flown to England (thus fulfilling Revelation 1:7), and now lives in London. Mr. Creme stated that this christ would meet the press, but the press conference was later postponed.

Creme, in his book *The Reappearance of the Christ,* ran true to New Age thought when describing the relationship of Jesus Christ to the New Age:

> The christ is not God, he is not coming as God. He is an embodiment of an aspect of God, the love aspect of God. He is the embodied soul of all creation. He embodies the energy which is a consciousness aspect of the Being we call God. . . . He would rather that you didn't pray to him, but to God within you, which is also within him . . . He said it himself. "The kingdom of God is within you."[7]

Such statements from New Age leaders characterize the spirituality as pointedly anti-Christian and particularly hostile to the unique claim of deity by the Lord Jesus Christ and confirmed by apostolic witness. In a fact sheet released by the Christian Research Institute dealing with the New Age movement, a report with which I concur, New Age spirituality has been described as

> the most common name used to portray the growing penetration of Eastern and occultic mysticism into Western culture. The words *New Age* refer to the Aquarian Age, which occultists believe to be dawning, bringing with it an era of enlightenment and peace. Encompassed within New Age spirituality are various cults which emphasize a mystic experience (including Transcendental Meditation, the Rajneesh cult, Eckankar, the Church

---

7. Benjamin Crème, *The Reappearance of the Christ,* 135. See also https://www.share-inter national.org/archives/M_teachings/i_M_teachings.htm.

Universal and Triumphant, and many others). The followers of various gurus, such as the late swami Muktananda, Sai Baba, Baba Ram Dass, and Mahareeshi Mahesh Yoga, personify the essence of modern New Age leadership. Other groups such as the "Human Potential Spirituality" exemplified in Est (now incorporated into Landmark Forum), Lifespring, Silva Mind Control, Summit Workshops, etc., and many (though not all) of the advocates of the various approaches to holistic health, accurately represent the spirit of the New Age.[8]

> New Age theology is pointedly anti-Christian and particularly hostile to the unique claim of deity by the Lord Jesus Christ.

Though the beliefs and emphases of the various groups and individuals who make up New Age spirituality can vary widely, they share a common religious experience and philosophical base. The theological similarity in the midst of diversity is much like the many traditions within historic Christianity that differ on peripheral doctrines and yet share a common experience with the Holy Spirit resulting from a common faith in Jesus Christ. Members of New Age spirituality share a common belief that "all is one," that is, everything that exists together composes one essential reality or substance. This ultimate reality is identified as God, usually seen as an impersonal consciousness and power.

The Divinity of All Mankind

The New Age derives its belief in the inherent divinity of man from this belief in the divinity of all things. Thus the separation of the human race from God which is obvious to the Christian church is treated differently by New Age spirituality. Whereas historic Christianity believes that man was separated from God by his transgression of God's law, New Age spirituality believes that man is separated from God *only* in his own consciousness. He is the victim of a false sense of separate identity that blinds him to his essential unity with God.

New Age spirituality advocates various methods of altering the consciousness (Yoga, meditation, chanting, ecstatic dancing, drugs, etc.) as

---

8. Christian Research Institute Fact Sheet, *The New Age*, n.d. For more information on Benjamin Crème quotes see *The New Age*, https://www.iclnet.org/pub/resources/text/cri/cri-jrnl/CRJ0035A.TXT.

the means of salvation. These enable man to consciously experience his supposed union with God, an experience defined as "enlightenment."

It also heavily emphasizes the ancient Hindu doctrines of *reincarnation* and *karma*. The law of karma teaches that whatever a person does, good or bad, will return to him in *exact* proportion in another existence. Since most people are not able to pay off in one lifetime all of the bad karma that they have accumulated for their bad deeds, they are compelled to return in new incarnations until all of their bad karma has been balanced by the good karma they achieve.

The Divinity of Earth

New Age spirituality embraces what has been termed *monistic panthe-ism*—all is one and all is God. Nature is divine and man is divine just as Satan once promised he would be in Eden (Genesis 3:5). Humans have a responsibility to protect nature or we will all face extinction.

Today, monistic pantheism fuels the rise of Eco-spirituality, a powerful ideology that has emerged as a political religion. It is rooted in the acceptance of the impersonal "Universe" as the ultimate *divine*, and the rejection of the God of the Bible.[9] Since God does not exist or is irrelevant to the present age, He cannot love or protect. Therefore, our world and our lives are in great danger as a result of human excesses and human waste.

What may once have been a philosophy of eco-love, drawn from the pages of the Hindu Vedas, has become the aggressive application of selected principles—a *religion* the Bible warned us about.[10] "They exchanged the truth about God for a lie and worshiped and served the creature rather than the Creator, who is blessed forever!" (Romans 1:18–25 ESV).

The advent of the twenty-first century revealed the rise of a fervent belief in a detached, divine Universe—a global Eco-spirituality whose theology is rooted in weakness and contradiction. The Universe is impersonal, with no emotional connection to people, but it can reward or punish personal evil through karma. The Universe is the blended mind or being of all

9. See the *Stanford Encyclopedia of Philosophy* for a discussion of Pantheism as a religious and metaphysical position: https://www.faculty.umb.edu/gary_zabel/Courses/Phil%20281b/Phil osophy%20of%20Magic/Phil%20100/Readings/stanford.eduentriespantheism.html.

10. Vikram Vishnu Shenoy, *Eco-Spirituality: Case Studies on Hinduism and Environmentalism in Contemporary India* (honors thesis, Bucknell University, 2016), https://digitalcommons.buck nell.edu/cgi/viewcontent.cgi?article=1355&context=honors_theses.

creatures, and yet it has no omnipotent power to prevent their destruction. Humans must create their own salvation by defeating the disaster of climate change.

In the face of this anti-biblical theology, what should the response of the Evangelical church be? Some, like the National Association of Evangelicals (NAE), appear to support the rhetoric and agenda of secular climate change, while others confront it.

The Cornwall Alliance, founded by Dr. Calvin Beisner, is an evangelical Christian nonprofit focused on providing answers to the arguments of climate "crisis." In its "Evangelical Declaration on Global Warming," the alliance states:

WHAT WE BELIEVE

1. We believe Earth and its ecosystems—created by God's intelligent design and infinite power and sustained by His faithful providence—are robust, resilient, self-regulating, and self-correcting, admirably suited for human flourishing, and displaying His glory. Earth's climate system is no exception. Recent global warming is one of many natural cycles of warming and cooling in geologic history.

2. We believe abundant, affordable energy is indispensable to human flourishing, particularly to societies which are rising out of abject poverty and the high rates of disease and premature death that accompany it. With present technologies, fossil and nuclear fuels are indispensable if energy is to be abundant and affordable.

3. We believe mandatory reductions in carbon dioxide and other greenhouse gas emissions, achievable mainly by greatly reduced use of fossil fuels, will greatly increase the price of energy and harm economies.

4. We believe such policies will harm the poor more than others because the poor spend a higher percentage of their income on energy and desperately need economic growth to rise out of poverty and overcome its miseries.

WHAT WE DENY

1. We deny that Earth and its ecosystems are the fragile and unstable products of chance, and particularly that Earth's climate system is

vulnerable to dangerous alteration because of minuscule changes in atmospheric chemistry. Recent warming was neither abnormally large nor abnormally rapid. There is no convincing scientific evidence that human contribution to greenhouse gases is causing dangerous global warming.

2. We deny that alternative, renewable fuels can, with present or near-term technology, replace fossil and nuclear fuels, either wholly or in significant part, to provide the abundant, affordable energy necessary to sustain prosperous economies or overcome poverty.

3. We deny that carbon dioxide—essential to all plant growth—is a pollutant. Reducing greenhouse gases cannot achieve significant reductions in future global temperatures, and the costs of the policies would far exceed the benefits.

4. We deny that such policies, which amount to a regressive tax, comply with the Biblical requirement of protecting the poor from harm and oppression.[11]

In the Aquarian age, peace, prosperity, love, and satisfaction are all within the grasp of those who are willing to exchange biblical revelation for Hindu speculation, and the Prince of Life for the Prince of Darkness. There can be little doubt that the rise of Eco-spirituality and the Bible have one common denominator: The Bible prophesies that at the end of the ages, false prophets, christs, and teachers will proliferate (Matthew 24) proclaiming, "'Here is the Christ!' or 'There he is!'" (v. 23 ESV).

In the words of the living Christ, "This day is this Scripture fulfilled in your ears" (Luke 4:21).

The Importance of New Age Spirituality

New Age spirituality is not important just because it has a multi-billion-dollar balance sheet, but because it reaches out to multiple millions of people who are dazzled by celebrities. It is penetrating our educational system as well as some of our state legislatures. It threatens not only the foundation of the Judeo-Christian religion, but challenges fundamental

11. The Wayback Machine, Cornwall Alliance, *Evangelical Declaration on Global Warming*, May 1, 2009, https://web.archive.org/web/20150722204817/http://www.cornwallalliance.org/2009/05/01/evangelical-declaration-on-global-warming/.

belief in the existence of objective truth. In New Age thinking, truth is perceived *individually*, and it is not uncommon for the New Age believer to say, "That's your truth—this is mine," as if truth, like beauty, exists only in the eye of the beholder.

The threat of New Age spirituality cannot be underestimated in our public schools, where children are taught *mantras*, meditation words, and meditation techniques like mindfulness and Transcendental Meditation (TM). They are subjected to "values clarification" in which moral, ethical, and spiritual values become purely subjective in nature and not subject to any meanings apart from those assigned by the child. In this jumbled scenario, reality becomes lost in a shuffle of conflicting vocabulary, and the law of the semantic jungle declares pragmatism: "If it works, use it; if it feels good, do it."

It is no wonder that *Time* magazine, quoting several Christian writers, noted:

> Humans are essentially religious creatures and they don't rest until they have some sort of answers to the fundamental questions. Rationalism and secularism don't answer those questions. But you can see the rise of the New Age is a barometer of the disintegration of American culture. Dostoyevsky said [that] anything is permissible if there is no God. But anything is also permissible if everything is God. There is no way to make any distinction between good and evil . . . once you've deified yourself, which is what the New Age is all about, there is no higher moral absolute. It's a recipe for ethical anarchy . . . it's both messianic and millennial.[12]

Sacrificing Biblical Revelation

The deification of man by New Age spirituality requires the abandonment of absolute truth, worship at the altar of relativism, and obsession with reincarnation. The spirituality is a growing threat to Christians and to those who take seriously biblical admonitions such as "I have made the earth . . . even my hands, have stretched out the heavens. . . . Thou shalt love the Lord thy God with all thy heart, and with all thy soul, and with all thy mind. . . . Thou shalt love thy neighbour as thyself. On these two commandments hang all the law and the prophets" (Isaiah 45:12; Matthew 22:37, 39–40).

12. *Time* magazine, Dec. 7, 1987, 72.

Biblical Perspective

There are many different answers that have been given to New Age teachings, for the Church has been on the front lines resisting the occult for almost 2,000 years. It is fair to say that most modern errors are only ancient heresies and doctrines in a different guise, tailor-fitted for the age in which we live.

Therefore, it should not surprise us that the old answers from the accumulated wisdom and theological expertise of the apostles, church fathers, and reformers are the best means of fighting ancient occultism in its modern forms. It is difficult, if not impossible, to improve on what the historic scholarship of the Christian church has to say about the revival of occultism in the New Age Cult.

The Personal, Triune God

In New Age theology, the triune God of the Bible cannot be properly described in personal terms. "He is not one individual, but an energy gestalt."[13] God is seen as an impersonal energy field whose only real personal structure is the sum of *its* parts. Both Judaism and Christianity abominate this essentially Hindu concept, affirming an unshakable monotheism—a personal, benevolent, and loving Deity who is immanent within His creation and yet transcends it by infinity because He is its Creator.

> The God of the Bible is a personal Being—He designates himself as Creator of the universe.

The greatest authorities on the nature and identity of God are His Son and His Word. Jesus Christ is the living Word of God, and the Bible is the written Word of God. Both testify that the highest of all truths is the unity of Deity. The great commandment is this: "Hear, O Israel: The Lord our God, the Lord is one" (Deuteronomy 6:4; Mark 12:29 NIV).

Christian scholars down through the centuries have recognized the fact that if Jesus Christ does not know God's nature, and someone else claims that he does, it is readily apparent that the challenger has placed himself above Christ. New Age gurus and avatars make this claim. The Christian must respond by reviewing the superiority of the life and influence of Jesus Christ upon this world, a world whose very calendar is dated by His birth.

13. Jane Roberts, *The Seth Material* (Englewood Cliffs, NJ: Prentice-Hall, 1970), 237.

That the God of the Bible is a personal Being, that He designates himself as Creator of the universe, and that the biblical view of creation is scientifically preferable to all versions cited by New Age leaders is clear evidence. The view of the world held by pagan sources upon which the New Age must draw fails all scientific criteria.

The characters and the attributes of the Creator are detailed in the Old and the New Testaments, and they bear repeating. In the third chapter of Exodus, Moses encountered God in the burning bush experience, and God identified himself as a personal being, saying, "I am the God of thy father, the God of Abraham, the God of Isaac, and the God of Jacob. . . . I Am that I Am" (Exodus 3:6, 14).

When Moses persisted in asking questions such as, "When I return to the land of Egypt, whom shall I say has sent me?" God responded by saying, "Thus shalt thou say unto the children of Israel, I Am has sent me unto you" (Exodus 3:14).

Jewish scholars have properly translated this as "the Eternal," since God affirmed "this is my name for ever and my memorial unto all generations" (Exodus 3:15).

Contrary to what the New Age Cult declares, God is a personal spirit (John 4:24). He has told us, "I am the almighty God; walk before me, and be thou perfect" (Genesis 17:1).

This eternal God revealed himself in the Bible as the Father, the Son, and the Holy Spirit (Matthew 28:19).

The God of creation has reflective memory: "For I know the thoughts that I think toward you, saith the Lord" (Jeremiah 29:11).

God affirms His uniqueness: "I am the Lord: that is my name: and my glory will I not give to another" (Isaiah 42:8).

The knowledge possessed by this all-powerful being is declared to be without limitation: "God . . . knoweth all things" (1 John 3:20).

He possesses a will (Roman 12:2) to which even His Son is subject: "Lo, I come . . . to do thy will, O God" (Hebrews 10:7).

Far from the triune God being "Father-Mother-Child" as New Age spirituality maintains, the personal living God proclaims, "I am the first, and I am the last; and beside me there is no God" (Isaiah 44:6).

God the Creator loves us; God the Creator remembers us and will tolerate no interference with His decrees. As the Lord Jesus said, "Thy kingdom come. Thy will be done in earth, as it is in heaven" (Matthew 6:10).

The God of the Bible is also the judge of the universe. Ezekiel writes, "Therefore thus saith the Lord God unto them; Behold, I, even I, will judge" (Ezekiel 34:20; Acts 17:31).

The Apostle Paul draws our attention to the fact that we must all appear before the judgment seat of Christ (2 Corinthians 5:10), and that all kingdoms will come under the absolute control of His kingdom, and His reign will be everlasting (Revelation 11:15).

These are just some of the descriptions given in Scripture, but they are more than adequate to reveal the sharp contrast that exists between gods fashioned in the image of men or Satan, and "the living God, who is the Saviour of all men, especially of those that believe" (1 Timothy 4:10).

Often New Age devotees will say that they reject the biblical concept of God and even the authority of the Scriptures, but their inconsistency surfaces because they persist in quoting Scriptures to buttress their own position. Why quote for proof what you say is untrustworthy? The truth is they find it impossible to function without some foundational reference to the eternal God, and we should not hesitate to cite examples of their use of the Bible as proof of inconsistency and lack of spiritual and scholastic integrity.

Jesus Christ

New Age teaching concerning Jesus Christ, though varied, has basic areas of agreement. No New Age follower will accept Jesus Christ "as the one and only Son of God sacrificed by His loving Father to save humanity from the results of its sins."[14]

The New Age Cult's attack upon the person of Jesus Christ—and an attack is surely what it is—concentrates on Christ's unique claim to deity. The Lord Jesus is indeed proclaimed in the New Testament as "the one and only Son of God" by virtue of the Greek term *monogeneses* (cf. John 1:1, 14, 18; 3:16). The second person of the Trinity does not share His throne with Krishna, Buddha, Mohammed, Zoroaster, or any of the endless assortment of gurus and gods. As the Savior of the world, He bore our sins in His own body upon the cross (1 Peter 2:24), and His miraculous powers have never been duplicated; He is indeed unique among the sons of men.

14. Benjamin Creme, *The Reappearance of the Christ and the Masters of Wisdom* (London: The Tara Press, 1980), 25.

In answer to those who challenged His identity and authority during His earthly ministry, the Lord Jesus stated, "Even though you do not believe me, believe the works" (John 10:38 ESV).

He let the facts speak for themselves. To a questioning John the Baptist in prison, Christ recited the miraculous works He had done. To dispel John's doubt, He said, "Go back and report to John what you hear and see: The blind receive sight, the lame walk, those who have leprosy are cured, the deaf hear, the dead are raised, and the good news is preached to the poor" (Matthew 11:4–5 NIV).

Even today, the verified miracles of Jesus of Nazareth proclaim Him as the Word of God made flesh. New Agers will search in vain for any guru in their history who fed 5,000 people with five loaves and two fishes, who in front of countless witnesses healed the sick, cleansed lepers, raised the dead, opened the eyes of the blind and the ears of the deaf, cast out demons, and demonstrated the love of God for the poor in so many wonderful ways. And how many of them have ever walked on water?

There is good reason for the great antipathy toward the historic Christ and biblical revelation in the New Age. Jesus simply defies all their categories and humbles all their works. This He does precisely because He is the unique Son of God. The New Testament record testifies that He received the worship of men (John 20:28), that He is our great God and Savior (Titus 2:13), that He conquered death itself (Matthew 1), and with the coming of His Spirit at Pentecost illumined the world as a flaming torch. That flame has spread to the ends of the earth and burns brightly, even now.

The man from Nazareth was not just an extraordinarily good person, prophet, or sage indwelt by the Christ or Cosmic Consciousness, as the New Age proclaims. He is the King of kings and the Lord of lords, Creator of all ages (Hebrews 1:1–3), and He remains the Way, the Truth, and the Life. No one comes to the Father but by Him (John 14:6).

The Fallenness of Mankind

It is a cardinal New Age teaching that man is born into this world both good and divine in his nature. Salvation depends upon his looking inward at his spiritual nature and recognizing that he is a god. One New Age writer declares:

Man as the image of God is already saved with an everlasting salvation. . . .
Man is God's image and likeness; whatever is possible to God, is possible
to man as God's reflection.[15]

The biblical record constantly reflects the fact that man is a sinner, that
he has transgressed the law of God. Jesus Christ recognized this and said,
"I am not come to call the righteous, but sinners to repentance" (Matthew
9:13).

The Apostle Peter informs us that Christ died for our sins with the
purpose of reconciling us, the unjust, to God (1 Peter 3:18). Paul agrees,
writing, "All have sinned and come short of the glory of God. . . . There
is none righteous, no, not one" (Romans 3:23, 10).

Sin, a transgression of the law, is described as "all unrighteousness"
(1 John 5:17), and Isaiah tells us that it was for our transgressions that
Jesus the Messiah suffered and died (Isaiah 53).

New Age spirituality denies the biblical doctrine of sin and substitutes
reincarnation as the means of atonement, evading the significance of the
cross. But as one New Age writer said, "No one who sees himself as guilty
can avoid the fear of God."[16]

It is not that New Age spirituality is ignorant of what the Christian
church has been talking about and what Jesus Christ did; it is rather that
they refuse to "fear God, and keep his commandments" (Ecclesiastes
12:13), and have chosen not to "work the works of God" as God prescribed
should be done (John 6).

The doctrine of personal redemption or salvation from sin is the core of
Judaism and Christianity, the oldest monotheistic religions. It is no wonder
that such conflict is inevitable, given New Age spirituality's definition of
salvation. The Apostle John spoke the final word on this when he wrote,
"If we say that we have no sin, we deceive ourselves, and the truth is not
in us. If we confess our sins, he is faithful and just to forgive us our sins,
and to cleanse us from all unrighteousness" (1 John 1:8–9).

Judgment, Heaven, and Hell

The problem of evil, judgment for wrongdoing, and reward for righteousness are all dealt with in New Age spirituality essentially under the

15. Mary Baker Eddy, *Miscellaneous Writings*, 183, 261.
16. *A Course in Miracles* (Foundation for Inner Peace, 1975), 594.

concept of reincarnation. According to the law of karma, stated in Christian terms, "whatsoever a man soweth, that shall he also reap" (Galatians 6:7). New Age teaching eliminates heaven and substitutes Nirvana, the Buddhist idea that all human souls will eventually be absorbed into the great "world soul." Hell is what we reap here in the form of "bad karma" or punishment for errors committed in our past lives. This is as close as New Age spirituality gets to the concept of divine judgment.

The Bible describes the judgment when the Lord Jesus Christ will preside and separate the sheep from the goats, the believers from unbelievers. The believers will enter the kingdom of God with heaven as their home, and the others will enter that realm that Jesus said was "prepared for the devil and his angels since the foundation of the ages." Christ also clearly said, "These shall go away into everlasting punishment, but the righteous unto life eternal" (Matthew 25:46).

The Problem of Evil

When discussing the problem of why evil exists and why God allows Satan and demonic powers to have any control in this world, New Age spirituality takes a very definite stand:

> It is important to see that Lucifer, as I am using this term, described an angel, a being, a great mighty planetary consciousness. It does not describe the popular thought form of satan who leads man down the path of sin and wrongdoing. . . . Man is his own satan just as man is his own salvation.[17]

In recognizing Lucifer as a "planetary consciousness," New Age writers acknowledge the biblical story of the origin of evil and, probably quite unconsciously, adopt biblical descriptions of Satan.

In New Age theology, Satan becomes the "other dark side of the Force," to put it in the vernacular of George Lucas's *Star Wars*. This Force fills the entire universe and sustains it by virtue of the fact that it is one with the universe. Benjamin Creme can thus write quite blithely:

> Of course, yes, the forces of evil are part of God. They are not separate from God. Everything is God.[18]

17. David Spangler, *Reflections on the Christ* (Moray, Scotland: Findhorn Publications, 1978), 39.
18. Creme, *The Reappearance of the Christ*, 103.

However, the Bible paints quite a different picture of the Force. The Bible emphatically describes Satan as "the god of this age" (2 Corinthians 4:4 NIV), or in the words of Jesus, "the prince of this world" (John 12:31). He is labeled "a murderer from the beginning" (John 8:44) and "the enemy of his Maker" (Isaiah 14:13–14). His titles "son of the morning" (Isaiah 14:12) and "covering cherub" (Ezekiel 28:14) tell us that he fell from a place of great glory and power. After his ejection from heaven, he assumed the title "prince of the power of the air" (Ephesians 2:2).

With his great power and alleged benevolence he entered the Garden of Eden and but for divine grace would have destroyed the Creation that God had designed in His own image and likeness.

Because of his evil acts, he will inevitably be defeated by the last Adam, the "Lord from heaven" (1 Corinthians 15:47–49), who is the manifest "seed" of the woman (Genesis 3:15). The New Testament proclaims the Lord Jesus Christ to be this seed who will finally defeat Satan and cast him into the lake of fire (Revelation 20:10).

The New Testament fairly bristles with the activities of a personal Satan, not the empty creation of New Age thinking. It was this personal entity who both tempted the Lord Jesus Christ and resisted Him during His years of earthly ministry (Luke 4).

The Lord Jesus has given the Church power over these demons in His name (Luke 9:1). Paul urges us to arm ourselves for spiritual warfare against the prince of darkness. Satan arrays himself as an angel of light so that if it were possible he would deceive even the chosen of God. The Apostle Paul describes his final deception as the man of sin "who opposes and exalts himself above every so-called god or object of worship, so that he takes his seat in the temple of God, displaying himself as being God" (2 Thessalonians 2 NASB). The thirteenth chapter of the book of Revelation catalogs his persecution of the Church during the first part of the tribulation that will test the whole earth, and John shows him broken and defeated eternally with all his followers (Revelations 20).

New Age spirituality fails to recognize that the so-called "higher beings" masquerading as divine avatars (messengers) or even as the spirits of the dead are in reality fallen angels directly controlled by Satan and his avowed enemies of the church of Jesus Christ.

Mahareeshi Mahesh Yoga, in his meditations, speaks of studying the Hindu scriptures and transcendental meditation for the purpose of getting in contact with "higher beings or gods" on other planes of spiritual reality.

The words of the Bible return with awesome force: "The things which the Gentiles sacrifice, they sacrifice to devils" (1 Corinthians 10:20) and "For though there be those that are *called* gods, whether in heaven or in earth . . . to us there is but one God, the Father, of whom are all things, and we in him; and one Lord Jesus Christ" (1 Corinthians 8:5–6, emphasis added).

New Agers employ the tools of the occult (tarot cards, crystals, Ouija boards, mediums or channelers, astrologers, and fortune-tellers) and are in reality seeking after the powers of "the god of this age." We need to remember the old proverb: "He that would sup with Satan had best have a long spoon." Practices such as astral projection—leaving your physical body during sleep to travel to other realms of reality, as taught by some New Age groups (Eckankar, for example)—place the soul in jeopardy and enter that dimension of spiritual darkness ruled by Satan, the enemy of all righteousness (cf. Ephesians 6:11–12).

The occultic prophet Nostradamus predicted that in 1999 a great and powerful world leader would arise, subduing all things to himself. It may well be that the Antichrist will be a figure like Maitreya, who will succeed in consolidating all authority and then reveal himself with "all power and signs and lying wonders" (2 Thessalonians 2:9), deluding the world with his evil charisma.

No matter how all these things may occur, they will come to pass, and behind it all will be those described by the Apostle Paul as "false apostles, deceitful workers, transforming themselves into the apostles of Christ. And no marvel; for Satan himself is transformed into an angel of light. Therefore it is no great thing if *his* ministers also be transformed as the ministers of righteousness; whose end shall be according to their works" (2 Corinthians 11:13–15). The New Age Cult fits that description, and only time will reveal the extent of its power.

The Second Coming of Christ

Down through the ages the doctrine of the resurrection of Jesus Christ has plagued the enemies of Christianity. It has been attacked vigorously in every era because it is both the cornerstone and capstone of the Christian faith. This doctrine is inextricably bound up with the doctrine of our Lord's second coming to deliver His church from persecution and to punish with flaming fire and everlasting ruination those who "obey not the gospel of our Lord Jesus Christ" (2 Thessalonians 1:6–10).

New Age theology attempts to blunt this cosmic event by either spiritual-izing it, connecting it with the appearance of "divine messengers" such as Maitreya, or attempting to point to a specific event as its fulfillment. David Spangler, a respected New Age writer, put it another way:

In a very real sense, Findhorn represents the second coming.[19]

This is perfectly acceptable from the perspective of the New Age world view, which ignores the historic person of Jesus Christ and the fact that He personally promised, "I will come again, and receive you unto myself; that where I am, there ye may be also" (John 14:3).

The picture of Christ descending from the clouds of heaven as John records in Revelation 1, and Paul in 1 Thessalonians 4, is directly dependent upon the doctrine of the resurrection of Christ. Repeatedly in the New Testament, Christ prophesied His bodily resurrection from the dead, not His reincarnation! (Matthew 20:19; Mark 8:31; 9:31; 10:34).

One of the most powerful passages on this subject and the only one that describes the nature of the Resurrection is found in the second chapter of John's gospel. After Christ had cleansed the temple in Jerusalem and the Jews sought a sign from Him to justify His authority in performing that act.

Since we may assume that the disciples and apostles of Christ were men like ourselves—capable of rational, logical thought—we can assume that if Jesus did not come back from the dead in His own body in three days, He would have been considered a false prophet by Old Testament standards and worthy of rejection by His followers. It is significant that John 2:22 reminds us that the apostles remembered this statement about raising the temple when Christ rose from the dead and appeared to them with "infallible proofs" (Acts 1:3).

New Agers tend to think that if the Resurrection took place at all, it was a spirit resurrection portending the future reincarnation of the Christ or Cosmic Consciousness. They are in no way prepared to confess Christ's bodily resurrection.

Since New Age writers talk about the spiritual survival of the Christ after the death of His body, the only records that they can turn to are the accounts of His appearances after that event. Considering Luke 24, we

19. Spangler, *Reflections*, 10.

must note that Christ said concerning himself that a spirit does not have flesh and bones as He had—and this came in response to the disciples perceiving Him as only a spirit. A rational person must reject the New Age redefinition of the Resurrection on the basis of what the Scriptures show us.

The gospel of John records that Christ appeared to His disciples and the apostles, even presenting *His body* for examination to Thomas the doubter (John 20:24–28), thus confirming the prophecy of John 2 with unimpeachable verification. In a word, Christ refuted all arguments about the nature of His resurrection and the fact of His resurrection by just being there! The Apostle Paul tells us in 1 Corinthians 15 that Christ was raised from the dead and "he appeared to more than five hundred of the brothers at the same time, most of whom are still living" (1 Corinthians 15:6 NIV). It is no wonder that Satan and those who are under his captive control (2 Timothy 2:26) fear the resurrection of Jesus Christ. It is the seal of the Church's redemption and of Satan's own judgment.

The Age of Aquarius fears above all else the preaching of the gospel of Jesus Christ and the fact of His resurrection. Hindu philosophy and Christian revelation stand face to face today on the spiritual battleground of time and eternity; but the battle is the Lord's (1 Samuel 17:47), God's kingdom will come, and His will be done on earth as it is in heaven.

Let us prepare "to give reason for the hope that lies within us"; let us study the Scriptures, our constant source of strength, under the guidance of the Spirit that inspired them and resist the devil, and he will flee from us. In the words of a great hymn of the Church:

> Crown Him the Lord of life, who triumphed o'er the grave;
> Who rose victorious to the strife for those He came to save.
> His glories now we sing who died and rose on high;
> Who died eternal life to bring and lives that death may die.

Christian Confrontation with New Agers

The practical side of learning about New Age occultic and cultic theology and those who have become its victims is to encounter them with the stark contrast between historic Christian theology and New Age beliefs. But in order to do this effectively, there are certain steps that must be taken and methods that must be applied to ensure maximum exposure and penetration of Christian evangelism and apologetics.

The Christian will learn almost immediately that after he witnesses to the truthfulness of the gospel message, he will have to introduce Christian apologetics, a reasoned defense of the validity of Christian truth.

Though some disagree with the need for the two-pronged approach, I have been successfully walking the line between evangelism and apologetics for over thirty-eight years. It is by no means an easy task, but from my own experience and study, I include the following suggestions. They can be extremely helpful, allowing you to get beyond the basics without the error of becoming a master of the obvious.

The Preparation of Prayer

The Apostle John reminds us that "if we ask any thing according to his will, he heareth us: and if we know that he hear us, whatsoever we ask, we know that we have the petitions that we desired of him" (1 John 5:14–15). Since we know this to be true and that His will is that everyone be saved (2 Peter 3:9), we must pray before we encounter the person we have been led to confront, continue to pray while we are speaking with them, and pray more after the confrontation. It must be specific prayer, calling to mind the promises that God has made, and asking Him to open the eyes and ears of the soul and mind of that person. We want the glorious light of the gospel of Christ, who is the image of God, to penetrate what is most assuredly spiritual and mental darkness. The Apostle Paul said:

> But if our gospel be hid, it is hid to them that are lost: in whom the god of this world hath blinded the minds of them which believe not, lest the light of the glorious gospel of Christ, who is the image of God, should shine unto them.
>
> 2 Corinthians 4:3–5

This should not surprise us because the Scriptures are clear in stating that "the natural man receiveth not the things of the Spirit of God: for they are foolishness unto him: neither can he know them, because they are spiritually discerned" (1 Corinthians 2:14).

We know, then, that if we are praying for God to open the eyes and ears of their minds and of their spiritual natures, our prayers are in accordance with His will. We are to plant the seed of scriptural truth just as the proverbial sower did, ever watering it with prayer, confident that "he which hath begun a good work in you will perform it until the day of Jesus Christ" (Philippians 1:6).

Repeat and Reword

We must cultivate with consistency the spiritual fruit of patience, and learn to state our position at least three times in different words (a dictionary of synonyms is very helpful here). People frequently simply do not "hear" the first time, but need the reinforcement of repetition. Should you find yourself losing patience, simply remember how difficult it was for you to accept the truth of the Gospel when you were in the same condition as the person you are talking with. Pray that the Lord would multiply this fruit during your time of encounter.

Communicate Your Love

Whenever possible, communicate your spiritual concern for the person, citing Leviticus 19:18 as your motive and go beyond the desire to make a statistic out of the person for some local congregation. New Agers are particularly sensitive to sincere love and concern for their well-being. Love demonstrates that concern. Medieval theologians had a saying: "The love of God conquers all things." Remember, the Lord would never have commanded us to love our neighbor as ourself if we did not have the capacity to do so. If you pray for this, it will manifest itself to that person.

Seek Common Ground

Find a common ground from which you can approach the controversial issues—perhaps from his religious background, his family, or certain goals or practices that you have in common with him. You might discuss abortion, Rotary, ecology, or patriotism. Whatever helps establish an amicable relationship facilitates communication, particularly if it is in the realm of spiritual values.

Define Terminology

Define your terminology in an inoffensive way, and when he is talking about God, love, Jesus Christ, salvation, or reincarnation, ask him to explain what he means. Try to arrive at a dictionary definition rather than a subjective judgment. There is a formidable difference between a dictionary definition and an encyclopedia of subjective comments. We can *communicate* with properly defined words in a context of objective truth, but a "feeling" about what a term means says nothing.

Be sure that you yourself are familiar with definitions, particularly when you get to the special terminology redefined by the cults and occult. These red-flag words can be easily defused with a dictionary reference. This is particularly true when it comes to such subjects as the nature of man, human sin, the problem of evil, and divine judgment or justice. Take care to keep the definitions simple.

Dr. Donald Grey Barnhouse once compared the communication of the Gospel to feeding cows. He said, "Get the hay down out of the loft onto the barn floor where the cows can get at it." Keep it as simple as possible. You are not there to impress the person with how much you know or how articulate you can be. You are there to be a representative of the Holy Spirit, whose task it is to "reprove the world of sin, and of righteousness, and of judgment" (John 16:8).

God has not called us to convert the world; God has called us to plant the seeds of the Gospel and water them with prayer. It is the task of the Spirit to bring those seeds to life, and He has promised that if we are faithful, He will.

Question, Don't Teach

Do not try to teach a New Ager, for the moment you don the teacher's garment, he will "tune out" just as he has been programmed to do. When the Lord Jesus Christ was teaching during His earthly ministry, He reasoned with people and consistently asked questions. When they could not answer what He had to say, then He began to teach them. His dialogue was more successful than if He had begun with teaching.

People are threatened by others who intimidate them with a professorial attitude that communicates an air of superiority, whether it is real or imagined. However, because our manner may be interpreted as haughtiness, the watchword is caution.

Jesus questioned the Pharisees, the Sadducees, the scribes, the Herodians, and even common men on subjects for which they had no real answers of enduring value. If incarnate Truth was that tactful, we could use a little sanctified tact ourselves. Jesus' encounter with the woman at the well (John 4) was a good illustration of our Lord's techniques, and the Holy

Spirit thought it important enough to record so that we might profit from the Lord's knowledge of human nature.

Read the Word

Wherever possible, use your Bible and ask the New Ager to read the specific passages under discussion. I call this technique "falling on the sword." Since the Bible is called the sword of the Spirit (Ephesians 6), we need only position the sword properly as they read and it will penetrate, even where all of our arguments and reasoning have failed.

The Bible reminds us again and again that "the Word of God is not bound" (2 Timothy 2:9), but it is "quick, and powerful, and sharper than a two-edged sword, piercing even to the dividing asunder of the soul and the spirit, and the joints and marrow, and is a discerner of the thoughts and intents of the heart" (Hebrews 4:12). You must consistently bring the New Ager back to the authority of what God has said, particularly in regard to the consciousness of personal sin.

Do not attack him with the sword of the Spirit, but rather permit the Spirit to use *His* instrument to cut through the scar tissue that sin has created on the minds and spirits of unregenerate men. The Spirit is the master teacher and the greatest of all surgeons; let Him do the work. You must simply prepare the patient for surgery.

Avoid Criticism

Avoid attacking New Age leaders or founders of specific groups, for even if the person knows that you are correct, he remains true to human nature and defends against what he considers to be unloving criticism. He or she is unaware that revealing truth is the most loving thing a person can do, but that truth must be spoken in love, and then only after much work has been done on your part to show that you speak not out of bitterness or an accusatory spirit, but simply from the perspective of historical fact.

Commend

Praise the zeal, dedication, and (wherever possible) the goals of New Age spirituality, because its basic nature is both messianic and millennial. New Age spirituality is seeking the right things, but with the wrong methods and with wrong reasons, sometimes merely because their vision is impaired by sin. Remind them that their quest for an end to poverty, disease, suffering, racial discrimination, inequalities, and economic and political tyranny are things with which Christianity has been concerned for almost two millennia.

Many New Age followers are genuinely seeking millennial conditions on the earth. But there will be no kingdom without the King, no love without justice, and no power without control. Point out to them from the Scriptures that those who follow Jesus Christ will inherit all these things as *a gift* from God and that the kingdoms of this world, when they become the kingdoms of our Lord and of His Christ, will reflect many of the values they now profess to hold sacred.

Take time to laud them for their efforts in the area of conservation and concern for the well-being of the planet as well as the creatures that live on it. Impress upon them your concern in these same areas, but use the opportunity to point out that no matter how hard we work, we still live in a world that is suffering from irremediable conditions caused by man's rebellion against his Creator.

Cite a few of the imperfections that demonstrate that fact: war, the oppression of minorities, and the abuse of human rights. These are all reminders of the fact that "all have sinned and come short of the glory of God" (Romans 3:23).

New Agers are sometimes disarmed by commendations because they have been incorrectly taught to believe that Christianity is so heavenly minded that it is of no earthly good and that the God of the Bible doesn't care about His creation. Let them see that you understand and that you care. Show that you care because God has shown us His concern in His Word.

Study the New Age

When dealing with New Age thinking, be sure that you can accurately quote New Age leaders, writings, and terms. New Age spirituality employs a mixed bag of an almost infinite number of occult practices. There are, however, words and phrases that may serve as warning signs that a particular belief, practice, or group is involved with something incompatible with the Christian faith. These include: Monism, Pantheism, Reincarnation, Karma, Evolution, Personal Transformation, Unlimited Human Potential, Reality Creating, Energy Alignment, Energy Healing, Energy Focusing, Attunement, At-one-ment, Enlightenment, Inner Power, Goddess Within, Mother Earth, Sensory Deprivation, Intuitive Abilities,

Near-Death Experiences, Chakras, Gurus, Tarot, Kabbalah, Pyramids, Crystals, Power, Auras, Color Balancing, Psychic Centering, Extraterrestrials, Brotherhood of Light, Higher Consciousness, Cosmic Consciousness, The Christ, Ascended Masters, Spirit Guides, Meditation, Yoga, Guided Imagery, Visualization, Astral Projection, Silver Cord, Inner Light, Out-of-Body Experiences, Mystics, Metaphysical, Holistic Healing, Therapeutic Touch, Biofeedback, Transpersonal Psychology, Hypnotherapy, Paranormal, Parapsychology, Higher Self, and Values Clarification.

If you do not understand or have not read what your opponent is talking about, make it a point to check it out before you check back with him. This will show him that you are consistent and interested in his well-being and truth as a whole. Be prepared to say, "Well I haven't seen or read that, but I certainly would like to look into it." Then do so.

Define "Jesus"

Ask the New Age believer if he can explain the difference between the Jesus found in the Bible and the Jesus who appears in New Age literature. Take him to 2 Corinthians 11 and pay particular attention to verses 3 and 4:

> But I am afraid that just as Eve was deceived by the serpent's cunning, your minds may somehow be led astray from your sincere and pure devotion to Christ. For if someone comes to you and preaches a Jesus other than the Jesus we preached, or if you receive a different spirit from the one you received, or a different gospel from the one you accepted, you put up with it easily enough. (NIV)

Let him see that the name *Jesus* means nothing unless it is defined within the context of New Testament revelation.

We can say anything we choose about Jesus, but an accurate portrayal of Him requires facts from the source documents, not from someone attempting to "restore" the "historical Jesus" hundreds of years or almost two thousand years later when in fact the only historical Jesus is the Jesus of the New Testament.

It is always helpful to show that the word *Jesus* is defined by the New Age completely differently than the context of history demands. Use the opportunity to exalt the Lord Jesus Christ, not as one of many messengers sent for a specific period in time for a specific set of needs, but rather as the Lord of the ages, *the* way to God, the embodiment of truth, and the incarnation of life itself.

Let the New Age follower understand that his view of Christ as merely an avatar, a messenger of God, is inconsistent with what Jesus said of himself and what the Church has believed. (At that juncture John 3:16–17 can be very helpful if you can read it with them.)

Reveal the Weakness of Moral Relativism

By asking questions, show how logically flawed it is to allow subjectivism and moral relativism to lead. Help him understand that he cannot live consistently with these principles. For instance, ask, "If your truth is your truth and my truth is my truth, how can we be certain about anything? Let us say that my truth happens to be that Einstein was wrong in the theory of relativity and the unified field theories, whereas you and objective truth in both mathematics and physics confirm that he was right. Does it make any difference whether the truth is based on facts or subjective feelings? Was Einstein wrong because I think he was wrong?" Relativism produces no truth.

A good method at this juncture is to point out what the great philosopher Mortimer J. Adler of the University of Chicago said concerning subjective "truth." Dr. Adler wisely observed that the Nazis' argument for killing Jews was a position that could not be refuted in a world of relative morality and ethics. Who could condemn Hitler for murdering six million Jews if their extinction was "his truth." To argue that he was wrong, if you are a relativist, is fallacious because your own definition of truth entitles Hitler as much right to his view as you have to yours.

But right and wrong are not determined by voice vote or social criteria; they are founded in abiding standards recognized universally as true— rightly designated as "moral absolutes." You can point out to the New Ager that speeding down Broadway in New York City at ninety miles an hour and failing to be influenced by red, yellow, or green traffic lights merely because he believes them to be irrelevant to the goal of reaching his destination on time will allow him to confront the objective truth that his action constitutes reckless driving when the police arrest him.

Show the Bible to Be Reliable

It is important to set forth the historic reliability of the Bible when discussing the concept of absolute truth. The Bible must be seen as a guide to truth superior to those with no credentials whatsoever. We can benefit from a study of biblical history and archeology to add credibility to our position. There are many excellent books on these subjects designed for the pastor and the layman.[20]

Reveal the Inconsistency of the New Age World View

Point out the underlying differences between Christian and New Age world views and show that the Christian world view is radically more consistent with the world and mankind as we find them.

The world view of New Age spirituality is a monistic pantheistic concept. Monistic pantheism, as noted previously, teaches that all is one and all is divine. It makes no division between God and His creation. This is inconsistent with logic and experience since billions of people can speak the personal pronoun "I" from the context of their own experience and lives. Each person is different from all the rest of his fellowmen. Mankind cannot even collectively account for the earth, life, or the problem of evil apart from divine revelation.

I was once talking to a New Age talk show host who, when I quoted Descartes' famous proof "I think, therefore I am," said, "Descartes was obviously mistaken. What he should have said is 'I think I think, therefore I think I am.'"

I replied, "It sounds good, but I can refute that in thirty seconds if you don't interrupt me."

He promised, "I won't interrupt you, but you're not gonna *hit* me to prove that I'm here, are you?"

We both laughed and I assured him that no violence would ensue.

He looked at his wristwatch and said, "Go for it."

"I have been carrying on a conversation with you for about fifteen minutes, have I not?" He looked at me in silence. "If you say that I have not been carrying on a conversation with you, and you have not been carrying on a conversation with me, then one of us is insane and people who talk to people that aren't there are not here very long."

He thought for a moment, then said, "That's a good point but truth is really as each of us perceives it."

I couldn't resist the argument Dr. Adler had made, so I said, "I'm glad to see that you agree with Adolf Hitler in his destruction of the Jews."

He recoiled in horror, but under the pressure of Dr. Adler's argument admitted vigorously that Hitler was wrong, that his perception was wrong.

20. See particularly *Evidence That Demands a Verdict* by Josh McDowell.

Yet the host, remaining consistent with his philosophy, could find no way to condemn Hitler. He concluded, "I've become illogical in the framework of my own views and must abhor as evil what Hitler did."

The New Age world view simply doesn't work in the hard, nitty-gritty world of everyday experience. It requires ideal conditions to find a place in the mind of the individual and in the events surrounding his life from day to day. Without this, it disintegrates under the hammer blows of sin and circumstances.

We must never allow ourselves to forget that God has planted three things in the minds of all men according to Romans 1. He has made us conscious of His existence as Creator, and it makes us uncomfortable. We are imbued with a conscience that constantly reveals the choices before us as good or evil. And He has made our spirits aware that since there is not perfect justice in this world, judgment must surely come from another one. Descartes called these "innate ideas," but they are actually imparted spiritual concepts that are part of our creation in the image and likeness of God (Genesis 1:26–27). The words of Augustine ring ever true: "Thou hast made us for thyself, O Lord, and our heart is restless until it finds its rest in thee."[21]

Provide Books or Audios

Refer the New Ager to some good Christian books, audios, videos, booklets, or tracts addressing New Age thinking (or you might give him one). If it is possible, find one that you think communicates effectively and fairly, and tell him that you hope he will seriously consider another point of view and pray about it, because God has promised, "You will seek me and find me when you seek me with all your heart" (Jeremiah 29:13).

A Note of Warning

As we think about encountering or confronting people in New Age spirituality, we ought to remember that Christians sometimes can be influenced and even led astray by their thinking. John Weldon and John Ankerberg have written:

Christians are being influenced by the New Age Movement (NAM) principally because of ignorance of biblical teachings and lack of doctrinal

21. Augustine of Hippo, *Confessions*.

knowledge. Because of America's emphasis on materialism, commitment to Christ as Lord in every area of life is sadly lacking. This brings disastrous results. Unfortunately there are Christians who love "the praise of men more than the praise of God" (John 12:43), who integrate the world's ways with their Christian faith (James 1:27; 1 John 2:15; 4:4), or who are ignorant of the extent of spiritual warfare (Acts 20:28–34; 2 Corinthians 4:4; Ephesians 6:11–23; 2 Peter 2:1; 1 John 4:1–3).

These sins of American Christianity open us to false philosophy such as the NAM. There are always some Christians who will actively embrace their culture. Whether they attempt to learn from it intellectually or borrow from it spiritually, or relish the enjoyment of worldly pleasures and pastimes, or attempt some kind of social reform along nominal Christian lines, the result is that their Christian faith becomes diluted or absorbed by an initially appealing but alien culture. This means that to the extent America turns to the New Age, to some degree there will be Christians who will adopt New Age practices or beliefs.[22]

In dealing with New Age Spirituality, we are in reality dealing with spiritual warfare against the forces of darkness, and we are told by God to put on the whole armor of heaven so that we will be able to withstand the forces of Satan (Ephesians 6:11).

There is no substitute in this conflict for knowledge of the Word of God and the proper use of the sword of the Spirit and the shield of faith to deflect all the flaming arrows of the evil one. The forces arrayed against us are great, the stakes are high: the souls of millions of people. But the promise of God stands sure—we can "overcome them: because greater is he that is in you, than he that is in the world" (1 John 4:4).

Prepare yourself for spiritual combat, study and show yourself approved by God, a workman who won't need to blush with embarrassment, rightly interpreting the word of truth. And above all, lift the shield of faith declaring, "Jesus Christ is Lord to the glory of God the Father." The Christian church looks to that glorious moment when "the Sun of righteousness will arise with healing in his wings" (Malachi 4:2), and the former things of the cursed earth will pass away and God will make all things new.

This is our blessed hope, the appearing of the glory of the great God and of our Savior Jesus Christ—this is the hope of the Church. This is the hope of the ages.

22. John Ankerberg and John Weldon, *The Facts on the New Age Movement*, 22.

─────────────────────── **Explore** ───────────────────────

Monistic Pantheism
Impersonal Universe
Deification of Man
Spiritual Combat

─────────────────────── **Discuss** ───────────────────────

1. What practices are forbidden to man and cursed by God?

2. What does the law of karma teach?

3. How is truth perceived in New Age Spirituality?

4. How does New Age Spirituality attack the Person of Jesus Christ?

─────────────────────── **Dig Deeper** ───────────────────────

See *The Kingdom of the Cults Study Guide* available at WalterMartin.com.

Answers to Chapter Questions

Chapter 1: The Kingdom of the Cults

1. The authority of the Scriptures is the criterion for measuring truth or error in all cultic claims. What is the *inerrancy* of Scripture? Are we required to defend it?

   The Bible teaches that it is God-breathed and without error in all that it teaches (2 Timothy 3:16). We are required to defend it (Jude 3).

2. The Bible is controversial—some call it a collection of stories and a "stumbling block" to belief. They avoid talking to unbelievers about creation, the flood, and other supernatural events the world calls *myths*. What approach did Jesus take? Which did Paul take?

   "I am the way, the truth, and the life: no man cometh unto the Father, but by me" (John 14:6). It should be carefully noted that Jesus did not say, "I am one of many equally good ways" or "I am a better way than the others, I am an aspect of truth; I am a fragment of the life." Instead, His claim was absolute, and allegiance to Him, as the Savior of the world, was to take precedence over all the claims of men and religions. Paul's strategy can be found in Acts 17.

3. How do liberal scholars take Gamaliel's advice out of context? How does God view someone who is a doctrinally sound teacher but has little money and few followers?

> Dr. Marcus Bach summed up the attitude of tolerance (see his quote). Liberal scholars have devoted themselves more to the way than to the why of the doctrines of the cults, and ignored the authority of the Scripture as a criterion for measuring either the truth or falsity of cultic claims.
>
> Biblically, the number of followers does not mean an automatic endorsement from God. We must examine the doctrine. Cults should be viewed in the light of what we know to be divine revelation, the Word of God, which itself weighs them, "in the sensitive scale of final truth" for it was our Lord who taught, "If you believe not that I AM, you will die in your sins" (John 8:24). And the final criterion today as always must remain, "What think ye of Christ; whose son is He?" (Matthew 22:42).

Chapter 2: Scaling the Language Barrier

1. What happens when historically accepted terms are redefined? In medicine? In mathematics? In theology?

> Truth becomes subjective, not absolute. A heart can be a lung, adding can be subtracting, and the identity of God can be altered.

2. When cult adherents redefine Christian terms, Christians must point to biblical verses and focus on *context*. Why?

> In context words mean just what they say. Cults spiritualize and redefine the clear meaning of biblical texts. They appear to be in harmony with the historic Christian faith but this harmony is, at best, a surface agreement based upon double meanings of words that cannot stand the test of biblical context, grammar, or sound exegesis.

3. Why is it important to talk about personal redemption from sin and the justice of God?

It is the responsibility of the Christian to present a clear testimony of his own regenerative experience with Jesus Christ in terminology that has been carefully clarified regarding the necessity of such regeneration on the part of the cultist in the light of the certain reality of God's inevitable justice.

4. Was Jesus polemic? If so, what biblical event demonstrates this? (chapter and verse)

Yes. Choose from many events in the gospels.

Chapter 3: The Psychological Structure of Cultism

1. Why are psychological factors important?

There are three regions or levels that psychologists generally recognize in any belief or disbelief system. An understanding of these factors can help in approach and dialogue.

2. What do cult belief systems have in common?

Similarities in thought exist in any group and can be analyzed and understood in relation to its particular theological structure (see the Examples section under Historical Perspective in this chapter).

3. What is conditioning?

Indoctrination—Almost all systems of authority in cult organizations indoctrinate their disciples to believe that anyone who opposes their beliefs cannot be motivated by anything other than satanic force or blind prejudice and ignorance. A cultist's encounter with Christians who do not fit this pattern can produce startling results. A discerning Christian who gives every indication of being unprejudiced, reasonably learned, and possessed of a genuine love for the welfare of the cultist himself (which is easily detectable in the Christian's concern for his soul and spiritual well-being) can have a devastating effect upon the conditioning apparatus of any cult system. (See Cult Belief Systems Share Much in Common section.)

4. What does the Bible say about the human heart and how does this influence our choices?

Start with Jeremiah 17:9 and expand to a biblical search on the word *heart*.

Chapter 4: Jehovah's Witnesses

1. Who was Judge Franklin Rutherford?

Upon Charles Taze Russell's death the helm of leadership was manned by Judge Joseph Franklin Rutherford. In comparing Russell and Rutherford it must be noted that the former was a literary pygmy compared to his successor. Russell's writings were distributed, some fifteen or twenty million copies of them, over a period of sixty years, but Rutherford's in half that time were many times that amount. The prolific judge wrote over one hundred books and pamphlets, and his works as of 1941 had been translated into eighty languages.

Thus, he was the Society's second great champion who, regardless of his many failings, was truly an unusual man by any standard. Russell and Rutherford are the two key figures in the Society's history, and without them it is doubtful that the organization would ever have come into existence.

2. Was Jesus ever inferior to God?

When Jesus said, "My Father is greater than I," He spoke the truth, for in the form of a servant (Philippians 2:7) and as a man, the Son was subject to the Father willingly; but upon His resurrection and in the radiance of His glory taken again from whence He veiled it (2:7–8). He showed forth His deity when He declared,

"All authority is surrendered to me in heaven and earth" (Matthew 28:18); proof positive of His intrinsic nature and unity of Substance. It is evident that the Lord Jesus Christ was never inferior—speaking of His nature—to His Father during His sojourn on earth. This is something Jesus emphasized when He said, "I and my Father are one" (John 10:30).

3. Who is the Jesus of the Jehovah's Witnesses?

Jehovah is not a Trinity. Jesus is not Jehovah God; he is the first and only direct creation of God and the agent through which Jehovah made all other things. He was raised from the dead but only with a spirit body.

4. Point to three Bible verses that teach the Christian doctrine of the Trinity.

What further proof is needed to show a threefold unity? Compare the baptism of Christ (Matthew 3:16–17) with the commission to preach in the threefold Name of God (Matthew 28:19) and the evidence is clear and undeniable. Even in the Incarnation itself (Luke 1:35) the Trinity appears (see also John 14:16 and 15:26). When Jesus said, "My Father is greater than I," He spoke the truth, for in the form of a servant (Philippians 2:7) and as a man, the Son was subject to the Father willingly; but upon His resurrection and in the radiance of His glory taken again from whence He veiled it (2:7–8). He showed forth His deity when He declared, "All authority is surrendered to me in heaven and earth" (Matthew 28:18).

Chapter 5: Christian Science

1. What happened when P. P. Quimby entered the Christian Science picture?

He became the father of Christian Science.

2. Why does plagiarism matter?

> Plagiarize: "to steal and pass off (the ideas or words of another) as one's own : use (another's production) without crediting the source" (Merriam-Webster Dictionary).

3. According to Mary Baker Eddy, Jesus, the disciples and apostles, and the early Christian theologians did not understand the meaning of the vicarious Atonement, but she did. How did the biblical atonement differ from Eddy's version of it?

> The material blood of Jesus was no more efficacious to cleanse from sin when it was shed upon "the accursed tree" than when it was flowing in His veins as he went daily about his Father's business (Science and Health, 25). –Mary Baker Eddy

> He atoned for the terrible unreality of a supposed existence apart from God (No and Yes, 55). –Mary Baker Eddy

> The efficacy of the crucifixion lies in the practical affection and goodness it demonstrated for mankind (Science and Health, 24). –Mary Baker Eddy

4. True or False: The death of Jesus upon the cross is more thoroughly substantiated from biblical and secular history than is His birth.

> True.

Chapter 6: Mormonism

1. Was God once a man?

> No. The Bible establishes God's identity and nature. Genesis 1:1— God is the Creator, not a creation. John 4:24—God is spirit. Numbers 23:19—God is not human.

2. Who is the Jesus of the Mormons?

Jesus was not conceived by the Holy Spirit; he is the half-brother of Lucifer.

3. Does the history of Joseph Smith Jr. matter?

Yes. Galatians 1:8 says, "But even if we or an angel from heaven should preach to you a gospel contrary to the one we preached to you, let him be accursed." Joseph Smith Jr. claimed an angel from heaven gave him a new gospel that contradicts the Word of God. In defense of the Christian faith, both his doctrine and his life are open to examination. Guard your doctrine (1 Timothy 4:16).

4. What does the DNA of Native Americans tell us about Mormonism?

Native American DNA is not of Semitic extraction and has the definite phenotypical characteristic of a Mongoloid. Joseph Smith Jr. taught that Native Americans were from the lost tribes of Israel—Jewish. This is a confirmation that his revelation was not from God.

Chapter 7: Spiritism—The Cult of Antiquity

1. What does Spiritism teach?

It teaches the continuity of life and the eternal progression of man toward perfection in the spirit realm.

2. Is there no such thing as a ghost?

There is no such thing as a ghost, but there are demons (fallen angels) who pretend to be ghosts in order to gain control over a person, possibly to the point of possession. They can form distinct images, as well as imitate the clothing, voice, and even the perfume of a deceased person.

3. What did Jesus teach us about demons during His ministry on earth?

The greatest authority on demon possession and exorcism is Jesus Christ. Though His ministry lasted only three years, and was recorded in just four New Testament books, these eyewitness gospels include 27 separate passages detailing Jesus' teaching on the subject of demons, demon possession, and exorcism. The number of passages discussing the same incidents emphasizes Jesus' interaction with demons: an interaction that was both frequent and confrontational. Demon possession is a common occurrence—not a rare phenomenon.

4. Is it possible to be a Christian and a medium?

(Acts 13:1–4, 6–11) The context of this chapter indicates that Paul and Barnabas were set apart specifically by the Holy Spirit (verses 2, 4) to preach the Word of God as the Spirit directed. In the course of discharging the duties assigned to them by the Holy Spirit, they found a certain magician or medium, a false prophet, a Jew, whose name was Barjesus (verse 6).

We learn from the account that this man deliberately obstructed the preaching of the Gospel to the deputy of the country, Sergius Paulus, a man of integrity who desired to hear the Word of God (verse 7). The judgment of God fell upon this man (verse 11). But it is not significant until it is noted that in verses 9 and 10 the judgment was preceded by the announcement that Paul was "filled with the Holy Spirit," when he set his eyes upon him. Paul's scathing denunciation of the medium identifies him as a destructive, mischievous son of Satan, the enemy of all divine righteousness, and the perverter or twister of the right pathway of the Lord.

Chapter 8: The Theosophical Society

1. Theosophy is mostly drawn from what three sources?

It draws its authoritative teachings from Hindu, Buddhistic, and early Gnostic sources.

2. How did Madam Helena Blavatsky change the meaning of reincarnation?

> In Hinduism and Buddhism, there is no guarantee that a person would reincarnate as a human (not an animal or insect). Blavatsky changed reincarnation to mean that humans only reincarnate as humans (the Law of Cause and Effect).

3. What does the Bible teach about sowing and reaping, and how is this different from reincarnation?

> Sowing and reaping is a natural cycle of life created by God. **It does not apply to salvation.** We do not reap any evil we may have sowed in life because Jesus paid the price for us.

4. What three beliefs do Christianity, Judaism, and Islam all confess?

> Christianity, Judaism, and Islam all confess a personal God and all believe in a resurrection of the body and in the authority of the Old Testament.

Chapter 9: Buddhism—Classical and Zen

1. Why did Buddha decide to leave Hinduism?

> He grew unhappy with the Wheel of Samsara and hoped to find a way off the Wheel.
> There seemed no escape from the fate of having to endure an endless succession of painful lives before one could be freed to merge for eternity with the "World-Soul"—a state known as Nirvana.

2. Was Buddha influenced by Hinduism?

> Buddhism shows a heavy influence of Brahmanism, gods, and goddesses in Buddha's history and teachings.

3. Who is God in Zen teachings?

The Nature of God (Pantheism)
"The eye by which I see God is the same as the eye by which God sees me. My eye and God's eye are one and the same—one in seeing, one in knowing, and one in loving. . . . When I have shut the doors of my five senses, earnestly desiring God, I find him in my soul as clearly and as joyful as he is in eternity. . . ."—Sohaku Ogata

4. What did Jesus say about Buddha?

"All that ever came before me are thieves and robbers: but the sheep did not hear them." John 10:8

Chapter 10: The Bahá'í Faith

1. Who is Bahá'u'lláh?

Bahá'u'lláh fulfilled a worldwide messianic calling, which equated him with other world religion leaders (i.e., Christ, Buddha, Mohammed).

2. What is the Unity of Threeness?

The Unity of Threeness is the very core of belief: "The Oneness of God, The Oneness of Religion, and the Oneness of Humanity," but it is also paraphrased as a Unity statement, The Unity of God, The Unity of Religion, and the Unity of Man.

3. Who is the Jesus of the Bahá'í?

"Moses, Jesus, and Mohammed were equal prophets, mirroring God's glory, messengers bearing the imprint of the Great Creator."[1] The blood of Jesus Christ is not efficacious to cleanse anyone of sin.

---

1. Marcus Bach, *They Have Found a Faith* (Indianapolis, IN: Bobbs-Merrill Company, 1946), 193.

4. What did Jesus teach in John 4:4–26 that proves all faiths are not the same?

> Jesus rebuked the Samaritan woman for thinking that her worship was the same as his. "You worship what you do not know; we worship what we do know" (John 4:22 NASB), so not all faiths are the same and they do not lead to God.

Chapter 11: The Unity School of Christianity

1. What is the principle Myrtle Fillmore embraced?

> Her conversion to Mary Baker Eddy's version of Phineas Quimby's theology came about when she realized that "I am a child of God and therefore I do not inherit sickness."
>
> Mrs. Fillmore credits her own appropriation of this principle with her healing from a variety of physical problems.

2. What is the all-encompassing mind?

> "The doctrine of the trinity is often a stumbling block, because we find it difficult to understand how three persons can be one. Three persons cannot be one. . . . God is the name of the all-encompassing Mind. Christ is the name of the all-loving Mind. Holy Spirit is the all-active manifestation. These three are one fundamental Mind in its three creative aspects."[2]

3. According to the Bible, reincarnation cannot be part of the cycle of life. Why not?

> The true Christian position concerning death is taught in numerous places in Scripture. For example, in 2 Corinthians 5:8, Paul emphatically states that "to be absent from the body [is] to be present with the Lord [or at home with the Lord]." And again, in Philippians 1:21–23, the great apostle anticipates his departure from this life to be with Christ, and certainly not to go through repeated lives.

2. Charles Fillmore, *The Revealed Word* (Lee's Summit, MO: Unity School of Christianity, 1959), 200.

To refute the Unity position, reincarnation vs. resurrection, see the fifteenth chapter of 1 Corinthians where the doctrine of the physical resurrection of the body to immortality is clearly stated.

4. Where in the Bible does it say that the physical body of Jesus was resurrected?

The Bible plainly states that Jesus arose from the grave in a physical form (John 20:27), that He was not raised a spirit (Luke 24:39–44) and that Christ Himself after He had risen, rebuked His disciples for their unbelief in His physical Resurrection (Mark 16:14). It is evident, therefore, that though Jesus Christ was raised physically, He had what the Bible terms a "spiritual body" (1 Corinthians 15:44–49), not a spirit form, but an immortal, incorruptible physical body possessed of spiritual characteristics forever exempt from death (Romans 6:9), a body the like of which all believers shall one day possess at His glorious return and our resurrection (1 John 3:2; 1 Corinthians 15:52–54).

Chapter 12: Armstrongism

1. What restores us to healthy Christianity?

Repentance, recommitment, prayer, and the study of God's Word. Add to this the fellowship of believers where "iron sharpens iron" (Proverbs 27:17 NIV).

2. How does Armstrongism redefine the nature of God?

The nature of God is spirit, according to Armstrong, but His shape, form, and stature is that of a man! In their correspondence course, he asks, "Does the Father therefore appear like a man? Comment: Christ clearly indicated that the Father has the general form and stature of a mortal man!"[3] The Plain Truth reveals, "We

---

3. Herbert W. Armstrong, ed., *Ambassador College Bible Correspondence Course (Lesson 9)* (Pasadena: Ambassador College, 1966): 8.

are made of material flesh, but in the form and shape of God. . . ."[4]
And, "Now notice once again Genesis 1:26: 'God (Elohim) said,
Let us make man in our image, after our likeness (form and shape).'
. . . God is described in the Bible as having eyes, ears, nose, mouth,
hair, arms, legs, fingers, toes."

3. Was Jesus referred to as the Son previous to His incarnation?

We find an affirmative answer in the Psalms: "Kiss the Son, lest he
be angry" (Psalm 2:12). Also, in Proverbs 30:4 (NKJV), the question
is asked, "Who has established all the ends of the earth? What is
His name, and what is His Son's name?" We must also remember
that Jesus was the "sent Son" (John 3:16) into the world, which
agrees with these Old Testament passages that He was the Son
before His incarnation.

4. How did Jesus prove He was alive?

When Jesus made His post-resurrection appearances He offered the
print of the nails in His hands (John 20:27) as proof that it was the
same crucified body. Otherwise, Jesus would have been deceiving
His disciples with imitation prints. He offered His hands and feet as
evidence (Luke 24:39). Of utmost importance, He denied that He
was other than "flesh and bones, as ye see me have" (Luke 24:39).
He proved His physical body by eating with His disciples (Luke
24:42; John 21:12–13). This is how Luke can assuredly tell us that
He showed himself alive with many infallible proofs (Acts 1:3).

Chapter 13: The Unification Church

1. What is Tao?

Beginning with God's essence, Moon teaches that God "exists
with His dual characteristics of positivity and negativity."[5] The
standard symbol representing Taoism is a circle with a curved "s"

4. Armstrong, "Just What Do You Mean: Born Again?" *The Plain Truth*, February 1977, 28.
5. Dr. Young Oon Kim, *Divine Principle* (San Francisco: The Holy Spirit Association for the Unification of World Christianity, 1960, third edition, 1963), 24.

division through the middle. The left side is white and the right side black. Each side contains its opposite color represented by a small circle. This symbol also underlies the Unification thesis for God. God is white and black simultaneously. He is positive and negative, male and female, subject and object, yang and yin. The god of Unification theology is dualistic.

2. What replaces the authority of the Bible in Unification?

Its authority is replaced by Moon's **Divine Principle**.
Moon held the opinion that science outdates the Bible. He counts it "impossible" in this "modern scientific civilization" to use "the same method of expressing the truth" as found in the New Testament. Therefore, he reasons, a "new truth must appear."

3. How does the Bible describe the Messiah?

He was one divine **person** who, from the incarnation and forward, possesses two **natures**, His eternal divine nature and his human nature. His human body came into being at His conception by the power of the Holy Spirit "overshadowing" the virgin Mary. The personal unity of Christ is indisputable throughout Scripture, as Christ said, for example, "Before Abraham was, I am" (John 8:58). Paul affirmed, there is "**one** Lord, Jesus Christ" (1 Corinthians 8:6). The apostle John declares, "The Word was God" (John 1:1) and "The Word became flesh" (John 1:14 NASB), so that we "beheld **his** glory" (John 1:14).

4. Who is the biblical Holy Spirit?

The word *Trinity* is used to summarize what we see of God's nature in the Bible. Therein we find one God and no others (Isaiah 43:10). God is personal as the Father (Matthew 6:9). God is personal as the Son (Matthew 3:17). God is personal as the Holy Spirit (Acts 5:3). And together the three persons are uniquely one God in Scripture (Isaiah 48:16; Matthew 28:19).

Chapter 14: Scientology

1. Who is the Jesus of Scientology?

> Christ is a legend that preexisted earth-life on other planets and was implanted into humans on earth. Jesus was just a shade above "clear" and was no greater than Buddha or Moses.

2. What is *homo novis*?

> The "clear" person is on the evolutionary journey to the next stage of man, a godlike being called *homo novis*.
>
> In Hubbard's evolutionary development of Homo sapiens, he teaches that man will evolve into *homo novis*, described as "very high and godlike."[6]

3. How is truth defined in Scientology?

> Truth for the individual in Scientology is often subjective and existential. To quote Hubbard, "Know thyself . . . and the truth shall set you free."
>
> The subjective nature of truth in Scientology allows variation on some items. Hubbard wrote, "What is true for you is what you have observed yourself." What one person perceives as truth may not be what another person perceives. So, what by normative standards would be called a contradiction outside of Scientology can be synthesized within the organization.

4. How does Jesus refute reincarnation?

> Jesus' bodily resurrection from the tomb refutes reincarnation because **He resurrected to the same body**.

Chapter 15: Eastern Religions

1. How many gods and goddesses are there in Hindu theology?

> An indefinite amount, numbering into the millions.

6. L. Ron Hubbard, *History of Man* (Los Angeles: ASHO, 1968), 38.

2. Give an illustration of the contradictory nature of Hinduism.

> An illustration of the pluralism or contradictory nature of Hinduism is found by comparing the god of the Gita with the god of earlier Vedic literature. God, as described by the Gita, is personal and often sounds even monotheistic (only one God who is personal and not a part of creation exists). However, when one reads earlier Vedic scripture, God is presented as being definitely pantheistic (all of existence is, in some way, divine) and perhaps even monistic (all of existence is one, whether any divinity exists at all).

3. Who is Jesus in Hinduism?

> Hinduism denies the Trinity, the deity of Christ, the Atonement, sin, and Salvation by grace through the sacrifice of Jesus Christ.

4. Is Transcendental Meditation secular?

> TM still wears its secular label in its own promotions today, and most Westerners are unaware of its religious presuppositions and nature.

Chapter 16: Islam—The Message of Muhammad

1. Who is Allah?

> Allah is one god in nature, not a Trinity. He has no son.

2. Compare Jesus and Muhammad according to the Koran.

> Jesus did miracles (Sura 3:49; 5:110), but Muhammad did not (Sura 13:8: "thou art a warner [of coming divine judgment] only"; also 6:37; 6:109; 17:59 and 17:90–93).
>
> Jesus was sinless (Sura 3:46), but Muhammad sinned and needed forgiveness (Sura 40:55: "ask forgiveness of thy sin"; 42:5: "ask forgiveness for those on the Earth"; 47:19: "ask forgiveness for thy sin"; 48:2: "that Allah may forgive thee of thy sin").

Jesus was called "the Messiah" and was even born of a virgin (3:45–57)! Yet Muhammad is supposed to be the greatest of the prophets.

3. Why do Muslims need to celebrate Ramadan?

Muslims must fast during the entire month of Ramadan; they are supposed to fast from all food and drink from sunrise to sunset in atonement for their own sins over the previous year.

4. Does the rapid spread of Islam prove it is of God? (Review Gamaliel's argument in chapter 1.)

Gamaliel counseled the Jews not to oppose the Christians for "if this counsel or this work be of men, it will come to naught: But if it be of God, ye cannot overthrow it" (Acts 5:38–39). Let it not be forgotten that Gamaliel's advice is not biblical theology; and if it were followed in the practical realm of experience as steadfastly as it is urged, then we would have to recognize Islam as "of God" because of its rapid growth and reproductive virility throughout the world. We would have to acknowledge Mormonism (six people in 1830 to 16 million in 2018) in the same category as Islam.

Chapter 17: The Jesus of the Cults

1. What is the foundation of the Christian faith?

The person and work of Christ is indeed the very foundation of Christian faith. And if it is redefined and interpreted out of context and therefore contrary to its biblical content, the whole message of the Gospel is radically altered and its value correspondingly diminished.

2. Should Christians oppose and criticize the beliefs of others? What is Christ's example?

We must first recognize that to oppose and criticize is neither unethical, bigoted, nor unchristian; rather, it is the epitome of proper Christian conduct where a very vital part of the Christian witness is concerned. "And He said to them, "Go into all the world and preach the gospel to all creation" (Mark 16:15) The pattern of Jesus' entire ministry was confrontational. He said what people did not want to hear, out of love for them.

We are required to preach the truth of the Gospel and to defend it: "Beloved, when I gave all diligence to write unto you of the common salvation, it was needful for me to write unto you, and exhort you that ye should earnestly contend for the faith which was once delivered unto the saints" (Jude 3).

Throughout His entire ministry, our Lord was constantly on guard against those who attempted to ensnare Him with trick questions and supposed contradictions between what He taught and the teachings of Moses and the prophets. Added to this, these professional interrogators masqueraded as religious, pious, and even tolerant zealots and professed that they were the descendants of Abraham, heirs to the covenant, and the servants of God. To these people our Lord addressed His most scathing denunciations, calling them, among other things, "whited sepulchers," "children of the devil," "dishonorers of God," "liars," "murderers," and "wolves."

The reasons why we must answer as well as be prepared to evangelize such people are quite clear. The church must do it because Christ and the apostles commanded her to do so, unpopular though it may be, and to this all true Christians should be unequivocally committed, for no other reason than out of respect for our Lord.

3. Some use Gamaliel to argue against evangelism and the defense of the faith. Why is this a false argument?

Gamaliel's advice, which he addressed to the Jews in the book of Acts (5:38–39) was this: "They, too, will say, 'Let them alone: for if this counsel or this work be of men, it will come to nought: But if it be of God, ye cannot overthrow it; lest haply ye be found even to fight against God.'"

The only difficulty, as we have noted earlier, is that the context clearly indicates the advice was given by Gamaliel to the Jews, and Gamaliel was not an inspired writer, an apostle, or even a Christian. The biblical text includes, at times, common sayings that were used among different cultures (see Paul's dialog on Mars Hill). So this appears to be one of these common sayings, argued by a man who was not a Christian.

4. What is the true nature of Jesus?

Jesus is incarnate God. He is the second Person of the Triune Deity: Father, Son, and Holy Spirit.

Jesus said to them, "Truly, truly, I say to you, before Abraham was, I am" (John 8:58 ESV).

Chapter 18: Cult Evangelism—Mission Field on Your Doorstep

1. Why is a cultist hostile?

"If the world hates you, you know that it has hated Me before it hated you" (John 15:18 NASB).

Indoctrination—Almost all systems of authority in cult organizations indoctrinate their disciples to believe that anyone who opposes their beliefs cannot be motivated by anything other than satanic force or blind prejudice and ignorance.

2. Why is it important to quote Scripture?

"I would profusely quote the Scriptures, and in actuality be preaching a three-minute sermonette, subliminally implanting the true Gospel of Jesus Christ."—Walter Martin

We must believe that God's Word will not return unto Him void, but will accomplish what He pleases and prosper in the thing whereto He has sent it (Isaiah 55:11).

3. What is prayer methodology?

"During my opening and closing prayers I would totally preach the Gospel, emphasizing the Deity of Christ, His death for our sins, the certainty of knowing that we have eternal life now, by faith in Him, and that salvation comes by grace alone, independent of human works. I would profusely quote the Scriptures, and in actuality be preaching a three-minute sermonette, subliminally implanting the true Gospel of Jesus Christ and, I might add, blissfully uninterrupted. For no one, not even the most zealous disciple of 'Pastor' Russell, Joseph Smith, or Brigham Young, can interrupt a prayer. I have seen such a methodology or technique of evangelism make a tremendous impact upon Jehovah's Witnesses and other cultists, because, for six minutes of the evening at least, the Christian has the opportunity to present the true Gospel of Christ without interruption."—Walter Martin

4. What does God say about His Word?

For the word of God is living and active, sharper than any two-edged sword, piercing to the division of soul and of spirit, of joints and of marrow, and discerning the thoughts and intentions of the heart (Hebrews 4:12 ESV).

It will not return void.

We must believe that God's Word will not return unto Him void, but will accomplish what He pleases and prosper in the thing whereto He has sent it (Isaiah 55:11).

Appendix A: The Satanic Temple

1. Why do organizations like The Satanic Temple redefine historical personalities like Satan?

Words are powerful; words mean things—they are either true or false. Once a false meaning is accepted, it causes delusion, and delusion causes damage (2 Thessalonians 2:11–12).

Example: Imagine going the hospital for heart surgery, and the cardiologist redefines the word *heart* to mean *lung*. He then removes your lung. Truth matters (John 17:17).

2. What is the biblical and historical identity of Satan, and what has he always wanted?

He is an ancient, created being who, by his very nature, can never be God (Ezekiel 28:13–17). Jesus said that Satan is a murderer and the father of lies—his nature is evil (John 8:44). He disguises himself as an angel of light (2 Corinthians 11:14). From the beginning, Satan wanted to be like God (Isaiah 14:13–14). He demands worship (Matthew 4:8–11). Historically, in every global culture, there is the teaching of an evil one, so the overwhelming, scientific evidence of history supports mankind's ancient acceptance of and experience with a personal evil being.

3. What do Christians and atheists have in common?

An atheist, like a Christian, believes that we can **know** whether or not there is a God.

4. What is Truth?

God's Word is truth (John 17:17). Jesus is truth (John 14:6).
"According to Psalm 119, the word of God is the way of happiness (vv. 1–2), the way to avoid shame (v. 6), the way of safety (v. 9), and the way of good counsel (v. 24). The word gives us strength (v. 28) and hope (v. 43). It provides wisdom (vv. 98–100, 130) and shows us the way we should go (v. 105)."[7]

Appendix B: New Age Spirituality—The Age of Aquarius

1. What practices are forbidden to man and cursed by God?

Astrology, numerology, witchcraft, crystal gazing, necromancy (communication with the dead), magic, and palm reading (Leviticus 20:6; Deuteronomy 18:9–11; Acts 19:19). Any practice that seeks to manipulate lives or control power by summoning forces

---

7. Kevin DeYoung, "3 Things We Must Believe about God's Word," *Crossway*, February 10, 2017, https://www.crossway.org/articles/3-things-we-must-believe-about-gods-word/.

that are not from God: He says that He has nothing to do with this kind of power—and neither should we.

2. What does the law of karma teach?

The law of karma teaches that whatever a person does, good or bad, will return to him in exact proportion in another existence. Judgment is dispensed by an impersonal "universe" that is NOT a deity, but somehow knows everything that happens—including personal thoughts.

3. How is truth perceived in New Age Spirituality?

Truth is perceived individually, and it is not uncommon for the New Age believer to say, "That's your truth—this is mine," as if truth, like beauty, exists only in the eye of the beholder. Truth is changeable—not absolute. So, in essence, there can be no right or wrong because there is no absolute standard. If this is true, the Nazis cannot be held accountable for the murder of 6 million Jews, since they were simply doing what they believed was right—following their own truth.

4. How does New Age Spirituality attack the Person of Jesus Christ?

The New Age attack upon the Person of Jesus Christ concentrates on Christ's unique claim to deity. The Lord Jesus is indeed proclaimed in the New Testament as "the one and only Son of God" by virtue of the Greek term monogeneses (cf. John 1:1, 14, 18; 3:16). The second person of the Trinity does not share His throne with Krishna, Buddha, Mohammed, Zoroaster, or any of the endless assortment of gurus and gods. As the Savior of the world, He bore our sins in His own body upon the cross (1 Peter 2:24), and His miraculous powers have never been duplicated; He is indeed unique among the sons of men.

Index

Bush, George W., 356
Buswell, J. Oliver, 241

C

Cane, Elisha, 162
Capon, Robert, 242
Carnell, Edward, 24
Cartwright, Nancy, 281
caste system, 191
catechism, 285
causation, 182
celebrities, 301, 385
celestial marriage, 154
chakras, 402
Chaldean occultism, 379
channelers, 394
Chan, Wing-Tsit, 194
character, 185
Chesterfield, 163
China, 26
Christendom, 42–43, 55
Christianity
  beliefs of, 253, 263–64, 417
  missionaries of, 19, 342
  restoration of, 44–45
  terminology of, 176
Christian Science
  definitions of, 29
  as Gnostic, 45–47, 351
  history of, 89–95
  interpretation of, 12
  Jesus of, 323–25
  on miracles, 108–11
  and New Age, 376, 379
  on the Trinity, 27
  vs. Unity School, 221, 227
Christology, 14, 253
Christotokos, 306n6, 314n20
Church of American Science, 274n10
Church of Jesus Christ of Latter-day Saints
  (LDS). *See* Mormonism
Church of Satan, 357
civilization, 126–28, 372
Clarke, Stanley, 281
Clayton, William, 139
clergy, 43–44, 55, 61, 341
climate change, 384–85
closed-mindedness, 35, 37

Collyridian heresy, 314n20
color balancing, 402
Colwell, E. C., 79
Colyer, Elmer, 242
common ground, 216, 347–48, 398
communism, 26, 318, 372
Community of Christ (RLDS), 138–39
compartmentalization, 39
conditioning, 42–44, 47, 411
Confucianism, 258
Confucius, 213, 379
confusion, 255, 352
conservation, 401
context, 30, 32, 410
contradiction, 41, 128–29, 213, 253, 283, 295, 372, 383, 424
conversion, 350
Cooper, I. C., 174
Cooper, James Fenimore, 162
Corea, Chick, 281
Cornwall Alliance, 384
cosmic consciousness, 402
counterfeits, 19, 104–5, 322
Counter-Reformation, 208
Cowdery, Oliver, 124, 130
creation, 178, 266
Creme, Benjamin, 381, 392
criticism, 327, 400
Crooks, William, 162, 164
Crossman, Richard, 39n5
Crowder, John, 242
Crowley, Aleister, 365
Cruise, Tom, 281
Crusades, 208
crystals, 377, 394, 402, 429
cults
  evangelism of, 332, 335–53
  language barrier of, 23–32
  Jesus of, 321–332
  psychological structure of, 35–49
Cushing, Alvin M., 93

D

darkness, 397, 406
Davis, John Jefferson, 242
Dawkins, Richard, 369, 370
Dawn Bible Students, 51
Day of Atonement, 133

M

About the Authors

Walter Martin is fondly and respectfully known as "The Bible Answer Man" and the father of modern Christian cult-apologetics. Many cult apologists credit him with their introduction to the field. He held four earned degrees, having received his Masters from New York University and Doctorate from California Coast University in the field of Comparative Religions. Author of a dozen books, a half-dozen booklets, and many articles, he founded Christian Research Institute and was its director for almost thirty years. Dr. Martin taught worldwide in churches, colleges and seminaries, and was a frequent guest on national television and radio programs. His work is continued today through Walter Martin Ministries located in Minneapolis, Minnesota (www.waltermartin.com).

Jill Martin Rische is the eldest daughter of Dr. Martin and an adjunct professor at the University of Northwestern-St. Paul, and Crown College in St. Bonifacius, Minnesota. She holds a BA in Old Testament Literature (Hebrew language emphasis), and an MA in Humanities (history emphasis). Jill is the managing editor for Walter Martin's classic work, *The Kingdom of the Cults*, and is coauthor of *The Kingdom of the Cults Handbook*, *The Kingdom of the Cults Study Guide*, *The Kingdom of the Occult*, and *Through the Windows of Heaven: 100 Powerful Stories and Teachings from Walter Martin, the* Original *Bible Answer Man*. She is the founder along with her husband, Kevin Rische, of *Walter Martin Ministries* in Minneapolis, Minnesota, and a cohost on Jan Markell's *Understanding the Times* radio program, heard on more than 830 stations across America.